An Ageing Population

For Sarah Carver and Kate Liddiard
who will be octogenarians in
the 2050s

An Ageing Population

A Reader and Sourcebook

Edited by Vida Carver and Penny Liddiard

HM
HOLMES & MEIER PUBLISHERS, INC.
New York

First published in the United States of America 1979 by
HOLMES & MEIER PUBLISHERS, INC.
30 Irving Place, New York. N.Y. 10003

Library of Congress Cataloging in Publication Data

1. Carver, Vida. 11. Liddiard, Penny.
   An Ageing Population
   1. Gerontology—Addresses, essays, lectures.
   I. Title
HQ1061.A43 1979   301.43′5   78–26607
ISBN 0–8419–0474–X

Printed in Great Britain

Contents

Part 6   The professional

Part 7   On working together

Part 8   Older people in care

'Kate'

'Kate', the writer of this poem, was unable to speak, but was occasionally seen to write. After her death, her hospital locker was emptied and this poem was found.

What do you see nurses
   What do you see?
Are you thinking
   when you are looking at me
A crabbit old woman
   not very wise,
Uncertain of habit
   with far-away eyes,
Who dribbles her food
   and makes no reply,
When you say in a loud voice
   'I do wish you'd try'
Who seems not to notice
   the things that you do,
And forever is losing
   a stocking or shoe,
Who unresisting or not
   lets you do as you will
with bathing and feeding
   the long day to fill,
Is that what you're thinking,
   is that what you see?
Then open your eyes nurse,
   You're not looking at me.
I'll tell you who I am
   as I sit here so still,
As I use at your bidding
   as I eat at your will.
I'm a small child of ten
   with a father and mother,
Brothers and sisters who
   love one another,
A young girl of sixteen
   with wings on her feet,
Dreaming that soon now
   a lover she'll meet:
A bride soon at twenty,
   my heart gives a leap,

Remembering the vows
   that I promised to keep:
At twenty-five now
   I have young of my own
Who need me to build
   a secure happy home.
A young woman of thirty
   my young now grow fast,
Bound to each other
   with ties that should last:
At forty my young ones
   now grown will soon be gone,
But my man stays beside me
   to see I don't mourn:
At fifty once more
   babies play round my knee,
Again we know children
   my loved one and me.
Dark days are upon me,
   my husband is dead,
I look at the future
   I shudder with dread,
For my young are all busy
   rearing young of their own,
And I think of the years
   and the love I have known.
I'm an old woman now
   and nature is cruel,
'Tis her jest to make
   old age look like a fool.
The body it crumbles,
   grace and vigour depart,
There now is a stone
   Where once I had a heart:
But inside this old carcase
   a young girl still dwells,
And now and again
   my battered heart swells,

I remember the joys,
   I remember the pain,
And I'm loving and living
   life over again,
I think of the years
   all too few—gone too fast,

And accept the stark fact
   that nothing can last.
So open your eyes nurses,
   Open and see,
Not a crabbit old woman,
   look closer—see ME.

Introduction

This book has been designed as a sourcebook for professional workers in the health and social services, and for volunteers and concerned members of the general public interested in coming to grips with what may be implied in the title, *An Ageing Population*. In particular, it is intended for the use of adult students following the Open University course* of the same title, and the aims of book and course are the same. They are: to identify the issues raised by the increasing number and proportion of older people in the community, to increase knowledge of the needs and circumstances of older people and of the skills required to anticipate and meet them; to point to ways in which the disadvantaging and handicapping effects frequently associated with age can be reduced; and to consider these issues in the context of attitudes, values and priorities in the community. These are wide aims and the papers selected for this Reader are drawn from a wide range of published material on both sides of the Atlantic. We have also included a number of previously unpublished articles. Both the topics covered and the approach to the topics vary widely. We have thought it appropriate to include theoretical and review studies, research reports and papers descriptive of good (and sometimes bad) practice drawn from the literature of sociology, psychology, medicine, social work, nursing and other relevant academic disciplines, side by side with personal accounts of the experience of ageing and disability, and of the problems of voluntary workers in the field – and even, in one case, a vision of a possible future as perceived by a science fiction writer. One important consideration, however, has guided the selection. If the many problems and challenges associated with ageing in modern societies are to be met by an adequate response from the community, then many individuals with widely differing backgrounds and experience need to be aware, involved and prepared to work together; and this in turn implies some understanding and appreciation by all of the aims and skills of others. To this end we have tried, as far as possible, to select papers which should be comprehensible to the attentive general reader, even where the content matter is necessarily specialized or technical.

With a view to assisting readers who may not be working through the book according to the plan suggested in the Open University correspondence text and broadcasts, we have grouped the individual items into sections, each dealing with a different topic. Part One provides the wider

---

* The Open University course *An Ageing Population* (P252) is the second of a series of courses developed in the Health and Social Welfare area of the OU Post-experience Courses Unit. The first is *The Handicapped Person in the Community* (P251) and the two courses in some respects complement each other. Intending students can obtain further particulars from the Associate Student Office, The Open University, Walton Hall, Milton Keynes MK7 6AA.

context for most of what is to follow. Part Two is concerned with the experience of ageing and with the values, myths and stereotypes of the society that structures the experience. Parts Three and Four deal, respectively, with some practical aspects of life in the community for older people, and with some practical problems for a community which seeks to ease the lives of its older members. Part Five is about sickness and disability as they may affect many people in later life, and Part Six about some of the specialized professions that seek to meet the needs of those who have experienced sickness, disability or social stress. Problems of coordinating services, and cooperation between caring individuals, professional and lay, are scrutinized in Part Seven, and the last part is concerned with improving the quality of life of older people in residential homes, hospitals and hospices.

Students of the related OU course should note that the course itself is rather differently structured. The reader is one component in a multi-media teaching plan which includes a guide to the use of the materials, correspondence texts, BBC television and radio programmes, personal tuition, student assignments, and additional 'set' books. No items from these books have been included in this Reader, but since they are complementary to it they are listed below:

BREARLEY, C. P. (1975) *Social Work, Ageing and Society.* London: Routledge and Kegan Paul.
HODKINSON, H. M. (1975) *An Outline of Geriatrics.* London: Academic Press. Published in the 'Monographs for Students of Medicine' series.
PUNER, M. (1974) *To the Good Long Life: what we know about growing old.* New York: Universe Books (UK edition Macmillan, 1978).

While the Editors must be held responsible for the final collation and selection of the material in this book, and particularly for its deficiencies, the items included were in nearly every case chosen, recommended, read and re-read by members of the Open University team responsible for the production of the course. We gratefully acknowledge their collaboration:

Members of the Open University Course Team:
Sheila Dale, Vic Finkelstein, Brian Gearing, Ros Greenfield, James Leeming, Robert Slater and George Watts.

Course Team Consultants:
Klaus Bergmann, Michael Fogarty, Averil Freeth, Malcolm Johnson and Ann Webber.

In the final stages of preparation we have also received valued help from Annie Clutterbuck, Roger Lubbock and John Taylor of the OU Publishing Division and from Lesley Timpson and Kirsty Wilson of the Post-experience Courses Unit. And for patient and painstaking secretarial assistance we owe thanks to Lesley Brazier and Elizabeth White.

Vida Carver
Penny Liddiard

Part 1 Ageing Populations

1 The history of ageing and the aged

Peter Laslett

The twentieth-century Englishman and indeed everyone living in an advanced industrial society seems to have a guilty feeling about the elderly and aged. We uneasily suspect that most of our millions and millions of old people live in reduced circumstances, not much cared about by such children and such kin folk as they have left to them and rather distant from the life of any family; solitary, very many of them, and as they grow to be really aged, miserably relegated to institutional living. The peasant and the craftsman of traditional England, so the common sentiment seems to be, provided far better for the familial life of the old than we do today. It is for us to learn from them.

Ageing in our society and ageing in the traditional world

Gerontology, the study of aging as a process and of the old as a social group, is the next most recent of the social sciences, the newest of all being historical sociology itself. An early achievement of the gerontologists, an achievement which could be said, as we shall see, to be itself historical in its character, is the demonstration that the beliefs which are so widely held in late-twentieth-century high industrial society about the situation of the aged are scarcely well founded. Gerontological publications in print or in progress* show that the majority of the aged are not in the position just described.

Retirement, so often regarded as a declaration of the unfitness of older people to perform what is required of a contemporary citizen, is certainly widespread and peremptory, and clearly distinguishes industrial society from pre-industrial society in respect of aging. But its effect varies with the

---

* See for example Shanas *et al.*, *Old People in Three Industrial Societies* (1968), the countries in question being Britain, the United States and Denmark. A recension of gerontological work on the familial situation of the aged is contained in vol. 1 of the *Handbook of Aging and the Social Sciences*, (1976) general ed. James E. Birren, vol. eds. Ethel Shanas and Robert Binstock, New York: Van Nostrand. This chapter is an adaptation and modification of a section contributed by the present writer to that volume and entitled 'Societal development and aging'.

Source: P. LASLETT (1977) *Family Life and Illicit Love in Earlier Generations*. Cambridge: Cambridge University Press, pp. 174–81.

job that has to be abandoned, with the skill of the individual concerned, with his health and his economic position. The old are not so drastically bereft of prestige and respect as the stereotypes imply; they have recognized functions, especially in relation to their children and grandchildren; they are supported, emotionally and otherwise, by their offspring, sometimes by their siblings, and even by more distant kin. They manage to live quite often in association with the families of their children, so combining what they most want to combine, interchange and independence. We must not suppose that the sufferings of some of the aged, and the miseries of the minority of the anomic amongst those who come into contact with the welfare services, are a proper indication of the condition of old people generally in our own society.

Nor must we suppose that there has been a single transition between pre-industrial, peasant society in which the aged were socially valued and enjoyed full family membership, and industrial, modern or even post-modern society where they have been exiled from the familial group. It is particularly inaccurate to identify such a change with the general process by which traditional societies become advanced societies. It is true that some traditional societies have in fact undergone a process during which the transition to industrial living was accompanied by a crucial change in the proportion of the aged in the social structure. Several of the many ethnic and economic regions which go to constitute the present U.S.S.R. are possible examples, as well as others in Central and Eastern Europe. Japan is another. In none of these, it may be noted, was the coincidence at all precise; and in the case of Western societies, in the case of England and Wales particularly, the two developments have been almost entirely separate in time.

One of the reasons why aged persons are thought to have been better appreciated in pre-industrial society is that there were fewer of them. But when we look at what actually happened when industrialization occurred, we find that the increase in the number of the old did not always or even usually coincide with technological and economic change. In France, the U.S.A. and especially England the really extensive changes in the proportions of the aged in the population took place a century or more after the onset of the dissolution of traditional society. This was because the demographic transition, during which the regime of high fertility and high mortality characteristic of traditional society gives way to the regime of low fertility and low mortality characteristic of modern industrial society, was not contemporaneous with the start of industrialization, but came some time afterwards.

In any case the sustained continuance of low fertility, which is responsible for the very high proportions of the aged in all advanced countries, could not in principle have had its full effect until fifty years or so after fertility began its definitive fall.* In England and Wales, we shall see, the decline in fertility commencing in the 1870s did not issue in a substantial rise in the proportion of the aged until the years after 1911 and did not bring about an outstanding alteration until the 1920s, 1930s and 1960s.

We shall also observe, to make matters more complicated, that England cannot be taken as necessarily typical of Western experience, except only during the final stages; certainly not as indicating in detail what happened in France. Indeed, we shall consider indications that the actual behaviour of old people in respect of residence may have differed from area to area in traditional European society, and that England may have been somewhat exceptional in its uniformity. This is what we might expect as a corollary to the homogeneity of English household structure [. . .].

But if it is unjustifiable to think of the aged as being always neglected and contemned in our world, it is equally unjustifiable to assume that they were always cherished by their families and by their kin folk in the pre-industrial era. It is true that the fragmentary though suggestive evidence which we shall cite indicates that the aged in pre-industrial England were more frequently to be found surrounded by their immediate family than is the case in the England of today. It is possible that they were given access to the families of their married offspring more readily than is now the case. This may be thought surprising in view of the infrequent occurrence of multigenerational and of complicated households of all kinds, which [were] characteristic of an earlier England. But we shall find that these circumstances can be persuasively accounted for without having to suppose that in the traditional era in England deliberate provision was made for the physical, emotional or economic needs of aged persons, aged relations or aged parents in a way which was in any sense superior to the provisions now being made by the children, the relatives and the friends of aged persons in our own day, not to speak of the elaborate machinery of an anxiously protective welfare state.

It cannot be shown, for example, that the English family group before the nineteenth century had any socially or legally recognized duty to give succour or family membership to aged relatives other than the parents of the head. The famous Elizabethan Poor Law of 1601 specifically confined

* See Roland Pressat, *Demographic Analysis* (1972), ch. 9, esp. pp. 277–82, for a demonstration that an increase in the numbers of the old in a population is almost entirely due to a decline in fertility leading, as cohort succeeds cohort, to a progressive diminution in the size of the younger age groups in relation to the older age groups. Increase in length of life (either as mean age at death or expectation of life, which are distinct in all historical populations and certainly in aging populations) is of little importance in this development. If mortality falls and fertility increases, or even if fertility stays constant, the proportion of older persons may actually go down. These are circumstances which it seems rather difficult to grasp without some very elementary demographic knowledge, but are essential to the understanding of how societies grow older.

responsibility for the relief of the elderly to their children alone. In Scotland, apparently, grandparents and grandchildren, perhaps sometimes the wider kin, could be required to repay Poor Law authorities for money spent on the relief of aged persons. In England, in spite of the supposedly bilateral character of English kinship, case law developed by the judges succeeded in confining such duties to 'natural' connections, and thus excluded all relatives by law, even stepfathers and stepmothers.

The behaviour of children in the matter of marriage does not seem to have been markedly affected by consideration of the welfare of their own parents. Family reconstitution reveals little or no disposition to wait until the parents died before their sons and daughters took spouses: in fact the marriage of orphaned children appears to have been later than that of those whose parents were alive. No doubt most daughters and some sons did conduct themselves so as to assure the comfort and security of their aging parents as far as they could, but we have found it difficult to confirm that they would return home for that purpose from their jobs or their holdings in other localities. Movement of failing fathers and mothers into the households of their married offspring undoubtedly occurred, but it was decidedly not a universal pattern in the evidence we have so far surveyed. Nor does it seem to have gone on at the demand of the parents themselves, certainly not at their command.

The authority of the father in traditional England was real enough, especially amongst the elite. He could order his children to marry or not to marry, and could decide where they should live, although his prospects of getting obedience depended to a large extent on whether they had property expectations from him. In practice, [. . .] English parents showed little disposition to keep children at home after marriage, or to require them to return after marriage or after being launched in the world elsewhere. The ordinary story of the family household after the child-rearing stage was of offspring leaving successively, though not necessarily in order of age, until, if the parents survived, they finally found themselves alone.

There is a telling contrast here with the traditional familial system of an area like South China, for example. There no child left the parental household except under clearly specified conditions, because the recognized rules of familial behaviour required co-residence wherever possible, and no father or mother of grown offspring would ever live alone. In China it would seem that the concept of the family group implied that there should be few persons who lived in what might be called unfamilial situations. It has not proved possible to identify such a concept in the English social structure.

If the stem-family arrangements so widely assumed, at least until recently, to have been common or even universal in traditional Europe had in fact existed in England, then the patriarch in charge, or even his widow, might have had the sanctions at hand to require a grown and often a married child to live at home, and to provide a supporting circle of family members when retirement arrived. But [. . .] this form of the domestic group seems to have been of little importance amongst the English in the generations just before traditional society began the process of transformation.

Where membership of the domestic group was conferred upon solitary, necessitous or infirm parents or kin folk in England in earlier times, therefore, it may be supposed to have been done for quite other reasons. The advantages of the presence of elderly relatives, or the dutifulness, the affection of the charitable disposition of the heads of the households concerned, seem to have been more important than any socially sanctioned expectation that such an action should take place. As for the advantages, they must have existed even before the rise of the factory took the working mother some distance away from the home during the whole of the day and created the need for perpetual child-minders. Many fathers of young children remarried with what seems to us like unfeeling alacrity when they lost their wives, but Janet Griffiths, who is studying remarriage, does not find that all of them did so. Sometimes, [. . .] a widower sent his orphaned youngsters to live with their grandmother, and occasionally he packed up and took the whole family back there until a new wife could be installed. These things confirm what common sense suggests, that the older generation were of use in child rearing. There are signs that widowed mothers were imported into the households of young and growing families; perhaps some widowed fathers were, too.

But so little was it the accepted thing that the parents of married persons should live with them that we have found such co-residents described as 'lodgers' rather than as family members, and even as 'lodger, receiving parish relief' (Laslett in Laslett and Wall (eds.) 1972: 35, n. 50; the lodger concerned was the aged father of the head of the household). We may recall from the study of what happened in Clayworth in the 1670s and 1680s that it was possible for a son to succeed to the family occupation and to the family dwelling and actually allow his widowed mother and his sister to live in the poor-law institution. But it would be unwise to judge the whole social system from the actions of such poverty-stricken individuals, as Jean-Louis Flandrin seems inclined to do (1976: 73, 77).

Nevertheless, it must not be overlooked that the legal duty of a child to assist his parents never seems to have been construed as an obligation to receive or to maintain him or her in the household. Nor did society require the compulsory joining together of families in order to make subsistence cheaper – society, that is to say, in the persons of the administrators of poor relief. These hardpressed volunteers would billet needy people on householders who could give them shelter, like 'Ruth Hurst, lodger upon charge of the town' in the house of Anne Scales, a widow of modest substance in Clayworth 1688. The *town*, that is, the village acting through the parish officers, would perhaps even have proceeded in this way so as to place the needy with neighbours, members of the community, rather than with relatives where relatives were likely to be unsatisfactory.

It would certainly not be justifiable, however, to suppose that the story of welfare relationships between the young and the old, between children and their aging or infirm parents, in traditional English society was one of indifference or neglect. There is convincing evidence that in medieval England the landholding peasant family had something like a set arrangement for the maintenance of old men, their wives and their widows no longer able to work for their livings. Such picturesquely named customs as 'widow's bench' indicate the extent to which these provisions were sanctioned by community tradition, which must surely have continued well beyond medieval times. Even in areas where partible inheritance was customary, there was apparently an expectation that the family plot would maintain successive holders in the family line throughout their lives.

This was so in spite of the fact that the man in possession seems to have been at liberty to sell on the market as suited his convenience, and can sometimes be seen to have done so in circumstances which suggest that his object was to ensure himself a living in his final years. In the sixteenth century and later the wills of such landed individuals, mostly with small or very small possessions, of course, but some of them fairly substantial, not infrequently provide for the remaining members of the generation about to relinquish possession and control, and even specify the house-room to be set aside for widowed mothers. It has not been found easy, in fact, to trace these old ladies dwelling in their allotted living spaces in those lists of inhabitants and residential arrangements which we have been able to study.*

But we can say little as yet about the everyday relationship between old people and their grown-up, independent children for any period earlier

---

* For the interesting issue about retirement and provision for the aged in Tudor and Stuart times, with reflections on the rarity of the retired old in listings of inhabitants, see Margaret Spufford, *Contrasting Communities* (1974), esp. pp. 114–15. References in the thirteenth century to payment for the support of old age and of needy family members, whether or not they had ever been responsible for working the plot, can be found in the doctoral dissertation of Richard Michael Smith. 'English peasant life-cycles and social–economic networks' (1974) and its references, particularly to the work of Ambrose Raftis and others. All these scholars insist that the evidence as to the aged is at present scanty, but that much remains to be analysed in the rolls of the manor courts, which continue right up to the seventeenth century and beyond. Sources of this kind for Suffolk manors in the thirteenth century provided Dr Smith with his remarkable information.

than recent times, at least in the matter of welfare and support. We are certainly in no position to estimate how much money was transferred, how often children visited their parents and how frequently and strenuously they exerted themselves to live near them or to find accommodation which would enable the parents themselves to come within easy reach. The wisps of evidence we have suggest that in some families elderly persons and children did live in close proximity, in others not. But we cannot hope to decide from the present state of our knowledge how successful our ancestors were in making such provisions.

Account would have to be taken of the very different situation of younger, independent people in that era of exiguous resources, poor communications and widespread illiteracy, which made keeping in touch with home and relations generally so much more difficult. The most likely conjecture from what we do know is that they behaved very much as we behave now in these respects, no better and no worse. In the list of the inhabitants of Corfe Castle, Dorset, as they were in the year 1790, a list which is one of the important sources for the present analysis of aging, the following entry appears for one of the households:

> 'Abner Croker, labourer   73
> Mary Croker, wife   73
>
> 'Abn. Croker is blind. He is maintained by his children etc.'

The Croker children, who do not seem to have been living in the village, may have been typical, or they may have been exceptional; we simply do not know.

Superficial as the comparision between past and present has to be, our knowledge is sufficient to show that the position of the elderly in late-twentieth-century social structure is historically novel. If the aged in our generation and in our society present a 'problem to be solved', it is a problem which has never been solved in the past, because it did not then exist. The value of historical sociology to the creation of policy in the present is in denoting how far we differ from past people and how much we are the same. With respect to aging, it is maintained that we are in an unprecedented situation: we shall have to invent appropriate social forms, for they cannot be recovered from our history. It could be said, with greater conviction if our knowledge had been greater, that the familial history of peoples other than the English, or of those in areas other than the Western European, does provide examples of the treatment of the aged and aging which might give us guidance and provide precedents. But in all of these areas and at all of the times we know about, the numbers of the aged were very much less than in high industrial society today. Our situation remains irreducibly novel: it calls for invention rather than imitation.

The facts which underlie the statements we have made about aging in the past and aging in the present have had to be painfully recovered, and must be described as few and somewhat desultory. They could be, and no doubt soon will be, enormously extended and enlivened by a search for references to the aged in the literature of the pre-industrial and industrializing West, and especially of England. [. . .]

References

FLANDRIN, J.-L. (1976) *Familles: Parenté, Maison, Sexualité dans l'ancienne Société.* Paris.

LASLETT, P. and WALL, R. (1972) *Household and Family in Past Times.* Cambridge: Cambridge University Press.

2   Ageing and modernization

Donald O. Cowgill and Lowell D. Holmes

Cowgill and Holmes and their colleagues who contributed to the book Aging and Modernization *made a series of studies of ageing in fourteen different societies, ranging from the mostly preliterate Sidam, Igbo and Bantu peoples of Africa, to the highly modern countries of Japan, Russia, Israel, Ireland, Austria, Norway and the United States; and between these extremes, in various stages of modernization, Samoa, Thailand, Mexico and the Pima Indians of Arizona. Their aim was to test certain propositions concerning the relationship between ageing and modernization. The following extracts are taken from the final chapter, 'Summary and Conclusions: The Theory in Review'. The propositions that survived the analysis of the findings are summarized at the end (pp. 25–7).*

Universals

Let us first review our case studies in the light of [our] propositions* as to those things which are found in all societies. All of the demographic principles appear to hold true for these societies. The aged are indeed relatively small minorities in all societies. The maximum per cent of age 65 and over among these societies was in Austria where we found almost 14 per cent. In all cases women also outnumbered men within the older population. Among these countries, the highest sex ratio for those 65 years of age and over was in Israel where there were only 95 males to 100 females. In all of the populations for which such information was available, widows predominated, the proportion of older females widowed ranging from half to three-fourths.

While we found varying criteria for classification, all societies had a category of people who were called 'old'. It also appears that the role expectations for such people are always different from those of their juniors and it is generally true that old people are graduated to less strenuous and less physically exacting pursuits. Even if there is no formal retirement, the old men are not expected to keep on being hunters or warriors or farmers; they are commonly promoted to become elders, headmen, or

* See pp. 25–7 below – eds.

Source: D. O. Cowgill and L. D. Holmes (1972) *Aging and Modernization*. New York: Appleton Century, pp. 305–23 (extract).

priests. In other words, they shift from roles requiring high physical exertion to sedentary, advisory or supervisor positions. In modern societies, this shift is viewed as 'retirement' carrying with it the expectation that the person ceases all formal occupational activity. For those who previously have been engaged in vocations requiring strenuous physical exertion, the shift is in the same direction, i.e. to less strenuous activities, but there is a vital difference: in the less modern societies, the new role, albeit less strenuous, is still important and honorific, whereas retirement in modern societies essentially means not only that the new role will be less active but so far as the society at large is concerned there is no role at all. Even when we find old people in different cultures performing the same functions, such as babysitting or keeping house, we find that they are valued in quite different ways; in preliterate societies these are likely to be viewed as vital social functions, while in modern societies they tend to be seen as peripheral and unimportant.

It appears to be true that some older persons continue to act as political, judicial, and civic leaders, but in modern societies these are the exceptions while among the Sidamo, the Igbo, the Bantu, and the Samoans these are the expected roles of older people.

In all of our societies we have seen evidence of mutual obligations and responsibilities between aged parents and their adult children, but these obligations appear to be less clear and less binding in modern societies with the possible exception of Ireland. Here the young, both rural and urban, feel a serious obligation to visit and to look after the parents. This results in part from traditional religious principles which admonish the young to honor one's father and mother. In all of the African societies we have noted the obligation of children to care for aged and infirm parents; in fact, this is seldom questioned and it is usually enforceable by the parent himself in view of his control of the property. But, even in the absence of such coercive power, the custom continues, as in Russia where McKain reports that older people usually live with their children, albeit with a pension check to ease the burden. Even in Austria, Norway, and the United States the mores, if not the law, carry such an obligation although there is considerable resistance to it, and state insurance and assistance programs have been instituted as partial substitutes for such filial responsibility.

While there is some concern about security in old age in all of these societies, it seems doubtful if we are justified in saying that there is a universal effort to save for old age. The social systems and cultural settings differ so widely and, in some, individual efforts to save are either irrelevant, meaningless or impossible. Is the elder's trusteeship of the tribal or family lands in Africa and Samoa the equivalent of saving? There may be some individual effort to save in the Soviet Union, but it seems neither to be expected nor often achieved. The notion of individual saving for old age appears to be mainly a western product derived from the Protestant Ethic.

On the other hand, we find no exception within our sample to the principle that all peoples value life and seek to prolong it, even in old age. In African societies where old people are so highly revered there is every reason to stay alive as long as possible. But even in modern societies where the elderly are not so highly honored, longevity is still prized. Russians boast about the alleged extreme longevity in some parts of their country and they are undertaking extensive research to find the secrets of it. As a matter of fact, one of the most unique features of modernized societies is their success in achieving their goals of prolonging life.

Variations

[. . .] We have stated that the concept of old age is relative to the degree of modernization; a person is classified as old at an earlier age in preliterate society than in a modern society. This principle appears to be supported by the cases we have surveyed [. . .]. The chronological age at the beginning of old age in the African countries can only be estimated, since the beginning of this period of life in those countries is determined by changes of status or function, not by the calendar. However, it appears that the onset of old age among the Igbo occurs somewhere between 40 and 50 and among the Sidamo at about 55. In Samoa the age is 50 and it shades up to 60 in Thailand and Japan. However, in all of the Western modernized countries it is 65 or 70. Thus it appears that the age of onset of old age does indeed increase with modernization.

But our observations lead us beyond this principle to another generalization. There is a strong indication that the use of chronological age to signal the beginning of old age is a modern development. It is characteristic of urban, industrial societies which are highly time-conscious and which have sophisticated methods of measuring the passage of time and keeping a record of its passage. These are also the societies in which social change is most rapid and the passage of time is therefore most noticeable. In preliterate societies where social change takes place at a slower pace, the passage of time is of less moment, is less attended to, and less accurately measured. [. . .]

There is no doubt that longevity is directly and significantly related to modernization. [. . .]

One of the more significant of the hypotheses of this study has been that the status of the aged is high in preliterate societies and is lower and more ambiguous in modern societies, and on this point we have abundant evidence which strongly supports the propostion. At the lower end of the modernization scale we find uniform testimony to the high regard for old people. In all of the African societies, growing old is equated with rising status and increased respect. Among the Igbo, the old person is assumed to be wise; this not only brings him respect, since he is consulted for his wisdom, it also provides him with a valued role in his society. The Bantu elder is 'The Father of his people' and revered as such. In Samoa too, old age is 'the best time of life' and older persons are accorded great respect. Likewise, in Thailand, older persons are honored and deferred to and Adams reports respect and affection for older people in rural Mexico. Apparently this was the situation in the traditional culture of the Pima Indians although it is now being undermined by changes in land tenure, urbanization, and the superior education of the children.

Plath * reports increasing ambivalence toward the aged in Japan; in the traditional culture they were accorded high status and respect and this is still the ideal, but increasingly the later years are being viewed as 'The Hateful Age' and the high suicide rate among the aged indicates that in this society old age is not always 'the best time of life'. In Austria, older persons apparently have relatively low and somewhat ambiguous status; filial duty is still observed albeit somewhat grudgingly. In Ireland the activities of the aged continue to be respected because the young tend to abdicate their social responsibilities or at least postpone them until they are well into middle age. In Norway, it is reported that the status of the aged has declined with urbanization and the dominance of the nuclear family, and that many old people complain about feeling 'useless'. Similarly, the status of the aged in the United States is at best ambiguous; perhaps it is not so much low status as it is no status; it is often described as a 'roleless role'.

Israel provides a very interesting and unexpected test of our hypothesis. Weihl reports relatively high status of old people among the migrants from Oriental countries and a relatively low status among those from western areas. It seems highly probable that most of those Oriental countries would fall toward the lower end of our modernization scale, and that the western countries would be among the more modern ones; thus, within one country we find the same correlation that we have been exploring through our cross-national comparisons. However, the finding of this contrast within the same country suggests that the differences of status are not a simple adjustment to technology and urbanization; presumably the two groups of migrants have approximately the same exposure to these influences within Israel. There appear to be persistent differences of cultural norms and family structure that are not immediately erased upon

* References are to authors of other chapters (not reproduced here) in *Aging and Modernization* – eds.

migration into a relatively modern situation. It is especially significant that the higher status of the aged among the Oriental migrants is associated with the persistence of the extended family, whereas the nuclear family was generally characteristic of western migrants among whom the status of the aged was relatively low. This suggests that the generalized status of the aged may be mainly a function of their status within the kin group.

Another perspective is provided by study of the status of the aged in Russia which appears to be an exception to the rule that the status of the aged declines with modernization. Certainly Russia is a modern nation and admittedly it is youth-oriented and yet McKain reports that the aged there are respected and loved and even though retired continue to lead useful and satisfying lives. Again it may be noted that these old people continue to live in an extended family situation, in fact, McKain reports an extension of the extended family – if the old persons don't have children of their own with whom they can reside, they may be adopted by another family. It appears that the Russians may have found a way of preserving the extended family, or at least the stem form thereof, in spite of modernization which usually pulls it apart and one suspects that the key ingredient in this is the economic security provided through their pension system and free public services. Under these conditions they are not a burden to the family with whom they live and they are not made to feel dependent or useless.

In our review of the relationship between status of the aged and modernization we have stumbled across some other variables which may have a bearing. One of these is power. It may have been noted that in all of the African countries under review old people not only had high status, they also had economic power. They controlled the ancestral land, they allocated the use of that land during their lifetime and, given the belief in the power of the spirits of the dead and given the greater access of the old to that spirit world, their power even extended beyond the grave. Such power in itself breeds respect and accords a certain status, although, as Shelton notes, it does not necessarily breed affection.

Rarely do the aged have such power in modern societies. The only modern society discussed [here] which would represent a contradiction is Ireland. In that society the father holds great economic power by virtue of the fact that he refuses to reveal his intentions concerning the inheritance of family property and is even reluctant to delegate responsibility concerning the operation of the family farm. Sons are kept in a subordinate position until they are 35 to 40 years of age. In most modern societies, however, young people have many alternatives and neither the economic power of their elders nor the threat of spiritual powers can hold them in subjection. [. . .]

If we have established that the status of the aged deteriorates with modernization and that the proportion of the aged in the population increases with modernization it follows that the status of the aged deteriorates as their proportion in the population increases. It is not suggested here that status declines because of the increase in supply; instead it appears that this negative correlation results from the fact that each is correlated with the same independent variable, modernization.

The rate of social change of a society is exceedingly hard to gauge and yet it is believed that the rate of social change is of great significance to the status and role of the aged. Impressionistically, it appears that change is slower and less disruptive in the societies at the lower end of the modernization scale, but there are evidences of change in all and the rate appears to be accelerating in all. Perhaps one of the major differences between the less modern and the more modern areas is related to the extent of urbanization. The rate of social change is usually greatest in the urban areas. In the less modern countries relatively low proportions of the total populations live in cities and hence are less affected by such change as is occurring; under these conditions the large rural population may continue to live in pretty much the traditional way, even though the small proportion of the population living in cities may be experiencing rapid change. On the other hand, modern countries are highly urbanized and thus much greater proportions of their populations are subject directly to the changes taking place in cities. Furthermore, communications are so efficient and migration so frequent that even their rural populations are subject to the same influences.

Change tends to undermine the status of older people for several reasons. It renders some of their skills and knowledge obsolete; not only can they no longer ply their trade, there is no reason for them to teach it to others. In a changing society, the young people are nearly always better educated than their elders and thus the latter lose their authority deriving from superior knowledge. In developing societies with relatively few literate persons and these mostly young there may be an increasing tendency for older leaders to be brushed aside. Modern societies have high mobility, both geographic and social, and both kinds tend to put distance between children and parents, to weaken the bonds of the extended family, and to undermine the authority of the elders. [. . .]

[. . .] Israel is an exceptional case, a country in which most of the people, including the aged, are migrants. Here nearly all of the older population have not only experienced the hardships and tragedies of two World Wars and much persecution in their countries of origin, they have also torn up roots in middle age or later to move to a new country. In the process they have experienced all of the disruption attendant upon migration and the problems of resettlement in a new area including in many cases the learning of a new occupation. [. . .]

There is some similarity between the situation of the aged in Israel at large and that of the aged in the *Kibbutz*. However, most of the aged in the *Kibbutz* are old migrants and pioneers in its organization and development. Feder notes that there is some difficulty in adjusting to reduced activity in old age in a society which is so strongly dedicated to hard physical labor. The *Kibbutz* has no institutionalized patterns for ageing; it is having to invent these as its members need them. It is experimenting with such devices as selective job assignment and gradual reduction of hours of labor. In other respects, the *Kibbutz* seems to provide some of the same economic, social, and emotional security characteristic of earlier agricultural societies. Although the older *Kibbutzim* contain many three-generation families within which the older generation enjoys close family relations, economic support comes from the *Kibbutz* as a whole.

Another of our hypotheses is that the status of the aged tends to be high in agricultural societies [. . .]. This is amply borne out in the cases under review. The African societies, Samoa and Thailand, are all basically agricultural and in all of them we find a high regard for the elderly. It also appears still to be true of the Mexican village although it is being undercut by modernizing influences and by migration of the young. On the other hand, we find a lower or ambiguous status of the aged in all of the urbanized countries except Russia and possibly Ireland. [. . .]

We have hypothesized that the status of the aged is high in those societies in which they are able to continue to perform useful and valued functions and it appears that the societies under review fit the hypothesis. In the African societies it appears that the older men are promoted from being farmers, hunters, or warriors to the positions of political, judicial, and religious leadership; they are the wise old leaders who guide, counsel, and teach the younger people of their society. The latter roles are valued more highly than the roles they performed when they were younger, hence they are more honored in old age. In Mexico and Thailand the shift of roles is more gradual and less clearly a promotion. The men reduce their physical labor on the farm as their health dictates; they remain heads of their households even when others must do the bulk of the work; but no new titles or functions are allotted to them as they withdraw from physical labor. However, in both countries most such people are living in small villages where they have lived all of their lives surrounded by neighbors and kinfolk and in such a circumstance one's status is less dependent on his work role than in American and European societies; he is known and valued as a person. Cessation of the work role has little effect on the status of a person in such a society; he is still the same person and still head of his household. Or, in the case of a woman, she is still grandmother, and in both of these societies this is an honored role. However, in the Mexican village, an economic factor affects the status of the old person; well-to-do people who can no longer work tend to be more respected than poorer ones, and they tend to have a more authoritarian position in their families.

By contrast, at the modern end of the scale, in the United States and the European countries where the work role is the chief determinant of status and where retirement is dictated by the calendar, the older retired person is left without valued roles to perform. To be sure they may keep busy gardening, babysitting, housekeeping, or fishing, but these activities are little valued in the society at large and are scarcely visible outside of the immediate circle of the nuclear family. Thus it is the old people in Norway feel 'useless' and those in the United States play a 'roleless role' In Ireland, however, the aged tend to control the importance of their roles through control of land and other forms of property. It should be remarked that it is not so much what the older person does as it is how that activity is valued in the particular society. Babysitting is an almost universal function of grandparents, but the value attaching to it varies widely. In societies maintaining the extended family [. . .] it is valued and they feel privileged in performing it. But in western societies where the nuclear family has become the mode [. . .] it has to be contrived and arranged, and its performance [. . .] accords no particular status and for some becomes a demeaning menial duty. The list of common activities of Russian grandparents reported by McKain does not differ much from the round of activities of many older Americans, but apparently there is a vastly different feeling about them in the two societies. The older Russian apparently feels comfortable, needed, useful, and loved while gardening, keeping house, shopping, or gossiping on a park bench while watching a grandchild playing in the park, whereas the same activities carry no such meaning or satisfaction for the older American. It is not evident that the work role is valued any less in Russia than in America but retirement seems not to involve the same trauma. Perhaps there is a cultural norm which in effect says at retirement, 'You have honorably fulfilled your obligation to society; you have earned the right to rest and enjoy yourself.' [. . .] Older Americans continue to be haunted by the spectre of dependency. The older Russian has no such fear and operating from the sanctuary of a three-generation household appears to have found psychological security and satisfaction in his status.

We have asserted that retirement is a modern invention found only in modern high productivity societies and this is true if we define retirement as total cessation of the main activity from which one obtained the major part of his income or livelihood, for reasons other than health. In this limited sense we find no retirement in African societies; one changes activity on becoming an elder, but this is certainly not the equivalent of retirement. Similarly in Samoa there is commonly a shift in the kind of activity, but definitely not a cessation of work for any other reason than physical incapacity and most continue to work even if seriously handicapped. In Thailand, there is compulsory retirement in the civil service, but this is a small proportion of the total population most of whom continue to work as long as they are physically able. We find essentially the same pattern in Mexico. But modernization has brought retirement to Japan; now about half of the older population is retired although most of them would rather continue working than be forced to live on their very low retirement incomes. In Israel the proportion working is somewhat lower, 43 per cent, but those who continue to work say they cannot afford to stop. In the other countries – Russia, Austria, Norway, and the United States – retirement has become the expected pattern although in Russia this seems to occur with less difficulty than in the other three countries.

From these cases it appears true that the status of the aged is high in societies in which the extended form of the family is prevalent and it tends to be lower in societies which favor the nuclear form of the family. In all of the African societies, the eldest male is head of the family which includes all of the direct descendants either of himself in patrilineal tribes or of his sister in matrilineal tribes. In either case he is highly revered, respected, and powerful. In all cases he is cared for and supported in his old age as a matter of course. The situation is analogous in Samoa where the *matai* are heads of extended families and claim support of their children even if those children are overseas. In Thailand, while the aged parent is less powerful, until the current generation they controlled the marital choices of their children and even yet have a claim for care in their old age, a claim that is usually satisfied by one or more children who maintain their residence in the parental compound.

Older parents live with their children in Mexico and the mores dictate that the children have an obligation to care for them. The situation in Japan is changing, but Plath reports that 80 per cent of older people live with their children, although usually in a separate room or house, and they have a legal right to support by their kin. Here we find the extended family persisting in a recently modernized country. Likewise the three-generation household persists in Russia where the traditional pattern has been reinforced by a pension system which makes the older person an asset rather than a liability in the household. In Ireland the nuclear family obtains, but due to late marriage of the sons and peculiar inheritance patterns it resembles the extended family in many respects.

In Austria, Norway, and the United States, the nuclear family is the mode and marriage is neolocal; the mores strongly favor independence of aged parents from their adult children in housing and financial matters. There are still affectional bonds, and children do in fact assume considerable responsibility for parents, but preferably not under the same roof.

Rosenmayr aptly describes the pattern in Vienna as 'intimacy at a distance', i.e. separate residence but close enough for frequent visiting and mutual assistance. In the rural areas of Norway, although it is tending to disappear, there is some persistence of the custom of primogeniture in the inheritance of land and the associated responsibility of the elder son to care for the aged parents. In the United States neolocal residence is prevalent, but there apparently is something akin to 'intimacy at a distance' in that most older people, although living separately, are visited frequently by children and other kin. This is so common that some students are referring to it as 'the modified extended family'. However, in the latter three countries it is evident that the kin relationships are more attenuated and it is precisely in these societies that we find the status of the aged ambiguous. In Ireland, the economic control exercised by the parents results in at least the youngest son remaining in the parental home until the death of the father.

Again in Israel we find contrasting situations which support the general proposition. Among the Oriental migrants who have maintained the extended family to a greater extent, the status of the aged is more secure, while among the western migrants the situation is comparable to that in Europe, i.e. the nuclear family is the expected form and the status of the aged is relatively lower.

There is very strong support for the proposition that with modernization the responsibility for providing economic security for dependent aged tends to be shifted from the family to the state. In the African countries no such programs have yet evolved as a part of governmental services; neither have they in Samoa. In Thailand there are meager pensions for civil servants but no general pension or social security program. Some public assistance based on need is available and there are already six governmentally operated homes for the aged. Furthermore, it is symptomatic of the very relationship which is being identified here that the Department of Social Welfare has begun to draft plans for a social insurance system as a part of their modernization program.

In most of the modern countries, from Japan to the United States we find elaborate pension, insurance, and assistance programs operated by the governments. Many of these also have extensive health services for the aged under the aegis of the government, and in Japan and Russia such public services extend to recreation, education, and cultural activities. Ireland again represents an exception among modern societies in that pensions and public assistance is extremely meager and in many cases if their children do not look after them the aged may be in serious economic straits. It has been suggested that this precarious economic situation has contributed to the high incidence of mental illness among Irish old people. [. . .]

Lopata provides us with further insights on role changes, in her analysis of widowhood. On the whole, it appears that in preliterate societies there is a strong tendency toward clear-cut ascribed roles for the widow. In some of these where there is widow inheritance or practice of the levirate there is much continuity of role and status. By contrast, in American society the widow, like the aged, is propelled into an ambiguous situation. Her freedom to choose among many potential achieved statuses becomes a social and psychological hazard. The difficulty of readjustment to such a 'roleless role' is exceeded only by the change to one which involves de-gradation of status or even death, as in traditional India. However, even in India social change is now in the process of eliminating the former ascribed roles of the widow and moving toward a greater freedom of choice, with all of the advantages and disadvantages of such freedom.

￫We hypothesized that the individualistic value system of western society tends to reduce the security and status of the older person and our cases tend to confirm the hypothesis. The individual is quite submerged within the family and lineage group in African societies and Samoa, and it is in these societies that we find the highest status of the aged and certainly the collective responsibility assures the aged of as generous support as the tribe can muster. There is a moderate degree of individualism in Thailand. [. . .] In Mexico and Ireland individualism is held in check by com-mitment to the family also. Individualism is increasing in Japan, but here too the family ties are still strong.

In Russia, individualism is deliberately suppressed in favor of the col-lective society and here we have a quite modern society which by main-taining its collective ethic at the expense of individualism also provides a security and a satisfying status for its elders. It is significant to note that this status is maintained even though there is probably as strong an em-phasis on the importance of work and the work role as in the West where this emphasis has sometimes been blamed for the disorientation of older people when they retire. Similar patterns are evident in the *Kibbutz* where the individual is subordinated to the group but in return they have greater security in the collective responsibility of the group for the welfare of its members, including its aged.

￫ By contrast, in Austria, Norway, and the United States where individualism is more pronounced, where the work role is largely divorced from the family, particularly the extended family, and where success is mainly through individual effort and failure is viewed as the individual's responsibility, the status of the aged appears to suffer most; it is here that old people feel useless, dread feeling dependent, and play empty roles.

Finally, we have asserted that disengagement is not characteristic of the aged in pre-industrial societies, but an increasing tendency toward disen-gagement appears to be an accompaniment of modernization. This proposition also appears to be confirmed by our cross-societal analysis. There is little semblance of disengagement in the African societies and Samoa, and such disengagement as occurs is more than balanced by reengagement as older people move into the roles of elders. Some disengagement occurs in Thailand, but it is usually very gradual and is seldom complete. Similarly the older person in Mexico may reduce the strenuousness of his physical exertions, but in many cases he remains fully involved in familial roles. Retirement from work is only one facet of disengagement, but it is a significant form which, as we have noted above, occurs only in modern societies. However, this form of disengagement apparently has different psychological consequences in different modern societies. Retirement seems to occasion little difficulty of adjustment in Russia or in the *Kibbutz*. Since both of these societies are as strongly work-oriented as western societies, we cannot explain the difference in terms of that value. Instead we are forced to look to the economic and psychological security afforded to older people in Russia and in the *Kibbutz*. In the more individualistic western societies, with fewer close family relations, the older person when he disengages from the most meaningful role of his life, the work role, is often left at loose ends without any other significant or satisfying roles.

Summary: a restatement of the theory

And so the theory with which we began this study has survived the test for the most part. In some cases we did not get adequate or relevant evidence. A few of our propositions were found wanting and must now be deleted or modified. These were more than balanced by serendipitous findings which we have not anticipated and were not looking for. Thus our theory has been extended and strengthened and is now ready for further testing.

Universals

1 The aged always constitute a minority within the total population.
2 In an older population, females outnumber males.
3 Widows comprise a high proportion of an older population.
4 In all societies, some people are classified as old and are treated differently because they are so classified.
5 There is a widespread tendency for people defined as old to shift to more sedentary, advisory, or supervisory roles involving less physical exertion and more concerned with group maintenance than with economic production.

6 In all societies, some old persons continue to act as political, judicial, and civic leaders.

7 In all societies, the mores prescribe some mutual responsibility between old people and their adult children.

8 All societies value life and seek to prolong it, even in old age.

Variations

1 The concept of old age is relative to the degree of modernization; a person is classified as old at an earlier chronological age in a primitive society than in a modern society.

2 Old age is identified in terms of chronological age chiefly in modern societies; in other societies onset of old age is more commonly linked with events such as succession to eldership or becoming a grandparent.

3 Longevity is directly and significantly related to the degree of modernization.

4 Modernized societies have older populations, i.e. higher proportions of old people.

5 Modern societies have higher proportions of women and especially of widows.

6 Modern societies have higher proportions of people who live to be grandparents and even great grandparents.

7 The status of the aged is high in primitive societies and is lower and more ambiguous in modern societies.

8 In primitive societies, older people tend to hold positions of political and economic power, but in modern societies such power is possessed by only a few.

9 The status of the aged is high in societies in which there is a high reverence for or worship of ancestors.

10 The status of the aged is highest when they constitute a low proportion of the population and tends to decline as their numbers and proportions increase.

11 The status of the aged is inversely proportional to the rate of social change.

12 Stability of residence favors high status of the aged; mobility tends to undermine it.

13 The status of the aged tends to be high in agricultural societies and lower in urbanized societies.

14 The status of the aged tends to be high in preliterate societies and to decline with increasing literacy of the populations.

15 The status of the aged is high in those societies in which they are able to continue to perform useful and valued functions; however, this is

contingent upon the values of the society as well as upon the specific activities of the aged.

16 Retirement is a modern invention; it is found chiefly in modern high-productivity societies.

17 The status of the aged is high in societies in which the extended form of the family is prevalent and tends to be lower in societies which favor the nuclear form of the family and neolocal marriage.

18 With modernization the responsibility for the provision of economic security for dependent aged tends to be shifted from the family to the state.

19 The proportion of the aged who are able to maintain leadership roles declines with modernization.

20 In primitive societies the roles of widows tend to be clearly ascribed, but such role ascription declines with modernization; the widow's role in modern societies tends to be flexible and ambiguous.

21 The individualistic value system of western society tends to reduce the security and status of older people.

22 Disengagement is not characteristic of the aged in primitive or agrarian societies, but an increasing tendency toward disengagement appears to accompany modernization.

3 Ageing in advanced industrialized societies

Jon Hendricks and C. Davis Hendricks

Introduction

[. . .] Significant improvements in human longevity did not take place until after the mid-seventeenth century; before that time, extension of life expectancy was slight indeed. The gradual increments eventually culminated in an unparalleled rise in life expectancy during the first sixty years of the twentieth century. The increase was of such magnitude in Western industrialized countries that individuals could expect to live twenty years longer if they were born in 1960 rather than in 1900. At the present time this rate appears to have slowed or stabilized, and future predictions suggest this will remain the case. To know whether or not this is a likely possibility requires a general overview of the dynamics of population changes.

The appreciable increase in longevity has been most noticeable among citizens of Western European nations, as well as in the United States. Several countries currently experience a more advantageous position in terms of life expectancy than the United States, among them France, Australia, Denmark, the Netherlands, New Zealand, Canada, Norway and Sweden. Since this rate of improvement has not occurred uniformly throughout the world, many Third World populations exhibit markedly lower life expectancies than their European counterparts. For example, during the period 1960–1970, life expectancy in advanced industrialized countries averaged over 65 years, while males in India could expect to live about 45 years, males in Iran 50 years, and the peoples of the African continent approximately 43 years.

Greater longevity has traditionally gone hand in hand with higher standards of living, reflected in a blending of medical breakthroughs with social advances. Those countries profiting most from improvements in these areas are represented by the lowest birth and death rates relative to the rest of the world. Although their combined population is small compared to the total world population, the hurdles confronting these societies portend those to be faced throughout the rest of the world as technological, economic and demographic profiles are modified. In 1970, the less-developed countries accounted for approximately 2542 million of the world's population, while the more developed numbered 1090 million – a

Source: J. HENDRICKS and C. D. HENDRICKS (1977) *Aging in Mass Society*. Cambridge, Mass.: Winthrop, pp. 51–65 (extracts).

ratio of 2·5 to 1 (United Nations 1971). The increased longevity experienced by part of the world also brings with it a larger proportion of individuals at the upper reaches of the life span. As population compositions shift, many institutions within a society must respond in order to meet the demand for additional or new services. The apparently simple fact of improved life expectancy implies a complex interweaving of social and biological factors that contribute to the additional years of life and are in turn modified by those added years.

The twentieth century has also witnessed the widespread urbanization of the industrialized countries of Europe, North America and Japan, coupled with the gradual industrialization of Eastern Europe. The population structures of these and other advanced industrialized countries of the world differ from those in Third World societies, the former having a larger percentage of people in adulthood, greater longevity and a lower birth rate than the latter. The increased life expectancy is due in part to adequate or better nutrition, health care and educational programs, plus advanced medical techniques. Those scientific discoveries that have added years to average life expectancy have not, however, offered answers to the problems currently facing the growing proportion of elderly in these populations.

Demography and ageing

Demographers often classify populations on the basis of the percentage of people age 65 and over. Thus, a young population is usually considered to be one in which those 65 or over constitute less than 4 per cent of the total population. Similarly, a mature population has between 4 and 7 per cent of its members in this age group, while an aged population has over 7 per cent 65 or older (United Nations 1956). The age structure of a population is an important indicator of many societal patterns. Demographers have found those countries in the world with young populations are characterized by economic underdevelopment, are often agricultural in nature, and have relatively high birth and death rates combined with comparatively short life expectancies. Nations with mature age structures include those undergoing rapid industrial transition and those experiencing high birth rates, declining death rates and a gradual upswing in longevity. Typically, many Eastern European countries fall into this category. To date, countries with aged populations still account for only a small proportion of the world population. Generally speaking, these countries demonstrate the lowest birth rates, lower death rates and greater longevity than the rest of the world. The most aged populations are found in the advanced industrialized societies of North and West Europe. As should already be evident, the aging of populations is a relatively recent phenomenon associated primarily with the growth of industrialism and the facilities available in technologically sophisticated societies. Although the rapid expansion of the proportion of the population age 65 or over began in the mid-nineteenth century for Sweden and France, the remaining countries illustrated in Figure 1 did not display such patterns until the present century.

Figure 1   Percentage of the population aged 65 and over for selected countries.

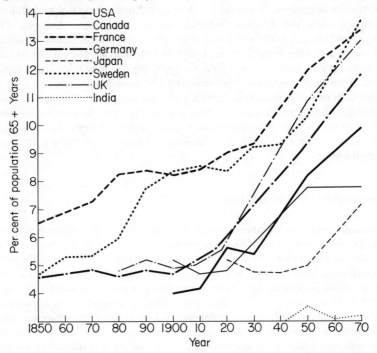

Sources: United Nations, *The Aging of Populations and Its Economic and Social Implications*, Population Studies, no. 26 (New York: United Nations 1956); United Nations, *Demographic Yearbook, 1973*, 25th ed. (New York: United Nations 1974). (Adapted from numeric data.)

One might easily assume populations age because of declining death rates, but in fact this is not necessarily the case. For example, despite the fact French mortality rates have not been reduced to the level of the Netherlands, France nevertheless has an older population. Why should this be so? Contrary to popular expectations, declining mortality is not sufficient in itself to bring about an aged population. We [have] noted that a lower birth rate does not immediately follow on the heels of declining mortality. In industrializing countries, reductions of fertility lag behind those of mortality, creating in the interval something resembling a baby boom. The reasons for this are twofold: First, and perhaps most significant, improvements in medical technology have been most successful in combating infectious diseases. Older people, however, are more likely to succumb as a consequence of the debilitating effects of chronic illnesses that sap their strength. Children on the other hand are more susceptible to the acute conditions of infectious diseases; hence, medical advances initially serve to inhibit aging of the entire population by swelling the numbers of the very young. Only after larger cohorts of children survive to adulthood does the age structure begin to shift upward. In all circumstances, the crucial variable is a declining fertility rate (United Nations 1956). Today many Third World countries have experienced a drop in mortality with the introduction of sophisticated medical techniques, yet their population age structures remain quite young due to continuing high birth rates. Since fertility is so closely tied to a host of social practices, demographic data must be considered with an eye to the intricate association of biological, psychological and social factors. Finally, a variable of considerable importance, but one beyond the scope of the present discussion, is migration. Migratory movements can alter the population age structure in a variety of ways. One example, detailed later in this paper, concerns the geographic relocation of young adults during the period of industrial expansion in the United States. Large scale international migrations, of less importance to today's industrialized societies, had, and to some extent have, a significant impact on societies that beckon in some way to younger, more mobile members of other cultures. Whether we select the colonization process by European powers, the influx of settlers in nineteenth century America or movement among Third World nations makes little difference. The crucial fact that must be assessed for each population in question is the intensity of the migratory movement, both for sender and receiver societies. Intensity must of necessity take into account age and sex distribution, but the interaction of migration with fertility and mortality involves even more complex and less certain relationships than the latter have with population age structures. [. . .]

Quality of life

Our evaluation of the relative position of the aged in society is made considerably easier in this century because of established census procedures in advanced industrialized countries. Although data are not always exactly comparable, a significant amount of information is available that enables researchers to provide a reasonably coherent description of the life situation of today's elderly. Any portrait of the elderly thus painted should also include a fine shadowing of the conditions that anticipated their current status. Since all segments of the population have grown, it is not enough to know there are more people over 65 now than ever before. The critical observer asks whether the *proportion* of elderly in mass society has shown a comparable increase. If the answer is yes, a glimmer of some of those factors influencing our social well-being begins to emerge.

The quality of life experienced by the elderly is directly related to their growing numbers, improving health status and changing societal values. As has been seen, the sheer numbers of people living beyond retirement age have multiplied dramatically since the turn of the century. The character of the lives they lead results from a wide spectrum of events and conditions impinging upon them. Among the more significant features to be discussed are sex and racial characteristics, residence and migration patterns, living arrangements, life expectancy, education, occupation, and income. [. . .] Let us highlight just a few of the trends.

Throughout the industrialized world women live longer than men. At birth the differences in expected longevity are in the range of two to eight years. The actual expectations vary, depending on such variables as local circumstances or racial background. In the United States, both white and black females generally live longer than their male counterparts, with life expectancy for white males and black females being nearly identical. Among whites, females outlive males by over seven years, while for blacks the interval is nearly eight and a half years. After age 24 there are more women than men in the population, with the sex ratio becoming further distorted after age 65. Right now in the United States there are 72 men for every 100 women past retirement age, and by the year 2000 this number will likely decline to about 67 men per 100 women.

In addition to changes in the average length of life, the composition of the work force has also undergone several fluctuations since the turn of the century. Most of the industrialized countries of the world have followed the lead of Germany and Chancellor Bismarck in establishing legal retirement at age 65. As a plank in its 1932 platform, the Democratic party of the United States came out in favor of inclusive Social Security coverage modeled after Germany's. Following the election and the inauguration of the Democratic administration, the first Social Security legislation was enacted in 1935, setting forth a federal program of supplemental income insurance for all workers reaching age 65. While such formal retirement policies inevitably meet with some criticism, they do allow a smoother transition of the labor force and more open access to upper echelon positions by younger workers. Of course, they may also become the basis for age discrimination. In 1890, over two-thirds of older American males were employed; today that figure has dropped to approximately 25 per cent. Among women, recent definitions of appropriate sex roles, periodic societal demands for workers and other economic incentives have contributed to a slight increase in the participation of older women in the labor force. The most dramatic change has occurred among women between 45 and 64 years of age. Their activity in the labor force has increased nearly fourfold, from 13 per cent in 1900 to more than 48 per cent in 1970. Over the course of the lives of today's elderly women, familial and household matters have constituted their chief responsibility, while their husbands were busy earning a livelihood outside the home. With the popularization of mandatory retirement, it was hypothesized by some gerontologists that men would find themselves deprived of what had been a major source of identity. Undoubtedly the psychological stresses attendant with the loss of a man's economic function are to be reckoned with, but [. . .] recent longitudinal research has questioned their severity. It may well be that loss of work, although previously constituting a central life role, is not nearly as devastating to the individual as once assumed. Nevertheless, retirement necessitates some type of accommodation among older people. The problem is not limited to male workers; older women may also suffer emotional distress as they live out the last several years of life unaccompanied by either spouse or family. Seventy years ago, few couples had much time left to themselves after launching their youngest child into adulthood; recently, however, they have come to enjoy close to fifteen years together after the marriage of their last child. In the United States at least, the wife then has an average of seven or more years in which she must cope with the realities of widowhood. If she is appreciably younger than her husband, and most wives are three to five years younger, this period may be even more extended.

Major population relocations have occurred as the emphasis on industrial production outdistanced that placed on agricultural. In the United States, the outmigration of young people from the Midwest has left behind vast areas where the proportion of the elderly in the population is far higher than the national average. Popular retirement states like Florida, Arizona and Nevada, or parts of California, also have an overrepresentation of the elderly. These shifts are reflected in the percentage of the country living in urban and rural environments. In 1900, over 60 per cent of the population resided in rural areas; by 1970 this figure was cut to about 26 per cent. The percentage of the elderly in smaller cities and rural areas is above the national average of one in every ten [. . .]. In urbanized regions, the elderly became concentrated in central city areas, as newer suburban neighbourhoods attracted young, mobile families. Patterns not unlike those presented here have been observed in other industrialized societies of the world. [. . .]

Old age and urbanization

[. . .] Even among those [countries] experiencing the slowest population growth, urbanization has proceeded at a rapid rate in the present century. Sweden and France, for instance, have had nearly stable growth rates for years, yet both have expanded their urban populations significantly, France by 15 per cent and Sweden by over 30 per cent. As younger people move to urban areas they leave behind parents and elders, eventually resulting in a disproportionate number of elderly in rural regions. In recent times this trend has been accompanied by younger workers settling in the newer, outlying suburban neighborhoods, thus contributing to an overrepresentation of older people in the inner city.

Urbanization is one by-product of the technological and economic changes fostered in part by the process of industrialization. The increasing size of our urban population is just one ecological manifestation of the technical and organizational requirements of industry. As more sophisticated means of production are created, new skills and knowledge are called for. Middle-aged and older workers have already established their occupational competence, and their educations were usually obtained in the distant past. As new opportunities become available, younger workers experience a selective mobility, both occupational and geographic. One of the apparent consequences of industrialization is a higher value placed on smaller family units that are more readily mobile, plus an emphasis on productive independence regardless of one's previous contributions.

References

UNITED NATIONS (1956) *The Aging of Populations and Its Economic and Social Implications.* Population Studies, no. 26. New York: United Nations.

UNITED NATIONS (1971) *The World Population Situation in 1970.* Population Studies, no. 49. New York: United Nations.

UNITED NATIONS (1974) *Demographic Yearbook, 1973,* 25th ed. Special Topic: Population Census Statistics 1. New York: United Nations.

UNITED NATIONS (1975) *Statistical Yearbook, 1974,* 26th ed. New York: United Nations.

4 Ageing and public expenditure in the United Kingdom

D. C. L. Wroe

Introduction

A major social problem today is how to provide for the large number of elderly people. Over the last fifty or so years the elderly population has grown substantially faster than the population of younger ages both on account of the fall in the birth rate in the early nineteen-twenties and on account of general improvements in health and social conditions which have led to increases in the proportions surviving to old age. At the same time the rise in the general level of economic prosperity has enabled more people to set up their own households so that, while the nuclear family has increased in importance, the elderly on the whole now receive less support from their families.

During the present century the state has gradually assumed a large measure of the responsibility for supporting the elderly which previously rested almost entirely with their families, charities and the elderly themselves, but voluntary organisations continue to accept responsibility for a wide range of services particularly in some areas of the country. Official statistics provide little information about the work of voluntary organisations and, partly for this reason, do not give a full picture of the services for elderly people. The statistics which are available nevertheless comprise a considerable body of information, and the purposes of this article are first to consider what they reveal of the circumstances and requirements of the elderly in respect of their incomes, housing, and so on, and then to examine the public expenditure incurred to meet those requirements.

The term elderly is used here to cover all persons at or above the minimum age at which a National Insurance retirement pension can be paid: for men this is age 65 and for women age 60. About 70 per cent of men and over 60 per cent of women with title to National Insurance retirement pensions retire within a year of reaching pensionable age. Attaining pensionable age therefore soon involves a radical change in the daily lives of most people previously in employment and is the stage at which many first become heavily dependent on social security expenditure, notably the retirement pensions for which they have contributed, as well as on the savings which they have accumulated. In contrast,

Source: D. C. L. WROE (1973) 'The elderly', *Social Trends*, no. 4, pp. 23–33 (extracts).

dependence on the health and personal social services increases gradually as people become older, and while some of those of pensionable ages – particularly persons over 75 – are heavily dependent on these services, there are nevertheless a large group capably and happily living independent lives.

Demographic aspects

In 1971 there were 2·8 million men in the United Kingdom aged at least 65 and 6·1 million women at least 60, in all 8·9 million elderly persons. This contrasts with 2·9 million in 1911, soon after the Old Age Pensions Act 1908 introduced a non-contributory pension of 5 shillings a week to persons over seventy and on an income less than £21 per annum. Since that time the number of elderly people has risen as in the third row of Table 1.

Table 1   Elderly persons in the UK. 1911–2001 (UK).

	Actual				*Projected*	
	1911	1931	1951	1971	1981	2001
Elderly population (thousands):						
Men aged at least 65	964	1,470	2,251	2,757	3,166	3,139
Women aged at least 60	1,915	2,950	4,599	6,141	6,545	6,313
Total elderly	2,879	4,420	6,850	8,898	9,711	9,452
Elderly as a percentage of total population	6·8	9·6	13·6	16·0	16·8	15·0
Elderly persons per thousand population of working age	110	145	213	267	280	244

Mainly on account of the high numbers of births in the years up to about 1921, the number of elderly people in the population will increase for the next two decades or so before the lower annual numbers of births between the wars lead to a slight decrease in the elderly population until the end of the century. [...] One of the effects of these changes in combination with other factors is that over the next ten years the number of persons of retirement ages will grow faster than the population of working ages, though not as fast as in recent decades. Past and projected movements in the ratio are shown in Table 1. One implication of the increasing ratio of elderly people to the numbers of working ages is that if the standard of living of the elderly is growing in line with earnings, an increasing proportion of each worker's earnings is required to support them.

The average age of the elderly will increase over the next few decades, adding considerably to the demands on the health and personal social services for the elderly, both statutory and voluntary. The percentage of elderly women aged at least 75 is projected to rise from 28·0 in 1971 to 32·0 in 1981 and to reach 37·6 by 2001. Table 2 also shows how the proportion aged at least 85 will increase. The proportion of elderly men aged at least 75 is likely to rise from 29·2 per cent in 1971 to 36·3 in 2001, but movements in this proportion and in the proportion aged at least 85 are substantially affected in this period by casualties in the First World War.

Table 2   Age structure of the elderly population (UK, percentages).

	Actual			*Projected*	
	1951	1961	1971	1981	2001
Men aged at least:					
85	3·1	4·4	4·4	3·8	5·5
75	30·7	32·7	29·2	31·3	36·3
65	100·0	100·0	100·0	100·0	100·0
Women aged at least:					
85	3·4	4·5	5·6	6·0	8·7
75	24·0	27·1	28·0	32·0	37·6
65	70·3	71·3	72·4	76·3	77·7
60	100·0	100·0	100·0	100·0	100·0

As women tend to outlive their husbands the problems of loneliness and adjusting to new circumstances faced by the elderly are confronted more frequently among women than men. Table 3 shows a considerably higher proportion widowed (or divorced) among elderly women than among elderly men. There are also substantial differences between age groups, especially for women. As may be seen from Table 3, over 80 per cent of women aged 75 or over are single, widowed or divorced. The proportions in each age group have varied noticeably in recent years, partly on account of war deaths.

As many more people have been able to establish separate households

Table 3   Elderly persons by marital status (UK, percentages).

	Married		Single		Widowed and divorced	
	1951	1971	1951	1971	1951	1971
Men						
65–74	72·2	78·9	8·9	7·5	18·9	13·6
75 and over	50·0	61·6	8·2	6·2	41·8	32·2
All elderly men	65·4	72·4	8·7	7·1	25·9	20·5
Women						
60–64	56·6	64·5	16·1	11·9	27·3	23·6
65–74	42·2	46·0	16·1	13·9	41·7	40·1
75 and over	19·8	18·1	17·0	16·2	63·2	65·7
All elderly women	41·2	43·3	16·3	14·0	42·5	42·7

Table 4   Elderly population in private households (Great Britain, percentages)[1].

	Living alone[2]			In married couple without others[3]
	1951	1966	1971	1966
Men				
65–74	6·5	9·0	10·9	53·2
75 and over	10·5	14·7	17·7	38·4
All elderly men—percentage	7·7	10·8	13·0	48·6
—*thousands*	*168*	*265*	*354*	*1,190*
Women				
60–74	15·6	23·1	27·0	34·7
75 and over	23·1	31·4	37·5	12·6
All elderly women—percentage	16·8	25·4	30·0	28·7
—*thousands*	*749*	*1,417*	*1,813*	*1,603*

[1] Excluding persons in household where no member was present on Census night.
[2] One person households as defined in the Censuses.
[3] The partner may not be of pensionable age, e.g. men 60–64 married to women in the same age group.

for themselves and their dependent children and more retired people are able to afford homes of their own, the proportion of elderly people who live alone has steadily increased (Table 4). In addition the pressures on working people to move to other areas where better opportunities exist have contributed to a situation in which families are less likely to provide company and care for the old. Thus, gradually the state and the community have taken over more responsibility, and considerable efforts are made by social service departments and by voluntary bodies to provide old people with company and activities outside the home in order to dispel the social isolation, boredom and vulnerability of many elderly people living alone. [. . .]

Public expenditure on the elderly

So far [. . .] the kinds of public services used by the elderly [have been discussed] and statistics have been presented to show the numbers of elderly people using such services in practice. This section extends the discussion by showing the results of an attempt to estimate, in broad terms, the financial and resource costs of providing certain social services used by the elderly and the changes in such costs over a period of years. This objective is fairly limited in scope, but it is nonetheless of some interest to examine the impact on an important demographic group of publicly provided resources, just as one may be interested in the impact of public expenditure on a particular income group or a particular region.

Summary of results

In the present state of knowledge we can only discuss public services consumed by the elderly in a few areas, particularly health and welfare services and income support. Table 5 provides a summary picture.

In 1971/72 when the elderly comprised 16 per cent of the total population, the proportion of public expenditure on social security, health and welfare absorbed by the elderly was 48 per cent.

The composition of rising expenditure

The total growth of expenditure on the elderly over time is composed of the effects of inflationary changes in prices generally, changes in the type and volume of services per head, and changes in the total number of elderly people consuming social services. Table 6 below illustrates the effect of each of these factors.

Table 5   Public expenditure on the elderly (Great Britain)[1].

	1963/64	1971/72
Social security expenditure on the elderly		
—£ millions	1,169	2,499
—as percentage of social security		
expenditure on all persons	62%	60%
—as percentage of GNP	4·1%	5·4%
Health and welfare expenditure on the elderly		
—£ millions	303	772
—as percentage of health and welfare		
expenditure on all persons	27%	28%
—as percentage of GNP	1·1%	1·5%
Total social security, health and welfare		
expenditure on the elderly		
—£ millions	1,472	3,221
—as percentage of social security, health		
and welfare expenditure on all persons	49%	48%
—as percentage of GDP	5·2%	6·9%
—per head of the elderly (£)	188	365
Elderly population as percentage of		
total population	15	16

[1] Expenditure figures are expressed at current prices.

Table 6   Composition of additional social service expenditure on the elderly, 1963/64–1971/72 (Great Britain, £ million)

	Social security	Health and welfare
Total additional expenditure	1,330	419
Higher benefits for 1963/64 numbers:		
To offset higher prices	595	221
Real improvements	448	114
Greater numbers:		
At 1963/64 costs per head	152	31
Increase due to applying 1971/72		
costs per head	135	53
of which real improvements	59	23

Table 7   Social service expenditure per head of elderly population at 1963/64 prices
(Great Britain, £ million).

	1963/64	*1971/72*
Social security	150	190
Health and welfare	38	47

The rise in the volume of expenditure *per head* of elderly population is shown in Table 7.

A detailed analysis of public expenditure is shown in Table 8.

Limitations of the results

The figures presented in this section do not cover all public expenditure from which the elderly benefit. Publicly provided resources are of various types:

(*a*) 'Public goods' consumed by everybody such as defence, street lighting and public administration: it is impossible to assign to individuals except in an arbitrary manner (equal per capita amounts, with or without adjustments for age, income, wealth, etc.) and they are ignored here; then there are services for which the elderly are eligible and which they consume to a knowable but unknown extent, e.g. housing subsidies, which have been ignored.

(*b*) There are also services provided for selected groups of people. These may be for (e.g.) the sick or the poor rather than the elderly *per se*, and we may have some knowledge of the share taken by the elderly, e.g. health services. Then there is provision specifically for the elderly, e.g. retirement pensions. Even excluding areas such as those outlined in sub-paragraph (*a*) above, what information does exist is often scattered among several government departments and other agencies, both central and local, and it is difficult to assemble. The present paper does not claim to have fully exploited the available scattered information.

Details of public expenditure on the elderly do not necessarily indicate the extent to which the resources of the rest of the community need to be reduced. In so far as pensions are saved or used to defray the running down of the existing savings of the elderly, pensions do not create a demand for resources. Part of pensions are subject to income tax and do not add to demand. More important in practice, part of the expenditure on the elderly does not create a demand for resources anyway, i.e. that part of expenditure out of State pensions which represents the indirect tax

Table 8   Social security, health and welfare expenditure on the elderly (Great Britain, £ million at current prices).

			1963/64	*1971/72*
Social security				
1.	a.	Retirement pensions and widows' benefits	986	2,091
	b.	National assistance and non-contributory pensions	111	—
	c.	Supplementary benefits	—	267
	d.	War pensions	52	68
	e.	Sickness, invalidity, injury and unemployment benefits	7	13
	f.	Disablement and industrial death benefits	10	25
	g.	Old persons' pensions	—	23
	h.	Attendance allowances	—	3
	i.	Death grants	3	9
		Total social security	1,169	2,499
Health and welfare				
2.	a.	Hospital inpatient/outpatient	192	430
	b.	Pharmaceutical	27	54
	c.	General practitioner	23	48
	d.	Dental and ophthalmic	10	20
	e.	Sub-total 2a.–d.	253	552
3.	a.	Domestic help ⎫	11	39
	b.	Health visits ⎭		
	c.	Home nursing	6	18
	d.	Ambulance	5	12
	e.	Chiropody	1	5
	f.	Residential accommodation	24	71
	g.	Welfare services for elderly and elderly handicapped	5	25
	h.	Sub-total 3a.–g.	50	170
		Total health and welfare	303	722

content of spending such as the duty on tobacco etc.* Further, if the State spends £x on the elderly it does not necessarily follow that solely as *a consequence of State actions* somebody else has £x less. If the State has not spent £x it is reasonable to assume that at least part of the £x would have been provided anyway voluntarily, e.g. via additional expenditure by the families of old people, charities, private insurance schemes, etc. Obviously we can argue about precisely what would have happened in the absence of State provision, but such argument is beyond the scope of this paper; all that is required in the present context is recognition that if the alternative to State provision is some private provision, then the expenditure of the State will tend to give an exaggerated impression of the resource costs of publicly supporting the elderly.

The estimates of public expenditure on the elderly do not indicate the extent to which income is redistributed towards the elderly from the rest of the community. In the first place, private transfers, e.g. within families or from numerous voluntary organisations, are excluded. Further, the figures in this article do not indicate what would have occurred in the absence of state provision, as explained in the previous paragraph, so that the 'incidence' on other households, i.e. the extent to which public provision simply replaces private provision, cannot be known. Finally, taxes paid by the elderly have not been taken into account.

* For a more extensive discussion of these points see *Public Expenditure White Papers: Handbook on Methodology* by HM Treasury, HMSO 1972.

5 Predictors of longevity: a follow-up of the aged in Chapel Hill

Erdman B. Palmore and Virginia Stone

An earlier analysis of longevity among the aged in Durham, North Carolina, found that the use of physical, mental, and social examinations can improve the accuracy of longevity predictions by one-third over predictions based on actuarial life expectancy alone (Palmore 1969a). A follow-up study found that work satisfaction, happiness rating, physical functioning, and tobacco use were the four strongest predictors of longevity when age, sex, and race are controlled by use of the Longevity Quotient (Palmore 1969b). However, it was noted that the Durham sample was a somewhat above-average group of volunteers and that the generalizability of these findings to other more typical populations would have to await testing with other groups.

The present paper reports the results of applying essentially the same techniques to prediction of longevity among most of the aged in Chapel Hill and Carboro, NC, in 1958.

Dr Stone attempted to interview all persons over 60 in 1958 residing in Chapel Hill or Carboro, getting basic demographic data as well as employment status, occupation, education, living arrangements, physical mobility, hearing, and condition of home furnishings (Stone 1962). Interviews were completed with over 900 persons. In 1971 this group was followed up to determine, among other things, place of residence for those still living and date of death for those deceased. This information was obtained for 864 of the original group. There were 388 still living and 476 dead, 325 men and 539 women, 661 whites and 203 blacks. In 1958, 520 were under 70 and 344 were over 70. Comparison with 1960 US Census data showed that those interviewed did include most of the target population.

The measure of longevity in this analysis is the Longevity Quotient (LQ), which is the observed number of years survived after initial interview divided by the actuarially expected number of years based on age, sex, and race. The LQ is thus analogous to an intelligence quotient which is the observed intelligence score divided by the expected intelligence score for the age group. An LQ of 1.0 means that the person survived exactly as long as expected, an LQ of 1.5 means that the person survived

Source: *The Gerontologist*, 1973, *13*, 1, pp. 88–90 (extracts).

50 per cent longer than expected, and an LQ of 0.5 means that the person survived half as long as expected. [. . .]

Use of the LQ has several advantages over other measures of longevity (Palmore 1969b, 1971). It controls for the known general effects of age, sex, and race on longevity and allows concentration on the less understood factors of health, mental, and social variables. [. . .]

The four significant predictors of longevity were physical mobility, education, occupation, and employment. The categories used in these predictors together with their mean LQ are as follow. *Mobility:* unimpaired (1.05), difficulty walking (.88), wheelchair or bedbound (.64). *Education:* PhD (1.23), MA or equivalent (1.13), BA (1.10), some college (1.04), high school or business school (1.00), 3–8 years elementary (.98), less than 3 years (.82). *Occupation:* professors (1.22), other white collar (1.06), blue collar (.95), housewife (.87), farmer (.77). *Employment:* employed (1.11), housewife (1.00), retired (.94). [. . .]

Education and occupation seem to exert substantial independent effects on longevity. Education and occupation are probably both indicators of the underlying dimensions of mental ability and socioeconomic status. There is substantial evidence that these indicators and underlying dimensions mutually reinforce each other in complex ways. Superior mental ability and higher family socioeconomic status both contribute to more education and all three of these contribute to higher occupational status. Thus they all probably increase longevity in direct and indirect ways. Superior mental ability probably increases longevity directly by allowing better problem-solving and adaptation to crisis and strain, as well as indirectly through its effects on education and occupation. Education probably increases longevity directly by increasing knowledge about health care, nutrition, safety, etc., as well as indirectly through its effects on occupation. Higher status occupations probably increase longevity by providing safer and healthier working conditions, more income for health care, nutrition, and housing. The psychological and social rewards of higher status occupations may indirectly increase longevity by contributing to more life satisfaction, better mental health, and preventing the psychosomatically dangerous effects of depression, alienation, and withdrawal.

When the effects of education and occupation are added together, they account for almost half of the explained variance in longevity. Thus; this complex of factors is substantially more important in predicting longevity than our single measure of health, physical mobility. [. . .]

Finally, continued employment had a modest but independent association with longevity. This is consistent with the Duke Longitudinal Study finding that work satisfaction was the third strongest predictor of longevity in our most recent analysis (Palmore 1972) [. . .]. Continued employment and work satisfaction may operate at three levels to increase longevity. On the physical level it usually provides regular exercise; on the mental level it usually provides cognitive stimulation; on the social level it usually provides the status, satisfaction, and social integration of a meaningful social role; all of which probably increase longevity. [. . .]

Several variables which might theoretically have been related to longevity showed no significant association. For example, marital status was not related to longevity. There was no difference in longevity between the married and the widowed, while single persons had a slightly higher longevity. This is contrary to other studies which show higher mortality rates for widowed and single persons, but consistent with the Duke longitudinal findings. Other variables with no consistent or significant association with longevity were number of years in the vicinity, living arrangements, being head of household, number of children in household, and hearing ability. [. . .]

References

PALMORE, E. (1969a) 'Physical, mental and social factors in predicting longevity', *Gerontologist*, 9, 103–8.

PALMORE, E. (1969b) 'Predicting longevity. A follow-up controlling for age', *Gerontologist*, 9, 247–50.

PALMORE, E. (1971) 'The relative importance of social factors in predicting longevity'. In E. Palmore and F. Jeffers (eds) *Prediction of Life Span*. Lexington, Mass.: D. C. Heath.

PALMORE, E. (1972) 'Social factors in predicting longevity'. Paper delivered at Southern Sociological Society Meetings, New Orleans.

STONE, Y. (1962) 'Personal adjustment in ageing in relation to community environment'. In *Proceedings of Seminars, 1959–61*. Durham, NC: Duke University Council on Gerontology.

6 Tomorrow and tomorrow and tomorrow

Kurt Vonnegut

The year was 2158 AD, and Lou and Emerald Schwartz were whispering on the balcony outside of Lou's family's apartment on the 76th floor of Building 257 in Alden Village, a New York housing development that covered what had once been known as Southern Connecticut. When Lou and Emerald had married, Em's parents had tearfully described the marriage as being between May and December; but now, with Lou 112 and Em 93, Em's parents had to admit that the match had worked out surprisingly well.

But Em and Lou weren't without their troubles, and they were out in the nippy air of the balcony because of them. What they were saying was bitter and private.

'Sometimes I get so mad, I feel like just up and diluting his anti-gerasone,' said Em.

'That'd be against Nature, Em,' said Lou, 'it'd be murder. Besides, if he caught us tinkering with his anti-gerasone, not only would he disinherit us, he'd bust my neck. Just because he's 172 doesn't mean Gramps isn't strong as a bull.'

'Against Nature,' said Em. 'Who knows what Nature's like any more? Ohhhhh – I don't guess I could ever bring myself to dilute his anti-gerasone or anything like that, but, gosh, Lou, a body can't help thinking Gramps is never going to leave if somebody doesn't help him along a little. Golly – we're so crowded a person can hardly turn around, and Verna's dying for a baby, and Melissa's gone thirty years without one.' She stamped her feet. 'I get so sick of seeing his wrinkled old face, watching him take the only private room and the best chair and the best food, and getting to pick out what to watch on TV, and running everybody's life by changing his will all the time.'

'Well, after all,' said Lou bleakly, 'Gramps *is* head of the family. And he can't help being wrinkled like he is. He was 70 before anti-gerasone was invented. He's going to leave, Em. Just give him time. It's his business. I know he's tough to live with, but be patient. It wouldn't do to do anything that'd rile him. After all, we've got it better'n anybody else, there on the day-bed.'

'How much longer do you think we'll get to sleep on the day-bed before he picks another pet? The world's record's two months, isn't it?'

Source: T. BOARDMAN (ed.) (1964) *Connoisseur's Science Fiction*. Harmondsworth: Penguin, pp. 64–6 (extract).

'Mom and Pop had it that long once, I guess.'

'When *is* he going to leave, Lou?' said Emerald.

'Well, he's talking about giving up anti-gerasone right after the 500-mile Speedway Race.'

'Yes – and before that it was the Olympics, and before that the World's Series, and before that the Presidential Elections, and before that I-don't-know-what. It's been just one excuse after another for fifty years now. I don't think we're ever going to get a room to ourselves or an egg or anything.'

'All right – call me a failure!' said Lou. 'What can I do? I work hard and make good money, but the whole thing practically is taxed away for defence and old age pensions. And if it wasn't taxed away, where you think we'd find a vacant room to rent? Iowa, maybe? Well, who wants to live on the outskirts of Chicago?'

Em put her arms around his neck. 'Lou, hon, I'm not calling you a failure. The Lord knows you're not. You just haven't had a chance to be anything or have anything because Gramps and the rest of his generation won't leave and let somebody else take over.'

'Yeah, yeah,' said Lou gloomily. 'You can't exactly blame 'em, though, can you? I mean, I wonder how quick we'll knock off the anti-gerasone when we get Gramps' age.'

'Sometimes I wish there wasn't any such thing as anti-gerasone!' said Emerald passionately. 'Or I wish it was made out of something real expensive and hard-to-get instead of mud and dandelions. Sometimes I wish folks just up and died regular as clockwork, without anything to say about it, instead of deciding themselves how long they're going to stay around. There ought to be a law against selling the stuff to anybody over 150.'

'Fat chance of that,' said Lou, 'with all the money and votes the old people've got.' He looked at her closely. 'You ready to up and die, Em?'

'Well, for heaven's sakes, what a thing to say to your wife. Hon! I'm not even 100 yet.' She ran her hands lightly over her firm, youthful figure, as though for confirmation. 'The best years of my life are still ahead of me. But you can bet that when 150 rolls around, old Em's going to pour her anti-gerasone down the sink, and quit taking up room, and she'll do it smiling.'

'Sure, sure,' said Lou, 'you bet. That's what they all say. How many you heard of doing it?'

'There was that man in Delaware.'

'Aren't you getting kind of tired of talking about him, Em? That was five months ago.'

'All right, then – Gramma Winkler, right here in the same building.'

'She got smeared by a subway.'

'That's just the way she picked to go,' said Em.

'Then what was she doing carrying a carton of anti-gerasone when she got it?'

Emerald shook her head wearily and covered her eyes. 'I dunno, I dunno, I dunno. All I know is, something's just got to be done.' She sighed. 'Sometimes I wish they'd left a couple of diseases kicking around somewhere, so I could get one and go to bed for a little while. Too many people!' she cried, and her words cackled and gabbled and died in a thousand asphalt-paved, skyscraper-walled courtyards. [. . .]

7 Speculations in social and environmental gerontology

D. B. Bromley

Most people would agree that Western industrial society is geared first to the needs and activities of its production and service workers, and secondly to the physical health and education of its juvenile members. It is only since the beginning of the twentieth century that the needs and activities of the elderly have made substantial and increasing demands upon the available goods and services. It is, therefore, not altogether surprising, particularly in view of the rapid changes in the age structure of the population and in world socioeconomic circumstances, that we have not yet learned to cope adequately with the many problems of human ageing. Even so, most people would agree that the health and living standards of the elderly have improved on average over recent decades and that the long-term trend seems to be set for continued improvement. The main problem, the main area of conflict and disagreement, concerns the *scale* and the *rate* of this improvement, although the *nature* of the resources to be provided is also a matter about which opinions differ (see Johnson 1976).

The British Society of Social and Behavioural Gerontology (BSSBG) could be expected to offer expert advice on the problem of what goods and services are *required* by older people. As yet, however, there are few economists, politicians and social administrators in its ranks who could examine questions of *feasibility* in relation to policy proposals based on social and environmental research.

Social and environmental gerontology is concerned with the adult part of the human lifespan, and with the relationships between juvenile development and adult ageing. It is concerned not only, or even mainly, with the individual psychological aspects of human ageing, but rather with its broader sociological, economic and environmental aspects. The BSSBG was established as, and continues to function as, a learned and scientific society. It is not a pressure group or even a 'charitable' society in the narrow sense of that term; so it does not hold dogmatic views about ageing, or engage in propaganda on behalf of the aged. Its functions are to advance knowledge, to question current beliefs and practices, and to disseminate what it believes, on the basis of the best scientific evidence and arguments, to be the correct facts and theories about human ageing (Bromley 1976a; and Bromley, 1976b).

Source: *Nursing Times*, 1977, *73*, 16, pp. 53–6.

The main functions of the BSSBG are scientific and educational; yet the BSSBG, as a socially responsible learned society, cannot evade the moral and practical issues associated with ageing and with the expected increase in the numbers of older and infirm aged people. Standards of living and health care for older people have been improving steadily, but the costs have risen steeply; and there has been a fall in the birthrate, and a relative decline in industrial productivity. This means that we are faced *not* with just a temporary socioeconomic difficulty that might be solved by a substantial but temporary shift of resources to the care of the aged. On the contrary, it seems that we are experiencing a firm evolutionary trend which could lead, in the not too distant future, to a society very different from the kind of society with which we are familiar – a society as different, in its age composition and social organisation, from the one we know as our present-day society is different from its Elizabethan period.

The broad ecological factors which govern the social evolution of a society like ours are not entirely beyond influence. Indeed many important ecological factors are associated with the industrial and institutional features of our environment, which are man-made. These include: urban living conditions, the age composition of our society, and our political system. We can, by rational and empirical inquiry, get to understand what is going on and attempt to bring these and many other factors under some degree of control, or at least anticipate their effects. But what we choose to do is not merely a matter of applying scientific knowledge; it is also a matter of adopting social policies which express moral values and political judgement. For example, we have heard a claim from one occupational group for an earlier retirement age for its workers, and we have heard the suggestion that there should be a common age of retirement for men and women. Such issues raise immediately manpower and economic questions. Could the retired members of the workforce be replaced in sufficient numbers to maintain output? Might the additional costs associated with a new common retirement age lead to substantial reductions in expenditure elsewhere? Experts in economics and manpower planning may be able to provide answers to these questions. But how do we decide whether such changes are desirable or whether they deserve higher priority than other socially desirable changes? How do we decide whether such changes are in fact in the best interests of the community as a whole or even of the people who will be most directly affected? Whose interests do the opinion leaders represent?

It could be argued that older people have not been given sufficient voice in the formulation of social and economic policies, even though the politicians, civil servants and advisers who make the policy may themselves be older people. The direct involvement of the aged in the formulation of social and economic policies may sound slightly absurd to some people. But this is an indication of the extent to which old age, and even late middle age, tends to lead to segregation, disengagement and dependence, and to a loss of the proper democratic procedures for securing consensus and the rights of minorities. Such segregation and loss of rights can be seen most clearly in certain kinds of institution for the care of the aged infirm.

The task of desegregating the aged infirm is one which occupies the severely undermanned geriatric medical, nursing and social services in this country. It is a task which has parallels in other disadvantaged sectors of the community, for example the disabled and the mentally retarded, and can be expected to meet with a certain amount of apathy and resistance. The problem is to find the resources and the methods whereby the diverse needs and functional capacities of the aged can be interlocked in a humane and effective way with the rest of society.

The successful *integration* of the elderly infirm *into* the community could be regarded as the touchstone for a comprehensive social and economic policy for later life, because the social attitudes and values, and the economic resources necessary to secure such integration, would have ensured that all other aspects of human ageing had been dealt with.

I cannot examine the large and fundamental issue of how to minimise segregation of the aged and how to integrate the elderly infirm into the wider community; but I can deal with a relevant issue – a delicate one – which is rarely mentioned in polite gerontological circles. Indeed, in comparison with other taboo topics it makes bereavement and euthanasia seem quite jolly. This delicate issue concerns what, for want of a more euphemistic term, we can call the 'aversive properties of the aged person' [. . .] and I believe that consideration of it helps us to appreciate the deep psychological processes that affect people in their dealings with the aged. The intensity that such feelings of aversion can reach is dramatically illustrated in an entry in Richard Crossman's diary for Tuesday, 20 December, 1966:

I was able to go to the Christmas party given by the Labour peers. As I walked in I saw, sitting on the left, the ghastly living corpse of Attlee, now virtually stone deaf and almost inarticulate. Patricia Llewelyn-Davies said to me, 'Do go and talk to the old man. He wants company.' I had to say to her, 'I'm sorry, I can't face it. He has always hated me and I now hate him.' I'm afraid I walked the other way.

Many people who have little direct contact with the elderly, experience something of that kind of aversion on encountering a physically and mentally deteriorated aged person. The reason for it probably lies in the way we have become conditioned to perceive and understand human beings. Briefly, what seems to happen is that early in life we become, in a sense, 'imprinted' with the image of the persons who look after us, usually our parents and older siblings. Through childhood we acquire a notion of what is normal and expected in relation to the appearance and behaviour of human beings. Close contact with any marked deviation from the norm tends to elicit anxiety, hostility and rejection, as may be seen by the initial reactions infants have to strangers and of young children to people with artificial limbs or facial disfigurement. (When I wore glasses for the first time, my own child refused to look at me for several minutes until she had got used to the idea that they could be removed and replaced and that it was the same face behind the glasses!)

The physical appearance and behaviour of an aged infirm person is markedly different from the norm to which we have been strongly conditioned. The isolation and segregation of the aged greatly reduces the frequency with which they are encountered, by younger adults and children, so that there is normally little opportunity through social interaction for us to become familiar with and adapted to them. There is, of course, interaction with aged parents or grandparents, but this is usually reduced if their physical appearance and behaviour deteriorate, and is unlikely to affect normal expectations and attitudes built up through life.

The frightening effects of distortions and caricatures of human behaviour and human appearance are easily demonstrated by the use of masks and simulation (as in acting). Animals, like chimpanzees, can be shown to exhibit fear when presented with something which caricatures chimpanzee appearance. The notion of what is normal and acceptable as 'human nature' has deep psychological and biological roots and this may have a bearing on the apparent lack of altruistic behaviour towards the aged. Anthropological studies of human ageing also have a bearing on this topic.

Aversion to the appearance of an aged and infirm person is not necessarily unavoidable or natural, but their very segregation and isolation deprives younger adults and children of opportunities for perceiving and understanding them as human beings; and hinders them, in effect, from learning to accept old age as a normal aspect of the human lifespan.

The only people who encounter the aged infirm in any sort of extensive and frequent way are physicians, nurses and social workers, and a few others whose work it is to care for the elderly. Their behaviour demonstrates that aversion is by no means universal and that even when it is present initially it tends to disappear or at least be lessened as a result of familiarity.

The relevance of all this to the *integration* of the elderly infirm *into* the community is that successful integration would mean that most people no longer had unfavourable attitudes towards old age, no longer avoided social interaction with the elderly, no longer accepted segregation of and degradation of the aged infirm.

This brief excursion into the psychology of social attitudes towards the aged perhaps reveals something of the extent and the strength of the feelings which hinder social integration. It suggests that age prejudice should be outlawed as are other forms of social prejudice.

How might we begin to redefine 'old age' and other 'stages' of life so that we can discard the highly unsatisfactory and outdated attitudes inherited from the Elizabethan and Victorian eras? (see Bromley 1974). There is not enough time to discuss the adult phase of life in detail, but a modern scheme should incorporate an attempt to discriminate different phases of middle age; it should incorporate a pre-retirement phase and a terminal phase. The positive aspects of all these stages need more emphasis than they currently receive. The psychological and sociological aspects of the menopause also need to be investigated more thoroughly as a critical period in the adult life of women.

Recognising that these stages of adult life have their own fairly distinctive features would help to focus attention on the relevant social, economic and environmental circumstances that attend them.

The notion of 'stages of life' is convenient, even if it does tend to oversimplify things, provided we do not lose sight of the widespread differences between individuals at any age. Allied to the notion of 'stages of life' is the notion of 'transitions in life', such as the transition from work to retirement, from health to infirmity, from companionship to isolation. Such transitions are important in personal adjustment and also have their socioeconomic and environmental aspects.

Popular beliefs about adult life and old age are old fashioned and inadequate; what we need is a more up-to-date and effective conceptualisation that fits the facts but offers a more positive view than the one Shakespeare left us with. Late middle-age, old age, and the terminal stage should achieve some kind of 'parity of esteem' with other stages of life.

In all this, of course, our concern is with the behaviour and circumstances of the average man and woman – a proper focus for social and environmental gerontology – rather than with the person whose physical and mental conditions results in a need for geriatric medical treatment. But the emphasis is one of degree rather than kind.

Social and environmental gerontology could make substantial contributions to 'designs for living' for ordinary people in later life. Indeed, contributions have already been made in respect of housing, furniture design and equipment, the provision of leisure and transport facilities; although, as we all know, much remains to be achieved in these and other areas.

The deterioration of our urban areas has brought to light serious deficiencies in some aspects of life for older people; these include social isolation, increased vulnerability to traffic hazards, loss of security against personal assault and robbery, and difficulties in alerting and communicating with others in case of need.

The increased isolation and passivity of people in later life tends to cut them off from public and private sources of information important to their own welfare and to exclude them from activities which they would find beneficial. Thus, when I use a phrase like 'designs for living in later life' I refer not just to the built-in environment and the delivery of services, but also to an effective system of interpersonal relationships into which the older person is integrated, not as a passive recipient but as a member functioning to the best of his ability.

The link between the sorts of applied social and environmental gerontology to which we have just referred and the more familiar geriatric medical and social services lies in what each can do to promote healthy living throughout adult life. Social and environmental gerontology should seek to promote congenial life-styles designed to promote physical fitness, social involvement, and personal adjustment throughout adulthood. Geriatric medicine should continue to develop preventive and screening measures, diagnostic procedures and remedial treatments for specific ailments which hinder functional capacity.

In one sense, academic and basic research is too far in advance of practical applications, and what we need now are extensive real-life experiments into long-range, broad-spectrum measures to prevent or retard functional incapacity. This should be accompanied by a re-examination of the value of existing policies affecting later life. So far we have considered, if only in general terms, what is *already* possible, given the necessary resources, in the way of *applied* social and environmental gerontology. What about the future? Perhaps the most important research exercise that social and environmental gerontologists could carry out is one that employs what is called the Delphi method (Ayes 1969; Smith 1975). This would take the form of a recursive survey in which people who are knowledgeable would be asked to speculate, in a realistic but creative way, about future developments relevant to human ageing. Their views would be collated, and then circulated to the same sample of individuals who would be asked to give their opinion on the likelihood and probable date by which each of the possible developments would have taken place. For example, will voluntary euthanasia for people over 65 years of age become legal? If so, by about what date? Could the menopause be retarded by biomedical intervention? If so, by how long? And when do you think this might be possible? The results of a Delphi survey are fed back to the respondents repeatedly until substantial agreement has been reached about a range of future developments and their most likely date of occurrence. Naturally, the method can be used to generate additional speculations about future events and the possible consequences of such developments. For example, we have already been warned by Alex Comfort about the serious effect on pension funds of even a small improvement in life expectancy.

A recent study in America describes an exercise of this kind using not the Delphi technique, but the extrapolation of statistical trends and legislative trends. I shall not repeat these findings, but adapt them as a set of speculations that *might* appear in a Delphi questionnaire about the future trends in this country. They are as follows:

(*i*) There will be a shift in political policy towards regionalism leading to wide geographical differences in provision for the elderly and to smaller social class differences.

(*ii*) Alternatively, certain institutional arrangements will be lifted out of regional into national or supranational control, e.g. adult education and geriatric medical services.

(*iii*) No comprehensive national policy for later life will be formulated in the foreseeable future because the problem is too complex, the resources required are too large, and the benefits to be derived are too nebulous.

(*iv*) Ageing as a political and economic issue, however, will become more prominent, partly because recently politicised younger cohorts will move through life's later stages and express their views more insistently than previous generations. The political voice of middle-aged and older people will be louder because there will be more of them, and there will be no shortage of spokesmen and spokeswomen.

(*v*) The gradual shift of wealth and income to higher age brackets will continue, adding to the economic and political strength of middle-aged and older people, but aggravating the conflict between generations. The producers of goods and services will have to deal with an older, wiser and more strongly consumer-orientated and consumer-protected society.

(*vi*) Although compulsory retirement will be retained, and the age of retirement perhaps lowered, age discrimination in employment will decrease and more opportunities will be found for earnings in retirement which are not severely penalised by taxation. Older people will compete for many kinds of work previously done by younger people.

(*vii*) The pressures on geriatric medical, nursing and social services will be eased by more liberal attitudes and laws relating to euthanasia and suicide.

(*viii*) The decline of religious beliefs – which have so far provided a kind of cushion against the harsh realities of human mortality – will not be accompanied by a growth of rationalism and humanism, at least not in the foreseeable future, but rather by a growth of alternative psychological defences and displacement activities, such as entertainment, millenial sectarianism, drink and drugs. (Perhaps television has replaced religion as the opium of the people!)

It is difficult to be both a gerontologist and an optimist. I have stressed the need for a positive and comprehensive social policy for later life based on a rational and empirical study of the normal human lifespan in relation to the resources available to the community. Its touchstone would be its adequacy in relation to the care of the aged infirm. The alternative to a scientific and humanistic management of human ageing threatens to bring unnecessary suffering, injustice, wasted lives, and social policies based on expediency and crisis conditions.

I have not spent a great deal of time identifying and describing the specific directions that research in social and environmental gerontology should take. We already have an abundance of research findings; there is no lack of ideas and methods for research; the technical literature provides ample evidence and easy access to them. However, unlike biomedical research, research in social and environmental gerontology does not have much coherence, so that it is difficult to frame a unified research policy.

As we have seen, the applications of research in social and environmental gerontology require changes in the existing socioeconomic framework; and it seems likely that substantial improvements in the quality of life for older people will come about only when political action by older people makes it possible to test these applications and to implement new social policies.

References

AYES, R. U. (1969) *Technological Forecasting and Long Range Planning.* New York: McGraw-Hill.

BROMLEY, D. B. (1974) *The Psychology of Human Ageing.* Harmondsworth: Penguin.

BROMLEY, D. B. (1976a) 'Research in social and behavioural gerontology.' In *Research in Gerontology: Problems and Prospects.* British Council for Ageing. London: National Council of Social Service.

BROMLEY, D. B. (1976b) 'Geriatrics in relation to the social and behavioural sciences', *Age and Ageing, 5.*

JOHNSON, M. (1976) 'That was your life: a biographical approach to later life.' In *Dependency or Interdependency in Old Age,* eds J. M. A. Munnichs and W. Van den Heuval. The Hague: M. Nijhoff [Chapter 14 in this Reader].

SMITH, J. M. (1975) 'Che sera sera: the future of psychology', *Bull. Br. Psychol. Soc., 28,* 1–9.

Part 2 On Growing Older: Myth and Experience

8 Ageism and common stereotypes

Jon Hendricks and C. Davis Hendricks

Gerontologists have coined the term ageism to refer to the pejorative image of someone who is old simply because of his or her age. Like racism or sexism, it is wholesale discrimination against all members of a category, though usually it appears in more covert form. The threatened cutbacks in Social Security, failure to provide meaningful outlets or activities, or the belief that those in their sixties and beyond do not benefit from psychotherapy are all examples of subtle, or in some cases not so subtle, appraisals of the old. Part of the myth, a fundamental if implicit element of ageism, is the view that the elderly are somehow different from our present and future selves and therefore not subject to the same desires, concerns or fears. Even our attempts at humor reveal the existence of largely negative attitudes about the elderly, with those referring to older women suggesting a particularly pernicious 'double standard' (Palmore 1971). Why should ageism have become a national prejudice? Probably because of the emphasis on productive capacity and technological expertise, or perhaps out of a thinly veiled attempt to avoid the reality that we will all one day grow old and die. Not to be dismissed is the fact that the early geronotological research that filtered into the public consciousness and reinforced existing misconceptions was based largely on institutionalized older people, who, however important they may be in their own right, are still a scant minority among the elderly (Butler and Lewis 1973).

Indicative of the range of commonly held stereotypes about the elderly is the belief that most older people are living isolated lives beset by serious health problems, causing them to be emotionally distraught. Just as widespread are the ideas that women experience psychological trauma with the onset of the so-called empty nest years, while retirement spells certain morale problems for men. That older people are no longer sexually active, that in fact they are no longer even interested, is another generally held view unsupported by the facts. Surely some or all of these themes can be observed among those over 65, but they can be found in any other age group as well (Palmore 1969; Maddox 1970). The realities of aging simply do not fit the stereotypes; however, despite the accumulation of new information the myths continue to thrive. Again, even older people who may not be experiencing the difficulties attributed to old age see them-

---

Source: J. HENDRICKS and C. D. HENDRICKS (1977) *Aging in Mass Society*. Cambridge, Mass.: Winthrop, pp. 14–16.

selves as exceptions to an otherwise dreary picture. By the nature of our misconceptions we do the elderly a great disservice, tending to cast them as just another problem rather than as a potential resource for resolving society's dilemmas (Harris *et al.* 1975).

Table 1   Differences between personal experiences of Americans aged 65 and over, and expectations held by other adults about those experiences.

	Very serious problems experienced by the elderly themselves (Percentage)	*Very serious problems the public expects the elderly to experience (Percentage)*	*Net difference*
Fear of crime	23	50	+27
Poor health	21	51	+30
Not having enough money to live on	15	62	+47
Loneliness	12	60	+48
Not having enough medical care	10	44	+34
Not having enough education	8	20	+12
Not feeling needed	7	54	+47
Not having enough to do to keep busy	6	37	+31
Not having enough friends	5	28	+23
Not having enough job opportunities	5	45	+40
Poor housing	4	35	+31
Not having enough clothing	3	16	+13

Source: L. Harris and Associates, *The Myth and Reality of Aging in America* (Washington, D.C.: The National Council on the Aging, Inc., 1975), p. 31.

To ascertain the public's attitudes toward aging and to measure the gap between the expectations and the experience of being old, the National Council on the Aging commissioned what may be the most extensive study of its type yet to be conducted. In all, over 4250 interviews were held with a representative cross-section of American adults by members of the Harris polling organization. As a group, only about 2 per cent of the respondents could conceive of the years after 60 as the best in life, while approximately one-third of those 18 to 64 and an even larger percentage of those over 65 saw them as the least desirable. It might be worth commenting, though, that while the majority in both instances did not perceive the later years to be any worse than, say, the teenage years, younger people consistently volunteered more negative views than did those who were actually over the age of 65. The discrepancy between the two age groups emerges dramatically in Table 1. As is clear, young adults expect the problems identified to be far more serious than they are for the elderly who actually experience them. As an illustration, somewhat less than one-fourth of the older respondents report fear of crime to be one of their most serious concerns, yet over twice as large a percentage of the general public thought crime constituted one of the biggest problems in the lives of the old. Granted, some older people might have been reluctant to admit to problems because of what it would suggest about their personal abilities; still, when other responses were included in the definition of problem areas, the differences did not disappear, though, for the most part, the magnitude of the gap closed and the problems identified were less overwhelming than most of us might think.

Despite the dire expectations about what life is going to be like, Harris and his associates found that for every older person who feels his or her life is worse than he or she thought it was going to be, there are at least three age mates who claim they are pleasantly surprised – it is better. Not unusually, there are those in every age category who are dismayed that things are not working out as they had hoped; the elderly can hardly be considered an exception. On the whole, income and racial background have been identified as having a greater impact on life satisfaction than does age. The more affluent respondents were not only more likely to express satisfaction with their current situation, but were more positively disposed toward the prospect of growing old. Though the sample does not differentiate among racial or ethnic groups other than between black and white, it appears as if there is a paradox among minority respondents revolving around the phenomenon of rising expectations. Older blacks feel more satisfied with their lives than do their younger counterparts, though a similar pattern tends to emerge among all respondents who are at the bottom end of the lower income scale. Regardless of financial levels, the black respondents felt less adequately prepared for old age than did the whites, yet, racial characteristics aside, most people over 65 express regrets for not having planned better for their later lives (Harris *et al.* 1975). Had they been more aware of what they would face and less insulated from the facts by the common tendency to shut the later years off from the rest of the life cycle, even those problems they do encounter might have been greatly ameliorated.

References

BUTLER, R. N. and LEWIS, M. I. (1973) *Aging and Mental Health.* St Louis: C. V. Mosby Co.

HARRIS, L. and associates (1975) *The Myth and Reality of Aging in America.* Washington, D.C.: The National Council on the Aging, Inc.

MADDOX, G. L. (1970) 'Themes and Issues in Sociological Theories of Human Aging', *Human Development, 13,* 1, 17–27.

PALMORE, E. (1969) 'Physical, mental and social factors in predicting longevity', *The Gerontologist, 9,* 103–8.

PALMORE, E. (1971) 'Attitudes Towards Aging as Shown by Humor', *The Gerontologist, 11,* 3, 181–6.

9 Sexuality in later life

Jon Hendricks and C. Davis Hendricks

Given the important role sex plays throughout life, it is too bad that it is an area of behavior more riddled with misconceptions than most. A generation ago sexuality did not create problems of the same magnitude for older people, as life expectancy seldom exceeded by much the reproductive years. With advances in longevity came the emergence of certain sex-related enigmas. One of the major impediments to a thoughtful appreciation of the place of sex in successful aging is that in nearly everyone's mind people tend to become neutered with the passing of the years. How many can imagine their grandparents engaging in sex? From the guffaws and general expressions of surprise the question often evokes, precious few; unfortunately neither can the grandparents. They see themselves as somehow beyond sex, but frustrated nonetheless because the idea still appeals to them. Most people openly acknowledge the value of basic sex education for adolescents or young marrieds, but what about later on, for the middle-aged and elderly who are just as much in the dark about what sex should be like at their ages? The taboos concerning the sex life of older people are ill-founded; after all, many of those who responded to the famous Kinsey studies after World War II, which told us so much about sexual practices, are themselves now past middle age. Yet cultural stereotypes continue to enforce a fictional view in the face of which the reality of the situation provides a substantial contrast.

Undoubtedly, physiological changes do alter sexual capacities in later life, yet their influence is vastly exaggerated. Psychological elements are probably far more consequential in determining the character of older people's sex lives. The myths proliferate, affecting women and men alike. Common opinion has it that middle-aged men fare somewhat better than women as far as sexual opportunity is concerned; they are allowed to seek out companions considerably younger than themselves – a prerogative not granted women. This is certainly true, but as long as they are presumed to be sexually active, older men are burdened with the onus of performance standards better suited to men 30 years their juniors, which they may be hard pressed to meet. Failing to recognize the basic facts of aging causes them, as well as their partners, to castigate themselves for falling short. Paradoxically, another ingredient of the myth of male sexuality is the widely held belief that the loss of a man's erective capacity is a natural

Source: J. HENDRICKS and C. D. HENDRICKS (1977) *Aging in Mass Society*. Cambridge, Mass.: Winthrop, pp. 304–11.

concomitant of aging. While men do indeed experience some delayed reactions in their sexual response cycle, the changes are functionally minimal compared to other physiological involutions. Most importantly, men do not naturally lose their capacity for erection as a result of these changes. An equally inappropriate stereotypic notion is that sex has lost its appeal to women by the end of their procreative years. Menopause is viewed as the great divide, and women on the other side are not supposed to be interested in sex. Again, the facts are quite the contrary. Among current generations of older women, concern with sex never seems to have been as prominent as with their male counterparts, though neither does it stop with their menses. All too often women fall into the trap of equating sexuality with reproductive ability. Like men, older women find themselves surrounded by sexual fallacies so strong they are hesitant to admit to anything other than socially prescribed norms. Physically, women retain their capacity to enjoy sex far more satisfactorily than men, and with mild hormone therapy there is no reason why postmenopausal women cannot remain active so long as they desire (Masters and Johnson 1970). As one well-known authority phrased it when remarking on society's tendency for 'hocusing' older people out of their sexuality in the same way they have been hocused out of other valuable activities:

... old folks stop having sex for the same reasons they stop riding a bicycle – general infirmity, thinking it looks ridiculous, no bicycle – and of these reasons the greatest is the social image of the dirty old man and the asexual, undesirable older woman (Comfort 1974).

Incidence and interest

One indication of the recency of scientific recognition of sexual interest and activity among older people is provided by the brief, two page summary made in the Kinsey study (1953). Only with the clinical investigations carried out by Masters and Johnson and the data gathered as part of the Duke longitudinal studies of aging has sexual activity among the elderly been given a significant measure of attention. Subsequent research has begun to augment these initial reports, although for basic information the earlier studies remain the most reliable and complete. Despite older people being enormously underrepresented among Kinsey's respondents, he reports an increasing incidence of male impotence over the years, coupled with declining activity levels. Notwithstanding this, the oldest men do not relinquish their activity levels with any greater speed than younger men. Sexual intercourse occurs less frequently among older women than their younger sisters; however, Kinsey suggests this is more a reflection of male than female processes. The Masters and Johnson and the Duke research illuminate what Kinsey barely implied. Together they provide a fairly broad overview of the effects of age on sexual interest and responsiveness. The following discussion is based largely on the information made available from these studies. It will focus first on incidence, then on some of the factors associated with male and female sexual functioning.

Sexual interest and involvement are clearly related to a host of variables, yet the single best predictors of whether or not older people will maintain their sexual activities turn out to be continuity and past behavior. Among both men and women, those who have enjoyed a long and recurrent sex life without lengthy interruption are most likely to remain active far longer than their age mates who have not experienced a similar history. Despite declines in the late sixties and seventies, there is no decade this side of 100 in which sexual activity is completely absent. As a rule, men are more active than women at every age. At 60 few men have ceased to engage in sex; by age 68 somewhat less than three-quarters continue to have sexual intercourse, although some portion of those who abstain are still interested – talking and speculating even when they are prevented from actual participation. By the time they reach their late seventies, only 25 per cent of the men are still active, and will continue to engage in some form of sex for the rest of their lives. In fact, there is even a moderate increase in the proportion of 80 and 90 year olds who acknowledge sexual activity; the slight upturn is probably a function of greater survival of the more biologically fit. Marital status apparently does not have much of an impact on men's activity levels; unmarried men are nearly as active and certainly as attracted as men who live with their spouses (Verwoerdt *et al.* 1970).

For women the situation is somewhat different. As with men, sexual interest is greater than actual incidence, even though sex is less often a topic of contemplation. Marital status proves to be the crucial factor in continued involvement; women who do not have a spouse have far fewer sexual outlets than their married counterparts. On the other hand, the number of outlets they have established persists far longer than for married women. Previous enjoyment more than simple frequency of sexual relationships is of particular importance for women in determining how they currently feel about sex – while for men both factors are equally relevant. A woman who has enjoyed her sexual experiences in earlier years, regardless of their regularity, will generally persist in those activities in her later years. Above all else, the presence of a sexually capable, socially sanctioned partner is particularly reflected in a woman's level of sexual involvement. In middle age, the years around 50, seven-eighths of all married women regularly engage in coitus with their husbands. Ten years later, participation has declined to about 70 per cent, and by age 65 only about half still engage in marital intercourse. Both members of the older couples in the Duke studies tend to attribute the cessation of intercourse to the husband, due to illness, lack of interest or impotence. Clearly coitus is not the only form of sexual activity, and reports issuing from the Duke investigations suggest masturbation is an alternative practiced by approximately a quarter of the women responding to the sexual questions (Christenson and Gagnon 1965; Pfeiffer, Verwoerdt and Wang 1970).

Table 1   Frequency of sexual intercourse in later life (percentages).

Group	Number	None	Once a Month	Once a Week	2–3 times a Week	More than 3 times a Week
Men						
46–50	43	0	5	62	26	7
51–55	41	5	29	49	17	0
56–60	61	7	38	44	11	0
61–65	54	20	43	30	7	0
66–71	62	24	48	26	2	0
Total	261	12	34	41	12	1
Women						
46–50	43	14	26	39	21	0
51–55	41	20	41	32	5	2
56–60	48	42	27	25	4	2
61–65	44	61	29	5	5	0
66–71	55	73	16	11	0	0
Total	231	44	27	22	6	1

Source: E. Pfeiffer, A. Verwoerdt and G. C. Davis (1972) 'Sexual Behavior in Middle Life', *American Journal of Psychiatry, 128*, 10, 1264.

Among that portion of the older population who are sexually involved in their later years, the frequency of intercourse gradually diminishes. The patterns shown in Table 1 were exhibited by participants in the Duke studies, yet they do not differ substantially from data reported elsewhere. What such overall trends generally mask is that married people, those from lower socioeconomic statuses and blacks are many times more active than are singles, those from the upper classes and whites (Newman and Nichols 1970). Judging from these data, there appears to be a slight increase in the occurrence of intercourse for the cohorts listed over what the Kinsey team reported nearly thirty years ago. One possible interpretation of this upward shift entails the presumed changes in sexual morality, implying that present generations of elderly are less conservative about sex than previous generations. Such an explanation would certainly be in keeping with Kinsey's (1953) own conclusions regarding generational differences in proclivity for orgasm and declining frigidity in women. It also implies that if contemporary trends toward more openly sensual relationships prove durable, future cohorts of older people should be even more sexually active. Despite the paucity of data on sexual functioning among elderly people, small scale research projects conducted around the world affirm the Duke findings and reiterate the call for more intensive counseling programs. For example, one Italian study reports a pattern of current sexual activity among older people almost identical to what has been observed in the United States (De Nicola and Peruzza 1974).

Sexual response cycles

In terms of the physiology of sex, Masters and Johnson (1970) indicate men experience more of an age-related deficit than women, though in neither case are the changes serious enough to interrupt the sex lives of the elderly. Clinically speaking, the four stages of the sexual response cycle begin to change sometime during middle age. The *excitation* stage, marked in men by the achievement of an erection and in women by vaginal lubrication, gradually requires more time than in previous years. The erection, which used to be achieved in seconds, takes minutes in later life, and even then it is neither as full or demanding as that of a young man. Because of hormonal changes and the involution of the vaginal lining, postmenopausal women do not lubricate as thoroughly, sometimes resulting in painful intromission. The *plateau* stage in older men is lengthened, pre-ejaculatory emissions are reduced and seemingly there is less urgency to reach orgasm. Women seemingly experience fewer age-related changes in the plateau phase. In spite of a modest reduction in the size of the clitoris with age, there is not any apparent loss of sensitivity. The *orgasmic* phase is roughly analogous in both men and women. For men, ejaculation can be divided into two steps. The first brings a sense of urgency marked by psychological readiness and recurring contractions of the prostate gland. In young men contractions come in regular intervals of less than one second, lasting up to four seconds. With advancing age this first step of the ejaculatory process may become less distinguishable; it can be either shorter or longer and might also include irregular contractions. The second step of the orgasmic phase is actual ejaculation. The normal pattern among younger men is a series of contractions that are relatively steady through actual emission. In men over the age of 50, however, the expulsive contractions may change rhythm earlier or be less severe, while seminal emissions are reduced. Middle-aged or older women may experience a shorter orgasmic phase compared to that of younger women, though hormonal treatments often inhibit significant alterations. As with men, women experience several contractions during orgasm, but among the aged these are of shorter duration or may even taken the form of spasms accompanied by some abdominal pain.

Finally, the *resolution* phase is again characteristic of both male and female cycles. For men over age 40, the refractory period may be considerably extended. During this time a man remains physically unresponsive to sexual stimulation and is unable to establish coital connection regardless of his emotional involvement. In young men the resolution phase transpires in only a matter of minutes and a limited erection may be maintained throughout, while for the middle-age or older man erections disappear more swiftly and hours may pass before intercourse is again possible. At any age the refractory period for women is far less than for men. Among middle-aged and postmenopausal women, return to a physiological equilibrium is fairly rapid and in many respects parallels that of the older male. For the man, reduced ejaculatory demand may translate into little need to ejaculate at all, thereby prolonging both immediate and long-term sexual functioning, and shortening the resolution phase as well.

Unfortunately, most people have little appreciation of their own bodily processes and any alterations in sexual functioning signal the beginning of distress. Impotence is the most common sexual disorder among men over 45, precipitating serious emotional turmoil accompanied by health or mental problems on occasion (Kent 1975). There is some evidence that men in their later fifties or sixties experience a kind of *climacteric* that is somewhat equivalent to menopause; as yet, however, little solid information is available with even less to indicate such a change might interfere with sexual activity. More likely, psychological predisposition plays a far greater role in declining sexual interest. Based on their extensive analyses, Masters and Johnson (1966) have isolated several integral components of male sexual inadequacies. Lack of prowess is often related to disenchantment and marital monotony, preoccupation with extraneous pursuits such as a career, emotional or physical fatigue, overindulgence in either food or drink, mental or physical infirmities, and finally, fears regarding sexual performance. All can effectively preclude any kind of sexual response. Another commonly expressed fear arises in the aftermath of heart attacks. People sometimes assume once a man has had cardiovascular problems, he should abstain from further sexual relations. Like many other ideas, this misconception finds little medical support and ought to be abandoned. Acually, sex requires no more exertion than taking a brisk walk or climbing a flight of stairs. Along with the cultural views of older people's sexuality, the lessening need and frequency of ejaculation contributes an additional personal strain insofar as a woman may inadvertently feel threatened by a partner who does not ejaculate. Both partners should understand changing sexual functions, learning to take more time to be emotionally demonstrative if they are to avoid confounding their relationship with unrealistic expectations (Masters and Johnson 1970).

Of all the aspects of human sexuality, the female menopause is a leading candidate for the most maligned. Why the termination of the menses is such a clouded issue is a complex question, yet overriding all other considerations is the fact that cultural conditioning is so pervasive. Behaviorally, the changes attributed to menopause are in many cases merely an accentuation of already existing tendencies previously held in check. Even the clinical features of the so-called menopausal syndrome are far from uniform. In the Western world, hot flushes, emotional turmoil, chronic fatigue, occipital headaches, neckaches, plus myriad other subjective factors are commonplace complaints. Externally there is a drying of the skin, changes in hair color and alterations in secondary sexual characteristics such as breast size and shape. Because of hormonal changes in the reproductive system, additional changes include an introversion of the vaginal walls and a loss of lubricating secretions which may occasionally result in painful intercourse. Lest the many fallacies surrounding menopause be reinforced, it cannot be stressed too strongly that psychological factors are equally, if not more, important with hormonal factors influencing subsequent sexual interests and functioning. Although depressed sex-steroid levels can be easily corrected by replacement therapy, sexual responsiveness, on the other hand, cannot be restored without appropriate psychological counseling. A woman's subjective perception of herself is most often what damages her sexual outlook; if she believes herself to be unattractive or too old, sex will in all probability become a thing of the past. On the physical side, menopause, or even a hysterectomy for that matter, has little effect on sensate pleasure – in fact many women experience a heightened sense of satisfaction once they are free of the pressures of preventing pregnancy (Masters and Johnson 1970).

It is improbable that future generations of women will repeat the sexual patterns of today's elderly women. As Masters and Johnson (1966, 1970) have noted, they will be exorcised of the Victorian belief that women should be sexually passive – sure to be a boon to men as well since the double standard of male dominance is an imposition on both partners. Women will also benefit from the advent of contraceptive security and estrogen replacement procedures developed over the past two decades; thus, menopause will mean neither new-found freedom nor hardship. Even the death or incapacity of male partners will not necessarily spell the end of sexual activity; already there is evidence to suggest masturbation is increasing among women in the 50 to 70 age range, and as social proscriptions against autoeroticism are eroded, more people will feel free to seek their own forms of sexual gratification. It should be remembered that intercourse is not the only means of expressing emotions, and it is a grave mistake to think of its termination as the end of sensuality. At all ages coitus is but a single element in the communication of love. It is not at all unusual for it to be of less importance than other manifestations of the sexual bond. For older couples, being physically or spiritually close, showing tenderness or respect can be valued in such a way that intercourse is hardly missed.

References

CHRISTENSON, C. V. and GAGNON, J. H. (1965) 'Sexual behaviour in a group of older women', *Journal of Gerontology, 20*, 3, 351–6.

COMFORT, A. (1974) 'Sexuality in old age', *Journal of the American Geriatrics Society, 22*, 10, 440–2.

DE NICOLA, P. and PERUZZA, M. (1974) 'Sex in the aged', *Journal of the American Geriatrics Society, 22*, 8, 380–2.

KENT, S. (1975) 'Impotence: the facts versus the fallacies', *Geriatrics, 30*, 4, 164–9.

KINSEY, A. C. *et al.* (1953) *Sexual Behaviour in the Human Female.* Philadelphia: W. B. Saunders.

MASTERS, W. H. and JOHNSON, V. E. (1966) *Human Sexual Response.* Boston: Little, Brown.

MASTERS, W. H. and JOHNSON, V. E. (1970) *Human Sexual Inadequacy.* Boston: Little, Brown.

NEWMAN, G. and NICHOLS, C. R. (1970) 'Sexual Activities and Attitudes in Older Persons.' In *Normal Aging*, ed. E. Palmore, pp. 277–81. Durham, N.C.: Duke University Press.

PFEIFFER, E., VERWOERDT, A. and WANG, H. S. (1970) 'Sexual Behavior in Aged Men and Woman.' In *Normal Aging*, ed. E. Palmore, pp. 299–303. Durham, N.C.: Duke University Press.

VERWOERDT, A., PFEIFFER, E. and WANG, H. S. (1970) 'Sexual Behavior in Senescence.' In *Normal Aging*, ed. E. Palmore, pp. 282–99. Durham, N.C.: Duke University Press.

10 The double standard of ageing

Susan Sontag

For a woman to be obliged to state her age, after 'a certain age', is always a miniature ordeal . . . Almost everyone acknowledges that once she passes an age that is, actually, quite young, a woman's exact age ceases to be a legitimate target of curiosity. After childhood the year of a woman's birth becomes her secret, her private property. It is something of a dirty secret. To answer truthfully is always indiscreet.

The discomfort a woman feels each time she tells her age is quite independent of the anxious awareness of human mortality that everyone has, from time to time. There is a normal sense in which nobody, men and women alike, relishes growing older. After 35 any mention of one's age carries with it the reminder that one is probably closer to the end of one's life than to the beginning. There is nothing unreasonable in that anxiety. Nor is there any abnormality in the anguish and anger that people who are really old, in their 70s and 80s, feel about the implacable waning of their powers, physical and mental. Advanced age is undeniably a trial, however stoically it may be endured. It is a shipwreck, no matter with what courage elderly people insist on continuing the voyage. But the objective, sacred pain of old age is of another order than the subjective, profane pain of aging. Old age is a genuine ordeal, one that men and women undergo in a similar way. Growing older is mainly an ordeal of the imagination – a moral disease, a social pathology – intrinsic to which is the fact that it afflicts women much more than men. It is particularly women who experience growing older (everything that comes *before* one is actually old) with such distaste and even shame.

The emotional privileges this society [U.S.A.] confers upon youth stir up some anxiety about getting older in everybody. All modern urbanized societies – unlike tribal, rural societies – condescend to the values of maturity and heap honors on the joys of youth. This revaluation of the life cycle in favor of the young brilliantly serves a secular society whose idols are ever-increasing industrial productivity and the unlimited cannibalization of nature. Such a society must create a new sense of the rhythms of life in order to incite people to buy more, to consume and throw away faster. People let the direct awareness they have of their needs, of what really gives them pleasure, be overruled by commercialized *images* of happiness and personal well-being; and, in this imagery designed to

Source: *Saturday Review*, 23 September 1972, pp. 29–38.

stimulate ever more avid levels of consumption, the most popular metaphor for happiness is 'youth'. (I would insist that it is a metaphor, not a
literal description. Youth is a metaphor for energy, restless mobility, appetite: for the state of 'wanting'.) This equating of well-being with youth
makes everyone naggingly aware of exact age – one's own and that of
other people. In primitive and premodern societies people attach much
less importance to dates. When lives are divided into long periods with
stable responsibilities and steady ideals (and hypocrisies), the exact number of years someone has lived becomes a trivial fact; there is hardly any
reason to mention, even to know, the year in which one was born. Most
people in nonindustrial societies are not sure exactly how old they are.
People in industrial societies are haunted by numbers. They take an
almost obsessional interest in keeping the score card of aging, convinced
that anything above a low total is some kind of bad news. In an era in
which people actually live longer and longer, what now amounts to the
latter *two-thirds* of everyone's life is shadowed by a poignant apprehension
of unremitting loss.

The prestige of youth afflicts everyone in this society to some degree.
Men, too, are prone to periodic bouts of depression about aging – for
instance, when feeling insecure or unfulfilled or insufficiently rewarded in
their jobs. But men rarely panic about aging in the way women often do.
Getting older is less profoundly wounding for a man, for in addition to the
propaganda for youth that puts both men and women on the defensive as
they age, there is a double standard about aging that denounces women
with special severity. Society is much more permissive about aging in
men, as it is more tolerant of the sexual infidelities of husbands. Men are
'allowed' to age, without penalty, in several ways that women are not.

This society offers even fewer rewards for aging to women than it does
to men. Being physically attractive counts much more in a woman's life
than in a man's, but beauty, identified, as it is for women, with youth-
fulness, does not stand up well to age. Exceptional mental powers can
increase with age, but women are rarely encouraged to develop their
minds above dilettante standards. Because the wisdom considered the
special province of women is 'eternal', an age-old, intuitive knowledge
about the emotions to which a repertoire of facts, worldly experience, and
the methods of rational analysis have nothing to contribute, living a long
time does not promise women an increase in wisdom either. The private
skills expected of women are exercised early and, with the exception of a
talent for making love, are not the kind that enlarge with experience.
'Masculinity' is identified with competence, autonomy, self-control –
qualities which the disappearance of youth does not threaten. Competence in most of the activities expected from men, physical sports ex-
cepted, increases with age. 'Femininity' is identified with incompetence,

helplessness, passivity, noncompetitiveness, being nice. Age does not improve these qualities.

Middle-class men feel diminished by aging, even while still young, if they have not yet shown distinction in their careers or made a lot of money. (And any tendencies they have toward hypochondria will get worse in middle age, focusing with particular nervousness on the specter of heart attacks and the loss of virility.) Their aging crisis is linked to that terrible pressure on men to be 'successful' that precisely defines their membership in the middle class. Women rarely feel anxious about their age because they haven't succeeded at something. The work that women do outside the home rarely counts as a form of achievement, only as a way of earning money; most employment available to women mainly exploits the training they have been receiving since early childhood to be servile, to be both supportive and parasitical, to be unadventurous. They can have menial, low-skilled jobs in light industries, which offer as feeble a criterion of success as housekeeping. They can be secretaries, clerks, sales personnel, maids, research assistants, waitresses, social workers, prostitutes, nurses, teachers, telephone operators – public transcriptions of the servicing and nurturing roles that women have in family life. Women fill very few executive posts, are rarely found suitable for large corporate or political responsibilities, and form only a tiny contingent in the liberal professions (apart from teaching). They are virtually barred from jobs that involve an expert, intimate relation with machines or an aggressive use of the body, or that carry any physical risk or sense of adventure. The jobs this society deems appropriate to women are auxiliary, 'calm' activities that do not compete with, but aid, what men do. Besides being less well paid, most work women do has a lower ceiling of advancement and gives meager outlet to normal wishes to be powerful. All outstanding work by women in this society is voluntary; most women are too inhibited by the social disapproval attached to their being ambitious and aggressive. Inevitably, women are exempted from the dreary panic of middle-aged men whose 'achievements' seem paltry, who feel stuck on the job ladder or fear being pushed off it by someone younger. But they are also denied most of the real satisfactions that men derive from work – satisfactions that often do increase with age.

The double standard about ageing shows up most brutally in the conventions of sexual feeling, which presuppose a disparity between men and women that operates permanently to women's disadvantage. In the accepted course of events a woman anywhere from her late teens through her middle 20s can expect to attract a man more or less her own age. (Ideally, he should be at least slightly older.) They marry and raise a family. But if her husband starts an affair after some years of marriage, he customarily does so with a woman much younger than his wife. Suppose, when both husband and wife are already in their late 40s or early 50s, they divorce. The husband has an excellent chance of getting married again, probably to a younger woman. His ex-wife finds it difficult to remarry. Attracting a second husband younger than herself is improbable; even to find someone her own age she has to be lucky, and she will probably have to settle for a man considerably older than herself, in his 60s or 70s. Women become sexually ineligible much earlier than men do. A man, even an ugly man, can remain eligible well into old age. He is an acceptable mate for a young, attractive woman. Women, even good-looking women, become ineligible (except as partners of very old men) at a much younger age.

Thus, for most women, aging means a humiliating process of gradual sexual disqualification. Since women are considered maximally eligible in early youth, after which their sexual value drops steadily, even young women feel themselves in a desperate race against the calendar. They are old as soon as they are no longer very young. In late adolescence some girls are already worrying about getting married. Boys and young men have little reason to anticipate trouble because of aging. What makes men desirable to women is by no means tied to youth. On the contrary, getting older tends (for several decades) to operate in men's favor, since their value as lovers and husbands is set more by what they do than how they look. Many men have more success romantically at 40 than they did at 20 or 25; fame, money, and, above all, power are sexually enhancing. (A woman who has won power in a competitive profession or business career is considered less, rather than more, desirable. Most men confess themselves intimidated or turned off sexually by such a woman, obviously because she is harder to treat as just a sexual 'object'.) As they age, men may start feeling anxious about actual sexual performance, worrying about a loss of sexual vigor or even impotence, but their sexual eligibility is not abridged simply by getting older. Men stay sexually possible as long as they can make love. Women are at a disadvantage because their sexual candidacy depends on meeting certain much stricter 'conditions' related to looks and age.

Since women are imagined to have much more limited sexual lives than men do, a woman who has never married is pitied. She was not found acceptable, and it is assumed that her life continues to confirm her unacceptability. Her presumed lack of sexual opportunity is embarrassing. A man who remains a bachelor is judged much less crudely. It is assumed that he, at any age, still has a sexual life – or the chance of one. For men there is no destiny equivalent to the humiliating condition of being an old maid, a spinster. 'Mr.', a cover from infancy to senility, precisely exempts men from the stigma that attaches to any woman, no longer young, who is still 'Miss'. (That women are divided into 'Miss' and 'Mrs', which calls unrelenting attention to the situation of each woman with respect to marriage, reflects the belief that being single or married is much more decisive for a woman than it is for a man.)

For a woman who is no longer very young, there is certainly some relief when she has finally been able to marry. Marriage soothes the sharpest pain she feels about the passing years. But her anxiety never subsides completely, for she knows that should she re-enter the sexual market at a later date – because of divorce, or the death of her husband, or the need for erotic adventure – she must do so under a handicap far greater than any man of her age (*whatever* her age may be) and regardless of how good-looking she is. Her achievements, if she has a career, are no asset. The calendar is the final arbiter.

To be sure, the calendar is subject to some variations from country to country. In Spain, Portugal, and the Latin American countries, the age at which most women are ruled physically undesirable comes earlier than in the United States. In France it is somewhat later. French conventions of sexual feelings make a quasi-official place for the woman between 35 and 45. Her role is to initiate an inexperienced or timid young man, after which she is, of course replaced by a young girl. (Colette's novella *Cheri* is the best-known account in fiction of such a love affair; biographies of Balzac relate a well-documented example from real life.) This sexual myth does make turning 40 somewhat easier for French women. But there is no difference in any of these countries in the basic attitudes that disqualify women sexually much earlier than men.

Aging also varies according to social class. Poor people look old much earlier in their lives than do rich people. But anxiety about aging is certainly more common, and more acute, among middle-class and rich women than among working-class women. Economically disadvantaged women in this society are more fatalistic about aging; they can't afford to fight the cosmetic battle as long or as tenaciously. Indeed, nothing so clearly indicates the fictional nature of this crisis than the fact that women who keep their youthful appearance the longest – women who lead unstrenuous, physically sheltered lives, who eat balanced meals, who can afford good medical care, who have few or no children – are those who feel the defeat of age most keenly. Aging is much more a social judgment than a biological eventuality. Far more extensive than the hard sense of loss suffered during menopause (which, with increased longevity, tends to arrive later and later) is the depression about aging, which may not be set off by any real event in a woman's life, but is a recurrent state of 'possession' of her imagination, ordained by society – that is, ordained by the way this society limits how women feel free to imagine themselves.

To be a woman is to be an actress. Being feminine is a kind of theater, with its appropriate costumes, decor, lighting, and stylized gestures. From early childhood on, girls are trained to care in a pathologically exaggerated way about their appearance and are profoundly mutilated (to the extent of being unfitted for first-class adulthood) by the extent of the stress put on presenting themselves as physically attractive objects. Women look in the mirror more frequently than men do. It is, virtually, their duty to look at themselves – to look often. Indeed, a woman who is not narcissistic is considered unfeminine. And a woman who spends literally *most* of her time caring for, and making purchases to flatter, her physical appearance is not regarded in this society as what she is: a kind of moral idiot. She is thought to be quite normal and is envied by other women whose time is mostly used up at jobs or caring for large families. The display of narcissism goes on all the time. It is expected that women will disappear several times in an evening – at a restaurant, at a party, during a theater intermission, in the course of a social visit – simply to check their appearance to see that nothing has gone wrong with their make-up and hairstyling, to make sure that their clothes are not spotted or too wrinkled or not hanging properly. It is even acceptable to perform this activity in public. At the table in a restaurant, over coffee, a woman opens a compact mirror and touches up her make-up and hair without embarrassment in front of her husband or her friends.

All this behavior, which is written off as normal 'vanity' in women, would seem ludicrous in a man. Women are more vain than men because of the relentless pressure on women to maintain their appearance at a certain high standard. What makes the pressure even more burdensome is that there are actually several standards. Men present themselves as face-and-body, a physical whole. Women are split, as men are not, into a body and a face – each judged by somewhat different standards. What is important for a face is that it be beautiful. What is important for a body is two things, which may even be (depending on fashion and taste) somewhat incompatible: first that it be desirable and, second, that it be beautiful. Men usually feel sexually attracted to women much more because of their bodies than their faces. The traits that arouse desire – such as fleshiness – don't always match those that fashion decrees as beautiful. (For instance, the ideal woman's body promoted in advertising in recent years is extremely thin: the kind of body that looks more desirable clothed than naked.) But women's concern with their appearance is not simply geared to arousing desire in men. It also aims at fabricating a certain image by which, as a more indirect way of arousing desire, women state their value. A woman's value lies in the way she *represents* herself, which is much more by her face than her body. In defiance of the laws of simple sexual attraction, women do not devote most of their attention to their bodies. The well-known 'normal' narcissism that women display – the amount of time they spend before the mirror – is used primarily in caring for the face and hair.

Women do not simply have faces, as men do; they are identified with their faces. Men have a naturalistic relation to their faces. Certainly they care whether they are good-looking or not. They suffer over acne, protruding ears, tiny eyes; they hate getting bald. But there is a much wider latitude in what is esthetically acceptable in a man's face than what is in a woman's. A man's face is defined as something he basically doesn't need to tamper with; all he has to do is keep it clean. He can avail himself of the options for ornament supplied by nature: a beard, a mustache, longer or shorter hair. But he is not supposed to disguise himself. What he is 'really' like is supposed to show. A man lives through his face; it records the progressive stages of his life. And since he doesn't tamper with his face, it is not separate from but is completed by his body – which is judged attractive by the impression it gives of virility and energy. By contrast, a woman's face is potentially separate from her body. She does not treat it naturalistically. A woman's face is the canvas upon which she paints a revised, corrected portrait of herself. One of the rules of this creation is that the face *not* show what she doesn't want it to show. Her face is an emblem, an icon, a flag. How she arranges her hair, the type of make-up she uses, the quality of the complexion – all these are signs, not of what she is 'really' like, but of how she asks to be treated by others, especially men. They establish her status as an 'object'.

For the normal changes that age inscribes on every human face, women are much more heavily penalized than men. Even in early adolescence, girls are cautioned to protect their faces against wear and tear. Mothers tell their daughters (but never their sons): You look ugly when you cry. Stop worrying. Don't read too much. Crying, frowning, squinting, even laughing – all these human activities make 'lines'. The same usage of the face in men is judged quite positively. In a man's face lines are taken to be signs of 'character'. They indicate emotional strength, maturity – qualities far more esteemed in men than in women. (They show he has 'lived'.) Even scars are often not felt to be unattractive; they too can add 'character' to a man's face. But lines of aging, any scar, even a small birthmark on a woman's face, are always regarded as unfortunate blemishes. In effect, people take character in men to be different from what constitutes character in women. A woman's character is thought to be innate, static – not the product of her experience, her years, her actions. A woman's face is prized so far as it remains unchanged by (or conceals the traces of) her emotions, her physical risk-taking. Ideally, it is supposed to be a mask – immutable, unmarked. The model woman's face is Garbo's. Because women are identified with their faces much more than men are, and the ideal woman's face is one that is 'perfect', it seems a calamity when a woman has a disfiguring accident. A broken nose or a scar or a burn mark, no more than regrettable for a man, is a terrible psychological wound to a woman; objectively, it diminishes her value. (As is well known, most clients for plastic surgery are women.)

Both sexes aspire to a physical ideal, but what is expected of boys and what is expected of girls involves a very different moral relation to the self. Boys are encouraged to *develop* their bodies, to regard the body as an instrument to be improved. They invent their masculine selves largely through exercise and sport, which harden the body and strengthen competitive feelings; clothes are of only secondary help in making their bodies attractive. Girls are not particularly encouraged to develop their bodies through any activity, strenuous or not; and physical strength and endurance are hardly valued at all. The invention of the feminine self proceeds mainly through clothes and other signs that testify to the very effort of girls to look attractive, to their commitment to please. When boys become men, they may go on (especially if they have sedentary jobs) practicing a sport or doing exercises for a while. Mostly they leave their appearance alone, having been trained to accept more or less what nature has handed out to them. (Men may start doing exercises again in their 40s to lose weight, but for reasons of health – there is an epidemic fear of heart attacks among the middle-aged in rich countries – not for cosmetic reasons.) As one of the norms of 'femininity' in this society is being preoccupied with one's physical appearance, so 'masculinity' means *not* caring very much about one's looks.

This society allows men to have a much more affirmative relation to their bodies than women have. Men are more 'at home' in their bodies, whether they treat them casually or use them aggressively. A man's body is defined as a strong body. It contains no contradiction between what is felt to be attractive and what is practical. A woman's body, so far as it is considered attractive, is defined as a fragile, light body. (Thus, women worry more than men do about being overweight.) When they do exercises, women avoid the ones that develop the muscles, particularly those in the upper arms. Being 'feminine' means looking physically weak, frail. Thus, the ideal woman's body is one that is not of much practical use in the hard work of this world, and one that must continually be 'defended'. Women do not develop their bodies, as men do. After a woman's body has reached its sexually acceptable form by late adolescence, most further development is viewed as negative. And it is thought irresponsible for women to do what is normal for men: simply leave their appearance alone. During early youth they are likely to come as close as they ever will to the ideal image – slim figure, smooth firm skin, light musculature, graceful movements. Their task is to try to maintain that image, unchanged, as long as possible. Improvement as such is not the task.

Women care for their bodies – against toughening, coarsening, getting fat. They *conserve* them. (Perhaps the fact that women in modern societies tend to have a more conservative political outlook than men originates in their profoundly conservative relation to their bodies.)

Nothing more clearly demonstrates the vulnerability of women than the special pain, confusion, and bad faith with which they experience getting older. And in the struggle that some women are waging on behalf of all women to be treated (and treat themselves) as full human beings – not 'only' as women – one of the earliest results to be hoped for is that women become aware, indignantly aware, of the double standard about aging from which they suffer so harshly.

11   Age discrimination

Robert Slater

[. . .] British attempts to pass legislation to prevent occupational age discrimination have had, at most, only a lukewarm reception. Yet in the United States, President Johnson signed the Age Discrimination in Employment Act back in December 1967.

This act involves virtually all employers of 25 or more employees and also applies to employment agencies and unions. Employers are prohibited from discrimination on the basis of age against individuals who are at least 40, but not more than 65, with regard to hiring, compensation and discharge. British legislation so far has amounted to private members' bills, to date put aside three times – all called the 'Age Level of Employment Bill'. The last of these bills, read on 5 May 1971, was 'to make it illegal for employers to refuse employment, on the sole ground that the person concerned is aged 45 years or over'.

The last reading showed that concern with the problem of unemployment had 'spread to the professions, the technical and administrative staffs, and higher executives'. Edward Milne, MP for Blyth, said, 'Most of us, if not all of us, know that the reason for the refusal of jobs rarely has anything to do with fitness for the job but has very much to do with the question of age.' He ended by remarking that, at present, the biggest single factor in securing a job on becoming unemployed is age itself. Corroborative evidence for this comes from other sources, the most recent being the HMSO publication, *Effects of the Redundancy Payment Act*, which shows that the older the man is, the more he feels his age is undoubtedly his biggest handicap in getting a job.

A major step in the legislative field towards an anti-discrimination bill is the suggestion that the Disabled Persons (Employment) Acts of 1944 and 1958 should be revised to include the old. Thus, employers would be legally obliged to employ a fixed percentage of disabled (and aged) persons in their work force. The current required figure for the disabled proportion of employees in a firm is 3 per cent. It has been suggested that the figure should be changed to 5 per cent, and that the term disabled should be altered to include men aged over 60. It has to be acknowledged, however, that the provisions of these acts are often evaded, even for the disabled.

There are other legislative possibilities – some of which are in force in Europe, and all of which are discussed in Bernice Reuben's book, *The*

Source: *New Society*, 10 May 1973, pp. 301–2.

Hard-to-Employ. Perhaps the second major step would be financial inducements to employers to take on older people. However, no one has yet formerly proposed to parliament any solutions along either of these lines.

Discrimination directly affecting the employment statistics takes effect at two places: in selecting those for dismissal, and in selecting those for employment. Although American legislation has been concerned with both, British bills seem more directly concerned with the process of hiring rather than firing. A British anti-discrimination bill introduced [in 1969] made no mention of the role of employment agencies in the problem, but the most recent bill sees employment agencies as the main sources of age discrimination through advertisements. American legislation takes exactly the same view as this.

Some years ago, Management Selection Limited found that 40 per cent of general management advertisements said men under the age of 40 were required; and advertisements for men in research development and design, in 86 per cent of the cases, restricted applications to men under 40. These two job areas represent the extremes. Evidence from America, before legislation came into force, suggested that more than half of employers used upper age limits of 45 to 55 in filling vacancies. In 1968, the Secretary of State for Labour said, at Senate hearings, that at least a quarter of all private job openings were barred to those over 45, and that half of all such job openings were barred to applicants over 55. One year later, when the Age Discrimination in Employment Act had been passed, estimates still suggested that the Secretary of State's figures for the previous year for age discrimination remained accurate. The obvious trouble is that, whereas discrimination in advertising is easy to detect, it is not so easy during selection – as candidates don't have to be told why they are being rejected.

A survey I made of advertisements appearing in the Professional and Executive column of the *Daily Telegraph* during August for the past sixteen years, shows how age discrimination in advertisements has changed. In 1957, 19 per cent of all advertisements mentioned that a man aged under 40 was required, but in 1970 this figure had risen to 32 per cent – an increase of 13 per cent. The percentage specifying that only men aged under 50 need apply was 26 per cent in 1957, but had risen in 1970 to 41 per cent – a rise of 15 per cent.

[Since 1971], however, there has been a small drop in age discrimination. It seems we may be on the brink of a decline in the number of advertisements with age discrimination.

The American legislation was meant to reduce age discrimination occurring at the time of hiring *and* firing. In Britain, the revision of the Redundancy Payment Act was intended to 'make the employer less willing to give him [the worker aged over 40] priority when redundancy lists are prepared ... the smaller rebate ... is certainly likely to encourage employers to concentrate their redundancies, when they come, amongst younger men with shorter service'. Roy Hattersley, in introducing the second reading of the amendment to the redundancy rebates system, on 30 January 1969, estimated that only one third of the massive increase in *per capita* redundancy payments was due to expanded earnings. The rest, 66 per cent, was considered to be due to an increase in the proportions of older men in redundancies. 'In 1963,' said Hattersley, 'the proportion of redundant workers over 40 was about 60 per cent. Last year [1968] it was 70 per cent.' An interesting explanation for these figures was given – namely that the higher payments received by older men were a higher inducement for them to volunteer for redundancy. Hattersley did not try to break down the proportion of the increase that was due to age discrimination by employers, or that due to 'self-selection' by older workers.

The redundancy rate (that is, the number of men made redundant in a year as a proportion of the male labour force) for older age groups before the amendment showed an increase, but now seems static. Although the proportion of older men being made redundant is no longer increasing, the actual rate for men over 40 is twice that for men aged under 40.

More information about discrimination in firing can be found in companies' dismissal policies. Most companies do not have a formal dismissal procedure but, of those surveyed by the British Institute of Management in 1969, only a very small proportion use age as the main reason for making a man redundant. Even when age is a consideration, it is mainly in the case of men who are over retiring age, and rarely men aged over 60. It seems that age discrimination is not a particularly crucial element in the selection of men for dismissal; although, of course, industries with a disproportionate number of older men in their labour force will probably continue to be those with the largest number of redundancies.

The facts about age and unemployment show up sharply in the employment statistics. The interpretation of these statistics is not simple, since there can be many explanations for the extent and length of employment among identifiable groups in the working population. It is not sensible to quote the employment statistics as evidence for age discrimination; instead, age discrimination must be taken into account when explaining the unemployment figures.

Certainly the unemployment rates can be partly explained in terms of overall economic trends, or structural changes in the occupational organisation of society. It may be true that the number of jobs needing characteristics possessed particularly by older men are now decreasing. It may also be true that technological societies are moving to a two-career system,

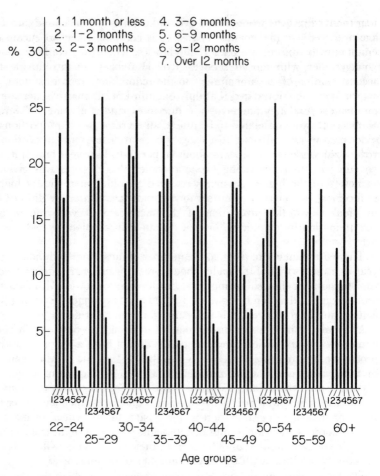

Figure 1   Unemployment levels for men by age-groups during March 1971, Professional and Executive Register.

with the young going up and the older going down – or at least sideways.

It has often been suggested that older men remain unemployed for longer than do younger men because older men are less willing to move home to get a job. A survey which I carried out in 1969–70, of 100 older unemployed executives, found that half said they would not move house to get a job 'even if the worst came to the worst'. Reluctance to move, performance at interviews, ambition and job-seeking strategies, all help explain the figures on length of unemployment and age.

In 1968, the American Secretary of Labour estimated that 'a disproportionate 20 per cent of the nation's unemployment and a disgraceful 40 per
cent of our long-term unemployed [defined as 27 weeks or more] are aged
45 or over'. In Britain, in the same year, people over 55 years of age were,
on becoming unemployed, likely to remain unemployed for four times as
long as those under 25. The *Ministry of Labour Gazette* for August 1968
commented that, even in times of low unemployment, there are large
numbers of people who have been on the register of wholly unemployed
persons for a long time and who have little hope of leaving it. This latter
group naturally contains a large proportion of older people. From 1951 to
1971 the proportion of older short-term unemployed men dropped by 16
per cent. In July 1970, for example, 84 per cent of the men who had been
unemployed for over one year were aged over 40, and 50 per cent were
aged 60 plus. The data for professional and executive unemployed persons
show the same features. The main reasons for discrimination against older
workers, taken from articles based on experience rather than on attitude
research, seem to be that older workers are thought to be: past their peak;
have less mileage in them; won't fit the pension plan; are inflexible and
hidebound; won't like taking orders from younger men; are expensive;
would be prime candidates for recurring redundancy. A further three
reasons often mentioned by American researchers are: the need to maintain policies of promotion from within; lack of skills, experience or education; and training costs and low productivity.

Negative attributes of the older managerial and executive employee
are usually lack of ruthlessness; failure to aim at higher goals; a desire for
an easy life; and failure of the man to maintain the job as the basis of his
life-style. Positive attributes are that older men are less accident-prone;
are more reliable; turn out better-quality work; have sounder judgment;
exhibit lower turnover rates; are more loyal to the firm; learn differently
but as well as younger men and remember more; in office work show
little, if any, decline in performance to age 60, and only minor decline to
age 65; require less supervision; and are more safe and responsible.

Much of the literature from the United States argues that age
discrimination is irrational. The supporters of British legislation agree.
Although older workers may be well thought of on the job, many economic myths may discourage employers from hiring them.

Would an anti-age discrimination act be an effective law? Or should
old age be a registered liability within an amended Disabled Persons
(Employment) Act? Should we continue thinking of older workers as a
special group at all? Neither form of legislation could provide a satisfactory solution. This is because the discrimination that exists is based on
stereotypes, and whereas legislation may to some extent affect people's
behaviour, it may have little effect on the attitudes which are the root of

the discrimination. The only potentially effective solution would be some form of campaign attacking the irrational stereotypes of the older worker.

References

BRENNAN, M. J. *et al.* (1967) *The Economics of Age*. New York: Norton.
Company Redundancy Policies. Report by British Institute of Management, 1969.
PARKER, S. R. *et al.* (1967) *Effects of the Redundancy Payments Act*. London: HMSO.
Promoting the Placement of Older Workers. Paris: OECD, 1967.
REUBEN, B. (1970) *The Hard-to-Employ: European Programmes*. New York: Columbia University Press.
SHEPPARD, H. L. (1970) *Toward an Industrial Gerontology*. Cambridge, Mass.: Schenkman.
SHEPPARD, H. L. (1971) *New Perspectives on Older Workers*. W. E. Upjohn Institute for Employment Research.
WEATHERBEE, H. Y. (1969) 'The older employee, a neglected resource', *Personnel*, 46, 1.

12 Compulsory versus flexible retirement: issues and facts

Erdman B. Palmore

Extent of compulsory retirement

The practice of compulsory retirement apparently became widespread only in this century and grew along with the swift industrialization and growth of large corportions in the early 1900s (Mathiasen 1953). A series of national surveys conducted by the Social Security Administration (SSA) and others show that compulsory retirement policies affect a large and growing proportion of older workers. A comparison of the reasons for retirement given in the 1951 and the 1963 Social Security surveys of the aged indicates that the proportions of male beneficiaries who retired because of compulsory retirement provisions doubled during those twelve years (11 per cent in 1951 and 21 per cent in 1963 for wage and salary workers retired within the preceding 5 years [Palmore 1967]). In their 1969 Survey of Newly Entitled Beneficiaries, the Social Security Administration found that 52 per cent of the nonworking beneficiaries, who had been wage or salary workers and who became entitled at age 65, had retired because of compulsory retirement (Reno, 1971) (those who retired before the reached 65, about $\frac{2}{3}$ of the new beneficiaries, usually gave poor health or job discontinued as the main reason, rather than compulsory retirement). A national survey of retirement policies found that 73 per cent of companies with pension plans (which includes most large companies) had compulsory retirement at a fixed age for some or all workers (Slavick and McConnell 1963). The majority of these had compulsory retirement at age 65. The 1966 SSA survey of retirement systems in state and local governments found that 79 per cent had compulsory or automatic retirement at a fixed age (Waldman 1968). This is an increase from the less than one-half of the systems in 1944.

Thus, it appears that compulsory retirement policies may affect about half of the male wage and salary workers retiring at age 65 and will affect more in the future if recent trends continue.

The case for flexible retirement

1 Compulsory retirement is by definition discrimination against an age

Source: *The Gerontologist*, 1972, *12*, 4, pp. 343–8 (extracts).

category, contrary to the principle of equal employment opportunity. [...]

Supporters of compulsory retirement might argue that such discrimination is as legal and justifiable as child labor laws and policies which restrict the employment of children. However, there seems to be a valid difference in that child labor restrictions are designed primarily for the protection of children while compulsory retirement policies are usually justified on grounds other than those of protecting older persons.

2 Age, as the sole criterion for compulsory retirement, is not an accurate indicator of ability because of the wide variation in the abilities of aged persons. Twenty years ago the National Conference on Retirement of Older Workers concluded that

Both science and experience indicate that the aging process and its effects show such wide variance among individuals as to destroy the logic of age as the sole factor in determining whether a person should retire or continue to work (Mathiasen 1953).

Recently the Gerontological Society's Committee on Research and Development Goals in Social Gerontology echoed this conclusion by stating

age limitations for employment are both socially and economically wasteful, since chronological age is rarely a reliable index of potential performance (Havighurst 1969).

All the available evidence agrees that despite the declining abilities of some aged, most workers could continue to work effectively beyond age 65 (Riley and Foner 1968).

3 Flexible retirement would better utilize the skills, experience, and productive potentials of older persons and thus increase our national output. [...]

4 Flexible retirement policies would increase the income of the aged and reduce the transfer payments necessary for income maintenance. [...] Thus the millions of aged persons with poverty incomes might be substantially reduced by flexible retirement, which would increase their employment opportunities. This in turn would substantially reduce the amount of old age assistance and other welfare payments currently given to the aged with inadequate incomes. [...]

5 Flexible retirement, in providing more employment, would improve life satisfaction and longevity of the aged. Most evidence indicates that retirement does tend to decrease life satisfaction. A recent review concluded:

Overall satisfaction with life is greater among older persons who are still working than among those who have retired. This pattern seems to arise in part (but only in part) because the kinds of people who remain in the labor force are very different from those who retire (tending to be healthier, better adjusted, more advantaged on the whole). Yet quite apart from such factors as health or socioeconomic status, the pattern of lower satisfaction among the retired persists. (Riley and Foner 1968).

Streib (1956) found that even for persons with similar levels of health and socioeconomic status, morale still tends to be comparatively higher among the employed. Thompson *et al.* (1960) found that decreases in satisfaction over two-year periods were somewhat greater among older persons who retired than among those who continued to work; and decreases in satisfaction were substantially greater among reluctant retirees. The Duke Longitudinal Study (Palmore 1968) found that reductions in economic activities including retirement were closely associated with reduction in life satisfaction. Dr Thomas Green (1970), of Syracuse University's Educational Policy Research Center, has concluded:

Surely there is nothing more damaging to the human spirit than the knowledge – or belief – that one's capacities are unused, unwanted . . .

There is less evidence supporting the idea that retirement has negative effects on health and longevity. Most of the association of poor health and greater mortality with retirement is probably due to the fact that people in poor health and with shortened life expectancies are the ones who tend to retire (Martin and Doran 1966; Riley and Foner 1968). However, we found that work satisfaction was one of the strongest predictors of longevity in our longitudinal study of normal aged (Palmore 1969). It may be that lack of work satisfaction, which can occur among the employed as well as among the retired, is the factor which reduces longevity.

6 Flexible retirement reduces the resentment and animosity caused by compulsory retirement. Apparently, many workers bitterly resent being thrown on the trash dump while they are still capable of working. Flexible retirement policies, by allowing such workers to continue work, eliminates this problem.

The case for compulsory retirement

1 Compulsory retirement is simple and easy to administer. Flexible retirement would require complicated tests which would be difficult to administer fairly and difficult to explain and justify to the worker. This may be the main reason for the popularity of compulsory retirement among administrators. Proponents of flexible retirement agree that it would be somewhat more difficult to administer, but many with experience in the administration of flexible retirement plans assert that the complications have been exaggerated and that adequate tests of retirement based on

ability are 'not the monsters they were made out to be' (Mathiasen 1953). Various groups have been working on improving techniques for measuring functional ability as a basis for retirement practices (Koyl 1970).

In fact, most organizations have implicit or explicit standards, more or less based on ability and merit, which they use to decide who should be hired, fired, transferred, or promoted among workers under 65. Flexible retirement policies can use these same standards, or somewhat more exacting standards, to decide who should be retained and who retired among workers over 65.

2 Compulsory retirement prevents caprice and discrimination against individual workers. Proponents of flexible retirement also grant this point, but point out that prevention of individual discrimination is bought at the price of wholesale discrimination against an entire age category. They argue that the net number of workers willing and able to work who are forced to retire would be much less under policies of flexible retirement.

3 Compulsory retirement provides predictability. Both employer and employee know well in advance that the employee must retire on a fixed date. Thus, both can plan ahead better. On the other hand, some predictability can be built into flexible retirement by requiring workers and management to give a certain amount of advance notice to the other party of any intended retirement.

4 Compulsory retirement forces management to provide retirement benefits at a determined age. Most compulsory retirement plans are accompanied by retirement pension systems (Slavick and McConnell 1963). On the other hand pension systems are often combined with flexible retirement policies with no great difficulty (Mathiasen 1953).

5 Compulsory retirement reduces unemployment by reducing the number of workers competing for limited jobs. This is especially important in declining or automating industries or plants with an over-supply of workers. On the other hand, it could be pointed out that compulsory retirement tends to increase unemployment among older workers by forcing them to leave one job at which they are experienced and seek another job in a new area in which they may be disadvantaged. Using compulsory retirement to reduce unemployment is analogous to firing all women or all blacks in order to reduce the number of workers competing for jobs. A better solution to the unemployment problem is for the government to stimulate the economy or to create additional jobs by being the 'employer of the last resort'. [. . .]

If a smaller work force is really desired, this could be accomplished by shorter work weeks, longer vacations, delayed entry into the labor market by more education, etc. (Kreps 1969).

6 Compulsory retirement prevents seniority and tenure provisions from blocking the hiring and promotion of younger workers. This is certainly true when seniority and tenure provisions are used to retain workers who have become less efficient and productive. A solution to this problem under flexible retirement would be to eliminate seniority and tenure provisions at a fixed age and require the older workers to compete periodically for their jobs on the basis of ability rather than seniority.

7 Compulsory retirement forces retirement in only a few cases because most workers 65 and over want to retire or are incapable of work. This claim is probably not true as shown by the surveys cited earlier.

It is true that 69 per cent of men over 65 not at work say they are not well enough to work and another 16 per cent say they are not interested in work, but many of these responses may be rationalizations for inability to find suitable employment (Palmore 1967; Sheppard 1969). The only way to accurately determine how many older workers are forced to retire, but willing and able to work, is to eliminate compulsory retirement and count how many take advantage of the opportunity to continue working.

8 Compulsory retirement saves face for the older worker no longer capable of performing adequately. The older worker does not have to be told and does not have to admit that he is no longer capable of working but can blame his retirement on the compulsory retirement policy. Such a face-saving device undoubtedly has important value for many workers, but the number of such workers should be balanced against the perhaps equal number of capable workers forced to retire by compulsory retirement and the resulting frustration, loss of status, reduction of income and of national productivity.

9 Most workers 65 years old have impaired health or only a few years of health left. The facts do not support this argument. Life expectancy for a 65-year-old person is now about fifteen years, and the majority of aged do not appear to have disabling impairments. Only 37 per cent of persons 65 and over report any limitation in their major activity (National Center for Health Statistics 1971).

[. . .] It appears probable that the majority of workers age 65 can expect a substantial number of years in which they will be capable of productive employment.

10 Most older workers are inferior and cannot perform most jobs as well as younger workers. This appears to be another of the stereotypes about the aged which has little or no basis in fact. A recent review of the evidence concluded,

Studies under actual conditions show older workers performing as well as younger workers, if not better, on most, but not all, measures. Thus, those men and women who remain in the labor force during their latter years are not making generally inferior contributions, despite their frequently poor performance under laboratory conditions (Riley and Foner 1968).

11 Compulsory retirement does little harm because most workers who are forced to retire could get other jobs if they wanted to. Again the evidence is contrary to this theory. When workers 65 and over lose their jobs, they have much more difficulty in getting another one than younger men. The proportions of older workers in the long-term unemployed categories are about twice as high compared to workers age 20–35 (Riley and Foner, 1968). Educational differences do not explain these differences in long-term unemployment (Sheppard 1969). [. . .]

12 Most workers forced to retire have adequate retirement income. Again the facts appear to be to the contrary. We do not know exactly what percentage of those forced to retire are in poverty, but 30 per cent of all retired couples and 64 per cent of the retired non-married persons have incomes below the official poverty level (Bixby 1970). And it is precisely those forced to retire early who have incomes substantially lower than those who retire early voluntarily (Reno 1971).

As may be obvious from the preceding review, I favour flexible retirement policies primarily because I conclude compulsory retirement is unfair to the capable older worker, psychologically and socially damaging, and economically wasteful [. . .]

In conclusion, I hope that this article may clarify the issues and facts involved and may become a basis for reducing the millions of cases of compulsory retirement and the resulting social and economic waste of our older citizens' talents and skills.

References

BIXBY, L. (1970) 'Income of people aged 65 and older', *Social Security Bulletin, 33*, 4, 3–34.

GREEN, T. (1970) 'Panel examines new technology', *New York Times*, Jan. 30.

HAVIGHURST, R. J. (ed.) (1969), 'Research and development goals in social gerontology, *Gerontologist, 9*, Part II.

KOYL, L. (1970) 'A technique for measuring functional criteria in placement and retirement practices.' In H. Sheppard (ed.) *Towards an Industrial Gerontology.* Cambridge, Mass.: Schenkman.

KREPS, J. (1969) 'Economics of retirement.' In E. Busse and E. Pfeiffer (eds.) *Behavior and Adaptation in Late Life.* Boston: Little, Brown & Co.

MARTIN, J., and DORAN, A. (1966) 'Evidence concerning the relationship between health and retirement', *Sociological Review, 14*, 329–43.

MATHIASEN, G. (ed.) (1953) *Criteria for Retirement.* New York: G. P. Putman's Sons.

NATIONAL CENTER FOR HEALTH STATISTICS (1971) 'Current estimates from the Health Interview Survey – 1969', *Vital and Health Statistics*, Ser. 10, No. 63.

PALMORE, E. (1967) 'Retirement patterns.' In L. Epstein and J. Murray, *The Aged Population of the United States*. Washington: Government Printing Office.

PALMORE, E. (1968) 'The effects of aging on activities and attitudes', *Gerontologist*, *8*, 259–63.

PALMORE, E. (1969) 'Predicting longevity', *Gerontologist*, *9*, 247–50.

RENO, V. (1971) 'Why men stop working at or before age 65: Findings from the Survey of New Beneficiaries', *Social Security Bulletin*, *34*, 6, 3–17.

RILEY, M. and FONER, A. (1969) *Aging and Society, Vol. 11* New York: Russell Sage Foundation.

SHEPPARD, H. (1969) 'Aging and manpower development.' In M. Riley and A. Foner, *Aging and Society, Vol. 11*. New York: Russell Sage Foundation.

SLAVICK, F. and MCCONNELL, J. (1963) 'Flexible versus compulsory retirement policies', *Monthly Labor Review*, *86*, 279–81.

STREIB, G. (1956) 'Morale of the retired', *Social Problems*, *3*, 270–6.

THOMPSON, W., STREIB, G., and KOSA, J. (1960) 'The effect of retirement on personal adjustment', *Journal of Gerontology*, *15*, 165–9.

WALDMAN, S. (1968) *Retirement Systems for Employees of State and Local Governments, 1968*. Washington: Government Printing Office.

13   On growing old

A. L. Vischer

Before people are old they must first grow old. From an objective point of view the transition from one phase of life to another is of course a slow and gradual process. [. . .] It is not possible to fix on specific ages, i.e. on specific points of time, as the periods during which people will pass from one phase to another. [Also] the transition from middle age to old age fluctuates far more from one individual to another than do the changes attendant on earlier periods of life. What we are interested in here is simply to discover why and how human personality undergoes a change of consciousness, for when we speak of 'growing old' we are in fact describing a condition which we ourselves experience and in which we are made aware of a change in our being. In the whole course of human life there is surely only one other transitional stage, in which there is a comparable emphasis on the formation of a new ego-consciousness, and that is puberty. Young persons are aware of a difference between themselves and children. They feel older. They have either left school or else they wish that they had left. They are intent on preparing, on building up and on organizing their chosen profession and their future life. When people pass from childhood to youth they see their lives stretched out before them awaiting fulfilment. 'All this is something entirely positive, for they expect something from the future; the future is to bring them fulfilment.' By contrast growing old seems to be a negative process and is always experienced as such, especially when it first sets in. As a result a dark foreboding enters into the consciousness of the aging, the foreboding that the progressive phase of life has come to an end. The feeling that one is growing old is a highly differentiated feeling with a wide range of nuances. There are times when it is quite intense and there are times when it is relatively weak. But it is always there, even though it may be hidden from sight. For there are those who are not completely conscious of growing old just as there are those for whom puberty is neither a critical nor a tempestuous period.

What sort of experiences first make people feel that they are growing old? A study by the psychologist Fritz Giese* has furnished us with some highly interesting data concerning such initial experiences. Giese's enquiry was based on questions which he put to the general public. He asked the readers of more than fifty German newspapers and periodicals

* 'Erlebnisfornen des Alterns', *Deutsche Psychologie*, 5, 4, 2.

Source: A. L. VISCHER (1966) *On Growing Old*. London: Allen and Unwin, pp. 30–5.

to answer the following two questions: 'Which factors first made you aware of growing old? Which were the first indications you received that you felt old?' The advantage of an investigation of this kind is that it reaches a broad public. Its disadvantage lies in the fact that very little is known about the people submitting answers to the questions. More answers were received from men than from women – sixty-nine per cent from men as compared with thirty-one per cent from women. As far as age-groups are concerned, there were very few answers from people between twenty and thirty years of age and the majority of these were from women. Nor were there very many answers from people between thirty and forty. Sixteen per cent of all answers came from people between forty and fifty, fifty-three per cent from people between fifty and seventy. The number of people over eighty who submitted answers was the same as those in the thirty–forty age group. The youngest person to reply, a woman, was twenty-five, the oldest was eighty-nine. The age at which most people felt they were 'old' was around about forty-nine.

But what was it that made these people feel old? Two-thirds of the attributes and experiences reported were physical whilst only one-third were psycho-spiritual in origin. It should be noted in this connection, however, that both the external and internal processes in which our bodies are involved nearly always take place beneath the threshold of consciousness. We are not normally aware of our bodies and if we do become aware of them, if they become an object of our experience, it is usually because some large-scale physical change has taken place or because certain physical functions have been disrupted. Giese reports that members of the higher professions often quoted psycho-spiritual phenomena as their first indication of age, but it is significant that psycho-spiritual factors were also not infrequently mentioned by manual workers (laundrywomen, storekeepers etc.). Giese has tabulated the physical properties and physical disturbances reported by his test subjects as the first indication of the onset of old age together with the various organs which they involved and the percentage of people affected.

1 Organs of movement (muscles, back, teeth, bones extremities)	... 17.4%
2 Nerves (including memory, sleeplessness)	... 15.7%
3 Organs of sense (eyes and ears)	... 14.6%
4 Skin (hair, wrinkles, etc.)	... 14.4%
5 Fatigue	... 10.5%
6 Sexual organs	... 9.2%
7 Circulation (heart, arteries)	... 7.1%
8 Metabolism (sugar, ghout, fat)	... 5.0%
9 Digestion (stomach, intestines)	... 3.2%
10 Urine (kidney)	... 1.7%
11 Respiration (lungs, chill, etc.)	... 1.2%

These data are striking in more than one respect. They do not readily agree with our general experience, above all in respect of the order of precedence which they follow. We are surprised to find that heart and circulation come only seventh in the list. When a doctor examines a patient of advanced years the first thing he will look at is the patient's circulation. But then patients often remain unaware over a considerable period of time of circulatory and heart trouble which is readily established by an objective examination. The reason for this is that of all the physical organs the heart is best able to adapt to changing conditions. A damaged heart can go on working on its own reserves of strength over a long period without giving rise to serious disturbances in other parts of the body. Disturbances, of which the patient is himself aware, such as shortage of breath and pains in the heart, occur only when the organ has reached the limit of its capacity. Until this happens there is no reason why the person concerned should feel anything that might lead him to suspect a faulty heart. Apart from this, however, it is of course quite probable that much of the malfunctioning of the organs of movement and much of the fatigue reported by Giese's test subjects was actually caused by disturbances to the circulatory organs.

Psycho-spiritual factors were mentioned only half as often as physical factors and there are various reasons why this should be so. In the first place the perception of psycho-spiritual changes in old age calls for a certain measure of self-observation, and not everyone is capable of this. On the other hand, there can be no doubt but that Giese's method is also partly responsible for this imbalance. People are naturally more inclined to admit to physical changes and to suppress their more intimate personal experiences. Stern is surely right when he argues that if we talk to people individually and gain their confidence, and especially if we are doctors, we discover that psychic factors occur more frequently than Giese's findings would appear to suggest. Enquiries based on questionnaires are valid only to a limited extent. But they do give food for thought and they do provide us with valuable hints. This is certainly true of Giese, who establishes three human types on the basis of the particular character assumed by the psycho-spiritual experiences of his test subjects.

The *first* type might be called negativist. He flatly refuses to be old and in his letter he protests that the very last thing that would ever enter his mind would be to feel old. He virtually takes offence at the mere mention of old age and we are left wondering why he should have bothered to answer the questions in the first place.

The *second* type feels that he is sinking, fading, becoming weighed down. These changes of spirit came about following specific experiences involving his environment and his fellow-men. A personal regression is established, whose source is felt to lie primarily in the field of work. Thus several subjects reported that their first intimation that they were growing old came from the shattering experience of failing to obtain a new post for which they had applied. With others the feeling that they were growing old was linked with the fear of redundancy, of dismissal from their profession, or with the fear of being pensioned off. It was primarily the white-collar workers who reported that the thought of giving up their positions in one or two years' time made them feel dull, oppressed and listless.

Quite apart from professional experiences of this order the words and deeds of his fellow-men, which are often both harsh and thoughtless, leave the aging person in no doubt as to his condition: you've grown old, you're not so young as you used to be. People who have lived their lives without a thought for the morrow, who have simply allowed themselves to be carried along by life and to whom self-observation is quite alien, suddenly find themselves confronted by specific observations made by their fellow-men. Often these observations are couched in the stereotyped phrases to which the aging person is exposed in trains and trams. But they might equally well appear in the polite forms of social intercourse, as, for example, when a mother says to her child, 'Stand up and let the old gentleman sit down!' A university lecturer was first made aware of his age – he was fifty-five – 'when (as he himself writes) a young girl offered him her place in the overcrowded tram'. And then there was the lady who was told by her hairdresser that she 'still had such beautiful hair'. A sixty-three-year-old tradesman writes, 'When I was fifty-one I learned to ride a bicycle. The onlookers said, "You can't teach an old dog new tricks!" Around about that time a tobacconist, to whom I happened to mention that I was not a heavy smoker, replied, "Most old gentlemen are very fond of their tobacco!" A few years later I was asked in connection with my trade, "How long are you going to keep it up? . . .".' A lady felt the first shock of old age when a child shouted after her in the street, 'Look Grandma's waddling.' Experiences of this kind constantly recur. They are quite stereotype in form and they can happen to everyone irrespective of their social background or breeding.

The reasons given by the *third* type for feeling old are based on certain intellectual or intuitive self-observations. He notices that his intellectual response to new experiences has been dulled and he finds himself extremely prone to the emergence of old memories. He often acquires a kind of spiritual clarity and subscribes to a philosophical or religious and more or less contemplative Weltanschauung. Both his emotional and his volitional actions become more elaborate. Pleasures such as those afforded by eating, dancing and travelling are felt to be less important. Many of the test subjects reported a general emotional impoverishment; the funerals of old friends no longer occasioned such grief, love and hate were becoming dormant and eroticism had receded. Only very few of the test subjects reported an unhoped-for revival of sexual desire and with those who did the object of their desire was nearly always a young person of the opposite sex. They were astonished to discover what they took to be a 'drive of old age', a last resurgence of passion.

The general conclusion which Giese drew from his study was that, whereas the physical symptoms which appear as people grow older tend to reveal a marked unanimity, in the spiritual sphere there are quite considerable typological differences.

14 That was your life: a biographical approach to later life

Malcolm Johnson

> 'Time passes. Listen. Time passes.
> Come closer now.
> Only you can hear the houses sleeping in the streets in
> the slow deep salt and silent black bandaged night. . . .
> Only you can hear and see, behind the eyes of the
> sleepers, the movements and countries and mazes and
> colours and dismays and rainbows and tunes and wishes
> and flight and fall and despairs and big seas of their
> dreams.'
>
> > *Dylan Thomas*
> > Under Milk Wood

Abstract

Social gerontology has over the past three decades generated a vast
amount of information and data about older people, but relatively little
real understanding and far less theory. [. . .]

   This paper suggests that more attention should be given to understanding the older person's self-perceived state, his own self-image and his own
needs and aspirations. In combining a concern for theoretical advance
and keener insight it is proposed that the sociological concept 'career' be
extended into an analytical tool for the examination of life biographies.
This would allow issues like dependency and independency to be seen in
their full and proper context – the life experience of the individual.

The rise of gerontology as a specialised area of academic work, has been
closely geared to appreciating and measuring the needs of older people in
the hope of being able to construct better social policies. Along the way
this pursuit has all but parted company with the larger concerns of the
process of ageing, with certain undesirable results. Much of the research
conducted in recent years has given attention to mapping what are seen as
the 'problems' of old age along with their medical, psychological and
social correlates. This research has tended to address itself to specific

Source: J. M. A. MUNNICHS and W. J. A. VAN DEN HEUVEL (eds) (1976) *Dependency or
Interdependency in Old Age*. The Hague: Martinus Nijhoff, pp. 148–61 (extracts).

topics, issues or problems, or to describing the experience of people in a particular age range, who are linked by some other social variable like income, class or ethnic origin. Its purpose has been to collect 'hard facts' about later life.

Amongst the most studied of all these areas are [. . .] Dependency and Independency. They are concerns thrust upon the developed nations as a direct result of developed status. Extension of life-expectancy due to better diet, better hygiene, and antibiotics, combined with the remodelling of family life and the growth of geographical mobility, has created an entirely new problem of the aged. Faced with a bulk of non-producers which is constantly being enlarged and which, in at least the economic sense, is also dependent, governments have encouraged gerontological research of a descriptive and epidemiological kind. The assumption underlying this research funding was that it would supply a sufficient data base for policy-makers to use the slender resources allocated to the care and support of older people in an effective and cost-efficient sort of way.

Even non-governmental research-funding agencies have tended to take this policy line and it has led social gerontology to a state where there is more data available of a particular positivistic kind, than any of us can hope to handle. What we have not got is a comparable body of knowledge which will allow us to properly interpret that data. Perhaps more to the point, the data has been constructed in such a way that it defies any other interpretation than as a rough guide to the possible *allocation of resources*. Theory is a very small part of the social gerontological literature (an issue we shall return to). Not only have there been very few attempts to produce new theoretical propositions, but researchers from sociological and policy backgrounds have studiously avoided contaminating their enquiries with theory from other areas of their discipline.

This article is one of several which have been produced over the past three or four years as a result of my disillusionment with current research (Johnson 1972, 1973, 1975). Having carried out a major study in the nineteen-sixties of the conventional type, it became apparent that it told us only what a score of studies before it had said. The planned and partly written book was never completed for lack of enthusiasm. Sadly, many more since have found their way into print only to rehearse the same unhelpful 'facts'. So the purpose here will be to offer a critique of some – though not all – of the literature and to discuss the consequences of the underdeveloped state of conceptual thinking about age. This assessment will lead into a consideration of a number of dynamic concepts in use in sociology and social psychology and some propositions about the use of biographical techniques, not only as ways of understanding life processes, but as necessary perspectives on such 'problems' as dependency and independency.

The literature – its life so far

Few people in the field will be offended if I describe social gerontology as being young and somewhat immature. I hesitate to call it adolescent or even pubetal, for fear of being placed in paradigms I wish to criticise, but as our concerns are with ageing a temporal/social analogy seems fitting.

Sociologists and those who use sociological methods and techniques of data collection have spent much of their efforts in the ageing field carrying out social surveys. In Britain this kind of work has long and honourable traditions, dating from the last quarter of the nineteenth century with the work of Booth, Rowntree, Webb and others. In America and (as far as my incomplete knowledge extends) in Europe and Australia, the bulk of research has been of this sort. Moreover, it is almost wholly directed towards the retired population, to the neglect of middle age and earlier life phases. Thus our information is skewed heavily in favour of those in a given ageband, and their myriad disabilities.

There have, of course, been attempts to construct theories about ageing, notably from Cumming and Henry (1961), Rose (1965) and Riley, Johnson and Foner (1972). However, these propositions are not universally accepted, though they are widely used in writings on gerontology, because they are among the very few systematic attempts to organize thinking about age. We shall give more attention to work of this sort subsequently; but for the present it is important to sketch out the dominant empirical tradition which has been most influential both in academic and in policy terms. The treatment will be thematic and at times historical. It will also be necessarily very selective.

Data-based studies fall into five general categories which cover what are seen to be the important aspects of later life:

(*i*) *Studies of social and physical morbidity*. These researches are of an epidemiological sort and set out to establish the extent to which identifiable social disabilities and physical illnesses are present in the retired population or sectors of it. The incidence of these conditions is determined in relation to pre-set standards and it is common for the study population to be classified into those who are in need of assistance of some kind and those who can manage without (e.g. Shanas 1962; Isaacs 1972).

(*ii*) A second category of enquiries might be contentiously labelled *Quality of life studies*. These are concerned with the elderly person's immediate environment; accommodation, public amenities, personal finances, transport, ownership of consumer durables, etc. This group also includes the many studies of special accommodation for the aged – sheltered housing, old people's homes and geriatric hospitals. Within this accommodation section there are several interestingly different sorts of investigation. But those who study the elderly in their own homes have tended towards a predictable inventory of the characteristics which are either explicitly or implicitly deemed desirable or undesirable (e.g. Brockington and Lempert 1966; Townsend 1968).

(*iii*) *Personal Relations* in later life have attracted a good deal of social science attention. There have been many studies of family relations, personal social networks, isolation and loneliness and formalised social activities (clubs and societies). These have tended to be somewhat more sensitive to the statements and views of older people if only because the researcher has greater difficulty in actually measuring human interactive processes. However, this has not stopped many students of gerontology from creating artificial scales of sociability by which to fulfil their desire to dichotomise their respondents into those whose personal relations meet with their approval and those who must be given aid (e.g. Kutner *et al.* 1956; Tunstall 1966).

(*iv*) *Social welfare services*. Whilst it will be argued later that the majority of studies on older people are resource based (i.e. concerned with finding ways of channelling existing resources, in their present or modified form), this category is the most aligned to this objective. Studies of this type are not unlike the screening studies in epidemiology, but where it is important to seek out those who are 'in need' of, say, meals-on-wheels or home nursing, but are not currently getting them. Such work is the predictable outcome of the very limited resources allocated to the care of older people in almost all countries and the unimaginative way in which these scarce resources are translated into 'blocks' of services (e.g. Van Zonneveld 1961; Rosow and Breslau 1966; Harris 1968).

(*v*) *Work and Retirement*. On the face of it, work in this field should be the most dynamic in the sense of dealing with a human process which takes place over a period of time. To a certain extent this is true, but a large proportion of retirement studies are more concerned with the adjustment or re-adjustment of actually retired individuals, rather than with explanation of social transitions. At the same time the retirement issue and the reconstruction of roles, relationship and perspectives has proved one of the most insightful areas of study (Crawford 1973; Donahue, Orbach and Pollack 1960; Maddox 1968).

Published work in the field of social gerontology cannot be neatly categorised under these five headings; not (I hope) because they are inappropriate, but because many studies include more than one or even all of these concerns. Therefore we shall look briefly at some studies which are concerned wholly or in part with these subjects. As the primary object is to make constructive proposals rather than to mount a full-blown literature review and critique, a selection of studies will be cited which exemplify different approaches and interests.

Social and health surveys of old people go back to the nineteenth century in Britain. A number of studies of importance were published between the wars. Following the Second World War, there was a rapid expansion of interest. Sheldon published his famous volume in 1948 and many astute observers of the field have said that most of the subsequent research has added very little to the findings of that simple but useful study. At the level of indicating the extent of a range of illnesses and some social disabilities, he set out a pattern which has not changed dramatically, despite the changes in affluence, life style and services. Along with Seebohm Rowntree's (1947) study, these two books were the precursors of a modest but steady growth of investigations.

In the 1950s and 1960s, the journals showed signs of the emergence of geriatrics as a hospital specialty and the enthusiasm for research that some of its early practitioners had. Ferguson Anderson, the founder of the specialism in Britain, entered the field early as did Exton-Smith, Geffen and Warren, Bransby and Osborne amongst others. These studies concerned themselves with the measurement of clinical morbidity and with such other issues as nutrition, incontinence and their relation to crude social variables.

By the late 1950s, interest had widened beyond health matters. In 1957 Barbara Shenfield published her *Social Policies for Old Age* (the same year as Peter Townsend's important book *The Family Life of Old People*), and seven years later Brockington and Lempert (1966) produced *The Social Needs of the Over Eighties*. From that time on there has been a steady flow of studies in socio-medical gerontology leading up to the more recent publications in the same tradition like Bernard Isaac's (1972) *Survival of the Unfittest* and Ann Cartwright's (1973) *Life Before Death*.

In one way or another these studies describe the illnesses and related social characteristics and problems of the chosen sample. In all the cited examples and in many more, there was no attempt to do more than describe the situation and deduce policy propositions from the data. This is quite legitimate activity and it proved itself worthy in that policy-makers are still interested in promoting work of this nature. However, it suffers from methodological deficiencies which are inherent in its conception rather than in its execution, i.e. it assumes that the standards of measurement used as a basis for describing good or ill-health or social disability are appropriate to all those studied.

If Holland is typical of the rest of Western Europe the picture there is similar to Britain. The Dutch way of dealing with its elderly since the last war has made the focus slightly different in so far as medical care is frequently provided in nursing homes rather than exclusively in hospitals or in the home (Munnichs 1976). So much of the research effort has gone into studies of nursing home care. Nevertheless, in a review article on the Dutch gerontological scene, Peter Coleman (1975) writes:

A number of surveys have taken place on the situation of the elderly in their own homes, in hospitals and in nursing homes. Some of these studies have concentrated on describing the health situation of the elderly (their pathology, symptoms, complaints, medical consumption, etc.) and relating it to other variables (age, sex, housing, social position, etc.).

American studies, because of their relative profusion, are more difficult to classify, but there is a strong tradition of the kind noted in Britain and the Netherlands. Ethel Shanas's (1962) well-known work *The Health of Older People* exemplifies the descriptive stream in U.S. research. It attempts little by way of sociological analysis, nor does it pretend to have a concern with theory. In the same way, George Rosen's (1960) essay in Tibbitts' compendious volume on social gerontology, shows clearly the nature of research – 'fact' based descriptive studies.

The great post-war outpouring of gerontological studies in America has been summarised in Volume I of *Ageing and Society* under the direction of Matilda White Riley (1968). There is little point in attempting an inferior substitute for that volume here. From that summary it is reasonable to deduce that sociological work on ageing has been in the main empirical and descriptive. Indeed, Riley *et al.'s* (1972) attempt to produce a theory of age stratification in the third volume is in itself an expression of the need to consolidate this vast range of research data.

Having very briefly and inadequately pointed to a pervading tradition in social gerontology – and being aware that assertion of this sort is no substitute for evidence – let us take a few specific examples of the kind of work which has so far been only implicitly criticised. The next section will suggest a greater prominence should be given to self-estimates of such things as are labelled 'need', 'problem', 'dependency', etc, the object of the present exercise being to demonstrate the way in which researchers neglect the individual's perceptions in favour of definitions constructed by themselves or other professionals. An interesting manifestation of this development can be seen in the growth of social indicators as applied to older people (Williams, forthcoming).

In a previous paper (Johnson 1972) I examined this problem in relation to self-perception of need, showing that many researchers had collected data on self-estimates of health status which were radically different from the professional judgements and that in all cases these enormous discrepancies were ignored. This means that the researcher feels either that he or she knows better than the respondent on the basis of 'objective' evidence or that the individual's assessment is of no account. In either event it seems that social gerontologists and sociologists of medicine alike are practising a huge arrogance. But more particularly, they are imposing values onto older people which may be appropriate to people of work age and who bear an obligation to work, but inappropriate to those whose time is, at least in theory, all their own.

This imposition of values is a feature which runs through most of the descriptive studies of later life. Of the other four categories of studies not discussed, three are heavily laden with this technique. Quality of Life studies are almost without exception based on preset standards of what is acceptable housing, adequate income, proper equipment and so on. In a similar way studies of the Social Relations of older people (particularly with their families) often employ traditional normative standards of desirable inter-generational relationships (Koller 1974), by which to measure the results of sociometric or other network analyses. Living alone in old age is certainly acceptable and even desirable for many people. But it is predictable that studies of such people will be overly concerned with imputing loneliness and may even go as far as to construct social contact scales as a basis for such judgements (Lowenthal 1964; Tunstall 1966).

Research based on the provision and uptake of social services is just as likely as that on health, to dichotomise study populations into 'need' and 'not need' categories. In Britain, classic examples of this sort of work would be Amelia Harris's (1968) *Social Welfare for the Elderly*, and Brockington and Lempert's work. The Fabian pamphlet by Michael Meacher and J. Agate (1969) is an archetypical case. On the American scene, the Post-White House Conference on Ageing Reports (1973) provide many examples of this approach. [. . .]

In the countries of Western Europe and America, there is a common set of possible services available to a given community. In some areas they are provided on a more generous scale than in others, but there is little national variation in the range of services and aids available. These are few in number and organized in such a way as to impose rigidity on their allocation. A list of the most important services would include hospital care, supervised or sheltered accommodation (including nursing homes), meals provision, home nursing, chiropody, income supplements (means tested), home helps, friendly visiting, supply of aids and house modification. To the best of my knowledge there is nowhere where these services are supplied in sufficient quality and quantity. In most places, the list of available services would be somewhat shorter.

Just as the social workers who disburse these social benefits are constrained by the nature of existing provision, so are many researchers, who cast their studies in the terms of what is, or might easily be, available. Thus there is a reinforcing process which lends a spurious legitimacy to giving older people the nearest thing you have from your minute range of provisions. Moreover, as budgets are universally small and the potential demand of older people on this basis is all but infinite, there operates an informal rationing system. Knowledge of this situation makes recipients feel grateful even for services which are useless to them, as they are numbered amongst the privileged few who receive these relatively expensive forms of aid.

One of the major flaws in this allocation process is the failure to properly diagnose the elderly person's true 'needs'. The other is the provision of services which are not of benefit to him and are wasteful both on social and economic grounds (Johnson 1972, 1975).

Life as a biographical career

So far we have talked of studies which set universal standards on such dimensions as health, income, housing, etc., and result in bad decisions about need. These decisions are bad in the sense that they are meant to result in an increased life satisfaction for the receiving party and often fail to do so. They are also bad at another level. They take little or no account of the individual's personal assessment and concentrate on decision-making, based upon the immediately *observable* and *present* features of his or her life. Such an approach denies the historical roots of personal 'needs' and implies an unrealistic homogeneity in the face of knowledge that as humans get older they become more idiosyncratic.

In order to overcome these deficiencies both in the diagnoses of such states as dependency and in the finding of appropriate and efficacious solutions, an alternative strategy is proposed. It is rooted in the development of dynamic concepts from sociology and social psychology on the grounds that being old (or just older) is the present manifestation of past experiences and processes. Underlying the proposal to use this thinking in the development of diagnostic techniques and as a result facilitating joint decision-making about outcomes, is the value-judgement that older people are entitled to select their own destiny, within given limits.

Social theories of ageing propounded to date have not given sufficient prominence to the uniqueness of the human biography, preferring to emphasize the commonality of certain characteristics and experiences. This is not surprising when one observes that the two major contributions, the Disengagement Theory of Cumming and Henry and the Theory of Age Stratification by Riley *et al.*, were conceived within the functionalist perspective. Both were grounded in the framework set out by Talcott Parsons. He in fact contributed a chapter to the Riley volume and added his imprimatur to Disengagement in his paper 'Old Age as Consummatory Phase' (Riley *et al.* 1968).

Cumming and Henry (1961) characterise old age as the phase when society and the individual prepare in advance for the inevitable disengagement which comes with death. Thus the two withdraw from each other in a mutually satisfying way, so that when the individual dies his departure does nothing to disrupt the orderly functioning of society. So disengagement is the period of withdrawal of those expectations and obligations which maintain the individual in equilibrium with society during his active life.

This theme is clearly identifiable in Riley's work too. Early in the first chapter she sets out the model:

Age, in the sociological view, affects both the *roles* in the social system and the *people* who act in these roles. Thus the conceptual scheme to be outlined in section I of this chapter will assume the existence of a role system and of a population of actors, and will concentrate on age-specific structural elements...

Although it would be untrue to say that either of these theories naively ignores the implications of life biography, they subjugate its importance in favour of the needs of society at large. Towards the end of the Riley (1972) volume John Clausen indicates one of the reasons why functionalists are disinterested in retrospective accounts as well as combating the proposition that people have the right to remain engaged with society if they wish:

Adequate understanding of a given person's life-history requires that one know both how that person viewed influential events at the time of their occurrence and how he subsequently interprets them. Ideally one would like to know the nature of the 'objective realities' that were encountered at any given time . . .

Arnold Rose (1965) has set out a clear critique of functionalist theories of ageing and suggests that not only are they poor interpretations of the facts, but that they are based on the unacceptable value-judgement that disengagement is a good thing. He goes on to say that these theorists are ethnocentric in their thinking and studiously avoid major social and historical trends in order to adhere to universal prescriptions about the necessity to adjust to death.

If Rose's criticisms hold water, then there is good reason for being dismayed not only at the overwhelmingly descriptive nature of studies in social gerontology, but also at the deficiencies of what important theoretical propositions exist. I would want to argue against the disengagement theory not only on broad theoretical grounds, but because it denies one of the things which research has clearly demonstrated, that older people mostly wish to remain living in their own homes and to retain choice.

Clearly Clausen was right when he said that ideally one would want corroborating evidence to support personal recall of events gone by, in order to reconstruct the past. However, in this paper we are primarily concerned with that category of issues, 'need'. In these circumstances –

given that you accept the right to determine one's own future – it is only the subjective that matters. It is how the individual composes his own reality that is the essence of his 'needs'.

In taking the line that 'clients' should be part of the process of diagnosing their own state and this having been done, exercising choice from a range of appropriate options, I am not suggesting a form of consumer sovereignty. Nor is it to be assumed that given a range of options, the client will always choose the most costly option. Indeed, one's suspicions are that they are most likely to choose the ones which mean staying home and options which include community rather than professional support. To take us closer to the reality of this diagnosis and chosen outcome we need to be aware of the factors which influence the presentation of problems in later life. It has been claimed several times so far that human lives are made up of dynamic processes and it is to these we must turn.

A biographical approach

Old Age as a notion has always been imprecise, but with the growth of post-retirement populations (now in Britain 16 per cent and in the U.S. 10 per cent) the age range has made any presumed homogeneity a nonsense. There are some very important realities which retired and old people have in common (e.g. the fact of being non-workers) but these features may not be of any significance to some, whilst imposing crushing limitations on others. Workers in the field of old age frequently point to this non-homogeneity argument, but as the pervading theoretical model is functionalist, the literature regularly implies commonality of experience. By seeing an individual life as a series of inter-related careers, intersected by transitions, reversals, conflicts and triumphs, we may, as Dylan Thomas put it, 'see behind the eyes of the sleepers'.

The term 'career' was for a long time used only in its conventional sense relating to occupations; but in recent years it has been liberated and expanded. Erving Goffman (1959) used it in his notable paper, 'The Moral Career of the Mental Patient', nearly twenty years ago. Through the work of Becker (1961, 1963) and others the term was employed widely in deviancy studies. McCall and Simmons (1966) write of 'the career of a relationship' in their book on role theory, and several years before, Julius Roth (1963) had introduced the notion of illness careers, in his perceptive study, *Timetables: Structuring the Passage of Time in Hospital and Other Careers*. What no-one seems seriously to have done so far is to extend the concept of career to its ultimate mortal extent, i.e. life careers.

Roth defined careers as '. . . a series of definable stages or phases of a given sphere of activity that a group of people goes through in a progressive fashion (that is one step leads to another) in a given direction or on the way to a more or less definite and recognizable endpoint or goal or series of goals'. This is a good beginning for thinking about life careers, except that it does not admit failure and set back. Stebbins (1970), and more specifically Glaser and Strauss (1965), have talked of the reversability of a career, denying that all careers constantly progress. Thus we may see a total life career and its component sectional careers as having an uneven and frequently internally conflicting passage.

What social gerontologists call 'the process of ageing', must therefore be seen not as a single dimension progression, but as a complex of strands running for differing lenths of time throughout a life biography and moulding its individuality. Thus an individual will experience many careers in his lifetime. Some of them will reach termination at an early age, e.g. the phase of pre-verbal communication, whereas his educational career in its formal and informal manifestations might run throughout his life. Other careers will begin later (though not necessarily at prescribed points on the temporal scale), like marriage and family of procreation. Some careers may be formally time-limited like an occupational career or a pregnancy whilst others may be of unspecified lengths, like those of particular interests, e.g. collecting, skiing, or even authoring conference papers.

Clearly we are using the term career very widely here to identify series of events which relate to a particular life activity. Inevitably, careers are of differing degrees of importance and those that the individual puts most store by will constantly override his interests in others. So a 'career man' might put his work career before his family career and a career in musical appreciation might suffer as a result of involvement in local politics. What is important about encompassing activities of different levels of significance is that those which are not highly valued by external observers may well be amongst the most significant, e.g. Marx's desires to live a thoroughly bourgeois life led him into a vast amount of journalism, which ultimately deterred him from completing *Capital*. Thus we must not make unsubstantiated judgements about the dominance of particular career lines.

In the biographical career of an individual there will be phases of his life which are likely to be problematic either because subjectively or objectively important careers are not progressing satisfactorily, or even regressing, or because important careers come into conflict with each other. A person at any stage of life may suffer damage to his self-image when events prove unsatisfactory. Life crises are shown in the psychiatric literature to occur as much for objectively minor as for major events. So the failure of an adolescent's early relationship with someone of the opposite sex might have a profound impact on his educational career with repercussions on his present family relationships and his future occupational status.

The intersection or conflicting of careers is capable of causing major transitions to occur in the overall biography. Marriage and occupation come to mind most readily. For women it has often meant the end of their occupational career, whilst for men marriage might have meant modifying their occupational practices to accommodate the demands of marriage. Whatever solutions worked out by marriage partners in setting their conjugal relationships, they are likely to cause a major life event which will temporarily disturb many career lines and completely end others (Fogarty, Rapoport and Rapoport 1971). Each relationship is a separate negotiation and as we know from the detailed analyses of family relationships developed by Elizabeth Bott (1957), there are few worthwhile stereotypes.

Later life tends to be the phase when careers are shed either voluntarily or compulsorily. Children grow up and leave home – what Glick (1947), in his work on the family cycle, misleadingly called the empty nest period. Retirement terminates the major occupational career, whilst growing infirmity might put an end to strenuous physical pursuits. In parallel with these, careers are closed off not through choice or compulsion, but because the stereotypical images which emerge from the functionalist/disengagement perspective strongly suggest to older people that these activities are no longer appropriate to them. As a result there are vast quantities of older people whose talents are socially suppressed and whose contributions to social life and their own life satisfaction are denied existence (Johnson 1975).

The arguments about the exclusion of older people from the system of social exchange have been discussed elsewhere. For the purpose of this paper it is important to link the complexities of life biography with the social situations which face older people. In most countries of the developed Western World it is easy to characterise the retired population as poor, sick and existing outside the mainstream of social life. As a result the present debates in social gerontology are about – to return to our theme – dependency and independency, need and problems. In response to these perceptions of the situation, the medical and social welfare machines have been aimlessly turned towards the elderly.

We do social welfare *to* old people and not with them. It is assumed that the professionals, both in medicine and in the social services, know what their needs are and how they can be resolved or ameliorated. But the present approach will die a natural death when policy-makers realise that the older sector of the population can consume infinite resources on this principle and still not be in a satisfactory state.

If it is reasonable to suggest that in their reflective moments, policy-makers and gerontologists seek a state of personal satisfaction for the older person, then it may be opportune to begin listening more to their clients.

This does not mean listening to more barren responses to swiftly delivered questions about 'what do you need' delivered by clip-board interviewers eager to press their instant replies into a computer. More appropriately, to listen to their reconstructed biographies, in order to identify the path of their life history and the way it has sculpted their present problems and concerns (Butler 1963; Earlix, forthcoming). In this way the individual's own *priorities* for the latter end of his life will emerge – his own losses and triumphs and fears and satisfactions and unfulfilled aspirations.

Only within this context of personal priorities is it reasonable for professional helpers of any sort to impose major changes on the lives of older people. Hospitalization, for example, should only be offered along with realistic estimates of outcome so that the individual may choose. So often the condition is preferable to the 'cure', as we know from old age institutions, full of people who end up there miserably as a result of 'being helped'. The biographical career approach to the understanding of the social realities of old age takes as one of its premises, the judgement that when an individual has made his major productive contribution to society, he should be free to seek a less constrained fulfillment in old age. So, too, this element of choice should be present in social policies designed to combat the problems he faces in later life. In all of this the subjective view of life takes paramount importance. What the 'objective reality' at the time was, would be fascinating to know for these purposes (though it is not entirely clear what constitutes objectivity), but it is the subjective view which has shaped his life and led it to its present position. His worries, failures, fond memories, satisfactions, frustrations and pride in the past are all his own self-estimates and part of cumulative self-image – all thoroughly 'non-objective'.

Retrospective life history studies may have their methodological drawbacks. Yet 'looking through a glass darkly' is a necessary corrective. Social policies for old age will be of limited effect if they continue to take into account only the *observable*. Social gerontology will hide from view so much of the rich fabric of old age if it persists in seeing later life as an event or a stage rather than the continuing of an intricate pattern of life careers.

References

BECKER, H. S., HUGHES, E., GEER, B. and STRAUSS, A. L. (1961) *Boys in White: Student Culture in Medical School*, Chicago.
BECKER, H. S. (1963) *Outsiders: Studies in the Sociology of Deviance*, New York.
BOTT, E. (1957) *Family and Social Network*, London, second revised edition, 1971.
BROCKINGTON, R. and LEMPERT, S. M. (1966) *The Social Needs of the Over Eighties*, Manchester.

BUTLER, R. N. (1963) 'The life review: an interpretation of reminiscence in old age', *Psychiatry, 26*, 1.

CARTWRIGHT, A., HOCKEY, L. and ANDERSON, J. L. (1973) *Life Before Death*, London.

CLAUSEN, J. (1972) 'The Life Course of Individuals'. In Riley *et al.* op. cit.

COLEMAN, P. G. (1975) 'Social gerontology in the Netherlands: a review of recent and current research', *The Gerontologist, 15*, 3.

COLEMAN, P. G. (1975) 'Social gerontology in England, Scotland and Wales: a review of recent and current research', *The Gerontologist, 15*, 3.

CRAWFORD, M. P. (1973) 'Retirement – a rite de passage', *Sociological Review, 21*, 3.

CUMMING, E. and HENRY, W. E. (1961) *Growing Old: The Process of Disengagement*, New York.

DONAHUE, W., ORBACH, H. L. and POLLACK, O. (1960) 'Retirement: The Emerging Social Pattern'. In Tibbitts, C. (ed.) *Handbook of Social Gerontology*, Chicago.

EARLIX, D. (in press) *A Study of Life Perceptions and Organization: Three Life Histories*.

FOGARTY, M., RAPOPORT, R. and RAPOPORT, R. (1971) *Sex, Career and Family* London.

GLASER, B. and STRAUSS, A. L. (1965) *Time for Dying*, London.

GLASER, B. and STRAUSS, A. L. (1971) *Status Passage*, London.

GLICK, P. C. (1947) 'The family cycle', *American Sociological Review*.

GOFFMAN, E. (1959) 'The moral career of the mental patient', *Psychiatry, 22*, 2.

HARRIS, A. (1968) *Social Welfare for the Elderly. A Study in Thirteen Local Authority Areas in England, Wales and Scotland*, London.

ISAACS, B. (1972) *Survival of the Unfittest: a study of geriatric patients in Glasgow*, London.

JOHNSON, M. L. (1972) 'Self perception of need amongst the elderly: an analysis of illness behaviour', *Sociological Review, 20*, 4.

JOHNSON, M. L. (1973) 'Old and young in the family, a negotiated arrangement'. Paper presented at the Bristol Society for Social and Behavioural Gerontology Conference, Keele.

JOHNSON, M. L. (1975) 'Old age and the gift relationship', *New Society*, 13 March.

KOLLER, M. R. (1974) *Families, A Multigenerational Approach*, New York.

KUTNER, B. *et al.* (1956) *Five Hundred over Sixty*, New York.

LOWENTHAL, M. F. (1964) 'Social isolation and mental illness in old age', *American Sociological Review, 29*, 1.

MCCALL, G. J. and SIMMONS, J. L. (1966) *Identities and Interactions*, New York.

MADDOX, G. (1968) 'Retirement as a Social Event in the United States'. In Neugarten, H. L. (ed.) *Middle Age and Ageing: A Reader in Social Psychology*, Chicago.

MEACHER, M. and AGATE, J. (1969) *The Care of the Old*, Fabian Research Series, 278, London.

MUNNICHS, J. M. A. (1976) 'Older People, Their Family and Use of General Provisions'. In Shanas, E. and Sussman, M. (eds.) *Older People, Family and Bureaucracy*, Durham.

PARSONS, T. (1968) 'Old Age as a Consummatory Phase'. In Riley, M. W. *et al.* op. cit.

Post-White House Conference on Aging Reports, Washington, 1973.

RILEY, M. W., JOHNSON, M. and FONER, A. (1968) *Ageing and Society: An Inventory of Research Findings*, New York.

RILEY, M. W., JOHNSON, M. and FONER, A. (1972) *Ageing and Society: A Sociology of Age Stratification*, New York.

ROSE, A. M. (1965) 'The subculture of the ageing: a framework for research in social gerontology'. In Rose, A. M., and Peterson, W. A. (eds) *Older People and their Social World*, Philadelphia.

ROSEN, G. (1960) 'Health Programs for an Aging Population'. In Tibbitts, C. (ed.) *Handbook of Social Gerontology*, Chicago.

ROSOW, I. and BRESLAU, N. (1966) 'A Guttman health scale for the aged', *Journal of Gerontology*, *21*, 4.

ROTH, J. (1963) *Timetables: Structuring the Passage of Time in Hospital and Other Careers*, Indianapolis.

ROWNTREE, B. S. (1947) *Old People*, London.

SHANAS, E. (1962) *The Health of Older People: A Social Survey*, Cambridge, Mass.

SHELDON, J. H. (1948) *The Social Medicine of Old Age*, London.

SHENFIELD, B. (1957) *Social Policies for Old Age*, London.

STEBBINS, R. A. (1970) 'Career: the subjective approach', *Sociological Quarterly*.

TOWNSEND, P. (1957) *The Family Life of Old People*, London.

TOWNSEND, P. (1968) 'Medical Services and Welfare Services and the Elderly'. In Shanas, E. *et al.*, *Old People in Three Industrial Societies*, London.

TUNSTALL, J. (1966) *Old and Alone: A Sociological Study of Old People*, London.

VAN ZONNEVELD, R. J. (1961) *Health of the Aged*, Assen.

WILLIAMS, A. (in press) *Development Possibilities for the Use of Social Indicators in the Health Field*, O.E.C.D.

Part 3   Living in the Community

15   The family life of old people: conclusion

Peter Townsend

The general conclusion of this book [*The Family Life of Old People*] is that if many of the processes and problems of ageing are to be understood, old people must be studied as members of families (which usually means extended families of three generations); and, if this is true, those concerned with social and health administration must, at every stage, treat old people as an inseparable part of a family group, which is more than just a residential unit. They are not simply individuals, let alone 'cases' occupying beds or chairs. They are members of families and whether or not they are treated as such largely determines their security, their health, and their happiness. [. . .]

We started by asking how far in fact old people were isolated from family life, and found that they often lived with relatives but preferred a 'supported' independence. Those not sharing their homes rarely lived alone in a literal sense. Three generations of relatives were generally distributed over two or more households near one another and old people had very close ties with their families. Those interviewed had an average of thirteen relatives within a mile and they saw three-quarters of all their children, both married and unmarried, once a week, as many as a third of them every day. We found old people getting a great deal of help, regularly and in emergencies, from their female relatives, particularly their daughters, living in neighbouring streets. The remarkable thing was how often this help was reciprocated – through provision of midday meals, care of grandchildren, and other services. The major function of the grandparent is perhaps the most important fact to emerge from this book. If confirmed elsewhere we may have to re-examine many of our ideas about the family, child-rearing, parenthood, and old age.

An individual's loyalties to the closely-knit group of relatives of three generations were potentially in conflict with those to his or her spouse. We found, in discussing first the economy of the home, and then the relationships with married children, how such conflict was reduced or regulated by marked segregation between man and wife in their financial and domestic roles, and by individual, rather than joint, associations with blood relatives. It was also reduced by acknowledgement of the special bond between grandmother, daughter, and daughter's child and of the pre-eminent place of the old 'Mum' in the family. All this helped to explain

Source: P. TOWNSEND (1963) *The Family Life of Old People*. Harmondsworth: Penguin, pp. 227–34 (extracts).

how the extended family was kept in being through time. Finally, in discussing relationships between parent and child, grandparent and grandchild, and one sibling and another over the course of individual life we saw the importance of the principles of replacement and compensation as applied to the family. An individual's relationships adjusted to variations in family composition. Sons took over part of the role of the father after the mother was widowed. When people had sons but not daughters they saw more of daughters-in-law, and when they had no children they saw more of siblings and nephews and nieces. Some without families tended to attach themselves to a friend's family. The functional or structural principles on which the extended family was based could therefore be summed up as those of continuity of membership through individual life; unity between grandmother, daughter, and grandchild; reciprocation of domestic and personal services between members; replacement of, or compensation for, lost or non-existent members; segregation between man and wife in financial, domestic, and family roles, and reserve between parent and child-in-law. Application of these principles allowed different interests, needs, and satisfactions to be judiciously composed.

The three-generation extended family, then, provided the normal environment for old people. By comparison with its ties of blood, duty, affection, common interest, and daily acquaintance we found that the ties of friendship, neighbourliness, and club and church membership were neither so enduring nor so indissoluble. Most people were very restrained in their relationships with neighbours; not many had even one close friend outside the family. The network of kinship supplied many links with the community but allowed few close friends. Moreover, in old age non-family activities diminished. Friends died or passed out of knowledge, money was shorter, and it was more difficult to get about.

These findings do not mean the course of ageing always ran smooth. They rather provided a frame of reference for assessing the problems of age. As we saw earlier, the fact that the old grandmother was usually such a dominant figure helped to explain why retirement was a particularly tragic event for most men, because they could not find much to justify their existence. The adjustment was all the greater because of the sharp fall in income which most people suffered upon giving up work – a fall of over two-thirds for single people and a half for married people. Even this does not take account of wives themselves giving up work or men taking a lighter job at lower pay in the years immediately preceding final retirement. Previous customs of life were hard to maintain, especially for the men, despite help from children and payments for family services.

The poorest people, not only financially, were those without an active family life. They had fewest resources in time of need. Yet many of them denied they were lonely, and in examining the reasons for this, a distinction was drawn between *isolates* and *desolates*. The hypothesis put forward was that desolation rather than isolation was the fundamental cause of loneliness in old age. Elderly isolates seemed likely to make disproportionately heavy claims on health and welfare services. A supplementary investigation of a geriatric hospital, of residential Homes, and of a local domiciliary service in fact showed this to be so. People with daughters at hand made least claim of all. [. . .]

How far are the findings from the working-class area of Bethnal Green applicable to the rest of the country? And how far do they apply to patterns of life fast disappearing? Questions such as these, which can be asked about most reports on field research, are as harassing as they are important. No clear answer can be given. Although there are general sociological and anthropological studies of urban and rural areas, and even studies of old people, which suggest, or hint, that in many respects family life may be very similar in other parts of Britain, they are not exactly comparable to this one. Moreover, neither this nor other studies tell us much about the patterns of life in specifically middle- or upper-class families or in suburban populations as a whole. So much is conjecture.

It may, however, be worth referring again to some of the facts about Bethnal Green which do and do not distinguish it from other areas. It is a long-settled working-class borough. Local industry is very mixed and, compared, for example, with some Yorkshire mining or Lancashire cotton towns, the same habits of work and daily routine do not spread through the length and breadth of the community. Roughly the same proportion of the population (fourteen per cent) as in London, and as in England and Wales as a whole, are of pensionable age. A small minority, less than one in ten, are Jewish. Largely because of the upheavals brought about by bombing and evacuation in the last war and by housing clearance and rebuilding that has gone on since, the total population is only half what it was twenty or thirty years ago. Thousands of people have been obliged to emigrate, many of them to housing estates on the eastern fringes of London. This has undoubtedly dispersed many families. Of the old people interviewed a quarter lived alone in the household; in the country as a whole the proportion seems to be one in eight. Taken together, these facts do not suggest that family relationships are likely, in general, to be much richer than in other mainly working-class areas.

The question of change is equally important. The presumption is that more of the present generation of people aged sixty and over have children and other relatives to look after them and are more secure than their children will be when they are old. In Bethnal Green forty-five per cent of the married and widowed people had no, one, or two surviving children, but thirty-one per cent had five or more. We found that those with fewer children saw relatively more of them. Against this we also found that children in smaller families had less chance of gaining relief from the strain of nursing an infirm old person.

In the country as a whole the prospect is rather more complicated and perhaps less gloomy than many people imagine. There are several reasons. Of women married in 1900–9, all of whom are now of pensionable age, eleven per cent had no live-born child. This proportion increased, for people married in later years, to about sixteen per cent or seventeen per cent in the mid-1920s but, according to what evidence there is, has not increased any further. Over the next ten years most of the remaining people who married in the first twenty-five years of this century will reach pensionable age and the proportion of married but childless old people will then remain about the same. But the proportion of unmarried men and women in the population is declining. More people marry than in the past. According to official estimates the proportion of men of pensionable age who are unmarried will decrease from nine per cent to seven per cent and of women from sixteen per cent to twelve per cent between 1954 and 1979.* And as there have been such immense improvements in mortality rates at the younger ages over the course of the last half-century, fewer of the people giving birth to one child or two are likely to lose them before they reach their sixties. At present it is estimated that twenty-one per cent of men and twenty-eight per cent of women of pensionable age are unmarried or childless. While these proportions are substantial and require careful verification so that class and area comparisons can be made, there is no prospect of their increasing sharply. The proportion of old people having only small families is likely to continue to increase steadily for about ten years but not thereafter. Of women married in 1900–9 thirty-four per cent had one or two live-born children and of those married in 1925 fifty-one per cent. It appears, however, that family size has not continued to fall for people married since, and, indeed, there may have been a slight increase in the years since the war.

The changes brought about by more marriage, smaller family size, and longer life are producing ramifications throughout the kinship system. More marriage may mean fewer isolated people in old age, but fewer uncommitted aunts who can, whenever they are needed, run to the aid of their kin. Smaller family size may mean not only small sibling groups, more manageable tasks for mother and grandmother, and the concentration of the responsibilities of parenthood into a shorter span of years, but that aged people will have fewer, and more elderly, children to look after them. The advantage of longer expectation of life, especially at the youn-

* In the same period the proportion of widowers over sixty-five is also expected to decrease slightly from twenty-six to twenty-three per cent and of widows from forty-three to forty-two per cent. Calculated from Table D of Appendix 6, *Report by the Government Actuary on the First Quinquennial Review of the National Insurance Act of 1946*, 1954, pp. 51–2.

ger ages, may produce the most significant changes of all in the structure and functioning of the family. A woman born in 1900 expected to live about forty-eight years; in 1951 seventy-one years. Such improvements suggest there are now more families in which there are grandparents, fewer marriages broken early by death, and more children having both parents alive throughout their childhood. One in five of all the old people in Bethnal Green had been widowed more than twenty years and over one in three lost at least one of their parents before the age of fifteen. The longer survival and the greater amount of marriage has given greater prominence to the relationship between man and wife in society, not only because husband and wife live longer together, but because people are less likely to have unattached relatives to whom they owe obligations. The general direction of change in family structure seems to be away from extreme diversities and towards more stability at the centre. As compared with fifty years ago family relationships now seem to be deeper (in generation depth), more symmetrical, and less collaterally extended. The full effects of all these developments on the position of the old need the most thoroughgoing investigation.

Other changes have taken place; of that there is no doubt. The people interviewed in Bethnal Green themselves gave cause for optimism about the present and future. When comparing the present with the past not all the advantage was on the side of the past. Most agreed, for example, that disputes between man and wife were rarer, that men helped more in the homes, that fathers more often took out young children, and that parents were less strict and less cruel; that people lived longer in one home, had steadier jobs, worked many fewer hours, and had a far higher standard of living; that family rituals, such as weddings and funerals, were now more extravagant affairs in which more people were involved, but that a Saturday sing-song, or 'knees up', was much rarer and families rather more dispersed. On the whole people seemed now to desire, and to achieve, a greater measure of personal independence and privacy while remaining members of a closely-knit extended family.

The evidence from this very limited inquiry suggests that the extended family is slowly adjusting to new circumstances, not disintegrating. To the old person as much as to the young it seems to be the supreme comfort and support. Its central purpose is as strong as ever. It continues to provide a natural, if conservative, means of self-fulfilment and expression, as the individual moves from the first to the third generation, learning, performing, and teaching the functions of child, parent, and grandparent.

16   Living with old age

Paul Harrison

Living with old age, both for the old themselves and for the rest of society, is continually out of step with present realities. Society has not yet found an acceptable way of 'dealing with' its old people, and is perpetually trying to catch up with its changing idea of their needs – an idea that the old themselves have little influence on. Nor do the old seem to have evolved a stable accommodation with the facts of their situation. Most are torn between their own values of a useful and sociable life, and the reality of isolation and enforced idleness. [. . .]

The supply of suitable residential accommodation is never in step with need. Local authorities are at least trying to remedy their earlier negligence. From 1945 to 1960, only 10 per cent of new council houses in England and Wales were one-bedroomed, but in the next eleven years the proportion rose to 27 per cent. Yet, in 1970, 368 housing authorities still had less than five one-bedroomed units per 100 people over 65, and 318 had between five and ten; whereas only 270 had more than ten. Sheltered housing has become increasingly popular. But Hugh Mellor, secretary of the National Corporation for the Care of Old People, estimates that double the present provision is needed.

Quality is as important as quantity; and as conceptions change, much of existing facilities comes to seem outmoded. [. . .] To get something of the spectrum of old people's own views, I talked to them in two very different parts of the country, Harrogate and the London borough of Southwark, both in their own homes and in institutions.

Off Sumner Road in Southwark I visited a sheltered housing scheme and a model home, both about two years old. Superficially, the sheltered scheme looked idyllic – thirty-five flats, round three courtyards with flower gardens and trees, benches to sit on, magnificent views of Tower Bridge and St Paul's. At one end there is a communal laundry; at the other, a lounge where food can be served; in the centre, the warden's flat with a panel of green alarm lights, one for each flat, worked by a buzzer near the bed. Yet the old people are, apart from daily contact with the warden, isolated. The scheme is perched on the fourth floor of a block of council flats. No one passes through. The old cannot sit at their windows watching the world go by. Nor do they even associate much with each other. The garden seats are invariably empty. The only time the lounge is

---

Source: *New Society*, 1 November 1973, pp. 265–8 (extracts).

used is for the twice-weekly bingo sessions, run in their own time by the warden and his wife. About half the residents turn up.

Rose Willis, who is 79, has been out only twice since she came a year ago from Dulwich: she has chronic osteo-arthritis. She has two sons in Birmingham and Southampton whom she hardly ever sees. She was on the housing list for twelve years before she got this flat. 'I've got a lot of friends in Dulwich and I really wanted a place there, where they would have come and taken me out in the wheelchair. But it's too far for them to come here.'

A few yards down the road is Ammon residential home, one of the new generation of small, comfortable homes. There are sixty residents; twenty-five of them are men and there are three married couples. The walled garden is overlooked by a pleasant, hotel-like dining room. Flowers everywhere, modern furniture, neat double and single bedrooms, four lounges with wall-to-wall carpets. Yet, even in a crowd, the old people are isolated. All the lounges have television (with at least one showing each channel, so there are no arguments), and the sets are on most of the day. There is very little talking. The residents sit round silently, watching, looking up with vague expectation when a stranger comes in. The hobbies room is tiny. Everything is done *for* the old people, even bathing – though some have odd jobs like cleaning the cutlery, for which they get a couple of bob extra. The residents have no say in the running of the place. Deaths, as in any old people's home, are frequent. Last year there were sixteen, though most occurred in hospital. Ammon is like a beautiful waiting room for the last journey. Mabel, aged 84, is one of the liveliest residents. She's carved out a position for herself mending the socks for the men who can't afford to pay the seamstress who comes in once a week. She plays the piano for the occasional singsong. Both her legs are paralysed and she's been advised to have one off. 'But my brains aren't what they used to be', she complains. 'They're not right, you see. I can't concentrate on much.' One of the nurses chucks her under the chin and behind the ears, like a baby; and Mabel looks up into her eyes. 'We do treat them like children', the nurse admits. 'That's what they *are* really, isn't it?'

There is a growing school of thought claiming that homes like Ammon, however comfortable, accelerate the helplessness and deterioration they exist to alleviate. In a recent report for Cheshire county council, Conrad Jameson wrote: 'Residents do not grow senile in spite of institutionalisation, but because of it.' He blamed this on the forcible uprooting of old people from familiar places and friends. However voluntary the move, there is always regret for what they left behind. Expectations in the homes encourage childish behaviour among residents, forcing them to compete for staff affections in their degree of grateful helplessness, and to fight over what remains of their privacy.

The *physical* facts of senescence are largely unavoidable. And these *social* facts – of income levels, types and amounts of residential provision – are also immutable as far as the elderly themselves are concerned. Living with old age, for the old themselves, is finding ways of coping with both these sets of facts. They are not free, either, in deciding how to adjust to them. They are conditioned by the norms they acquired earlier in their lives: concepts of a child's duty to its parents, from an age when mobility was less and there was no welfare state; concepts of financial independence, from the time when state handouts *were* charity; concepts of privacy and intrusion, acquired during a lifetime absorbed in the family.

How, in practice, do they manage? In many cases they don't. But few of the old people I spoke to, either in 'homes' or at home, were bitter about their own situation. One lady summed up for many when she said, 'I thank God I get what I've got, although I've got nothing.' Their expectations are low enough to preempt disappointment. But they become perilously dependent on one or two little things: the television, the radio, the library. 'If it wasn't for . . . I don't know what I'd do', was repeated by practically every one. Only the 'for what' bit changes.

One of the most difficult things to adjust to is retirement – thought of, in advance, as the long-deserved rest from toil. As one old man put it: 'Retirement is all right if you've got plenty of money. It looks like a chance to do the things you've always wanted to. But when it comes to doing them, you find you can't afford it.' Harry Schofield, aged 82, from Harrogate, has never succeeded in filling the gap left in his life when he retired from train-driving seventeen years ago. 'I had an allotment at first. But I had to give it up when my back got bad. My eyes are going, too. I can't see the telly any more. But I do my little jobs. I keep myself pottering about doing this and that.' He does the shopping, while his wife Edith, aged 80, does the housework. George Cox, who lives in the sheltered housing in Southwark, was a printer's reader on the old *News Chronicle* when he retired, fifteen years ago. At first he played bowls 'pretty well all the time'. Then his breathing got bad, and he had to give it up. 'I'm sorry now I did. I get bored a lot. I go out to the corner shop for a walk. Often I go through the *Daily Telegraph*, marking it up – a lot of errors creep through these days.'

Some 30 per cent of men, aged 65 to 70, do still carry on with some form of employment, to combat the problem of having too much time on their hands. Boredom may, in fact, be one cause of their earlier death. For most wives, life goes on much the same, with no sudden break-off point. At 65, men can expect to live another twelve years, women another sixteen. There are 114 women to every 100 men aged between 60 and 65. Above 75, the ratio rises to 215 women per 100 men. [. . .]

Some 1.7 million aged in Britain live alone – about one in five. The numbers living alone are increasing far faster than the total numbers – by about 40 per cent between 1961 and 1966. The degree of loneliness due to family neglect is often exaggerated, and varies a great deal from place to place. There are signs that it is increasing. In Bethnal Green in 1957, Peter Townsend found that 96 per cent of old people were visited at least once a week. But two surveys in the past two years (one in Hillfields, Coventry; another by PEP, based on a nationwide sample) found that a little over 60 per cent of old people were visited by relatives once a week or more. Estimates of how many actually *feel* lonely vary from Townsend's 1957 estimate of 27 per cent, to a 1972 Age Concern survey, quoting 58 per cent.

Today's old people undoubtedly expect their children, if not to care for them, at least to visit them regularly. The two million old people with no children have an advantage in this respect. At least they will never feel embittered at infrequent visits. Eva Deighton, aged 79, from Harrogate, complains that her daughter never visits her, though she lives only eight miles away in Ripley: 'If I want to see her, I've got to go there; and I can hardly walk since I broke my hip.' She lives alone. [. . .]

The day centre offers one answer for both of the main problems: boredom and isolation. Southwark has no less than thirteen of these, more than any other London borough. Yet only 1,400 of the borough's 34,000 people over 65 attend – about 4 per cent. People have to be referred there by a doctor or social worker, and most centres have a waiting list. I visited the day centre in Caroline Gardens, where fifty people have lunch every day, knit, paint, make stools and soft toys, have singsongs and quizzes. Some 200 people come each week. But those who are handicapped are rationed to one day a week, because of the shortage of transport. The centre means a great deal to them. Alf Williams, who attends every day, is 75: 'When I leave here, I don't see anybody else all day. All I've got to look at is the four walls. I'd have a thin time of it if I wasn't interested in crosswords.'

The most adventurous activity of Southwark's day centres is film making. They have an annual festival, which Caroline Gardens has won for the past two years. Their entries show that old age pensioners' aspirations, when allowed free range, are simply older versions of everyone else's. In one, called *High Hopes*, an old-age pensioner syndicate win the pools, go off to the boozer to celebrate, and each one dreams about what they would do with the money: the ladies go on a shopping spree, buying jewelry and dresses; one man buys a car, another a hi-fi set. But when the envelope arrives, they open it and find just £1.

The day centre appeals to the predominant view of retirement, as a time that must be filled to the brim with ceaseless activity, to prevent old people from reflecting unhealthily on the unpleasantness of their basic situation. Southwark's organiser of activities, Rose Button, summarises this attitude: 'Idle hands make idle minds, don't they? If they're doing something, they're not thinking about themselves. And they love it, they love to feel they're making something, however small, that might bring some joy to somebody.'

For most old people the choice is between a growing lethargy, or a frenzy of pointless activity, both an escape from thinking too much about the predicament in which social change has stranded them. One man who rejects either is Maurice Clements from Dagenham. Now 72, he found his retirement from inspecting London buses a great shock: 'At 11.59 on Sunday night, I was somebody. At midnight, I was nothing and nobody, and nobody wanted me. After a few months I came to a dead stop. I saw no point in getting up, and no point in going to bed. Then I said to myself: I can't go on like this, or I'll be just sitting here, waiting for the undertaker.'

He got himself a job as office messenger three days a week. Then he became church treasurer and secretary, looking after arrangements for weddings. He is now an instructor in St John's Ambulance Brigade, and a voluntary welfare visitor for Barking borough council, visiting ten old people each week, helping them with financial and health problems. 'My wife often says: if you want to see me, you've got to have an appointment.' Yet he has scant regard for most people's approach to old age: 'They're only out for what they can get, not for what they can do for other people. But if they would only look outward instead of inward, they'd be surprised what they would find. If they were more clannish together, there'd be no need of old people's clubs.'

Neighbours, in general, play a less important part in old people's lives than relatives or voluntary agencies. The PEP survey found that, of all regular visits mentioned by old people in its sample, 419 were organised by statutory authorities or voluntary agencies, and only 232 were social or informal. The largest category were voluntary visitors – 130, as against 89 by relatives and 78 by neighbours.

But, once again, the collapse of neighbourly kindness to old people may be generally over-estimated. I came across plenty of examples of practical help. Florence Vandeeper, at the day centre, told me about the 'angel of Alcott Lane', who comes knocking to see if old people are all right. But her two companions at the day centre said her street must be exceptional. 'Next door they don't even nod to me'; 'I've been there four years and they've not spoken to me once.'

Daily contact, as you can still find it in some terraced streets, has two main functions – to keep a constant eye on old people in case of emergency, and to provide small services like daily shopping. These functions are beginning to be taken over by voluntary groups. This movement is not yet widespread, outside organisations like Task Force and Community Service Volunteers, who deal mainly with younger volunteers. A few local authorities are sponsoring good-neighbour schemes, and there are about twenty 'Fish' schemes, offering emergency help of all kinds. These are sponsored by local churches – hence the early Christian symbol of the fish – but with lay volunteers. Harrogate has one of the best-developed of these. Though it has only been going for two years, it has a network of 5,000 volunteers (out of a total Harrogate population of only 64,000). There is a central telephone number anyone can ring for help. The nearest suitable volunteer is then contacted and sent along. Harrogate is divided up into eleven sectors, each under a chairman; and there are 42 area organisers and 500 or so street stewards. The stewards keep a day-to-day eye on their streets. In an emergency, old people without a phone can put a card with a fish symbol in the window to call for help. The scheme costs £400 a year to run, mainly because the volunteers never claim back their expenses, such as phone calls or petrol. Even the central phone is manned by a rota of volunteers. The three who take the main brunt are severely handicapped. The scheme helps out with hospital visiting, taking people to relatives in emergencies, picking up prescriptions. It has organised the opening of a jar of pickled onions, the translation of Finnish washing instructions on a pair of trousers, someone to sleep alongside an old lady after a bereavement, and the collecting of old people into each others' houses for warmth during the miners' strike.

Joyce Topley, secretary of Harrogate Fish scheme, believes Fish is not simply a substitute for, but an improvement on, 'natural' neighbourliness: 'Fish spreads the time among so many people that it's no longer a burden. And it's often easier to help, or accept help from, a stranger. It doesn't look like interference.' It looks as if in the future, neighbourliness will move away from being a spontaneous function to something much more organised. Voluntary help, in many ways, makes more sense than the chance bonds of blood or residence. Yet even this sees old people as the passive receivers of help.

The fact is that our society has no positive conception of a *role* for old age, either in the community or in the life of the individual. [. . .] Old people are physically hived off into ghettoes where they can no longer play even the modest role of baby-sitting. Mentally, too, old age is a cul-de-sac. Ask most old people what they think old age is *for*, and they reply with a blank stare. After a lifetime of work and rearing families, they continue to feel they should be some use to somebody; yet they are largely condemned to passivity. The doctrine of self-help has not yet been extended to them, though they represent a huge reserve of manpower. The active old could easily be occupied in looking after those who are physically incapacitated. In a society of mixed-age groups and mixed degrees of agility, such a role could be encouraged. Without a role, the old even condemn themselves as useless.

17 Old people at home: their unreported needs

J. Williamson, I. H. Stokoe, Sallie Gray, Mary Fisher, Alwin Smith, Anne McGhee and Elsie Stephenson

One of the most striking and distressing features of work in a geriatric unit is that patients are so often admitted in a very advanced stage of disease. Many have pressure sores or permanent joint contractures, and show signs of prolonged neglect and subnutrition. Yet the family doctor may write: 'I saw this patient for the first time yesterday', or 'the last time I saw this old lady was two years ago when her husband died'. Careful history-taking will establish that timely medical or social intervention might have prevented much of the disability. Why then was it not forthcoming?

Surveys of the elderly have largely neglected this problem and give little information as to whether the abnormalities they uncovered were already known to the general practitioners. Since the general practitioner must usually be the prime mover in ensuring that the medical and social needs of his patients are recognised and met, it seemed worth determining how well informed he is about the health and welfare of his older patients. With this end in view we made a study of physical and psychiatric disability in older people in Edinburgh and district in 1962–63.

Methods

Our team included two specialists in geriatrics, a psychiatrist, and a social worker. Coordination of the study was the responsibility of a medically qualified member.

We studied a random sample of persons aged 65 and over on the lists of three general practices. Two of these practices were in Edinburgh and the third in a small mining town nearby. The practices were chosen partly because of the willingness of the practitioners to cooperate and partly because they had a suitable age-register from which to take the sample. The quality of general-practitioner care was thus probably above the average.

In each practice the listed people aged 65 and over on a specified date were numbered and a sample taken using a table of random numbers. The list of sampled numbers was kept by one of us (M.F.), and the identified individuals were chosen in sequence so that an appropriate

Source: *The Lancet*, 23 May 1964, pp. 1117–20.

number was regularly taken from the register for the examinations planned for the ensuing fortnight. Their names were then given to the family doctor who visited them, explained the study, invited their cooperation, and gave appointments to those willing to take part. Summaries were prepared of the information in the practice records, and the doctor was interviewed to supplement the summary with any information which had not been recorded in writing.

Some of the people in the sample were dead or had left the district. Ten were excluded because they were temporarily away from home staying with relatives. Forty-eight declined to participate and one was excluded because she was closely related to the psychiatrist in the team.

The study was continued until 200 people had been examined. Each was given a full clinical examination by a specialist in geriatrics and a screening examination by a psychiatrist. Urine was examined for sugar and albumin and microscopically for blood or pus cells. Venous blood was taken for hæmatological examination, blood-urea nitrogen estimation and leucocyte culture for karyotype analysis. So far as possible examinations were made in the doctor's surgery. Fifteen people were examined at home, two in general hospitals, two in long-stay geriatric units, one in a geriatric assessment unit, and one in a geriatric outpatient department. No-one in the sample was in a welfare or voluntary home at the time of the study. A medical social worker visited the home of each person and prepared reports.

Since the practices were selected and so many subjects refused examination, it is important to see how far the sample is representative of the related population.

The distribution of the sample by age, sex, marital status, and whether examination was accepted or refused was compared with that of all Edinburgh residents age 65 or over.[1] Although the refusals included a disproportionately high number of single and widowed women, the distribution of examined persons does not differ from that of the total

Table 1   Age and sex of those examined and those who refused.

Sex		Age-groups (yrs.)					
		65–69	70–74	75–79	80–84	85+	Total
M	examined	41	25	12	8	5	91
F		43	28	21	16	1	109
M	refused	5	4	1	1	1	12
F		15	9	6	5	1	36

population by more than could be accounted by random sampling error (Table 1). The sample examined contained relatively fewer women at all ages (especially single and widowed) and relatively fewer elderly males.

Physical findings

Our most striking observation was the frequency of multiple disabilities. Men had a mean of 3·26 disabilities, of which 1·87 were unknown to the family doctor; women a mean of 3·42 disabilities, with 2·03 unknown (Table 2). The severer disabilities were more likely to be known to the

Table 2   Disabilities known (K) and not known (NK) to doctors.

Grade of disability	Sex	No. of disabilities			Mean no. of disabilities per subject		
		K	NK	Total	K	NK	Total
Slight	M	49	118	167	0·55	1·30	1·84
	F	68	136	204	0·62	1·25	1·87
Moderate	M	37	25	62	0·41	0·27	0·68
	F	26	40	66	0·24	0·37	0·61
Severe	M	23	8	31	0·25	0·09	0·34
	F	23	2	25	0·21	0·02	0·23
Not graded*	M	18	19	37	0·20	0·21	0·41
	F	35	43	78	0·32	0·40	0·72
All disabilities	M	127	170	297	1·40	1·87	3·26
	F	152	221	373	1·39	2·03	3·42

* Varicose veins and psychiatric disorders other than dementia.

general practitioners, although even some of these were not. Six men and two women had no detectable disability, and nineteen men and seventeen women had only slight disabilities. All the others (156) had at least one moderate or severe disability.

Mobility

Of the 200 people examined, four were immobile or bedridden, fifteen were capable of indoor activity only, 71 were capable of limited outdoor mobility; 110 had normal mobility. Independent assessments of mobility were made by the clinician and the social worker, taking into account the circumstances in which the old persons were living. Of the four who were bedridden, one was unknown by the family doctor to be in this state.

Vision and hearing defects (62 men, 83 women)

Visual and hearing defects were classified according to functional assessment.

Slight visual defect denoted some limitation of ability to read or do fine work; moderate visual defect denoted inability to read even large print, but the subject could still get about freely and safely; severe visual defeat denoted that the subject was seriously handicapped in his daily activities. When the person ordinarily wore spectacles, the assessment was based on his performance with this aid.

For hearing, slight defect denoted that the subject could understand ordinary conversation with the voice only slightly raised; moderate defect denoted that ordinary conversation was feasible but difficult; severe deafness denoted that verbal communication was extremely difficult or impossible. When the person was wearing a hearing-aid, the assessment was made with it in use.

Eighteen men and thirty-eight women had slight or moderate visual defects and most were unknown to the general practitioner. Three out of seventeen with severe visual defects or total blindness were unknown.

Thirty-seven men and thirty-five women had some degree of deafness; four men and five women were severely affected. Most of the slight and moderate defects were apparently unknown to the family doctors, but these were not specifically asked about minor degrees of deafness.

Respiratory system disability (39 men, 14 women)

There was a higher prevalence of respiratory disability in men (43%). Eight were unknown to the practitioners, all in the slight or moderate grades. Women showed a much lower prevalence (13%) and there were no severe cases. Thirty men (7 unknown) and ten women (3 unknown) had chronic bronchitis.

One of the practices was in a mining area and this may explain some of the sex differences in prevalence; for there were several cases of pneumoconiosis in the sample from this practice.

Heart-disease (15 men and 22 women)

Thirteen patients with this disability were unknown to the doctor, including a man of 73 with atrial fibrillation, hypertension, and congestive failure, who was attending a hospital for physiotherapy for an arthritic condition.

Alimentary system disability (31 men, 9 women)

Disability associated with peptic ulceration was the commonest finding, but some disability was also due to hernia, and some followed gastrectomy. Sixteen cases were unknown to the doctor, including a 70-year-old man living alone and in very poor health due to hepatic cirrhosis. He had severe generalised oedema but had not consulted his doctor though he was feeling very miserable.

Central nervous system disability (9 men, 8 women)

Six cases were unknown to the doctor. The illnesses of these patients varied from mild diabetic neuropathy to hemiplegia associated with stroke. Included in this category was cerebrovascular disease.

Genitourinary system disability (23 men, 16 women)

The main forms of disability were those associated with undue frequency of micturition. Simple prostatic enlargement was not classified as disability unless accompanied by symptoms. Rectal examination was done in all men, but it was soon found that it caused distress to the women. In the mining town the high refusal-rate was at least partly due to this. It was therefore omitted. Vaginal examinations were also not done; hence some gynaecological disorders probably went undetected. Accordingly our estimate of the prevalance of disability may well be too low. But it is noteworthy that of the thirty-nine persons whose genitourinary disability was recognised, in only eight (4 men and 4 women) was it known to the practitioner before the study. The commonest disability was that associated with prostatic obstruction, often complicated by pyuria. One man was receiving oestrogen therapy for prostatic carcinoma, but he had an undetected urinary infection as well.

Locomotor system disability (25 men, 49 women)

Because of the very high prevalence of disorders of the feet in old people, separate tabulations were made for these. Clinical evidence of abnormal joints, such as enlargement and marked crepitus on movement, was not interpreted as disability unless there was pain or stiffness or other interference with the patient's daily life. The disability of ten men and twenty-two women was unknown to the general practitioner. The commonest condition was osteoarthritis of knee and hips, which caused a good deal of pain and discomfort and often made the old persons much less mobile, particularly those living upstairs.

Foot disability (25 men, 61 women)

There was a very high prevalence of disability associated with feet among the women (52 were unknown to the general practitioner). Although none was severe and most were slight, clearly a more effective chiropody service is needed. Most of these old people accepted foot trouble as an inescapable accompaniment of ageing, for few had ever consulted their doctor about it.

Anaemia (5 men, 11 women)

Haemoglobin levels were estimated by photoelectric colorimeter. Results were expressed as a percentage using 14·6 g per 100 ml as 100 per cent. Any level lower than 80 per cent was classed as anaemia. Estimations were not done for three people. Of the other 197, sixteen had anaemia by the rather low standard used (Table 3). Only two were known to the

Table 3   Cases of anaemia.

Sex	70–79 (Hb %)		60–69 (Hb %)		< 60 (Hb %)		Total		Hb not done
	K	NK	K	NK	K	NK	K	NK	
M	0	3	0	1	0	1	0	5	2
F	2	8	0	1	0	0	2	9	1

general practitioner. In addition twenty-three men and forty-three women had haemoglobin levels of 80–89 per cent. An 86-year-old man who had severe anaemia unknown to his general practitioner had severe osteoarthritis and was known to have diverticulitis. His haemoglobin was 48 per cent and his anaemia was due to blood-loss from his bowel. He responded well to hospital treatment and after discharge attended the day hospital with great benefit.

Other abnormalities

Blood-pressure readings were taken for all the sample, based on one or two estimations with the patient supine. As isolated readings are unreliable it would be unwise to draw firm conclusions, but six men and fourteen women had diastolic pressures of 120 mm Hg or more. Three men and seven women were known to have hypertension.

In assessing the degree of arteriosclerosis, we used as criteria abnormal thickening and tortuosity of the peripheral arteries and the presence or absence of arterial pulsation of the femoral, popliteal, dorsalis pedis, and posterior tibial arteries. Specific inquiry was made about intermittent claudication. Fifty men showed signs of arteriosclerosis (40 unknown) and thirty women (21 unknown). Where intermittent claudication was present and pulsation below the popliteal arteries was absent, the condition was classified as severe. In this category there were six men (4 unknown) and one woman (known).

Seventeen men and thirty-seven women had disabling varicose veins, but these had been recorded by the general practitioners in only nine of the men and sixteen of the women. In most the disability was slight, but some had healed ulcers: retirement from active work may have helped some longstanding lesions.

Diabetes mellitus was found in six persons (2 men and 4 women). In two women this was previously unknown. Another man, who was dying of carcinoma of the pharynx, showed persistent glycosuria and mild hyperglycaemia.

Body build

As an index of body build, measurements of height and weight proved misleading because of the loss of height in people with osteoporosis. Classification was therefore based on general appearance only. Fourteen men and nine women were on the thin side of average, and thirty-five men and fifty-two women were obese (Table 4). The term 'gross obesity' was only

Table 4   Body build.

Sex	Emaciated	Thin	Average	Obesity Slight	Obesity Moderate	Obesity Gross
Males	1	13	42	16	16	3
Females	0	9	48	12	28	12

applied in extreme cases, most of whom were suffering considerable disability from their condition. Gross obesity was much commoner in women.

Psychiatric findings

The psychiatric examination took the form of a semi-structured interview with brief psychological testing, incorporating the paired associate learning test of Inglis.[2]

Neurosis (7 men, 26 women)

The condition of sixteen of the women and of four of the men was unknown to their general practitioner.

Depression (8 men, 13 women)

In ten of the women and six of the men their depression was unknown to their doctor. These findings show the importance of being on the lookout for depressive illnesses in old people, since this condition is often amenable to treatment.

Dementia (29 men, 26 women)

The organic mental impairment found was mostly slight or moderate, but in twenty-five men and twenty-three women it was unknown to the general practitioners (Table 5).

Table 5   Prevalence of dementia.

Sex		Slight		Moderate		Severe		Total	
		K	*NK*	*K*	*NK*	*K*	*NK*	*K*	*NK*
Males	..	2	19	1	5	1	1	4	25
Females	..	2	16	0	7	1	0	3	23

The man with severe dementia which was unknown to his doctor was 80 and had been bedridden at home for nine months. He also suffered from aortic incompetence, Paget's disease, neglect, subnutrition, and was frequently incontinent. He lived in a miserable old tenement with his son who was out at work all day. He had last consulted his doctor twenty-two months previously when still mobile.

It might be argued that many of the cases of slight dementia were of little practical significance and that it made no difference whether or not the doctor knew of the failure in mental powers. Certainly many patients were adequately cared for by their families. But among the city patients with dementia more than two-thirds were in some degree socially deprived, and were thus in a potentially dangerous predicament. None of the patients with dementia in the small-town practice was socially deprived.

Other abnormal conditions

The psychiatrist found hypomania in one woman, paranoid states in two women, and alcoholism in three men.

Assessment of needs

Medical needs

The amount of unmet need for general-practitioner care was high, as is shown by the number of unknown disabilities.

It was considered that seventeen men and twenty-one women would have benefited from referral to a hospital specialist for investigation or treatment of physical illness. Of this group, five men and seven women needed referral to the geriatric service, and three of the men had to be admitted forthwith to the geriatric unit (one for investigation and rehabilitation and two for long-term care). Two other men and six women were considered to need specialist psychiatric help.

Chiropody was needed by twenty-nine men (of whom only seven were receiving it) and sixty-six women (of whom nineteen were receiving it).

Nursing needs

Nursing care for old people in their own homes is provided by the health visiting and district nursing services. In the areas studied these services were separate. Three men and two women were being visited by health visitors. The team held that an additional twenty-six men and fifty women would have benefited from this service. The health visitor's help had not been requested for any of these.

District nurses were attending two men and no women at the time of the inquiry. A further three men and three women were thought to be in need of this service, but it had not been requested.

Social needs

The housing of twenty-three men and twenty-five women was unsatisfactory. Conditions varied very widely, and included men living a meagre existence in common lodging-houses, and couples in decaying tenements (whose worn, dark, and winding stairs were so dangerous as to render them housebound). A widow was living in a detached stone-built house in a residential area, but because of her disabilities (and the presence of a schizophrenic son) she lived in genteel squalor worse than that of many slums.

Only one of the fifty-two old people in the small town was badly housed. In this case rehousing had been arranged, but the family had elected to return to their old dwelling.

The basic financial needs of sixteen men and nineteen women were not being met. In reaching this conclusion the team took many factors into account such as special dietary needs, exceptional laundry bills, and need for extra heating.

Twenty-two per cent of the old people in the city were in financial need and only two per cent in the mining town.

Social contacts ranged from complete isolation to complete integration in family and community life. Nineteen men and thirty-two women had social contacts which were classified as inadequate. About 30 per cent of the city patients lacked adequate human contacts, compared with only 10 per cent in the small town.

Discussion

Our study was made in three practices, two in the city and one in a small mining town. We did not try to compare the results in the different practices, but the small-town patients seemed to enjoy much better social standards than their city contemporaries. The doctors in the small town were more aware of the disabilities of their patients, and no severe disability was unknown to them. In the close-knit community almost everyone knows everyone else and almost everyone is on the one practice list. The doctor is able to recognise almost everyone in his practice, and as he goes about his rounds he picks up information from patients about other patients who might not themselves come to him. This unofficial system of ascertainment of disability and need, combined with better social conditions, puts the old person in this small town in a far more favourable position than his city counterpart.

The three practices studied were more likely to be above than below average in the standard of medical care provided. Probably, therefore, the degree of unawareness of morbidity among doctors in the country as a whole is not less than that recorded here. Most of the unknown disabilities are slight or moderately severe. This suggests that most old people do not report their complaints to their doctors until the condition is advanced. Thus a general-practitioner service based on the self-reporting of illness is likely to be seriously handicapped in meeting the needs of old people. It might be argued that many of the unknown disabilities we detected are degenerative and progressive, and therefore not amenable to curative measures. This is unjustifiably pessimistic; preventive medicine is at least as important in old age as it is earlier in life, and there are few conditions in old people which medical and social measures, applied soon enough, will not help. Indeed, in many of these degenerative states, further progress of disability can be arrested or at least slowed down.

For example, an obese old lady with osteoarthritis of hips and knees who lives up three flights of steep stairs in an old tenement is in grave danger of becoming housebound, lonely, depressed, and eventually neglected and bedridden. Energetic measures to reduce her weight, physiotherapy for her arthritis, and rehousing on the ground floor may enable her to lead an independent existence in the community for many more years. Similarly, an old widowed man living alone and beginning to show signs of dementia is in danger of lapsing into self-neglect, malnutrition, and accidents.

If self-reporting of illness fails to meet the needs of old people, what can replace it? There seems much to be said for periodic examination. Ideally such an arrangement should include all old people, but meanwhile it may be possible to identify those who are in special danger of deterioration. Macmillan suggests that old people living alone, especially those recently bereaved, are particularly vulnerable.[3]

Family doctors should make special efforts to keep in touch with their older patients, and the first step towards this would be to keep up-to-date registers. Admittedly the present organisation of general practice does not favour this, but the health visitor might prove a useful ally. She could undertake periodic visiting of old people and carry out screening on behalf of general practitioners. All old people could be visited in the first instance and the timing of later visits could be determined by individual need. The health visitor could ascertain the degree of mobility of the old person and inquire into the cause of any deterioration. She could examine for oedema or other evidence of heart-failure and she could inspect the patients' feet. Specimens of blood could be taken for laboratory examinations and particular inquiries made about dysuria, nocturia, or other likely pointers to pathological processes. There seems no reason why the health visitor could not carry out simple tests for mental deterioration or depression and gather corroborative evidence from relatives, neighbours, local shopkeepers, and others. She could put the old person in touch with appropriate social services and could advise about diet, budgeting, and the avoidance of accidents in the home. It may be that follow-up visits could be made by less highly trained nursing staff, already the policy of some authorities.

The use of health visitors in these ways would call for a substantial increase in the proportion of their time given to old people. The report of the Royal College of Physicians of Edinburgh [4] shows how small a proportion of health visitors' time is at present spent on old people, and recommends widespread development of arrangements for health visitors to be attached to specific general practices. Where such attachments have been made the number of visits paid by health visitors to old people has increased sharply.[5] Some general practitioners already have clinics for antenatal care, child welfare, and immunisation. They might also open geriatric clinics for patients sent to them by health visitors, who would of course attend and help at each session.

A necessary corollary of these suggestions is that health visitors should have adequate instruction in modern geriatric practice. The health-visitor service was started to meet the crisis of high infant and child morbidity which is now a thing of the past. Instead our society faces an equally serious crisis of ill-health and disability at the other end of life.

References

1 Census for 1961. Scotland County Report, vol. 1, part 1. Edinburgh: HMSO.
2 INGLIS, J. (1959) *J. ment. Sci.*, *105*, 440.
3 MACMILLAN, D. (1960) *Lancet*, *2*, 1439.
4 Royal College of Physicians of Edinburgh. Publication no. 22, 1963.
5 Report of the Medical Officer of Health for Oxford for 1962.

18 Tolerance of debility in elderly dependants by supporters at home: its significance for hospital practice

J. R. A. Sanford

Abstract

Some 12 per cent of all geriatric admissions to University College Hospital and Whittington Hospital are for patients whose relatives or friends can no longer cope with them at home. The person principally involved with home support was interviewed in fifty such cases. The causes of inability to cope were identified on a quantitative and qualitative basis. The supporters were asked to assess which of the problems identified would have to be alleviated to restore a tolerable situation at home; forty-six (92%) were able to do so. Identification of the 'alleviation factors' forms a therapeutic and prognostic guideline in this type of admission and may have far-reaching social and economic implications.

Introduction

To some extent social considerations affect all patients admitted to a geriatric unit and in many cases they predominate. For example, admissions are sometimes undertaken to enable relatives to take a holiday or because the patient can no longer manage alone. Another consideration, which forms the subject of this study and which gives rise to a large proportion of all geriatric admissions, is that those who live with and support the patient at home may no longer be able to cope.

There is little documented information on the type and frequency of problems encountered by supporters or their attitude to the long-term welfare of their dependant. Which problems do they feel able to cope with? Which do they regard as an absolute barrier to home management? Until these questions are answered in individual cases it is not possible to organize therapy or make a rational assessment of prognosis. Until the pattern as a whole is established, resources and research cannot be directed efficiently.

The present study

The study was undertaken in the geriatric units of a teaching hospital and

Source: *British Medical Journal*, 1975, *3*, pp. 471–3.

a district general hospital in London between April and November 1974. Fifty cases were investigated. None were included in which admission was for a medical emergency. There were two reasons for studying the supporters rather than the dependants: firstly they have been largely ignored by formal research and, secondly, the supporter is the 'hub' around which the future of the patient revolves.

The information was obtained from the person principally supporting the dependant at home. There was rarely any difficulty in deciding which of the family this was. In thirty-six cases (72%) only one person lived with the dependant. In the remaining cases, in which two or more people lived with the dependant, the burden of care was evenly distributed in only one family. Of the principal supporters twenty-two were spouses (16 F., 6 M., mean age 74 years), twenty-three were offspring (19 F., 4 M., mean age 56 years), two were sisters (mean age 76 years), two were unrelated (women, mean age 67 years), and one was a daughter-in-law (age 60 years).

All fifty supporters were interviewed by me. The information was recorded on a standard form rather than a questionnaire, which might have limited the amount of information obtained.

Problems encountered by the supporters, which in some cases were intolerable, fell into three groups: (1) dependants' behaviour patterns; (2) their own limitations related to the dependant; (3) environmental and social conditions.

Once the problems had been elucidated and classified the supporter was asked to state which ones would need to be alleviated to restore a tolerable situation at home. The problems thus identified were termed 'alleviation factors'. Identification of these made it possible to express the degree of tolerance shown by the supporters to each problem.

Results

All the supporters interviewed were able to define the problems encountered in managing their dependant at home. Forty-six (92%) could envisage a situation in which they could accept the patient home and could identify the problems that would need to be alleviated – that is, the alleviation factors. Only four of the supporters (8%) would not consider having the patient at home again under any circumstances.

The frequency with which group 1 problems were identified (patients' behaviour patterns) and the proportion of supporters able to tolerate them (and who did not, therefore, include them as alleviation factors) are shown in Table 1. Calculation of tolerance makes it possible to gauge the overall degree of severity with which the supporters regarded each problem and adds a qualitative measure of the problems to the quantitative measure of their frequency. Tolerance is derived, using whole numbers, from the following equation:

$$\frac{\text{Problem frequency} - \text{alleviation factor frequency}}{\text{Problem frequency}} \times 100$$

For example, twenty-two supporters identified inability of the dependant to dress unaided as a problem. Five indicated this as an alleviation factor, and seventeen were able to tolerate it; seventeen expressed as a percentage of twenty-two gives a tolerance of 77 per cent (Table 1).

Of the group 1 problems sleep disturbance was the most common,

Table 1   Analysis of group 1 problems identified (dependants' behaviour patterns).

	Frequency (% of Cases)	Tolerance (% of Supporters Able to Tolerate Problems)
Sleep disturbance	62	16
Night wandering	24	24
Micturition	24	17
Shouting	10	20
Incontinence of faeces	56	43
Incontinence of urine	54	81
Falls	58	52
Inability to get out of bed unaided	52	35
Inability to get into bed unaided	50	40
Inability to get on commode unaided	36	22
Inability to get off commode unaided	38	21
Dangerous, irresponsible behaviour	32	58
Inability to walk unaided	18	33
Inability to walk at all	16	13
Personality conflicts	26	54
Physically aggressive behaviour	18	44
Inability to dress unaided	44	77
Inability to wash and/or shave unaided	54	93
Inability to communicate	16	50
Daytime wandering	12	33
Inability to manage stairs unaided	10	60
Inability to feed unaided	12	67
Blindness	2	0

Table 2   Analysis of group 2 problems identified (supporters' own limitations).

	Frequency (% of Cases)	Tolerance (% of Supporters Able to Tolerate Problem)
Anxiety/depression	52	65
Personality conflicts	26	54
Insufficient strength for lifting	22	73
Rheumatoid/osteoarthritis	12	67
Back strain	8	100
Bronchitis	6	33
Embarrassment	4	0
Other	12	67

Table 3   Analysis of group 3 problems identified (environmental and social conditions).

	Frequency (% of Cases)	Tolerance (% of Supporters Able to Tolerate Problem)
Restriction of social life	42	57
Inability to leave dependant for more than one hour	28	71
Stairs within accommodation	26	85
Financial disadvantage	4	0
Other	4	0

Table 4   Diagnoses in dependants which contributed to their debility.

	No. of Dependants
Senile dementia	31
Rheumatoid/osteoarthritis	14
Hemiplegia	6
Diffuse cerebrovascular disease	4
Parkinson's disease	4
Obesity	4
Diabetes	2
Amputee	2
Other	2

Table 5   Numbers of cases in which social services were used and in which there
was a shortfall of use.

	Service Used	Shortfall
District nurse	26	6
Meals on Wheels	8	2
Incontinence laundry service	1	15
Home help	19	7

being mentioned in 62 per cent of cases. It was often included as an alleviation factor and was therefore poorly tolerated (tolerance 16%). Urinary incontinence (54% of cases), however, was rarely included as an alleviation factor and was therefore well tolerated (tolerance 81%). Group 1 contained the largest number of *different* problems in the three groups (20; 57%) and 75 per cent of *all*, problems encountered. It also contained 80 per cent of the alleviation factors identified.

The group 2 problems (supporters' own limitations related to the dependant) are set out in Table 2. Nine different ones were identified (26%), and 16 per cent of all the problems encountered were in this group. Group 2 contained 11 per cent of the alleviation factors.

In group 3 (environmental and social conditions) (Table 3) six different problems were identified (17%); 12 per cent of all the problems in the study and 9 per cent of the alleviation factors were in this group.

The total number of different problems in the three groups was thirty-five and their overall numerical frequency was 452. Thus each supporter had a mean of nine problems. Of the 452 problems, 221 were alleviation factors, giving a mean of 4·4 for each supporter and showing that approximately one in every two problems identified was an alleviation factor.

The diagnoses in the dependants thought to have contributed to an intolerable situation for the supporters are given in Table 4. Thirty dependants were women aged 70–94 (mean 83) years and twenty were men aged 69–92 (mean 79) years.

The use made of social services is shown in Table 5. 'Shortfall' refers to cases in which there was a partially or completely unfulfilled need.

Discussion

The alternative to home management in almost all of these cases was long-term hospitalization, most patients being too debilitated for part III accommodation. Most supporters were clearly devoted to the dependants and had suffered considerable strain over a prolonged period.[1]

Interestingly forty-six (92%) were able clearly to evaluate the problems at home which they could and could not cope with, even during the crisis period surrounding hospitalization of the dependant.

Most of the problems the supporters felt unable to cope with in future home management – the 'alleviation factors' – fell into group 1 (80%). In this group the most frequent problem was sleep disturbance (62 % of cases), in which the supporter was woken regularly at night by the dependant for various reasons. This was poorly tolerated (16%). This may not be the only type of dependant relationship in which sleep disturbance causes stress; for example, it may be a factor in the battered baby syndrome. Despite the fact that sleep disturbance generated much animosity in the supporters, however, no evidence of 'granny battering' was found. The causes of sleep disturbance were night wandering, inability to get on and off the commode unaided (usually for micturition), and irrational shouting. Night wandering is a feature of senile dementia. Clinical experience suggests that a moderate dose of a phenothiazine in the evening may be effective in its control but there are no published data on the subject. The problem of nocturnal micturition may be approached in three ways: either by reducing frequency or by positioning the commode to enable the dependant to reach it unaided or by providing a receptacle for use in bed. The first approach entails treating disorders such as urinary tract infections or congestive heart failure and discouraging fluids in the evening. The second and third approach require common-sense measures but are often neglected.

Another frequent (56%) and poorly tolerated (43%) factor in group 1 was faecal incontinence. As might have been expected, urinary incontinence, while almost as frequent (54%), was well tolerated (81%). Most cases of faecal incontinence were associated with senile dementia, but inability to get to the commode unaided was, of course, another factor. Treatment is unlikely to prove successful unless a local cause is found – for example, impaction – but efforts should be made to re-establish continence by training and to increase mobility. Because of the difficulty of treatment, faecal incontinence when listed as an alleviation factor implies a bad prognosis for future home management. Fifteen supporters, however, thought that an incontinence laundry service would be of value, and there may be a case for making this service more widely available.

Other frequent and poorly tolerated factors in group 1 were those of general immobility; interestingly, inability to get in and out of bed and on and off the commode were more often encountered and regarded as more of a problem than inability to walk unaided. This indicates a need, both at home and in hospital, to explore the advantages of aids such as low beds and handrails.

Dangerous irresponsibility was mentioned in 32 per cent of cases though most supporters felt able to contain it by such measures as turning off the gas at source, locking outside doors, and having high-wall electric fires. Advice on these matters can be given to supporters when necessary.

Falls, another problem in group 1, were fairly well tolerated by the supporters if not by the dependants. Worry about the possibility of injury to the dependant was, perhaps surprisingly, overshadowed in most supporters' minds by the difficulty of picking the dependant up, which often required the help of a neighbour or the police.

Frequent though well-tolerated factors in group 1 not often identified as alleviation factors included urinary incontinence, inability to wash unaided, and inability to dress unaided. Most supporters felt able to cope with these problems, often in the case of washing with the aid of a district nurse. Washing the dependant was particularly well tolerated (93%), and in this the supporters received the most help from the social services. This does perhaps suggest that outside help for other problems might be of value in enabling supporters to cope.

Factors less often encountered were physically aggressive behaviour by the dependant or specific personality conflicts attributed by the supporter to the dependant's behaviour. A number of different personality conflicts were present including demanding behaviour (8%) and a continuing sexual interest (2%). Only 16 per cent of the supporters identified inability to communicate as a problem, and the tolerance of this was 50 per cent.

Group 2 contained only 16 per cent of all the problems identified and only 11 per cent of the alleviation factors. The most common problem was anxiety or depression or both (52% of cases), which was usually attributed to looking after the dependant. Tolerance of this was, perhaps surprisingly, fairly good (65%). Eleven of the supporters (22%) considered that they were just not physically strong enough to cope with lifting, but again this was well tolerated (73%). Two supporters, both sons, identified as a problem factor embarassment in dressing and attending to their mothers on the commode, and both listed this as an alleviation factor, tolerance, therefore, being nil. Interestingly, despite the fact that over half (59%) of the supporters in this study were over 65 years old, relatively few problems (16%) were identified in group 2. This suggests that we would be mistaken to regard age as synonymous with debility and indicates that it is the old who lead the frail in our society rather than the 'frail who lead the frail', as has been suggested.[2]

Group 3 was again much smaller than group 1 and contained only 12 per cent of all the problems identified and 9 per cent of the alleviation factors. Restriction of social life was identified in 42 per cent of cases, and the tolerance of this was 57 per cent. Many supporters had not had a holiday or even an evening out for years and welcomed the idea of a 'granny sitter'. This was a real unfulfilled need. Fourteen supporters (28%) felt unable to leave their dependant for more than an hour, which precluded all activity outside the home except for a quick visit to the shops. Surprisingly few supporters thought that their environment made matters more difficult. Thirteen (26%) identified stairs within their accommodation as a problem, but they usually managed to alleviate this by such measures as bringing the dependant's bed downstairs and obtaining a commode. Tolerance of this problem was therefore high (85%). Two supporters (4%) considered that they were financially disadvantaged by looking after their dependant, and this was due to having to give up work. A number of supporters were entitled to, but had not been receiving, an attendance allowance.

Conclusion

The population of England and Wales over 75 years of age is likely to increase by 20 per cent in the next decade.[3] There is a deficiency of resources within geriatric units to meet existing needs. This study examines the problems of a group of people who have the potential to reduce the geriatric ward-patient population by as much as 12 per cent. At present their problems are neglected and they are unable to cope with their dependants at home. We would be well advised to consider their needs most carefully for the future.

References

1 ISAACS, B. (1971) *British Medical Journal*, *4*, 282.
2 CRESSWELL, J. et al. (1972) *New Society*, *20*, 410.
3 Registrar General (1974) *Quarterly Return for England and Wales, No. 501*. London: HMSO.

19 Domiciliary care for the elderly sick: economy or neglect?

L. J. Opit

Abstract

This paper reports an investigation of the costs of domiciliary care for 139 elderly sick patients under the care of the home nursing service. The data suggest that there may be little economic advantage in home care for seriously disabled elderly people. The revenue cost of domiciliary care was equal to or greater than the average associated with residential or hospital custodial care in such patients. Even so, the cost of services received at home did not disclose the real need for domiciliary care, since at present this is obscured by compulsory rationing and the separation of responsibility between health and social services. It is suggested that the supposed economic advantage of domiciliary care will depend increasingly on restricting such services, thus increasing the degree of neglect to some patients.

Introduction

Studies of the cost of domiciliary care [1,2,3] have mainly used population groups and standard statistical costing returns. Hence these rely on average costs over a large range of disability and illness and may be misleading if the object is to appraise the cost of alternative strategies of care for similarly disabled elderly people. But what proportion of severely handicapped patients require less expenditure or help to manage at home or indeed prefer staying there? Here I report an attempt to measure the use of resources by a sample of the elderly sick living at home.

Methods and comments

District nurses attached to thirty-six general practice panels in the Central Birmingham Health District were asked to provide data about a representative sample of six to twelve elderly patients whom they were attending from 1 August to 31 October 1974. Of the 581 patients aged 65 and over

Source: *British Medical Journal*, 1977, *1*, pp. 30–3.

then receiving attention from the nursing service, 139 were chosen for study. They were not a random sample, but since the study was determining the level of service (and its cost) to individual patients, I felt that the sample should be representative of a wide range of social and medical problems.

Data collection

The nurses were given a structured inquiry form for each patient asking for data relating to housing, social contacts, disability, and medical condition. They were also given a detailed list and asked to score those activities provided for each patient and to estimate the time per visit that these needed during a week. They recorded distance of each patient's home from base; the number of visits by nursing staff members; the degree of family, neighbour, and volunteer help; and the use of social services, laundry, and equipment or aids. These data were checked at the social service agencies as well as the community services division of the area health authority.

Much of these data were converted into average visiting time per patient per week and assigned a monetary value.

Categorisation

Each patient was categorised into an illness group, as follows:

Stroke – when the notes recorded stroke or evidence of hemiplegia or aphasia.

Dementia – patients with appreciable intellectual or behavioural disturbance without evidence of stroke.

Incontinence – patients who had no evidence of stroke or dementia but who had frequent incontinence of bladder or bowel without apparent cause.

Terminal – patients dying of malignancy.

Multiple pathology – the remaining patients, many of whom had varied conditions such as arthritis, obesity, leg ulcers, or heart failure, were divided into two groups according to the presence or absence of recorded moderate to severe blindness or deafness.

All patients were further classified by activity ability. The nature and source of the data prevented the use of a refined classification of disability such as that used by Harris *et al.*[4] Instead, three groups were identified: those bed-ridden or chairfast (bedfast); those ambulant and largely able to care for themselves (self-care); and the remainder partial self-care groups.

Time study

During the study three nurses kept a detailed time study of actual nurse–patient contact for twenty days.

The sample – characteristics and comment

Demographic characteristics. One patient (a male tetraplegic) was under 60 while twenty-six were 60–69, forty-nine 70–79, fifty-six 80–89, and seven 90 or older. The overall proportion of women to men was 6·7 to 1. Forty-four patients lived alone, and of these thirteen had unsuitable or unsatisfactory housing. Fifty-three patients lived with other old people, mostly a spouse. Two patients lived with mentally defective children. The housing conditions were unsatisfactory on nine occasions. The remainder of the patients were living within family groups, although a few stayed with friends or in trust houses; in eight cases this accommodation was 'unsatisfactory'. 'Unsatisfactory' ranged from accommodation with only an outside lavatory to filthy and neglected conditions, and no source of hot water other than a kettle.

Disease and disability characteristics. Some twenty-eight patients had had

Table 1   Direct costs of care.

Diagnostic category	Activity state		
	Bedfast	*Partial self-care*	*Self-care*
(a) Stroke	£23·10 (14)	£9·20 (12)	£16·60 (2)
(b) Dementia	£34·80 (4)	£10·40 (15)	£12·70 (6)
(c) Multiple pathology No recorded major visual or hearing defect	£26·10 (12)	£9·00 (28)	£7·60 (19)
(d) Multiple pathology Recorded major visual or hearing defect	£36·00 (2)	£9·50 (7)	£6·70 (7)
(e) Incontinence	£8·40 (2)	£8·20 (2)	
(f) Terminal	£26·50 (5)		£10·20 (1)
Activity average	£25·60 (39)	£9·40 (64)	£8·90 (35)

The cost figures are £ per week average and exclude costs associated with outpatient or inpatient attendance, social-worker time, blind welfare services, or day centre attendance. One patient not classified.

strokes (Table 1), and half of these were bedfast or totally dependent on other people. About the same number had disturbances of behaviour with confusion. A further ten patients had intermittent behavioural disturbances and, of the total, twenty-one had intermittent or persistent incontinence. Sixteen patients had deafness and blindness without stroke or dementia; these often had additional recorded handicaps, such as severe arthritis or obesity. In all, twenty-three patients had some visual defect, thirty deafness, and ten both. Among the blind were four patients who had diagnosed cataracts, two of whom had been on hospital waiting lists for some time.

Some ten patients of the twenty-three with visual disturbance were diabetics. Six patients had terminal malignancy, five of them seriously ill. The largest group of patients, multiple pathology, included a wide spectrum of categories. Among the bedfast patients were three with Parkinson's disease, two with fractured lower legs, a tetraplegic, one with prostatism with indwelling catheter, and one with multiple sclerosis. Many of the less disabled were obese, suffering from osteoarthritis and congestive heart failure, while a few had no clear diagnostic label except old age.

Quality of care. The nurses' purely subjective classification of the quality of care showed 97 patients as receiving satisfactory care and 41 unsatisfactory care. Analysis of these assessments showed that the designation of unsatisfactory was associated particularly with increasing total average nursing work load per patient (Table 2).

Table 2   Estimated patient–nurse contact time per week.

	Cases classified as satisfactory	Cases classified as unsatisfactory	Total
< $\frac{1}{2}$ hour	21	5	26
> $\frac{1}{2}$ hour and ≤ 1 hour	28	6	34
> 1 hour and ≤ 2·5 hours	26	17	43
> 2·5 hours and ≤ 5 hours	15	7	22
> 5 hours and ≤ 10 hours	7	4	11
> 10 hours	1	2	3

Direct costs

Nursing costs. Nursing costs were estimated from the average nurse contact time for each patient. The usual method of assigning costs per visit, as used by the Institute of Municipal Treasurers and Accountants was believed to be unreliable, since visits may range between three minutes and several hours. The cost of contact time was obtained from the nursing award rates available in November 1974 adjusted to allow for the cost of area nursing and geriatric supervision, area administration, superannuation, and the maintenance of plant and buildings. It included the cost of uniform allowance, drugs, stationery, and telephone.

In addition an increment for central administrative costs was made. No allowance for mileage was included since these data were available for each patient–nurse contact. The self-recorded work study carried out by three nurses showed that on average only $3\frac{1}{4}$ hours a day were spent on actual patient contact so that the cost per hour visiting was then doubled to include the assumption that one hour of patient contact required two hours of a nurse's time. This estimate can be confirmed from a detailed study of district nurse work by Hockey and Buttimore,[5] which gives an average of $3\frac{1}{2}$ hours a day for time spent on visiting (Table 3).

Table 3   Nursing cost distribution. Corrected cost distribution using (b) and including mileage at 7·5p per mile.

£ per week average	Total
< £5	61
> £5 ≤ £10	35
> £10 ≤ £15	21
> £15 ≤ £20	8
> £20 ≤ £30	7
> £30 ≤ £50	4
> £50	9

(a) Deduced costs an hour for employment. SRN grade £2·24. SEN grade £1·51, and nurse attendant grade £1·18.
(b) Deduced costs an hour for visiting corrected for proportion of time spent visiting. SRN grade £4·48, SEN grade £3·02, and nurse attendant grade £2·36.

Home help. Since most home helps are part-time and are paid only for the help provided, the hours of work for which pay is received is very close to the hours of home help provided, so that no allowance was made for the discrepancy in assessing nursing costs. The latter include allowance for pensions, national insurance, transport, supervision, and administration. No allowance for overtime or central administrative costs was readily available, and the costs as given in most social service costings were almost certainly too low.

Other social service functions costed included meals on wheels, chiropody, night watch, and attendance by social-work aides. Cost components included salary, administrative costs, and transport.

Health service functions costed were laundry services, Marie Curie Foundation nursing, and day-hospital attendance.

Equipment costs. The home-nursing service provided nursing aids and equipment while the social services department supplied some additional aids – such as fitted handrails, shower equipment, and telephones. Additional equipment was available from the blind welfare section of social services.

So far as possible the items provided for each person were costed and the administrative costs of stocking, providing, and maintaining this equipment was added pro rata to the capital cost of the equipment (Table 4). For equipment such as a telephone it is easy to associate a weekly cost with the equipment but for most items, which may have been collected over several years, this can be done only by estimating the annual cost of the capital investment and by using some simple depreciation schedule.

Table 4   Use of domiciliary services

Service	No. of patients receiving service	Average cost per patient week of service
Laundry	29	£2·08
Equipment:		
Telephone	9	38p/week
Other aids and equipment	83	{ Total £6·02 33p/week
Home helps	63	£3·23
Meals at home	35	{ £1·14 (2 meals) gross £0·84 nett
Social worker contact	67	?
Social-work aide visiting	4	£0·20
Occupational therapist	3	?
Chiropody	14	£0·16
Hospital service (4)		
Domiciliary service (10)		
Blind welfare services	4	?
Day centres	3	?
Night watch	3	£14·85
Marie Curie Foundation nursing	3	£11·15
Day hospital attendance	23	£5·93

Neither of these schemes is entirely realistic. The cost of capital was set at 14 per cent and depreciation schedule was over five years. Services that were not costed included social worker services, occupational therapy, blind welfare services, and day centres.

Indirect costs

Family, neighbours, and volunteers in the care of the elderly sick were important for two categories of patients. The first were those living alone and, of these 44, twenty-four were receiving almost daily support from these groups. The second category were those living with an aged relative, spouse, or child and, of the 53, twenty-four were supported in this way.

I expected that no realistic costs could be assigned for this help, even though this support spared the nursing and social services. It seemed important, nevertheless, to provide some rough guide to these sources of help.

Social security

The final component of cost was that associated directly with payment of money. Almost all these patients were pensioners, some received supplementary payments to cover such items as fuel, while others were cared for by their family, who might receive attendance allowance payments. I identified five such cases.

It was difficult to obtain reliable estimates of this cost directly from patients, and information about individuals cannot be obtained from the Department of Health and Social Security. Nevertheless, these payments have a particular significance when comparing the cost of domiciliary care with that in an institution, because there is a loss of the attendance payments on admission and a graduated loss of pension with increasing length of stay.

Results

Home helps

The major social service support was provided by the home-help organisation and of our sample patients, 63 were recorded as receiving home-help, with an average of 3·8 hours per person a week (individual maximum twenty hours a week, modal three hours). By using data provided by the social services accountant the gross cost of this service was estimated as 85p an hour. Patients might be asked to contribute but for the whole city the average was only 3p for an hour's service.

The distribution of home help to patients was skew: 76 of the patients received no help, while five received eight or more hours a week. These five patients represented only 3·5 per cent of the sample but they received almost a quarter of the home help provided. The home help was concentrated on those patients living alone, with 3·9 hours a week for those receiving help (66%). Patients receiving nursing support received less than average home-help support. Thus the bedfast or totally dependant group (27% of the sample) received 16 per cent of all the available home help. Details of some individual cases suggested that in cases with heavy nursing loads the district nurses were providing domestic rather than technical services, and their use was inappropriate to their skills. If nursing help and home help are substituting for one another, then the use of nurses at £4 an hour to carry out home-help duties that can be purchased for less than £1 an hour suggests some obvious deficiency in the integration of the organisations that supply these resources.

Social workers and occupational therapist contact

Files existed in the social work departments for 67 patients in the survey. Only fourteen files were classified as open or active, and, of these, only six patients were receiving regular social work or welfare aid visits. One had several visits scattered over a month mostly at his own request in a successful bid for residential accommodation, and one case was attended by a social work trainee. Three people had occasional visits from the occupational therapist.

Superficially, therefore, one might be tempted to assume that the cost of this service for these patients was negligible even given that the cost of a half hour visit from a social-work aide is £1·80 and from an occupational therapist £2·00. The files themselves are, however, a testimony to time spent writing, travelling, telephoning, and talking even if little visiting is identified. Any field social workers cost a lot even if the care of the elderly has a relatively low priority in their work, so that the inability to cost satisfactorily the work of social workers is a serious deficiency in this study. To achieve such a costing needs a detailed work study of social work, and this is currently being examined by the Research, Planning, and Development Section of the Birmingham Social Service Department.

Costs of patient care at home

Direct costs. Direct cost data for individual patients, and relating this cost (and its implied measure of the use of resource) to patient disability, are inevitably inexact because of the method of costing and the complexity of much illness in the elderly (Table 1). The data suggest that the activity status indicator is more useful than the diagnostic class in classifying these costs. The latter for all bedfast groups was £25·60, close to the average for all diagnostic groups except incontinence. The range of cost values a week for bedfast patients was £2·95–£83·75; twenty patients in this category had costs of £20 a week or more, while eight had weekly costs of over £30 a week.

For those classified as partial self-care, the activity class average was again similar to the averages within diagnostic groups (range per week £1·14–£35·02). In over half (36) the cost was £8 a week or less, while in seven cases it was over £20.

The self-care patients had average weekly cost values that varied little among diagnostic classes except for stroke patients, when the sample numbers were very small. The values for self-care patients ranged from £0·56 to £26·02 a week; in just less than half of the sample (15) the cost was £4 or less, while for two-thirds (23) it was less than £8. Two cases had costs greater than £20.

Indirect costs. Cash costs associated with living at home must be taken into account, particularly if the costs of domiciliary care and institutional care are to be compared. These costs were not available for individuals but may be estimated in two ways. One method is to add to the direct costs the cash value of maintaining a house: it includes upkeep, heating, rent, rates, and food. This approach was adopted by Rickard[3] and would increase the direct costs in my analysis by £16 to £30 using data from pensioners' household expenditure.[6] An alternative approach is to regard pension, benefit, and attendance payments as part of the cost of domiciliary care, particularly since these payments are reduced or abolished on admission to an institution. This 'saving' may be estimated for the social service institutions by looking at the difference between the nett and gross costs. In Birmingham this amounted to an average of £15 a patient week in 1974.

One other important indirect cost is the use of labour and goods obtained from neighbours, friends, and family. There is no credible way of assigning a money value to this activity but this study suggests that it could be considerable, and valuable (cases 1 and 2).

Case 1 – An 83-year-old widow was living alone with no social contacts in a large neglected house. She had evidence of severe dementia with incontinence and was receiving $3\frac{1}{2}$ hours of nursing and 15 hours of home help a week. The total cost assigned to this patient was £30·10 per week.

Case 2 – A 78-year-old widow was living alone but receiving daily visits from her neighbours. She had severe blindness and had been on the waiting list for cataract extraction for two years. She was also deaf and frail, having difficulty in walking without help. She received only about 15 minutes of nursing visits a week and three hours of home help. The weekly total cost assigned for the care of this patient was £6·09.

Discussion

This study shows that domiciliary care of severely handicapped old people is not cheap, even given that the level of care provided was probably often inadequate. Often workers have claimed, however, that this is not so.[3] Nevertheless, it is difficult to validate my results from other costing studies. Each depends on the nature of the data collected, the sample, and the assumptions made. These variables are determined at the outset by the objectives of the costing exercise.

My study was concerned with determining the costs of health and social services in caring for individuals and this differs from other studies.[2,3] A study reported by Wager[7] has some similarity. Although his sampling was different, he used a classification of disability and provided data that related disability to the use of some domiciliary services. Once again, data relating to nursing contact were limited and costed per visit. The social workers were asked to make recommendations about additional social service or nursing help required, and these were also costed. Wager concluded that the marginal cost difference between residential care and intensive domiciliary care was small or negative for some groups of people.

All studies have one serious limitation in their reliance on an estimate of cost at one point in time and failure to consider the dynamic nature of the patients' state. Equally important, the data in this and other studies relate to cost at the current level of provision, and the latter does not imply that the care provided is the best. Thus, the cost of domiciliary services has largely been depressed by rationing of scarce resources. The use of money to indicate the use of resources does not disclose the limited availability of staff time or equipment. Hence, some patients who are receiving large amounts of social service or nursing care at home are in competition with other patients who also need these resources.

I found that there was a waiting list for laundry services and that far more were needed than were provided. Similarly, the number of blind or partially sighted patients known to the blind welfare services is only a fraction of those entitled to this aid.[8]

Clearly the demand for domiciliary services is already greater than can be provided with present resources and some assessment of benefit or quality of service is needed. Unfortunately, no objective assessment of the quality of care is available. In my study, however, I asked the domiciliary nursing staff to provide a subjective assessment. They identified almost 30 per cent of their cases as receiving either inadequate or inappropriate care, and I found it difficult not to agree with their assessment in most instances. Many of this 'unsatisfactory' group were severely disabled with serious irreversible conditions such as stroke or dementia and in spite of the considerable degree of support, I doubt whether a satisfactory environment could have been maintained for them at home. Since some of these cases could have been suitable for transfer to residential or custodial beds, it is interesting to compare the costs with the estimated revenue costs of this care. In the Birmingham region the cost per week for geriatric hospitals varies from £21 to £54 (1973–4). These costs include specialist staff and diagnostic and therapeutic facilities, and money can be subtracted to correspond to these. If this is done the probable average cost for 1974–5 would be about £45 a week, although this estimate is mainly guesswork. Similarly, the average gross cost per patient week in residential homes was £34 in Birmingham (1974–5). If these values are compared with the average cost for bedfast patients of £26 and allowance made for an average indirect cost of £15, some 20 per cent of this study sample were more expensive to manage at home than in a geriatric hospital. No allowance is made for capital costs of these institutions.

If the work created by this sample of patients represents half of the total nursing work (although it is only for 25 per cent of the patients) then for the whole nursing area 5 per cent of all patients would actually cost more to support at home than in hospital. Moreover, about 10 per cent would cost more than in residential care, even given the present inadequate level of domiciliary support. Of course, any decision to treat patients in home or hospital should not be made mainly on economic grounds. But it is equally unrealistic to ignore this factor completely, for compulsory rationing deprives some patients of adequate care when the limited resources are used heavily for some other persons.

It is quite possible to keep many seriously disabled old persons at home, but to do so without neglect will require a large investment in the support services. Even then, the quality of life for some of these patients or their families may be far from compatible with any civilised humanitarian standards. Whatever may be said about the quality of care for the elderly sick at home it is not cheap to provide, if the data in my study are representative of those elsewhere. Thus, services for a patient receiving four hours' visiting a week, four hours of home help, and two meals will cost as much as the cost of non-medical resources given to a person in a residential home and about two-thirds of that given to a patient in an established geriatric inpatient unit, if the assumptions about the graduated loss of pension and other allowances with hospital or residential home admission are valid.

During this study I found it difficult to avoid the conclusion that some of the cost incurred could have been reduced by appreciable changes in the organisation of the health and social services. If the present policy of passively transferring the elderly chronic sick from hospital to home continues by limiting the various types of accommodation available for them, a substantial additional financial allocation for domiciliary care will be needed. If this does not occur then domiciliary care for the elderly sick will be increasingly 'economic' simply because the level of care provided becomes increasingly inadequate.

References

1 ECONOMIST INTELLIGENCE UNIT (1973) *Care with Dignity.* Horsham: National Fund for Research into Crippling Diseases.
2 HUTTON, D. S. S., IMBER, V. and MITCHELL, H. D. (1974) *Journal of the Royal Statistical Society A, 137,* 4, 483.
3 RICKARD, J. H. (1974) *Journal of the Royal College of General Practitioners, 24,* 839.
4 HARRIS, A. I., COX, E. and SMITH, C. R. W. (1971) *Handicapped and Impaired in Great Britain.* London: HMSO.
5 HOCKEY, L. and BUTTIMORE, A. (1973) *Cooperation in Patient Care.* London: Queens Institute of District Nursing.
6 CENTRAL STATISTICAL OFFICE (1975) *Social Trends No. 6.* London: HMSO.
7 WAGER, R. (1972) *Care of the Elderly.* London: Institute of Municipal Treasurers and Accountants.
8 BRENNAN, M. E. and KNOX, E. G. (1973) *British Journal of Preventive and Social Medicine, 27,* 154.

20   Falling through the social services net

Anon

Ellen (93) and Jane (81), both retired professional women, are sisters who live together in their own home. Ellen, who is registered blind, is visited by 'my nice social worker' from the local Social Services Department. She enjoys Talking Books and says that if anything goes wrong with her machine 'a wonderful mechanic' calls to repair it promptly. A volunteer gardener comes once a month to work in the sisters' garden, and – before the pressure of exams – they used to be visited by two schoolgirls.

The sisters are both very appreciative of the attention and help they receive from friends which enables them to continue to live in their own house. However, a recent experience, which separated them and so deprived them of the mutual support which must be their main prop, has shaken their confidence in the ability of the statutory services to provide a safety-net in emergencies. The disabilities of old age are accepted with cheerful courage; accidents will happen, and pain, discomfort and upheaval can be endured, but when this is aggravated by worry and uncertainty for both of them, this is a shattering experience.

They tell the following story:

Jane   I set forth one Saturday morning – ten days before Christmas – about ten o'clock, having only made my bed and washed up and thinking I could just do the shopping before finishing the rest of the housework. I went up the road with my push-basket to our nice friendly greengrocer, but on leaving the shop I think I must have slipped on a cabbage leaf and I sat down very hard and sudden on the step. I was taken into the room behind the shop; a doctor was fetched and he said nothing was broken. I should rest for an hour and then go home. I thought Ellen would be demented so the greengrocer's wife went to tell her I would be home shortly. But when I tried to rise I could not stand and so the greengrocer sent for the ambulance. When it came the men said they could take me to the hospital but they could not take me home. So I said 'In that case you can't take me anywhere.' They relented and brought me home and carried me indoors.

The doctor who saw me at the shop had phoned my doctor and in course of time she arrived – at about three o'clock. She said I must go to

Source: *Age Concern Today*, 1975, no. 15, pp. 19–20.

hospital as she was almost sure I had a fracture. She ordered an ambulance and very kind men took me off to hospital, and my last words to Ellen were 'I hope they will look after you all right.'

Ellen The doctor said she would arrange for Social Services to call. Jane, distressed at leaving me alone, said I was to be sure to get the social worker to phone the hospital to let her know what arrangements had been made. I was left alone in the house, very incapable and decrepit, with all sorts of disabilities – I can't see to telephone, don't hear the front door bell.

Late that afternoon a social worker came and asked what I wanted him to do, so I said 'I don't know – I would like someone to come and stay in the house for a day or two to look after me.' He said he couldn't do anything till Monday but then he would see about meals on wheels and perhaps a home help. I felt that even on Monday he wouldn't be able to do anything, and I knew that if I let him go I would be stranded. So I asked him to do a little telephoning and suggested one or two numbers he might call, including a nurse friend's but she was not there. I thought if I tell him to ring the hospital and say he will come again on Monday Jane will go off pop and if I do not ring the hospital she will also go off pop, so I gave him the number of a friend who lives not far away and she responded and came almost at once. That was lucky as she might have been out.

I asked this friend, Mary, whether she could sleep in the house that night but she said she could not do that but would be very pleased to take me home with her so I thought I had better opt for that. She had commandeered a friend with a car but because she was in a great hurry I had no time to pack anything – I had to go straightaway and Jane was told that I was staying with Mary.

I thought the young man from Social Services would report to my nice social worker and I thought she would come on Monday and arrange something because I had once been told by her that they kept some emergency beds in their homes. Although Mary was full of engagements she waited in the house on Monday to see the social worker – but she did not come. On Tuesday I suggested she should ring up Social Services and she spoke to my social worker who had had no message and could not come that day. She called on the next day but had nothing to offer. There were no emergency beds because decorations were being done. She rang round to various nursing homes but they all had long waiting lists. She could not do anything.

Mary was extremely busy and had no time to look after me; she went to a lot of trouble to see if there was anyone who could either sleep in our house or take me in. She asked the Vicar of the church to which Jane belongs and he produced a retired nurse. Mary rang up this nurse, Miss Jones, who explained that though she had volunteered to help in cases of need, she had in mind such things as relieving relatives for a few hours; she could not live in as she had an invalid sister who could not be left at night.

My social worker did not know what to do with me. She pressed Mary to keep me and poor Mary had to succumb but she said she was going away on Christmas Eve and that was the absolute limit. Miss Jones was then pressed and she agreed to take me on Christmas Eve so that Mary could go off. I did not know at all what I was going to, but as Jane would still be in hospital we would both be provided for at Christmas. Then, to my horror, I got a message that Jane was being turned out of hospital, still needing care and not able to walk. I told my social worker I was desperately unhappy about this; she rang up the social worker at the hospital and was told that Jane was pressing to go home, and patients could not be stopped if they wanted to leave.

Miss Jones and her sister had a nice, comfortable house with two large bedrooms – one each – and one very, very small spare room – and now they were pressed to take Jane as well. They finally agreed to take Jane for Christmas Day and Boxing Day although this meant that they not only had to share a room but they had to share a bed. And so we went together there for the two days and we were all happy together except that the sisters obviously hated sharing a bed.

Jane Now, let me tell you my side of it. I was borne off to hospital with inadequate packing and dumped on a stretcher there and after hours and hours and hours and hours and hours, it seemed to me, by which time I was absolutely starving incidentally, I got to the X-ray. The surgeon said nothing to worry about. I had cracked a bone in my pelvis; there was no treatment – just wait until it got better. I asked if I should do it any injury if I moved it about and he said 'No.' That was the only time it was examined by a doctor. He said they would keep me until Monday. I said I could not go home as I could not walk, but it was obvious that, with Christmas approaching, they were very anxious to clear the beds.

The nurses were very kind to me. Eventually the social worker came to see me. I told her that I could not go home until I was better and able to run the house, and yet she made out that I was pressing to go home. I quite understand that the hospital wanted to clear the beds because somebody told me that round Christmas they always had such an awful lot of accidents.

Local friends – very, very kind friends – would call to see me in a hurry; they were all making arrangements for Christmas involving families or going away and I could never get a straight tale of what was happening to Ellen; I think they didn't want to worry me but I would rather have known just what was happening. One of the nurses told me that Ellen was all right with Mary, and eventually I was told that the Jones's were going to have me at Christmas but I did not know how absolutely desperate everybody was to find somewhere for us to go. I could not get any straight news of Ellen.

When the surgeon looked at me, (my face not my pelvis), and said I was to get up, he said physiotherapy would help me to walk again. But the physiotherapist was too busy to help me much. I learnt to walk with a frame and then that was taken away and I was landed with two sticks which was really rather terrifying. Have you ever walked with two sticks? The physiotherapist showed me how to get upstairs but there were no twiddles on these hospital stairs and I had only one practice on them. But I learnt to walk on the level with the two sticks and I could go to the loo by myself without being frightened to death.

It was arranged that two friends of ours would be told when I would be arriving home so that they could be around. On that morning breakfast was late I was just beginning to dress, very, very slowly, of course, when a youth arrived with a push-chair and said I was to be taken to the ambulance. I said I could not go immediately and he fetched a nurse who said they couldn't wait. She said she would pack my bag and I was to go as I was. She bundled everything into my case and the youth pushed me into the entrance hall where I waited at least half an hour. At last I was put in the ambulance with three old ladies bound for the cottage hospital. The ambulance man had no instructions about me apart from the address to which I was to be delivered and he was prepared to leave me at the gate. But I said I could not get up the stairs and they grumbled a bit and then lifted me upstairs and lit the fire for me.

I was alone in the house as my friends had not expected me to be home so soon but they arrived not long after, saw I had something to eat, and left the door key on a string so that people could get in. I found it very difficult on two sticks and I was marooned upstairs. Once the ambulance men left me I might have been a skeleton for all the official help I had. A friend down the road brought me hot vegetables every day at lunch time, and other friends came to see me. They were all close friends who had been helping us for years. The people at the shop on the corner were very kind – lucky it wasn't a supermarket . . .

On the Sunday morning suddenly in came Ellen, Mary and another friend who drove them in the car.

Ellen I had asked to go home to try to pack a suitcase before I went away for Christmas.

Jane The first thing she did was to say to me 'Why, oh why did you insist on coming home?' There was much confusion and in the middle of it the doctor came and said she was glad to see me home, and then she went. One of Mary's neighbours who heard about our plight offered to come and help me downstairs; he was a vet and he said 'I'm used to carrying cows', and when the time came for us to go to Miss Jones, he carried me down without the slightest difficulty.

We are vegetarians which was another horror for Miss Jones but she was very, very kind in agreeing to have me. They were so kind to us, and very generous and so we made some new friends. But the Social Services didn't even help us with transport.

Ellen   I think there was nothing the Social Services could do. It seems to me that in a crisis you want some kind of place where you can either take people or send someone to them. It seems to take about a fortnight for the Social Services to get going. The service is too large; too bureaucratic.

Jane   If only there had been someone to coordinate. What we needed was one hefty relation. On our return home, Ellen organised the whole thing. She said 'Write to Nora.' That's a friend in Yorkshire who used to live near us. I wrote to her and asked if she could possibly come and help us out and she came at once. Ellen said 'Ring Joan'. Joan was our daily help for five years and had left eight years ago. A friend phoned her and she agreed to come and has been coming ever since.

After I had got to the point of getting up and down stairs and we got Nora, our friend, and Joan, there was a ring at the door and it was the Health Visitor to ask how we were getting on. It seems to me so absurd that they can do nothing but advise.

Other cases

The sisters were very impressed and touched by the great kindness they received from so many people – 'Nothing could be more heart-warming than the way people all rallied round' – but Jane said that she feared that if they had only had the statutory services to call on, two skeletons might have been found in their house.

Their anxiety about an official emergency service, about the lack of coordination between social workers, sometimes even when they are working in the same department, and about the failure of social workers in some instances to give information and reassurance to clients, has been reinforced by another case they have heard about at first hand.

'We had a friend, old but active, whose eyesight was failing. She came to see my Talking Book machine as she had been advised to be registered blind so that she could have one. About a month later she phoned us, very distressed, as she had gone completely blind and was alone in the house. Jane phoned Social Services and asked if they could send someone to see our poor friend. About a fortnight later we heard she had died – and after that we had a call from Social Services, asking us for particulars about her. Presumably they wanted to collect as much information as possible before they visited.

'It is immediate help that is wanted in a crisis.'

Part 4   Community Needs and Problems

21 Poverty and the elderly

David Jordan

In the late 1950s and early 1960s a series of studies were made in Britain of the financial and other needs of the elderly. All the studies used the National Assistance (now Supplementary Benefit) level or some proportion of it as a standard of low or poverty income. Thus in 1962 Dorothy Cole and John Utting reported that 'the most important finding which emerges from this study is that in addition to that quarter of all units in the sample who were already receiving national assistance there were more than as many again with incomes little higher and, in some cases, actually lower than those with assistance . . . we found that 27 per cent of the units were at or below these levels (i.e. approximating to national assistance) of income but without help from the Assistance Board'. Taking into account the offsetting effect of savings and certain other resources on entitlement to national assistance, Cole and Utting concluded that 'over 12 per cent of old people units, nearly half as many again as are at present receiving assistance, are entitled to help from the Assistance Board but are not getting it'.[1] These findings were confirmed a few years later by a further study:

As many as 11 per cent of our sample had financial resources actually below national assistance scale rates, although they were not receiving national assistance. This was not a calculation about entitlements to national assistance and as the regulations stand such old people would not necessarily be entitled. But the financial resources of this group were clearly minimal. Then there were another 13 per cent of income units at or above the scale rates but with resources no higher than those units receiving national assistance. Altogether, taking those with and without national assistance, it appears that nearly half of all elderly income units have financial resources at the current administratively defined 'subsistence' levels.[2]

Three further studies cemented the impression that old age was a major cause of poverty. The Allen Committee reported in 1965 that 800,000 retired heads of households were apparently eligible for national assistance but not getting it.[3] A re-analysis of Family Expenditure Survey data carried out by Abel-Smith and Townsend found that 'thirty-five per cent of the persons in low income households were older persons with pensions as their primary source of income' in 1960. The definition of low income used as a 'poverty line' was 140 per cent of the then national assistance level.[4]

Source: previously unpublished paper, written for this Reader.

Finally, in 1965, the Ministry of Pensions and National Insurance conducted its own inquiry which revealed that 'rather more than 700,000 pensioner households (about 850,000 pensioners) could have received assistance if they had applied for it'.[5] At the time there were 1,560,000 retirement pensioners receiving national assistance out of a total 6,360,000 retirement pensioners.

The alarm caused by the findings of these studies and particularly the official confirmation of the earlier independent results spawned a series of new pension schemes, culminating in that introduced in April 1978, the effect of which seems to have been to curtail the investigation of the poverty and hardship of today's pensioners. As in the past the 'impression has sometimes been given that attention was being paid rather to some distant pensioner of the future than to the pensioner of today'.[6]

If we use the same yardstick as that utilised in the past,[7] the supplementary benefit (formerly national assistance) level, we can learn from official figures the extent of poverty amongst today's elderly. The justification for using the supplementary benefit level, quite apart from its comparability, is that it does at least have some form of official sanction being 'the minimum standard of living that the Government considers necessary at a particular time'.[8] Moreover it provides, particularly since automatic upratings were introduced in 1975, a relative standard of poverty.

Supplementary benefit is a means-tested benefit designed to bring the recipient's income up to a certain level. If it falls short of that level the difference is made up by the supplementary benefit payment. In November 1977 the long-term rates of supplementary benefit were increased to £17.90 per week for a single pensioner and £28.35 per week for a married couple, plus the payment of rent and rates in full. These scale rates 'are regarded . . . as covering all normal needs which can be foreseen, including food, fuel and light, the normal repair and replacement of clothing, household sundries (but not major items of bedding and furnishing) and provision for amenities such as newspapers, entertainments and television licences'.[9] Such a budget leaves little room for manoeuvre. Townsend described the lives of two pensioners living on National Assistance:

Mr Preeley was a cripple in his late seventies and he lived alone in a two room flat. He was unmarried and socially isolated. He was very deaf. He lived on a non-contributory pension and supplementary assistance of £2 10s 6d. His rent was 10s 6d, coal about 6s . . . No money, Christmas or other club. Insurances – an endowment policy costing him 2s 0½d a week. 'It covers everything and every now and then I can draw on it. When the man called he said I could draw on it again in June. It's an all in. I had it (the sum of money) three years ago when I drew £1 for the radio licence.' Radio rental 2s 3d. No pets. . . . It was quite clear he was in poverty. The outgoings mentioned amounted to about £1 2s to which must be added a few shillings for electricity and gas. He had no more than £1 4s a week left for his food, clothing, household sundries, and everything else. 'I don't have any breakfast. I mostly have boiled beef when I get meat, and with it I have carrots or parsnips or brussel sprouts and potatoes. Sometimes I make myself a pease pudding. Oh yes, I'm a great one for tea. I can't do less than a quarter lb every week. I drink more of that than I ought to. I used to like drink, I used to be terrible about drinking. [. . .] I can't afford it now.'

Mrs Docker was a widow with a single daughter. She had a retirement pension of £2 plus assistance of 5s. (Her daughter had a low wage and contributed £1. 10s to her keep). . . . 'The money goes like anything. It cost me £1 for my rations. . . . We can't afford luxuries. I just have a bit of toast for breakfast and a cup of tea. I can't afford eggs.' Her daughter came in from work for a midday meal and in the evening 'I usually have just a bit of toast and tea and then we might have a cup of cocoa before we go to bed.'[10]

Although these impressions were recorded two decades ago they may not differ drastically from the lives of those dependent on supplementary benefit today. Table 1 shows the proportions of expenditure made on certain items by pensioners at supplementary benefit level.

Table 1   Expenditure by pensioners at supplementary benefit level expressed as a percentage of total expenditure.

Goods and Services	Married couple	Single Female	Single Male
Food	46·7	44·7	40·9
Clothing	3·9	4·3	3·1
Fuel	14·0	21·4	17·6
Basic	7·5	8·0	7·0
Services	1·9	3·4	2·5
Durables	5·2	5·3	4·3
Entertainment	3·2	3·1	2·0
Alcohol and tobacco	8·3	2·2	15·2
Travel	3·5	2·1	2·2
Other	5·9	5·5	5·2

Source: Churchill, R. C. 'Expenditure patterns of retired persons at or immediately above their supplementary benefit level in October 1972', *Economic Trends*, December 1974, HMSO, Table B.

In none of the three cases shown did expenditure on food and fuel alone fall below 60 per cent of total expenditure (excluding housing). Moreover, the figures were recorded before the massive rise in fuel prices occasioned by the oil price increase and the higher relative increase in food prices which has characterised recent years. Nevertheless the comparable average expenditure on food and fuel made by the average household revealed by the latest Family Expenditure Survey was of the order of 27 per cent of total expenditure.[11] Undeniably, therefore, living on incomes at or around the supplementary benefit level imposes severe constraints on the expenditure, and consequently the lifestyle, of the elderly poor.

Table 2 shows the totals of elderly people claiming supplementary

Table 2   Persons in receipt of supplementary benefit (not including dependants).

	1948*	1951*	1961*	1971	1972	1973	1974	1975	1976
Over pensionable age	638	969	1295	1919	1910	1840	1810	1680	1687
Under pensionable age	373	493	549	990	840	720	720	810	1253
Total	1011	1462	1844	2909	2750	2560	2530	2490	2940

* National Assistance – became Supplementary Benefit in 1966.
Sources: Field F., *Poverty: The Facts*, Poverty Pamphlet 21, Child Poverty Action Group, 1975, Table 1.2; *Hansard, Written Answers*, 22 November 1976, Columns 1001–2; Supplementary Benefits Commission, *Annual Report 1976*, Cmnd 6910, HMSO, 1977 p. 20 and Table 2.1.

benefit for a number of years since 1948. In addition, some elderly claimants support another person of pensionable age on their supplementary pension. Thus, in 1975, there were a further 150,000 pensioners dependent on supplementary benefit. According to the Supplementary Benefits Commission 23 per cent of the just over 8 million pensioners were claiming supplementary benefit at the end of 1976 (their total numbers are shown in Table 2) – a figure which would be even higher were it not for the scheme introduced in 1974 to switch pensioners automatically to rent and rate rebates when they would be rendered better off by doing so. But, in addition, there are still a huge number of elderly people eligible for supplementary benefit but not claiming it. Table 3 shows the most recent official estimates of their numbers.

Thus, in 1975, a further three-quarters of a million of the elderly were living on incomes below the officially sanctioned poverty line, and failing to claim, according to the Supplementary Benefits Commission, an aver-

Table 3   Number of pensioners eligible for supplementary benefit but not claiming (000s).

	1972	1973	1974	1975
Claimants over pension age	760	690	450	590
Dependants over pension age	220	170	100	150
Total persons	980	860	550	740

Source: *Hansard, Written Answers*, 22 November 1976, columns 1001–2.

age of £2. 10p per week (though 30 per cent of potential elderly claimants would get less than £1 a week).

Why are so many of the elderly in poverty? The answer lies partly in the derivation of the income upon which the elderly rely in retirement and partly on their reluctance to apply for and accept means-tested help. The Ministry of Pensions survey[12] estimated the number of retirement pensioners without any source of income other than the retirement pension itself (and national assistance): one-fifth of retirement pensioners received income from no other source and this proportion increased dramatically to 44 per cent for all aged 85 and over (50 per cent in the case of single women). Had the original Beveridge scheme been fully implemented the lack of alternative resources would not have been serious: 'Any plan of Social Security worthy of its name . . . means providing, as an essential part of the plan, a pension on retirement from work which is enough for subsistence, even though the pensioner has no other resources whatever.'[13] But at no time since the retirement pension was introduced has its level exceeded that of supplementary benefit. Consequently any pensioner reliant on his pension alone is automatically beneath the State-defined subsistence level. Though retirement pensioners have shared the rewards of economic growth, there has been virtually no improvement in their relative position since 1948, when the standard rate of retirement pension as a proportion of average male manual earnings was 18.9 per cent for a single person and 30.5 per cent for a married couple. In 1975 the comparable figures were 19.5 per cent and 31.1 per cent respectively.

Moreover, while there has been a considerable growth in the number of occupational pensioners, the value of occupational pensions can easily be overestimated. In 1974, though the average occupational pension paid to men and women over retirement age was £8. 80 per week, 38 per cent of occupational pensions paid amounted to less than £4 a week[14] and in 1975 almost a third of occupational pensions were worth less than £3.[15] At the same time the importance of earnings as a source of income to the elderly has declined rapidly. One measure of this fall is the number of increments to the retirement pension earned in recent years (each increment requires the deferment of retirement for nine weeks). In 1955, 51.4 per cent of men retired with increments to their pension. By 1965 this figure had declined to 36.1 per cent and by 1975 it had plunged to 15 per cent.[16] Both the chances of receiving income from earnings and from an occupational pension were found to decline dramatically with age, and far fewer women than men received income from this source according to the Ministry of Pensions Survey. Table 4 summarises the results

Despite the smallness of some of the sums received from occupational pensions, they could make a significant difference to the likelihood of

Table 4 Proportions of pensioners with income from earnings and occupational pensions (percentages).

	Earnings %	Occupational Pension %
Married Couples		
All Ages	26	52
65–69	31	60
70–74	28	50
75–79	18	43
80–84	7	36
85 and over	5	39
Single Men		
All Ages	11	40
65–69	15	53
70–74	15	40
75–79	11	38
80–84	5	32
85 and over	1	32
Single Women		
All Ages	13	15
60–64	35	20
65–69	19	19
70–74	8	16
75–79	3	10
80–84	1	6
85 and over	–	6

Source: Ministry of Pensions and National Insurance, *Financial and other Circumstances of Retirement Pensioners*, HMSO, 1966, Table II.5.

poverty. Thus the incomes of 22 per cent of those with occupational pensions fell below national assistance level as compared with 60 per cent of retirement pensioners without an occupational pension. Not unsurprisingly, therefore, the chances of falling short of the national assistance level of income was found to be considerably higher amongst single women – 62 per cent of them had incomes below the national assistance scale as compared with 40 per cent of single men and 34 per cent of married couples. 'There was also a marked tendency for the proportion with incomes below the national assistance scale to rise with age. . . . This is particularly true of married couples for whom the proportion falling below was over twice as high among those aged 85 plus as for those in age group 65–69. . . .'[17]

If the likelihood of poverty increases with age, so too does the probability that the elderly person will view means-tested benefits as unwanted charity: 'I don't like the idea of going to ask for it. Your pension now, you have a right to that. . . . The supplementary benefit is not like something you're entitled to';[18] 'I'm not down to brass tack yet – I can still hold my head above water. I just have the pension. I don't want to go on to Social Security if I can help it – it's just like taking charity.'[19]

The reluctance to claim supplementary benefit is mirrored in the take-up figures for rent and rate rebates and rent allowances. The take-up of rent rebates (which are paid to council tenants) is much higher than for rent allowances (paid to tenants of private landlords). Official government estimates put the take-up of rent rebates at 70–75 per cent, rent allowances (for unfurnished tenancies) at 30–35 per cent and rate rebates at 70 per cent.[20] For furnished tenancies an earlier estimate for rent allowance take-up was 10 per cent.[21] But evidence from a number of local studies suggests that these estimates are, in any case, far too high.[22] Wherever the truth lies, take-up is certainly lowest in the forms of tenure most frequented by the elderly in the privately-rented sector.

The shortfall in take-up is not only a function of the reluctance of the elderly to claim. The problem is compounded by a widespread ignorance of social security and welfare benefits. This is illustrated by a small study of the take-up of extra needs payments (ENPs) amongst supplementary pensioners in Coventry. ENPs can be made by the Supplementary Benefits Commission to cover unforeseen items of expenditure which are not expected to be catered for out of the scale rates of supplementary benefit, for example the provision of new bedding or furnishing. Out of 96 supplementary pensioners successfully interviewed 80 'had apparently insufficient knowledge to allow them to make a reasonable application (including 35 with virtually no knowledge whatsoever)'. Twenty-five were ineligible for ENPs because of the savings limit applied, but 34 subsequently successfully applied for an ENP for some outstanding need.[23] Further evidence that the system of ENPs is not working and that the scale rates are inadequate is furnished by Butcher and Moore. They interviewed 120 pensioners in London and Bristol to discover what the £10 Christmas Bonus paid to pensioners in 1973 was spent on. They found that

Many old people had spent all their money on electricity or gas bills that were due for payment. Others paid for their winter coal delivery or had part of their money in coins for the meters. Under the heading of 'clothing' we included specific mention that people had bought warm underclothes, winter coats and new shoes. The fact that so many supplementary pensioners spent at least part of their money on fuel or clothing suggests that the system of discretionary grants and additions is not working. Pensioners either don't know of them, don't apply or don't succeed in their application. Altogether 86 per cent of the supplementary pensioners mentioned either fuel, clothing, rent arrears, bedding, curtains, towels or household repairs. All of these are items of expenditure that could have been met by the SBC.[24]

All this evidence adds up to a depressing picture of resources failing to meet needs even amongst those of the elderly who have applied for and are receiving means-tested benefits (often said to be designed to help those most in need). Whereas working families and households can dig into savings at times of difficulty, this is not a luxury afforded the elderly poor. Of the 1,679,000 supplementary pensioners at the end of 1975, 842,000 had no recorded capital assets and 352,000 had less than £200.[25] Not surprisingly

most of the old people living below the poverty line had not been able to add to their 'capital' since retirement. Mrs Sparrow was unusual in having bought a carpet on the HP: 'I kissed the carpet when it was paid for, and said it's mine.' Others had to make do with the furniture they had even if it did more or less fall to pieces, and put patches over the lino when it finally wore away in front of the sink or by the door. It was the same with clothing, which had to be secondhand – 'I go to jumble sales to keep myself clean and tidy'. Mrs Jasper, aged 72, said she wore the same clothes she had when she finished working many years before.[26]

The same lack of capital assets which prevents the replacement of worn-out furniture and clothing also inhibits the renovation or improvement of property. Moreover, just as the oldest are, in general, the poorest, so too do the oldest occupy the housing most in need of repair and rehabilitation. Table 5 shows how the age of dwelling and lack of amenities coincides with the age of the occupier, and the General Household Survey has

Table 5   Age of dwelling and amenities by age of head of household (1971).

Percentage of households in accommodation:	*Age of head of household*				
	25–44	*65–69*	*70–79*	*80 and over*	*All 65 and over*
built before 1919	24	37	39	42	39
lacking fixed bath	5	14	16	20	16
lacking internal w.c.	9	19	21	23	20
without central heating	57	73	77	82	76

Source: Wroe, D. C. L., 'The Elderly', *Social Trends*, No. 4, HMSO, 1973, Table VI.

reported that 'chronic sickness was more common amongst people living in housing built before 1919, in accommodation without central heating, without a fixed bath and without a lavatory; and in accommodation with a lavatory it was most common where the entrance to the lavatory was outside the building'.[27]

Old housing is also the most likely to lack insulation. Not surprisingly, despite the high proportion of expenditure devoted to fuel (see Table 1), a positive correlation has been discovered by one authoritative source between lack of income and low body temperature and hypothermia. An attempt to relate the incidence of a low body temperature or hypothermia to a number of social and economic factors revealed that 'the only significant factor to emerge is the receipt of supplementary pensions. This factor broadly distinguishes the poorest one-third of the sample and therefore strongly suggests that low income is associated with low body temperature'.[28] 'Fifty per cent of those with low body temperatures and seven out of nine hypothermic subjects were receiving supplementary pensions.'[29]

Heating, in winter, was a problem for almost all who did not live in centrally heated flats and for some who did where the heating broke down. Mrs Namier gave herself a treat only once a week. 'On a Sunday afternoon I'd have the electric fire on, but other times I couldn't afford to have the fire all the time.' Mrs Ayer said that 'you don't get much gas for your money. It doesn't last more than five minutes.' People like her with slot meters had to pay more per unit, but at least they did not have to face large quarterly bills which are not easy to save up for each week. For Mrs Tinberger the electricity bill is the biggest worry . . . 'I sit in misery sometimes at night when I'd like the light on.'[30]

Thus far attention has been concentrated on the elderly at or below the poverty line. But the point has long been established that the feeling of poverty need not be strictly related to absolute level of need. The decline of resources available after retirement is often so dramatic as to create the feeling of relative poverty even amongst those comparatively well off. For virtually everyone the onset of retirement marks a drastic drop in income. In 1976 the average weekly household income of a one-adult household aged over 65 was £25.70 compared with £52.06 for a similar adult aged under 65. For a single man over 65 the comparable figure was £27.24 in contrast to his younger counterpart's average income of £65.62 and a single woman over 60 averaged an income of £26.45 compared with £46.77 for a woman of working age. The average weekly income of elderly couples (i.e. with a head of household aged 65 or more) was £48.54 compared with £98.16 for couples headed by an adult under pensionable age. Of course, the entire drop in income may not occur at the time of retirement. It is well documented that the earnings of older workers tend to be lower than those of their younger colleagues, but this is often because older workers have already sought, or been forced to accept, lighter, less arduous and less well paid jobs in the prelude to retirement.[31]

In this way some of the inevitable fall in income may be taken early. Indeed, according to Peter Townsend's study of old people in East London 'the income of some people had already plunged before retirement'. His enquiries revealed that the incomes of the single and widowed elderly fell, on average, by 68 per cent, and by 52 per cent for married couples, when they retired. 'Amongst those interviewed a fall in income of over a half and often as much as two-thirds was certainly felt as poverty' and necessitated a curtailment of expenditure 'not only on such things as cakes, newspapers and periodicals, betting and drink, but also on meat, milk, fruit and clothing'.[32] More recently Paul Lewis has described the vulnerability of those formerly able to rely on their own resources to cope with old age. The value of their extra income from savings, employers' pensions and investments has dropped rapidly and the financial protection with which they had surrounded themselves is vanishing. . . . It is the twin blows of falling income and the loss of independence which makes these pensioners feel so poor.'[33] At the same time falling tax thresholds have trapped more of the elderly into paying tax despite the special protection afforded the elderly by the age allowance (formerly age exemption). Whereas an elderly single person paid no tax until his income reached 41.2 per cent of average earnings in 1958/59, by August 1976 this proportion had dropped to 25.7 per cent. For a married man a similar reduction occurred – from 66 per cent to 38.5 per cent.[34]

But if inflation has undermined the security of those who had previously cushioned themselves against the risks of retirement, its consequences have been felt even more keenly by those in the grips of poverty. The retirement pension is now increased, usually every twelve months, in line with prices or earnings (whichever is rising faster) but at recent rates of inflation even this much-needed protection seems scanty. Between July 1974 and November 1975 the Retail Price Index rose by 31.4 per cent. Despite an increase in April 1975, both the single persons and married couples pensions had lost over a tenth of their real value by the time they were uprated again in November 1975. Unlike those workers who are able to win wage increases, or work overtime or switch jobs or participate in a phoney re-grading exercise to increase their relative rewards and blunt inflation's cutting edge, the pensioner is virtually defenceless. Inflation at that level literally means a real decrease in spending power of over 10 per cent. Moreover, the effect is likely to be greatest on those least able to afford it.[35] The differential impact of inflation has been shown to discriminate against low income families who spend a higher proportion of their income on necessities like food and fuel which have risen in price particularly quickly. According to the Supplementary Benefits Commission between March 1974 and March 1977 the price of gas went up 50 per cent, paraffin and heating oil nearly 70 per cent, coal and coke

100 per cent, and electricity 125 per cent. The average 'real' increase in fuel prices (in relation to other prices) in the same period was of the order of ten per cent. This means that to maintain the same warmth as hitherto a pensioner would have to increase spending on heating by a tenth on average and considerably more if using an expensive form of fuel. As we have already seen, a single female supplementary pensioner was already devoting 66 per cent of her expenditure to food and fuel alone long before the energy crisis (see Table 1).

Conclusion

We have tried to suggest some of the reasons why 23 per cent of retirement pensioners find themselves living at the officially defined subsistence level and hundreds of thousands more below it. It has been suggested that occupational pensions have failed to make good the cessation of earnings and that the retirement pension has failed to shoulder the burden Beveridge originally intended for it.

It has been shown that the chances of poverty increase with old age, despite the introduction in September 1971 of an extra allowance of 25p to pensioners over age 80 (the sum has remained the same ever since) and of the old person's pension in November 1970 at a level well below that of the retirement pension. The chances of poverty are also greater for women. More than twice as many elderly women as men rely on supplementary benefit, partly reflecting the lack of occupational pensions held by women (and the non-transferability of those held by their husbands) and partly the fact that women tend to live longer. An additional factor may also be the onset of disability in old age. Out of the 730,000 people over age 65 estimated to be severely, very severely or appreciably handicapped by the Amelia Harris survey, 530,000 were women.[36] The risk of poverty is far greater for the sick and disabled than for others, and the likelihood of sickness and disability increases with age.

Despite the overwhelming evidence that hardship and need increase with age, the system of income maintenance has never been geared to providing more for the oldest. Instead the oldest have had increasingly to resort to the overworked safety net of supplementary benefit. Nor does the new pension system attempt to cope with this anomaly. Twenty years on from its introduction in April 1978, when it reaches maturity, we may still be wondering why.

Notes and references

1 D. COLE and J. UTTING (1962) *The Economic Circumstances of Old People*. Occasional Paper on Social Administration No. 4, Codicote Press, pp. 65 and 98.

2 P. TOWNSEND and D. WEDDERBURN (1965) *The Aged in the Welfare State*, Occasional Paper on Social Administration No. 14, Bell, pp. 124–5.

3 *Report of the Committee of Inquiry into the Impact of Rates on Households*, Cmnd 2582, HMSO, 1965.

4 B. ABEL-SMITH and P. TOWNSEND (1965) *The Poor and the Poorest*. Occasional Paper on Social Administration No. 17, Bell, p. 42.

5 Ministry of Pensions and National Insurance (1966) *Financial and other circumstances of Retirement Pensioners*, HMSO.

6 D. COLE and J. UTTING (1962) *The Economic Circumstances of Old People*, Occasional Paper on Social Administration No. 4, Codicote Press, p. 7.

7 It is not exactly the same because in 1966 a long-term rate of supplementary benefit was introduced for which all persons of pensionable age are automatically eligible – the long-term is higher than short-term rate.

8 A. B. ATKINSON (1974) 'Poverty and income inequality in Britain'. In Wedderburn (ed.) *Poverty Inequality and Class Structure*, Cambridge University Press, p. 48.

9 Department of Health and Social Security (1977) *Supplementary Benefits Handbook*, SBA Paper No. 2, HMSO, p. 26.

10 P. TOWNSEND (1963) *The Family Life of Old People*, Penguin, pp. 178–9.

11 Department of Employment (1977) *Family Expenditure Survey 1976*, HMSO, Table 1.

12 Ministry of Pensions and National Insurance (1966) *Financial and Other Circumstances of Retirement Pensions*, HMSO, Table 11.4.

13 *Social Insurance and Allied Services* (The Beveridge Report), Cmnd 6404, HMSO, 1942, para. 239, p. 92.

14 Letter from the late Brian O'Malley, Minister of State for Health and Social Security, to Dafydd Thomas MP, 15 March 1976.

15 Department of Health and Social Security Paper to Conference on Priorities for Social Security, 1977.

16 A. B. ATKINSON (1973) 'Poverty and Pensions – The Financial Needs of the Elderly', Table 2, in R. W. Canvin and N. G. Pearson (eds) *The Needs of the Elderly for Health and Welfare Services*, Exeter University; Department of Health and Social Security (1977) *Social Security Statistics 1975*, HMSO, Table 13.43.

17 A. B. ATKINSON (1969) *Poverty in Britain and the Reform of Social Security*, University of Cambridge DAE Occasional Paper 18, CUP, p. 49.

18 P. TOWNSEND (1963) *The Family Life of Old People*, Penguin, p. 184.

19 Age Concern (1974) *The Attitudes of the Retired and the Elderly*, p. 64.

20 *Hansard, Written Answers*, 13 April 1976, Columns 471–2.

21 *Hansard, Written Answers*, 18 February 1975, Column 304.

22 For a review of the evidence see R. LISTER (1974) 'Take up of means-tested benefits', *Poverty*, No. 18, Child Poverty Action Group, and R. LISTER (1976) 'Take up: the same old story', *Poverty*, No. 34, Summer 1976, Child Poverty Action Group.

23 B. GEARING and G. SHARP (1973) *Exceptional Needs Payments and the Elderly*, Coventry Community Development Project, Occasional Paper No. 10.

24 M. BUTCHER and P. MOORE (1974) 'The Christmas Bonus', *Poverty*, No. 28, Spring 1974, Child Poverty Action Group.

25 Department of Health and Social Security (1977) *Social Security Statistics 1975*, HMSO, Table 34.56.

26 L. SYSON and M. YOUNG (1974) 'Poverty in Bethnal Green'. In M. Young (ed.) *Poverty Report 1974*, Temple Smith, p. 113.

27 Office of Population Censuses and Surveys, Social Surveys Division (1973) *The General Household Survey, Introductory Report*, HMSO, p. 287.

28 R. H. FOX, P. M. WOODWARD, A. N. EXTON-SMITH, M. F. GREEN, D. V. DONNISON and M. H. WICKS (1973) 'Body temperatures in the elderly: a national study of physiological, social and environmental conditions', *British Medical Journal*, 27 January 1973, quoted in Memorandum from Age Concern, England, in *Paying for Fuel, National Consumer Council, Report No. 2*, HMSO, 1976, p. 184.

29 Memorandum from Age Concern, England, in *Paying for Fuel, National Consumer Council, Report No. 2*, HMSO, 1976, p. 184.

30 L. SYSON and M. YOUNG (1974) 'Poverty in Bethnal Green'. In M. Young (ed.) *Poverty Report 1974*. Temple Smith, p. 113.

31 See N. BOSANQUET and R. J. STEPHENS (1972) 'Another look at Low Pay', *Journal of Social Policy*, No. 3, July 1972.

32 P. TOWNSEND (1963) *The Family Life of Old People*, Penguin, pp. 176–8.

33 P. LEWIS (1975) 'Pensions, savings and inflation'. In Paul Lewis *et al. Inflation and Low Incomes*, Fabian Research Series 322, p. 18.

34 *Hansard, Written Answers*, 26 January 1977, Cols 649–50, and 7 April 1976, Col. 223.

35 See C. POND (1977) 'Inflation'. In Frances Williams (ed.) *Why the Poor Pay More*, Macmillan for the National Consumer Council.

36 AMELIA I. HARRIS *et al.* (1971) *Handicapped and Impaired in Great Britain Part 1*, Office of Population Censuses and Surveys, Social Surveys Division, HMSO, Table 10.

22 Mobility and the elderly: a community challenge

Jonathan Barker and Michael Bury

Variations in human experience across generations have received little systematic attention. The fashionable public debate on the so-called 'generation gap' has now subsided. Even during its popularity the emphasis was on the development and significance of 'youth culture'. Continuity and change among different generations over periods of time are, apparently, of less interest. Yet, if we are fully to understand the outlook and aspirations of older people in our communities, the influences over their life experiences need careful documentation. This is just as true for studying mobility as for any other area of life, for it is more than just a static question of the ability to move: it is also a matter of the purposes and activities being pursued. Without the ability and resources to be mobile, the individual cannot participate in social life; without an adequate range of social experiences, the ability to be mobile is undermined. There is a need, therefore, to sustain an analysis which grasps both the physical and material prerequisites for mobility and the structural and cultural determinants operating in a given place and at a given point in time.

Viewed historically, the opportunities for increased levels of mobility have expanded significantly, and for increasing proportions of the community, this century. For those who have grown up in the last twenty years, a relatively high rate of mobility has become commonplace. Holidays abroad, for example, are part of the experience of wide sections of the population. Young people following their football teams can be seen travelling to Paris or Milan, by plane or train, with hardly a second thought. School trips to the continent, at one time available only to children of the rich, are now widespread. For working-class populations brought up in the years following the turn of the century, only the first signs of this increased mobility and independence were emerging. As Robert Roberts describes so well in his book *The Classic Slum* (1971), the arrival of the tram and later the bus gave whole sections of working-class populations their first opportunity to travel regularly outside the immediate neighbourhood. It brought a sense of perspective largely absent from traditional city life, marking, as it did, the improving economic prospects of the mass of people during the period.

In this paper we explore the influences of social structure and culture on mobility in the modern context, as well as the apparently more clear-

Source: previously unpublished paper, written for this Reader.

cut medical and physical factors affecting individuals. We hope to show that mobility is rarely an end in itself, that it depends both on material resources and on complex social patterns which, though bound up in practice, are analytically separable. The implications for health and social policies and the supportive services are explored alongside the wider challenges to communities which such issues raise.

In focusing on mobility amongst the elderly, we necessarily draw on a particular conception of what the term 'elderly' means. We reject a 'problem-oriented' view of all retired persons. Like Johnson (1976) and Philipson (1977), we conceive of life after retirement as a process, as part and parcel of the life-cycle, involving different stages and different kinds of experience. We also accept Philipson's finding that the major proportion of retired persons at any one time are relatively free from difficulties. Retirement can be and often is a period of life to which increasing numbers of people look forward. The potential for a fulfilling retirement is by no means limited, given adequate material and social facilities. We therefore look for the development of enabling rather than helping structures. The question of mobility should be approached in a similar positive manner, so that while we inevitably highlight shortcomings and difficulties in being mobile, these are not approached in an absolute or negative way. Although we know, for example, that three-quarters of retired people live in households where there is no access to a private car (Norman 1977), the extension of access for many to free or cheap public transport through the development of bus passes has doubtless benefited large numbers of those over retirement age.

However, to place such matters in context, let us first consider in a little more detail the nature and extent of physical restrictions facing those over retirement age, and mobility-related health problems facing particular groups. From there we can then build up a more complete view.

Disability among the elderly

In 1971 the first national survey of disability in Britain was published (Harris 1971). It found that there were at least 3 million people with impairments in Britain, half of the men and two-thirds of the women being over 65. Only those over 16 years of age were included. The criteria for inclusion in the categories of impairment and handicap largely concerned locomotor restrictions and self-care measures, so that handicap arising from conditions such as deafness tended to be under-estimated. Nonetheless the survey provides a national picture of disability which, by and large, has been confirmed subsequently by local surveys (Brown and Bowl 1976).

By relating the figures of disabled persons to the populations from which they were drawn, we can estimate the degree of disability amongst the elderly in Britain. The Harris survey showed that of the total population over the age of 65 in Britain, 27 per cent suffer some form of impairment which interferes with daily life. Translated into actual numbers this means over 1,700,000 people. Just over 11 per cent of the over-65s are at least appreciably handicapped, that is 713,000 men and women. These are *minimum estimates*, because they are based on a survey of households. They therefore exclude those over the age of retirement in various forms of residential and long-term hospital care; clearly, those in such accommodation will tend to be the more dependent or vulnerable individuals, and, as Jolly and Wilkins (1978) have shown in a recent survey, the level of disability amongst such residents and patients is increasing.

However, if we concentrate, here, on the position at the community level and use the broad findings of the Harris survey as a backdrop, a number of implications for mobility amongst the elderly emerge. Studies which have investigated functional and medical characteristics of such populations have displayed the influences which affect self-care and mobility. Thus, Leeming and Ross (1967), in their survey of geriatric services in Bolton, found that whilst incontinence and severe mental deterioration are 'not very common' amongst the elderly at home, problems such as defective vision, arthritis, oedema, forgetfulness, pallor, unsteadiness, breathlessness and slowness of movement were particularly common amongst women and deafness particularly common amongst men. All of these symptoms will naturally affect a person's ability to maintain a mobile life. Deafness, for example, will make a person far more cautious in being alone outside the home and the authors make a special note of the 'high overall incidence of unsteadiness and slowness of movement', both of which, of course, relate crucially to mobility, in limiting the amount of exercise a person will undertake. The ability to tolerate sustained exertion, a necessary prerequisite for a fully mobile daily life, is thus also involved.

These problems, in themselves, go some way to explain the high rate of accidents affecting the elderly outside the home, particularly as pedestrians, as documented recently by Age Concern (Kellagher 1977). Even more important to our concern is the *perception* of such risks by the elderly themselves. Those who suffer from unsteadiness or slowness of movement are likely to be apprehensive about outings which involve negotiating busy roads. A range of perceived difficulties encountered in community settings, for example a fear, exacerbated by media stories, of assault, will also increase tendencies towards a restricted lifestyle.

So far we have discussed 'the elderly' in somewhat global terms. When we look a little more closely, we find, as predicted, that particular groups and sections of the elderly population have greater problems with mobility than others. Any arbitrary distinctions that we might make in this connection are equally open to question but nonetheless prove important to a clearer understanding of the ageing process. The first relates to levels of mobility, or the stages through which an elderly person passes. Evidence is accumulating to indicate that the over-75s face far more problems than the under-75s. Secondly, those with particularly severe health problems will also be at a higher risk of increased restriction.

If we return, briefly, to the national survey we can immediately find some broad evidence on disability and mobility problems amongst the over-75s. As was stated earlier, 27 per cent of all those over 65 were found to be suffering from some form of impairment. For those persons over 75 the figure rises to 37 per cent, while 17 per cent of those over that age are at least appreciably handicapped to such a degree that they need help in carrying out routine self-care tasks and might be able to go out only with difficulty. The position of women over 75 years of age is worse. Of all women aged 75 and over, just over 40 per cent are impaired and half of these at least appreciably. The consequences of such disability were documented by the survey in a number of ways, including an estimate of those who are housebound. We calculate, from the figures given, that at least 5 per cent of those over 65 in Britain are housebound and so, significantly, are 13 per cent of women over the age of 75.

As we have stated, there are a number of reasons to be cautious in the use of such figures, both from the point of view of their accuracy and from the point of view of their use to create categories which depict the elderly as a 'social problem'. This latter point is examined in more detail below. But there can be little doubt that, for some amongst the elderly, the position is even worse than these national figures portray. Bradfield and Leeming (1978), for example, found in a group practice in Manchester that in a total of 365 over-75s surveyed, 107 were housebound, 87 of whom were women. Nearly a half of those surveyed were assessed by health visitors as being unable to cross the road fast enough to negotiate traffic, and over a third were short of breath on walking a hundred yards on the level. In relating such problems to the nature of the community itself, the survey found that a third of the patients did not have any access to shops within a quarter of an hour's walk.

The older person in the community

At this point the need to bring the characteristics of particular communities into the discussion is highlighted. By looking at what features of the environment add to, or create, restrictions for the elderly person we will then be able to build a bridge to a consideration of the social and cultural conditions in their own right. Fundamental changes in the environment are, in the first instance, a consequence of corporate planning decisions and economic determinants. The economic and physical decay of many traditional city communities needs no reiteration here, though we are concerned to draw out the sociological implications of these changes. These are discussed below. Firstly, however, we need to explore a little more fully the specific environmental issues which relate to mobility.

Perhaps one of the best ways of doing this is to focus on a group of people who, by virtue of their ill health, are at risk of a loss of mobility. In a recent study of a group of 120 arthritic patients in Leeds a number of environmental factors were documented and are worthy of note here (Chamberlain *et al.* 1978). Those who were classified as handicapped were mainly elderly women, very few of whom lived in any form of adapted housing even though half of the houses concerned had two steps or more to reach street level. The authors state, 'One in three respondents could not walk beyond their gate (one in two of those aged 75 and over).' They continue, 'Nearly one in three respondents could not walk to their nearest shop in comfort, a quarter were unable to reach a park.'

The availability and accessibility of local facilities emerged as severely limited in the survey. The nature of shopping in modern towns itself constitutes a major difficulty. The development of shopping precincts presupposes a high degree of mobility, both in terms of being able to get to and from the town centre and of negotiating the variety of architectural barriers found there. Distance is not the only problem of access. Lifts and escalators in large stores may frighten those who are not fully agile. Uneven surfaces, steep slopes and difficulties with kerbs and steps are all barriers to considering such outings, particularly in poor weather. Many studies, for example the comprehensive Islington Access Project survey (Denby *et al.* 1978), show how many buildings, floors or shelves are inaccessible to slightly-disabled, 'stiff' or easily-tired people. Shops, especially the cheaper ones, have become bigger, involve more queuing, are less personal and are often further away. The local corner shop has, in many places, disappeared and large new estates often have few or none at all. Local chemist's shops are also a thing of the past in many inner-city areas, which tend to house concentrations of older people (e.g. North Southwark Community Development Group, 1975). This tendency to centralise facilities is also true of many local services, including the general practitioner; the move from the small 'lock-up' doctor's surgery to the new, big and efficient Health Centre, while offering many advantages for the diary-keeping, mobile young family, may render the doctor more unapproachable for older people and the experience of visiting him more confusing. In addition, the loss of familiar, old cottage hospitals (though often ill-equipped, grubby and depressing) in favour of brash new District General Hospitals may have added to the forbidding nature of a hospital stay.

The character of public transport is an important element in this picture. Yet the development of appropriate transport systems for those particularly at risk of being 'cut off' (e.g. the elderly disabled person with limited finance) has been virtually non-existent. In the Leeds study, the practical difficulties for those using public transport, especially buses, included the distance to bus-stops, getting on and off the vehicle and maintaining a hold when it accelerated. Frailer people also complain of long waits and of the anxiety involved in having to change buses. Recently there has been a move towards 'Dial-a-bus' schemes but, for many people, a taxi is the only available expedient, obviously one to which the majority will only resort in dire need such as for a visit to a husband in hospital.

Categories and labels

Is it realistic under these circumstances to talk about mobility and the elderly in simple functional terms and, for example, to define some people as 'housebound'? Those who are usually housebound are, as we have stated, a small minority of the population of retired people – less than one-third of people over 80 and only about 6 per cent of those aged 65 to 74.* It is important here to distinguish between people who are temporarily housebound and those who are housebound permanently. The use by Tunstall (1966) of the classification housebound only if someone had been confined to home for at least six months, lopped nearly a third off the numbers in this category. An alternative distinction might be between mobility from home to meet survival needs (to see a doctor, buy food, or collect a pension), for social contact or to satisfy emotional needs, or for recreation (to go to a park, have a holiday, or go to the pub). The problem with such distinctions is that, for instance, people living with relatives or even just with a spouse will have significantly different needs from those who live alone. In any case, some activities, like going to a Day Centre for lunch or going for a weekend with grandchildren, fall into

---

* Note that there are two ways of looking at these data. First, they show that most pensioners are mobile well beyond the bounds of their homes even though some may have chronic or acute conditions which limit their levels of activity. But it could be that houseboundness itself is often a short-term state which could itself increase morbidity and mortality rates. Data on 'survivors', that show that housebound people are most likely to be over 80, female, and of non-manual social class, ignore the fact that men and working-class people die earlier. In the age-group 70–79, there are more manual-class men and women who are housebound.

several categories. But some features of the experience of being temporarily housebound must be similar to those found by those who stay at home all the time, especially for the many old people who stay at home for most of the time through the winter months from October until May.

Perhaps there is yet another distinction to be made, between *routine mobility* and *exceptional mobility*. The difficulty with these abstract definitions is that it is the simpler ones that tend to be widely used and which encourage stereotyping. Social and health service categories combine with people's expectations and norms to ensure that one either fits the label 'housebound' or the label 'mobile', even though this is a travesty of reality given the range of abilities, biographies, health statuses, anxieties and aspirations to be found among older people.

Many of the barriers to mobility to which we have referred are daily overcome by some people. An individual's capacity to do so is determined not only by his health but also by his *commitment* to active life, his *horizons* and his readiness and ability to improvise or experiment. These factors, in turn, depend on past experiences of mobility and on the expectations that he and other people have of him. If his friends and relatives have moved away or have died, he may feel that he has less to go out for. Or he and his contemporaries may have succumbed to some image of what is 'appropriate behaviour' for someone of their age. Much will relate to his own *life biography* and to life-long desires, perhaps to avoid dependence or to be sociable; for a life spent making friends will be unlikely to stop at some arbitrary point. But absence of work or some other 'peg' on which to hang a friendship may lead to a more inward-looking life especially, for instance, for the shy person recently bereaved from a spouse who found it easier to make the necessary contacts. In the same way, the person who has rarely taken risks or who has experienced frequent frustration or anxiety (or accidents) is more likely to say, 'I'll stay at home: there I know that I can control my own world'. However, it has to be recognised that staying at home all day is a *deviant* thing for people to do both in terms of their own life norms and in terms of community norms at any one time. It is only 'not deviant' in terms of a stereotype which speaks of a person who is old, non-contributing, ill, and in receipt of care. The moment someone decides, in the face of whatever affliction or anxiety, to stay at home most of the time, except when taken out by someone else, he can expect all the other constituent labels in the stereotype to be applied to him.

For mobility is the key to *active access* to community, neighbourhood or friendship involvement. To be housebound, even if relatively active and healthy, is to be seen as a passive or receiving member of the community. So, houseboundness tends to be a state of non-participant dependence, while mobility means self-sufficiency and engagement.

Staying at home

What, then, happens to people when they retreat within their own thresholds? It may be that the retreat itself, by rendering people dependent and deviant, leaves them both diminished in self-respect and stigmatised by others. Add to this the loneliness that is a frequent concomitant of the isolation involved, and the result is a recipe for low morale or depression. as illustrated, for younger people, by Brown's work on young mothers bound to the home by infant children (Brown *et al.* 1975).* Similarly, Tunstall shows that the worst aspects of being housebound seem to be the loss of activities such as walking in the fresh air, going to visit people and shopping rather than the loss of mobility itself. And Blau (1973) points out that numerous studies (e.g. Maddox 1963; Havighurst *et al.* 1963) in a variety of communities and in institutions for old people 'report that activity . . . and sociability . . . are the most stable and consistent correlates of high morale in old age' and that the pattern that she calls 'retreatism' (analogous to what Cumming and Henry (1961) describe as 'disengagement') is therefore not normal, typical, inevitable, desirable or healthy. People who continue to work after retirement maintain higher morale (see Streib 1956) and there is evidence from the U.S.A. (Spiegelman 1966) that disability and other factors which could lead to immobility and houseboundness do not increase so rapidly with age among people who are in work as in the general population of comparable age.

With low morale and depression comes a reduced belief in one's own capacity to break free of illness or other constraints and, as horizons are further reduced, we can postulate that a downward spiral can begin. Ironically, these are the conditions for the 'careless mishaps' that arise in people's own homes and which further reduce self-confidence and the ability to cope on one's own. Cooking accidents, burnt meals, falls on the stairs or in the bath, as well as having a less tidy or clean home, are all things that can give rise to feelings of 'shame', including being ashamed to let other people into the home to see 'the state I've got myself into'.

At the same time, the inertia which follows feelings of depression and such home accidents may lead to other medical problems that derive from inactivity. And these ailments will often be compounded by poverty – it is expensive to keep a house heated all day, something that people who go

* Several studies have failed to find people who admit to extensive loneliness even when often isolated. Furthermore, home-help or meals-on-wheels organisers attest to the evidence, found by Tunstall, that most housebound people do see relatives frequently. They are somewhat less likely to live alone than other old people and are more likely to be widowed or single. Nearly half the housebound and bedfast lived with a married daughter or unmarried child. Similarly, Townsend *et al.* (1968) show that, according to a national British survey, 80 per cent of housebound older women have living children and only 7 per cent admit to having seen no child in the last week.

out do not need to do. Difficulty in reaching a doctor or a belief in the incurability of even minor ailments may exacerbate a worsening situation.

What, then, triggers someone to become 'housebound'? It is clear that absolute incapacity limits a relatively small group. In Tunstall's four-area study, many housebound people did their own housework and were active around the house and garden. Other studies show that they may play an important role as babysitter for grandchildren with whom they live. The precipitating health factor for half of them was arthritis. Snellgrove's Luton study (1963), involving medical assessment, found that the most common complaint among the housebound was osteo-arthritis (40%), followed by coronary disease, hypertension, rheumatoid arthritis, bronchitis, mental conditions and stroke, and that half of the household had three or more of these complaints. But, in answer to the question, we must emphasize the importance of the notion of *control* over the familiar, set against a fear of images of greater unfamiliarity, distance and speed in the outside world. Someone in his seventies is usually acutely aware of how an 'old person' is expected to behave; yet many do not see themselves as belonging to the reference group 'old' until a *turning point* is reached.

The turning point may take the form of something as dramatic as the death of a wife, an experience with deep emotional significance compounded by practical implications. It may relate to a more gradual realization that few contemporaries are still alive. The disappearance of a familiar face or distant acquaintance in the locality, or even an advertisement hoarding designed to elicit sympathy and money for old people, could draw someone's attention to his own '*old identity*'. An accident, the closure of a shop, rowdy children in the street or offspring moving away or appearing rejecting – all these lesser *life events* could trigger the decision to stay at home. So, indeed, could preventive health education material pointing to the danger of fractured femurs in the elderly. Research led one of us to meet a sprightly lady in her mid-80s who never goes out because the nearby Oxford Street in London's West End, an extreme example of hustle and bustle, terrified her, as did the people who lived around, 'not my kind' (Barker 1978).

Many people who come out of hospital, even having spent time there for relatively minor complaints which in themselves need not affect mobility or threaten life, say things like 'The experience has taken years off my life. I'm an old man now. I've got to be careful . . . I mustn't go out any more or do anything too risky or demanding.' Other people make prognostic remarks such as 'I'm never going to be able to do things like I did before. I'll have to ask people to come and look after me now' (Barker 1976). Being re-housed, falling off a bus, tripping on a kerb or being laughed at by younger people may also trigger the decision to 'stay home and keep safe'. Dame Eileen Younghusband (1977) speaks resentfully of the way shop assistants 'inaccurately diagnose my tendency to drop the change as being due to senility of the brain rather than arthritis of the fingers'. Less resolute people could be put off shopping by such an experience. This concept of the ageing affect of life events is further illustrated among young arthritics. Research has shown that premature ageing fears accompany chronic illness and could even become self-fulfilling (Bury 1978).

Most people are afraid of death. Many people are perhaps even more alarmed by the prospect of separation. But some people view the prospect of dependency or powerlessness or bed-fast, even mind-fast illness with an even greater abhorrence. For everyone in their 70s or 80s, such prospects must seem very real and imminent. From our different backgrounds, we react according to our own experiences, expectations, personalities and circumstances. But protectiveness of oneself, albeit often self-defeating, may be the most attractive option. People will tend to react to protect whichever goal they most value, be it health, independence, control, dignity or life, and will sometimes do so even though fully aware that the protection of one goal may conflict with others.

Policy and education

In this situation we are presented with a dilemma when it comes to policy implications, especially in relation to the planning of health education programmes. This dilemma is well summed up by Beattie (1977) in a discussion on falls in the home:

The proposal by Jacobson (1974) seems plausible; that is that (whatever biophysical liability to fall may be present in the aged person) the degree of risk of a fall is increased insofar as he 'cannot accept the limitations of ageing and denies his inability to perform everyday activities as well as before'. In the light of this suggestion, a topic that should be given high priority in education programmes for the elderly is 'ageing' itself; that is, the changing capabilities of the human organism in later years of life, the limits of biological fitness and the need for psychological and social readjustment. The outcome that could be anticipated from such a programme would be an improvement in the 'health preserving' behaviour of the elderly and a more ready assumption of the 'at risk' role. This would have two implications. The first is that elderly people would be less 'stoic' in the face of disability and less 'unwisely sparing of medical services' and a fuller use of health professionals and a more rational compliance with their recommendations should ensue. The second is that elderly individuals and their relatives could review the habits, routines and schedules of everyday life of the old person so as to modify behaviour patterns in the interests of risk reduction.

The emphasis in this paper is that the 'stoicism', the unwillingness to comply and the readiness to take risks may be important keys to mobility and to the protection of such valued characteristics as dignity, control and independence, and that policy needs to take these goals seriously.

Other policy implications are demonstrated by Bytheway (1978). He shows that older people are more likely to be pedestrians and they tend to be more law-abiding than other pedestrians. He turns the familiar arguments on their heads by showing that traffic accidents involving the elderly are more often than not attributable to careless driving and speed and to road regulations and designs that give greater priority to cars than to pedestrians. He comments, 'If one thinks of the driver as the person responsible for the machine which causes the injury, then these figures [which show that older people and especially the over-80s, account for an apparently disproportionate number of pedestrian casualties] are highly relevant to the politics of age. . . .' And he concludes, 'Pavements, as much as roads, are the arteries of our cities and towns. Users of pavements are helping to keep cities and towns alive as much as the container lorry, full of newly-imported food. It is not just in "their" interests that we should strive to make older people feel safer when away from their homes.'

Another set of policy implications is illustrated by Wolff (1976). He points to the way that engineering and design are geared for the convenience of the young affluent consumer and of industry. But he shows how the direction of a little engineering ingenuity towards the creation of *enabling* facilities for the disabled or elderly can reap rewards. He cites the examples of a simple gadget that enables a grandmother to pour her tea, thus making it possible for her to retain a 'giver' or 'host' role with her relatives and friends, and of a device that could enable people to pump themselves gently out of a chair thus rendering them mobile within the home. He points out that school workshops have all the equipment to make such products and that changes in school curricula in this and other ways could make independent and mobile life more readily available to older people. He also calls for more 'Unexciting Research into Necessary Equipment'.

Conclusions

As we have attempted to show, older people have very particular transport and mobility characteristics. For example, 86.5 per cent of the population over 65 do not hold a driving licence and 76 per cent do not live in car-owning households. Bytheway (1978) further shows that over half of all road accidents casualties who were drivers were males aged under 30, while none were females or males over 80! So, as Norman (1977) remarks, 'elderly people are far more dependent on their feet for getting to the shops or reaching public transport than the rest of the population'. To ensure that everyone feels secure in going out and being mobile for whatever reason, social policies have to take these factors into account. Almost anyone can be discouraged from being mobile by being frequently at risk of being run over by a car, tripping on dangerous paving stones or being unable to afford fares. As Norman says,

Obstacles to mobility such as congested or uneven pavements, high kerbs, fast traffic, traffic lights with no pedestrian phase, subways and footbridges become important to you if you are laden down . . . pushing a pram, lame from an injury, pregnant or ill. . . . Elderly pedestrians may suffer from any of these temporary disabilities (apart from being pregnant) but a considerable proportion will also suffer some degree of chronic disablement which makes walking permanently slow and painful and therefore heightens the severity and danger of the obstacles which they meet.

It is to minimize the risk of becoming 'voluntarily' limited to the bounds of their home that is the responsibility of policy-makers – especially those who also speak of the need, albeit sometimes for somewhat spurious economic reasons, to keep older people in the community, physically and socially active (e.g. *Priorities for Health and Personal Social Services – A Consultative Document*, DHSS 1976). The functions of social policy here should be to enable people confidently to live the kind of life they choose with a minimum of stigmatizing or disabling obstacles. We have sought to show that mobility is more than a purely mechanical function and depends on an enabling environment, the ability to continue to achieve personal goals and the development of social life in the community.

References

BARKER, J. (1976) 'Going into Hospital: a result or contributory cause of ageing'? Paper to Conference of British Society of Social and Behavioural Gerontology.

BARKER, J. (1978) 'The Relationship of Informal Care and Formal Social Services: who helps people cope with social and health problems in old age'? In *Teamwork*, London: Personal Social Services Council; New York: Syracuse University Press.

BEATTIE, A. (1977) 'The Planning of Preventive Programmes for the Elderly'. M.Med.Sci. Dissertation, Department of Community Medicine, University of Nottingham.

BLAU, Z. S. (1973) *Old Age in a Changing Society: New Viewpoints*. New York: Franklin Watts.

BRADFIELD, C. J. and LEEMING, J. T. (1978) Personal communication.

BROWN, G. W., NI BHRÓLCHÁIN, M. and HARRIS, T. (1975) 'Social class and psychiatric disturbance among women in an urban population', *Sociology*, 9, 2, 225–54.

BROWN, M. J. and BOWL, R. (1976) *Study of Local Authority Chronic Sick and Disabled Persons Surveys*. Social Service Unit, Birmingham University.

BURY, M. (1978) 'Living with a Chronic Illness'. Paper to London Medical Sociology Group.

BYTHEWAY, W. R. (1978) 'Accidents and Accidents', *New Age Concern Today* (forthcoming).

CHAMBERLAIN, M. A., BUCHANAN, J. and HANKS, H. (1978) *Mobility of the Arthritic in an Urban Environment* (forthcoming).

CUMMING, E. and HENRY, W. D. (1961) *Growing Old – The Process of Disengagement*. New York: Basic Books.

DENBY, E., TAYLOR, P. and PEACH, M. (1978) *Guides 1–5*, Islington Access Project. Department of Health and Social Security (1976) *Priorities for Health and Personal Social Services – A Consultative Document*. London: HMSO.

HARRIS, A. I. (1971) *Handicapped and Impaired in Great Britain*. London: HMSO.

HAVIGHURST, R. J., NEUGARTEN, B. L. and TOBIN, S. S. (1963) 'Disengagement, Personality, and Life Satisfaction in the Later Years'. In P. F. Hansen (ed.) *Proceedings of the 6th International Congress of Gerontology*. Copenhagen: Munksgaard.

JACOBSON, S. B. (1974) 'Accidents in the aged: a psychological and psychiatric viewpoint', *New York State Journal of Medicine*, 74.2417.

JOLLY, D. J. and WILKINS, D. (1978) *A Comparative Study of Behavioural Problems in Hospital and Residential Care for the Elderly* (forthcoming).

JOHNSON, M. L. (1976) 'That was your life: a biographical approach to later life'. In J. M. A. Munnichs and W. J. A. van den Heuval (eds.) *Dependency or Interdependency in Old Age*. The Hague: Nijhoff (Chapter 14 in this Reader).

KELLAGHER, L. (1977) *Profiles of the Elderly 5: Accidents*. London: Age Concern.

LEEMING, J. T. and ROSS, A. T. (1967) *A Survey of Geriatric Services*. Bolton County Borough, The Medical Officer, August 1967.

MADDOX, G. W. (1963) 'Activity and morale: a longitudinal study of selected elderly subjects', *Social Forces*, XLII.

NORMAN, A. (1977) *Transport and the Elderly*. London: NCCOP.

North Southwark Community Development Group (1975) *Campaign for Chemists*.

PHILIPSON, C. (1977) *The Emergence of Retirement*. Department of Sociology, University of Durham.

ROBERTS, R. (1971) *The Classic Slum*. First published by University of Manchester Press, Manchester. Reprinted 1973 in Pelican Books, Harmondsworth.

SNELLGROVE, D. R. (1963) *Elderly Housebound*. Luton: White Crescent Press.

SPIEGELMAN, M. (1966) *Significant Mortality and Morbidity Trends in the U.S. since 1900*. Bryn Mawr, Pa.: The American College of Underwriters.

STREIB, G. F. (1956) 'Morale of the retired', *Social Problems*, III, 270–6.

TOWNSEND, P. (1968) 'The Structure of the Family'. In *Old People in Three Industrial Societies*, eds E. Shanas, P. Townsend, D. Wedderburn, H. Friis, P. Milhøj, and J. Stenhower. New York: Atherton Press; London: Routledge & Kegan Paul.

TUNSTALL, J. (1966) *Old and Alone*. London: Routledge & Kegan Paul.
WOLFF, H. (1976) 'Practical Design for the Elderly'. In *Old Age Today and Tomorrow*, Report of Proceedings of Symposium, British Society for the Advancement of Science, London.
YOUNGHUSBAND, E. (1977) 'Is old age a good age?' *Community Care*, 7 December 1977.

23 Role of day hospital care

J. C. Brocklehurst

Geriatric medicine initiated an early form of progressive patient care in hospital – through acute admission ward, to rehabilitation ward, and continuing care ward. The geriatric day hospital is a logical extension of this system and forms a bridge between the hospital and the community. The ever-increasing numbers and proportion of elderly people, particularly the very old, in our society inevitably increase the incidence of disabling disease. The provision of day care for the treatment and support of elderly disabled people has been an attempt, attended with a good deal of success, to prevent the admission to hospital of more and more of these old people.

Day care for the elderly includes a wide variety of social and hospital provisions which must be clearly distinguished. Social day care is provided either by local authorities or by voluntary organizations (for example, old people's welfare committees) – or occasionally by thoughtful employers. Social day care itself offers a whole spectrum of facilities.[1] Anderson's definition of social day care is as follows: 'Clubs and social centres exist for all old people, to increase social contact and to give scope and facilities for new pursuits in retirement.'

Several main types of day care are now available. Day care centres, most usually instituted by local authorities, provide a substantial amount of personal care to at least a small proportion of clients. Referral is usually through general practitioners or social workers. There are a wide range of services, including bathing, chiropody, meals, and provision of low priced foods. Psychogeriatric day care centres are similar to day care centres but require a greater degree of supervision. Their purpose is more that of a crèche than a club. Since it is now the Department of Health and Social Security's policy to support old people suffering from dementia, who are neither physically handicapped nor pose behavioural problems, in the community, the importance of psychogeriatric day care centres is likely to increase.[2]

Both these types of social day centres may be provided by local authorities under the 1968 Health Services and Public Health Act and both require transport to bring the clients to them.

Social centres or social clubs come in many varieties; some are open seven days a week, others only one half-day a fortnight. They usually have a regular membership and are often organized by the retired people

Source: M. WARE (ed.) (1974) *Medicine in Old Age*. London: British Medical Association, pp. 57–62.

themselves. Shelters (rest centre or drop-in) may be provided by local communities or employers and serve simply as a communal meeting place which elderly people may use as they wish.

Communal rooms in sheltered housing and other housing schemes clearly offer a great opportunity for day care, in which both residents in the sheltered housing and other people living in the area may join together. A most important development for the future will be the provision of a restaurant so that residents in sheltered housing may have at least one communal cooked meal a day, where they may be joined by elderly people from the local community.

Lunch clubs are an important and desirable alternative to meals-on-wheels. Work centres may be provided either by the local authority, commercial organizations, or voluntary bodies. Essentially, retired people come here to engage in productive work for which they are paid. This has, of course, very important social and emotional advantages.

These various types of social day care available at present must be clearly distinguished from the geriatric day hospital.

Day hospitals are part of the hospital service and are generally situated within a district general hospital in close relationship to the geriatric rehabilitation department. In many cases, day hospital and geriatric rehabilitation department share the same premises and facilities. This is a particularly desirable concept, which allows patients who have been undergoing rehabilitation to return to their homes and yet have the security of a continuing contact with the hospital and so with their therapists, until they are firmly settled back at home. Though day hospitals have many uses other than this, this is one of the most important, and one which guards against waste of hospital resources.

The concept of a geriatric day hospital must now be extended to include the psychogeriatric day hospital. Though not many are so far available it is part of the clearly defined policy of the Department of Health and Social Security to provide two places per one thousand people over 65 for geriatric day hospital care and an additional two places per one thousand people over 65 for psychogeriatric day hospital care. The psychogeriatric day hospital may be established adjoining the geriatric day hospital and share several facilities. Alternatively, and hitherto more commonly, it may be set up within a psychiatric hospital, though in future, of course, these will be replaced. A further possibility is that the psychogeriatric day hospital may be situated within the community hospital or general-practitioner hospital, particularly in rural areas.

Geriatric day hospitals first developed from occupational therapy departments. The first purpose-built geriatric day hospital was opened in Oxford at Cowley Road Hospital, and this has served as the model for subsequent development. The day hospital at Oxford was opened in 1958 and by the end of 1970 there were 120 geriatric day hospitals in the U.K. Now most geriatric departments include a day hospital, and increasingly purpose-built day hospitals are superseding adaptations of various other hospital premises.

Elderly patients come to a day hospital for one of four main reasons: rehabilitation; maintenance treatment; medical or nursing investigation; or social care.

Rehabilitation is an important part of geriatric practice since so often the problem is one of physical disability: there is prospect of improvement, though often not of recovery. It is helpful to see rehabilitation as a finite process to which there is usually an end – reached when the patient achieves his maximum degree of independence.

Maintenance treatment is important in old age since having once achieved maximum independence many elderly people will deteriorate slowly (and sometimes quite rapidly) once they are cut off from the stimulus of the geriatric rehabilitation department. Much important and laborious work can thereby be undone, particularly if relatives are over-protective or the old person poorly motivated. Once-weekly day hospital attendance perhaps for an indefinite period often ensures that the state of independence achieved is maintained.

Medical and nursing procedures in the day hospital form a very variable part of current geriatric practice. In a few departments great stress is laid on these;[3] in most some use is made of the day hospital for procedures such as sternal marrow punctures, the supervision and treatment of faecal incontinence, glucose tolerance tests, etc. On the other hand, obviously it is not appropriate to bring elderly people up to a day hospital simply to carry out procedures which might equally well be done by the district nurse or the family doctor in the patient's home.

The distinction between social day care and the geriatric day hospital has already been emphasized, but a few elderly people are so physically disabled as to be unsuitable for social day centres and yet have needs for companionship and relief of their isolation. Its nursing care makes the geriatric day hospital the appropriate place for such patients. In some day hospitals severely disabled younger patients are brought for this purpose. Another, if uncommon, aspect of social care is when a disabled elderly patient may be discharged home from hospital and looked after at night and at the weekend, but when the relative on whom he depends has to work. Discharge may then be possible only if day hospital attendance can be arranged.

In a national survey of day hospitals Brocklehurst[4] found that consultant geriatricians placed most importance on physical rehabilitation and physical maintenance (89% and 78%, respectively, of respondents). Half laid stress on the social care of physically disabled people as important, 36 per cent on medical or nursing procedures, and 21 per cent on the social care of mentally confused old people. In a more detailed survey of five day hospitals the numbers of patients actually attending for these various purposes were as follows: rehabilitation 27 per cent, physical maintenance 42 per cent, social reason 26 per cent, and other 5 per cent.

This survey also noted the source of referral of 465 day hospital patients as follows: in-patient geriatric ward 32 per cent, medical ward 7 per cent, other wards 2 per cent, geriatric outpatient consultative clinic 29 per cent, domiciliary or assessment visit 13 per cent, and by direct negotiation with the general practitioner 17 per cent. Most people attending the day hospitals surveyed were aged between 75 and 84 and the major diagnostic categories were stroke (30%) and arthritis (26%).

The day hospital should be regarded as a ward within the hospital – in fact, Andrews has suggested that it should be called a day ward rather than a day hospital. This emphasizes that staffing should be on similar levels of that of an inpatient ward and that management should be along similar lines. The day hospital is generally in charge of the consultant geriatrician and consists of three main departments – nursing, physiotherapy, and occupational therapy – with a smaller involvement of speech therapists, social workers, volunteers, and administrators. A doctor must attend daily to maintain records and to initiate investigation and treatment of patients. There should also be a case conference of the whole medical, social and therapeutic team at least once weekly to review the patients' progress. To be dynamic a day hospital must be continually discharging and accepting new patients and there should never be a waiting list. It is a great advantage if there are clear pathways between the day hospital and the various social day care facilities so that those who no longer need the therapeutic aspect of day care may continue to enjoy its social benefit.

The advantages of the geriatric day hospital lie first in allowing the treatment of many elderly people without hospital admission, particularly when outpatient attendance at a physiotherapy department would be unsuitable. The need is for a continuing therapeutic environment where the pace is slower but activity continues throughout most of the day. The day hospital also allows the earlier discharge of patients and their subsequent supervision until they are safely settled at home. Another advantage is that the hours are attractive to staff and recruitment of suitable staff is often easier than to the inpatient wards.

Day hospitals are not without their problems. Probably the greatest of these lies in the provision of ambulance transport. It is exceptional for any patient needing day hospital treatment to be able to come independently. A few can be brought by relatives in cars, and in the occasional area taxis are hired for this purpose, but generally day hospitals must depend on the ambulance service for the delivery and returning home of their patient. This requires special and appropriate transport – for example, a vehicle with eight to ten seats with a hydraulic or other lift, good visibility for the passengers, safe seating, and good heating. Such a vehicle is likely to take between an hour and an hour and a half to collect its complement of patients and so those collected first may well spend upwards of an hour in the vehicle. For most of them this is of no hardship provided that the vehicle is appropriate, since it is likely to be the only time that they get out of their own homes.

It is essential that ambulances should bring patients to the day hospital and take them home according to a pre-arranged time-table and that vehicles are not used which are apt to be diverted for other purposes. The whole professional team in the day hospital awaits the arrival of the patients and if ambulance services are erratic there is an enormous waste of these professional resources. It is equally frustrating for the old person sitting for two or three hours awaiting the ambulance's arrival. Furthermore, patients coming to day hospitals are often relying on this as their only source of food that day, and perhaps of heating and other care. If the ambulance does not collect them they may suffer great hardship, as was shown in a survey of the effect of industrial action by the ambulance service on day hospital patients.[5]

Finally, what of the future? The day hospital is now firmly established and in due course every geriatric department will have one as an essential part of its service. There may be an increase of specialization within day hospitals, some developing more as day wards for medical and nursing treatment, others becoming the local stroke rehabilitation unit or orthopaedic rehabilitation unit for elderly people. Possibly some smaller day hospitals may be set up in association with community hospitals, where the emphasis will be on maintenance and social treatment. The day hospital serves as an excellent focus bringing together community medical care (the general-practitioner team) and the geriatric hospital team. The day hospital is in many ways a shop window for the geriatric service, and undoubtedly a good one adds immeasurably to the morale of the whole geriatric department.

References

1 ANDERSON, D. C. (1972) *Report on Leisure and Day Care Facilities for the Old.* London: Age Concern.
2 DAVIDGE, J. L. (1972) in *The Elderly Mind.* London: British Hospital Journal/ Hospital International.

3 ANDREWS, J., FAIRLEY, A. and HYLAND, M. (1970) *Journal of the American Geriatrics Society*, *18*, 378.

4 BROCKLEHURST, J. C. (1970) *The Geriatric Day Hospital*. London: King Edward's Hospital Fund for London.

5 PRINSLEY, D. N. (1971) *British Medical Journal*, *3*, 170.

24 Homes for old people: toward a positive environment

Alan Lipman and Robert Slater

Since the National Assistance Act was promulgated in 1948, local (public) authority Homes for old people in England and Wales have been planned with the specific intention of providing hotel-like service for residents. Seeking to abolish workhouses, the legislators envisaged substituting accommodation modeled on residential hotels:

The workhouse is doomed. Instead, local authorities are busy planning and opening small, comfortable Homes where old people, many of them lonely, can live pleasantly and with dignity. The old 'master and inmate' relationship is being replaced by one more nearly approaching that of an hotel manager and his guests (Ministry of Health 1950).

Dignity appears to have resided in being a guest for whom day-to-day services, often of an intimate nature, are provided by others.

We believe the hotel model to be inappropriate. Even if Homes have functioned in this manner, and the evidence suggests overwhelmingly that they have not (Meacher 1972; Townsend 1962), in our view dependency is inherent in the notion. In particular, it fails to take into account the pressures militating against independence in prevailing staff/resident relationships. It ignores the asymmetric distribution of power in these relationships. It discounts the discrepancies between the parties' authority-based relationships and the contractual, the voluntary, manager/guest relationship posited by the model. In addition, by proposing a reliance on hotel-like personnel, the notion tends to entrench dependency. It subverts the expression of such potential for self-help and mutual assistance as might exist among residents. The proposals described in this paper seek to exploit such potentialities. Rather than viewing residents as passive recipients of daily services, we have assumed that, with the aid of supportive physical settings, they can be induced to exercise the self-maintenance skills acquired throughout their lives. That is, we have sought to foster their independence.

In so doing, we have interpreted the somewhat nebulous concept of independence as meaning 'not contingent on . . . the action of others' (Onions 1972). Independence has been viewed as an ideal state in which residents are not bound or subject to staff for conducting the four broad

Source: *The Gerontologist*, 1977, *17*, 2, pp. 146–56.

categories of customary activity we have observed in some thirty-seven Homes: the clusters of daily activities that surround sleeping, toileting and bathing, preparing and eating food, and socializing.

Resident independency and institutional life

Attempts to implement this stance give rise to congregate living conditions. They call for forms of grouped accommodation, if only in consequence of the anticipated mutual help furnished by fellow residents which we consider desirable. And this is reinforced by the necessity, we contend, for maintaining at least the present standards of care afforded to residents by 'domestic' and 'care attendant' staff (Personal Social Service Council 1975).

Here we are in a dilemma. Both these circumstances – group living and the presence of staff – are conducive to the dependent situations we have noted (Lipman 1970; Slater 1968) and which have been attributed to the qualities of 'total institutionality' of Homes (Bennett and Nahemow 1965; Meacher 1972). A preferred resolution of the dilemma probably lies in efforts to maintain the independence of 'at risk' old people before they qualify for admittance to Homes. It lies in social policies that obviate the grounds for residential care (Meacher 1972; Townsend 1962; Tunstall 1966). Action of this nature has been urged, usually in the form of domiciliary services (Committee on Local Authority and Allied Personal Services 1968; Townsend 1962). To date, however, such services as exist have left the demand for residential care unabated (Age Concern 1973; Townsend 1975). The quandary remains. At best, and this is the purpose of our proposals, efforts can be made to remove some of the factors that facilitate institutional dependency.

Thus, given the current emphasis in social policy, and forecasts of its persistence, we have, perforce, focused on the Homes. Further, given the similar expectation of a continued shortage of trained staff (Personal Social Service Council 1975), our efforts have tended to center on physical design. We have sought to draw on residents' resources, to enhance their opportunities for self-sufficiency, and to minimize staff intervention. On the basis, principally, of our participant observation studies (Harris, Lipman and Slater 1977), attention has been directed to the following areas of accommodation:

1 The current provision of so-called bedsitting rooms (for individual or multiple occupancy) that are insufficiently large to be used as such and the layouts of which (e.g. positions of doors, windows, and built-in fittings) prohibit a variety of furniture arrangements.

2 Toilet and bathroom accommodation arranged in centralized blocks (i.e. communally).
3 Centralized dining rooms and food preparation areas to which access is not customarily available to residents.
4 Lengthy internal corridors.
5 Doors opening directly into bedrooms (i.e. unscreened personal accommodation).

Each of these points is indicated by the appropriate numeral on a ground floor plan of one of the Homes we studied (Figure 1).

Social and organizational issues

In addition to this commitment to resident independency, our research experiences have led to three other, related, value orientations. Expressed, as they are, as articles of faith, these comprise the beliefs:

(a) that activity, social and physical, on the part of the residents is likely to be more beneficial for them than the types of inactivity we have observed (Lipman 1968) and which others have reported (Anderson 1963; Meacher 1972);
(b) that privacy is a right, and that opportunities for personal and social privacy – for being alone or with chosen others – are, if exercised, likely to be beneficial (Pastalan 1970; Schwartz 1975); and
(c) that 'integrating' physically able and rational with frail and confused residents is likely to be advantageous for all – benefits for able and rational residents lie in the opportunity to accept responsibility for the care of their frail and confused fellow residents and for the latter in the assistance and stimulation afforded by the presence of the former (Meacher 1972).

Activity

Our proposals are intended to provide physical settings in which residents' resources can be mobilized to counter symptoms of what has been described as institutional neurosis, 'a disease characterized by apathy, lack of initiative, loss of interest, especially in things of an impersonal nature, submissiveness . . .' (Barton 1966). Following Maslow's (1943) thesis on human motivation, among such resources we stress what he termed self-actualizing motives, acting in accord with desires, needs, to give expression to, to fulfil one's capabilities. In short, the proposals are intended to help foster, or reinforce, residents' abilities to 'do-things-for-themselves', hopefully by minimizing the necessity for staff assistance.

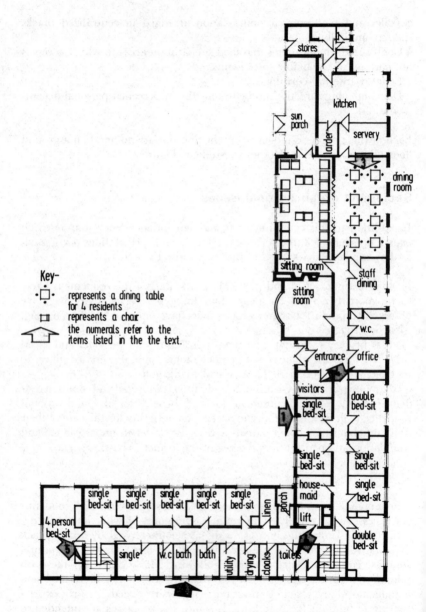

Key—

·□· represents a dining table
      for 4 residents
▢ represents a chair
⬆ the numerals refer to the
      items listed in the the text.

Figure 1   Ground floor plan of a conventional Home for old people.

For these reasons the proposed designs exclude centralized accommodation of the type shown in Figure 1; namely the recommended communal sitting-rooms and dining areas (Ministry of Health 1962, 1973). These, we found, readily subject the occupants to staff surveillance and attention. Thus, we have sacrificed large, public areas, such as the dining room for thirty-two people and the sitting-room for twenty-three in the Home on the accompanying plan, for smaller, dispersed, accommodation. Further, we have exceeded the recommended sizes for single and two-person bedrooms, 10 and 15.5 square meters respectively (Ministry of Health 1973). This is to provide personal space and facilities that will enable residents individually to engage in the four categories of daily activity mentioned above.

In an analogous context, designing for young mentally handicapped people, Gunzburg and Gunzburg (1973) furnished an apt framework for indicating the detailed implications of our intentions. Elaborating their suggestions for developing and maintaining appropriate levels of functioning among patients living in mental institutions, they urged that suitable opportunities for activity be made available. To this end, they argued for physical settings that can be used as 'tools' for experiencing 'complete activity cycles'. Taking the daily activity of eating as an example, they described such a cycle:

... eating must not merely come to mean chewing food and swallowing it in a socially acceptable form, but must be associated with shopping, preparing food, cooking, laying the table, serving, washing hands, washing dishes, clearing away, cleaning the kitchen, washing tea towels, using washing powder, hanging up towels for drying, taking them down, ironing them and putting them into a cupboard till required again.

As well as illustrating the types and levels of activity we envisage, this detailed description highlights the deficiencies we noted while working as quasi care-attendants during the participant observation stages of our studies. Dining, we found, conformed to the hotel-service notion. None of the routines mentioned above were carried out by residents; the act of choosing food was confined to selecting items served to them at dining tables. Bathing, dressing for bed or on waking, and even toileting took place at prescribed times with, especially in the case of bathing, staff in attendance. Bedrooms, designated on the architects' drawings and referred to by staff as 'bedsitting rooms', were, in the main, only used for sleeping. And since the residents spent most of their waking hours in 'their' chairs in the communal sitting-rooms, conversations tended to occur among those in immediately neighboring seats (Harris *et al.* 1977; Lipman 1967). Consequently, social exchanges, particularly those with affective content, tended to be limited to members of dyads or triads considered compatible by the staff who had directed the residents to the chairs they then occupied habitually.

Considering their lifetime experiences, it seems reasonable to presume that at least some of the activities that comprise these everyday cycles fall within residents' capabilities. And considering the adverse physiological and emotional effects that have been attributed to inactivity in old age (Bromley 1974), staff shortages apart, opportunities for residents to participate appear in and of themselves to be desirable.

Privacy

From the various definitions of this concept that are available (Altman 1975), we have opted for a socially rather than an individually orientated formulation; one suited to congregate living conditions. In the course of an extended argument, Bates (1964) claimed that privacy might most simply be described as,

. . . a person's feeling that others should be excluded from something which is of concern to him, and also a recognition that others have a right to do this.

This view assumes that the value placed on privacy is shared. It posits some minimum degree of consensus; an agreement usually associated with the social integration, or cohesion, held to characterize community-like collectivities (Suttles 1972).

For Bates then, privacy is, as it were, the obverse of sociability. Without the shared, the normative, understandings that flow from communal social relations, the concept has little social meaning. In this sense, the two notions are inseparable; the one can scarcely be conceived without invoking the other. If the tensions of collective life are to be managed, or accommodated, then – the argument runs – rights to personal and group privacy are to be both recognized and exercised. Access to privacy, in other words, can be regarded as a buffer between the pressures met in everyday social intercourse and people's abilities to manage them.

In our view, the relevance of this argument to the experience of shared living in Homes is immediate and central. If, as intended (Ministry of Health 1950), the experience is to approximate the solidarity of the community ideal, the privacy of those who occupy the Homes must be allowed scope for being exercised. And the more so since such approximations appear unattainable in institutional settings; since the already fragile cohesion of their fortuitous, nominal, nature as communities is threatened by the uneven, the divisive, distribution of authority between staff and residents.

These rights should be extended to all the parties concerned – to resident and staff groups and subgroups, and to each individual. Given the stresses of congregate living, all are likely to require opportunities to be private as well as public. In formulating our design proposals, however, attention has centered on efforts to enhance residents' opportunities. It is they who are at risk. As Meacher (1972) noted, prior to being admitted to Homes, it is their views of personal autonomy that, in most instances, have been undermined by being defined as requiring residential care. And once in, it is their privacy that tends to be jeopardized by the institutional circumstances they encounter; by, chiefly, staff intrusions into and control of their daily activities (Brocklehurst 1974). Once in, our studies indicate (Harris 1976), it is their enforced social contacts with staff and fellow residents that call for buffers.

Again we confront the contradiction described earlier. How, in staffed and congregate living situations, can residents' independent access to privacy be fostered and maintained? How can the effects of this contradiction, an apparently inherent facet of institutional life (Bennett 1964) be mitigated?

In lieu of excluding care attendant staff completely, we anticipate that their influence can be minimized most effectively by limiting the range and scope of resident/staff contacts, by attempting to maximize resident initiative. Although, compared with changes in the authority relationships prevailing in Homes, physical design can only contribute marginally to such a state of affairs, this seems insufficient grounds on which to discount its potential for providing appropriate physical settings. Appropriate, that is, in that they enhance opportunities for residents to exercise choice vis-à-vis their social contacts. For this reason, our proposals seek to separate resident accommodation from major areas of staff activity, to decentralize residents' dining and sitting accommodation, and to facilitate resident self-reliance by making amenities such as personal toilets, showers, and dining spaces readily available. Additionally, with reference to resident/resident contacts, our efforts have been directed to presenting opportunities for solitude as well as company; for individuals and groups to choose independently when and with whom they might seek companionship.

Integration

Our reference to this notion stresses its connotations of 'making up of a whole by adding together . . . separate parts' (Onions 1972). Accordingly, having attempted to forestall staff aid, we have sought to enable residents to compensate for their deficiencies in carrying out the day-to-day activities referred to earlier by calling on the assistance of their peers. Here the intention is to capitalize on the reciprocity involved in exchanges of goods, services and sentiments that anthropologists (Levi-Strauss 1964) and sociologists (Parsons and Shils 1964) claim lies at the core of social relations.

Thus, our design proposals depart from current practice. Contrary to present segregationalist policies, whereby so-called confused and rational, and, on occasion, physically frail and active, elderly people are separately housed (Meacher 1972), our proposals are intended to help effect residential integration. To this end, they comprise grouped accommodation for small numbers of individuals drawn from both these frail and active categories. And to this end, they include communal as well as personal accommodation in which reciprocity of services might occur readily among members of these groupings.

Following his study of three 'separatist' and three 'integrated' Homes for old people, Meacher (1972) emphasized the advantages of life in integrated venues. The chief benefits for confused residents, he argued, lay in the aid and stimulation afforded by the company of their rational co-residents, and for the latter in the opportunities to take responsibility for the care of their less able colleagues. In so arguing, Meacher touched on one of the central issues in gerontology: retarding or compensating for the mental, physical, and social deterioration experienced by elderly people, confused, rational, frail, and active alike (Bromley 1974). Especially in institutional conditions, it has been claimed that such retardation or compensation can be assisted by providing opportunities for maintaining the mental, physical, and social competences residents exercised before entry (Lawton and Nahemow 1973).

To what extent does integration take place when residents are mixed? Our recent study of eight Homes – sampled, among other criteria, to maximize the difference in proportions of confused to rational residents – provided some suggestions. As reported elsewhere (Harris *et al.* 1977), we examined two types of information: locational and interaction data. Analysis of the former indicated that residents are unlikely to live in what might be described as a spatially integrated manner. On the contrary, they can expect to encounter spatial segregation; if not in their sleeping arrangements, then by or within the sitting-rooms they occupy habitually and, to a lesser degree, where they take their daily meals. The interaction data showed a similar trend. Logged recordings of conversations among the three categories of resident that were identified – rational, moderately confused, and severely confused – showed, on analysis, that they occurred primarily within rather than across the categories. Despite their mixed populations, life in each of the Homes appeared to be characterized by segregation.

Seeking to account for this situation, we concluded that it was largely a consequence of the administrative regimes prevailing in the Homes. Spatial segregation, our participant observation records indicated, had been established and was maintained in order to facilitate the daily services staff administered to residents. And the availability, the ubiquity, of these services contributed to the interactional segregation our analyses disclosed. They remove the grounds on which inter-resident exchanges of services or sentiments might be founded. They precluded reciprocity.

To recapitulate: on three counts – resident activity, privacy, and integration – we wish to minimize the institutional dependency implicit in the hotel model of residential care. For this purpose we have referred to another image, an apartment model: one akin to self-serviced 'digs' – like accommodation for young people (Allen 1968), one akin to the notion of 'grouped flatlets' for old people (Ministry of Housing and Local Government 1966). However, like merely changing the nomenclature, the changes in built form this model might evoke carry with them no certainty that the relations between those who serve and those who are served will change. As our study indicated (Harris 1976; Harris *et al.* 1977), despite disparate spatial settings, the effects of staff-imposed regimens appear to be uniform. Thus we found that resident inactivity was maintained in each of the Homes – on occasion with the aid of drugs. Access to privacy was denied, for instance, by the simple expedient of removing bedroom, bathroom, and toilet locks or keys. And integration was undermined, for example, by demarcating specific bedroom wings, sitting-rooms, and dining tables on the basis of administrative categorization of residents.

In these circumstances what seems necessary are attempts to limit staff services. While not anticipating that physical design, of itself, will guarantee the success of such efforts, we believe that it can offer a means of facilitating them. As well as providing environments that can support residents' capacities for mutual and self-care, design can help discourage the dependence induced by staff attention.

The design proposals

Staff/resident separation

Complying with the trend in government policy for England and Wales which our colleague Barrett (1976) has traced, we favor 'small' Homes. We accept Korte's (1966) recommendation that, where her suggested optimum of twenty-five is exceeded, the number of residents in a Home be limited to approximately forty who are accommodated in 'family groups' of some eight individuals. We do not, however, accept her stipulation that:

Figure 2   Exterior view of prototype Home for old people.

Staff accommodation and facilities should not be strictly separated from residents'
accommodation, but should be situated so that residents feel they can have ready
access to staff.

In outline then, our proposals comprise, as a case-in-point, five single-
person bedsitting rooms; each, as well as providing a personal shower and
toilet, allowing for the activities involved in the daily cycles of sleeping,
food preparation and eating, and socializing. Together with, say, a two-
person bedsitting room designed for wheelchair users (Goldsmith 1975),
these individual rooms are grouped in 'units' that include spaces for group
sitting, food preparation, and dining. Such combinations of private bedsitting accommodation and group spaces can be arranged in at least one of
three manners. They can form the individual floors of, for instance, a
multi-story building, they can be detached single-story units, or they can
take the form of double-story 'pavilions' consisting of two units. In each of
these, the units are to be separated from the staff accommodation, access

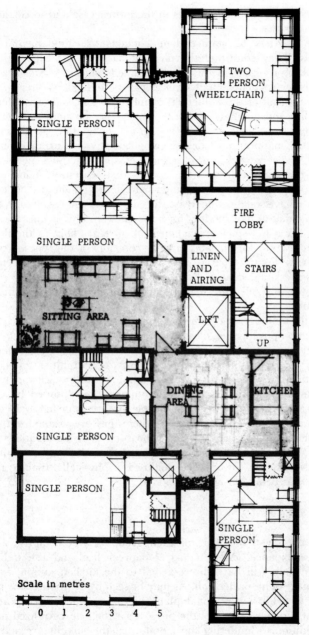

Figure 3   Second and fourth floor plan of Home shown in Figure 2.

being restricted to stairs and lifts in the former case and to corridor-links in the latter two.

These barriers to staff/resident contacts are fundamental to the proposals. They constitute the physical bases of our expectation that, given other propitious factors (such as amenable staff regimens and physical aids for residents), staff services can be limited. We recognize that where most staff or the influential members of staff and/or residents wish to establish and maintain residents' dependence on staff, they will do so. Moreover, as we have noted (Harris *et al.* 1977), they will do so despite apparently inappropriate or inconvenient physical arrangements. We contend, however, that in negotiating their spatial settings, people tend to prefer what may be termed the line of least resistance. Thus, adapting Zipf's (1965) notions about 'human behaviour and the principle of least effort', we have sought to increase the efforts staff are required to make in providing day-to-day services for residents. On this count, we favor a vertical, say a five-story arrangement (Figure 2). This, as the floor-plan indicates (Figure 3), obviates lengthy corridors of the type encountered customarily (Figure 1). And, if areas of staff activity such as centralized kitchens are situated at a distance from stairs and lifts, these means of access probably offer the maximum discouragement of ubiquitous staff attendance.

Notwithstanding our commitment to this separation, we anticipate that at times, and possibly for considerable periods, some residents may wish to 'feel they can have ready access to staff'. Consequently, and consistent with our intention of furthering residents' opportunities for exercising choice, the proposals incorporate a communal sitting space and a serviced dining area in proximity to staff accommodation. Limited by virtue of their size to use by some eight people, we recommend that these be situated at ground level, preferably where they are visible from publicly accessible areas (Figure 4). Such measures, our observations suggest (Harris *et al.* 1977), may well reduce the likelihood of staff confining them to exclusive use by, for instance, confused or physically disabled residents they view as being 'unsightly'.

The grouped units

Ideally the seven members of each grouping will comprise a 'rough numerical balance' (Meacher 1972) between frail and able individuals, each of whom will have direct access to the kitchen, dining area, and sitting space of his or her unit. As may be seen by comparing our proposal (Figure 3) with a traditional plan (Figure 1), these shared amenities highlight a major feature of the proposals – their decentralized nature.

In addition to hindering the monitoring, the surveillance activities of

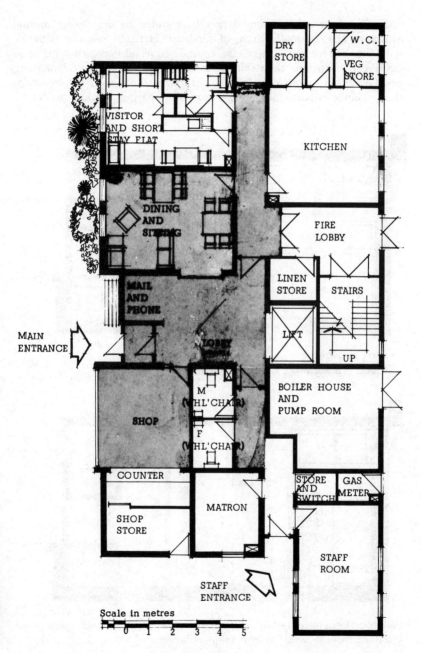

Figure 4   Ground floor plan of Home shown in Figure 2.

staff, this dispersed accommodation is intended to help foster mutual assistance among small groups of residents. Here, in contrast with the hotel-like service encountered in centralized conditions, those who so desire can contribute their skills to activity cycles of the type Gunzburg and Gunzburg (1973) described in our extract from their recommendations. They can participate in the tasks of preparing, serving, and clear-

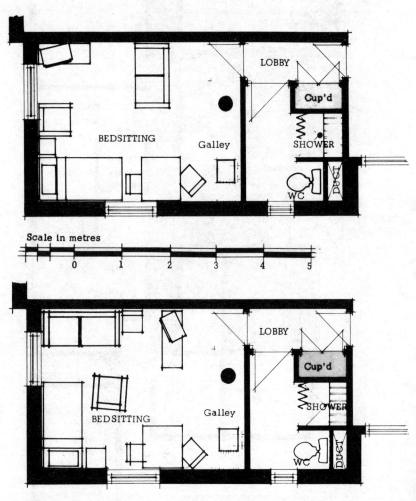

Figure 5   Example of bedsitting room arrangement: narrow front, single person bedsitting room showing alternate furniture layouts.

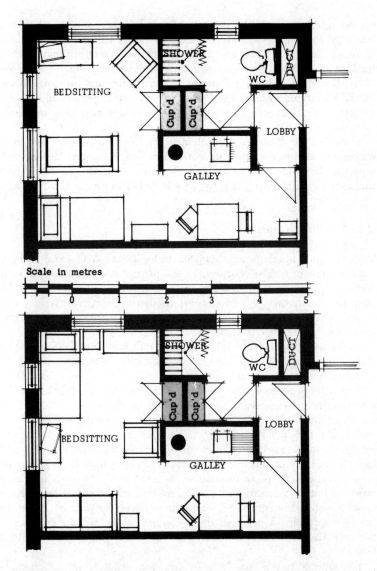

Figure 6   Another example of bedsitting room arrangement: wide front, single person bedsitting room showing alternate furniture layouts.

ing-up after meals, tasks that usually, our observations indicate, are restricted to members of staff and some two or three 'privileged' residents. Here too, in sitting areas specifically designed to seat approximately the number in a unit, those who wish to can experience small group sociability. Rather than having to adapt to the institutional, the formal, sociospatial situations exemplified by the seating arrangement illustrated in Figure 1, they can seek companionship in settings of a more domestic, a more informal scale.

These 'social' spaces are supplementary to the analogous but smaller spaces provided in the residents' personal accommodation. And it is to this aspect of the proposals that attention now turns – to the schematic bedsitting room layouts represented by the selected examples in Figures 5 and 6.

The bedsitting rooms

With the individual shower cubicles, toilet areas (W.C.) and entry hall (lobby) shown on these room plans, the private food preparation, eating, and sitting areas in the bedsitting rooms are intended to serve two related purposes. First, they should support residents' efforts to care for themselves. Second, they should help counter the institutional effects of traditionally designed Homes.

Fitted with appropriate aids – such as movable hand-operated sprays, slatted seats, and grab-rails (Goldsmith 1976) – shower cubicles seem more likely to lend themselves to independent use by elderly people than bathtubs do. Showers can be negotiated by those frail or disabled residents who require help in getting in or out of baths and are convenient for use by those for whom incontinence necessitates frequent washing without undressing fully. With similarly equipped toilet compartments, their provision as personal amenities should minimize routine, time-tabled bathing and a toileting by staff. Even if this does not occur, rather than being acknowledged communally, as evidenced by the queues we observed outside centralized bath and toilet blocks, these services need not be administered openly. They can take place in the privacy of residents' personal quarters, a privacy which, we anticipate, will be enhanced by the individual entrances, the domestic 'hall-like' quality afforded by the lobbies.

The galleys marked on the plans are intended to comprise sinks, hot-plates, work-surfaces, and storage for foodstuff and cooking and eating utensils. These will enable residents, independently to prepare snacks or meals for themselves and for the two or three guests they can accommodate in the dining and sitting areas in each room. Consequently, as well as receiving visitors in this manner, residents will be able to withdraw from the tensions that might be engendered by the shared activities envisaged for the occupants of the units.

The final major feature of the bedsitting room design we propose is illustrated by the alternative furniture layouts shown in Figures 5 and 6. In stressing this factor we hope that, contrary to the uniform arrangements found during our studies, residents will be encouraged to vary, to personalize, their accommodation. Here we are seeking to counter the homogeneity imposed, we believe, by the nursing attention which staff appear to associate with residential care (Kosberg and Gorman 1975); in particular, their tendency to insist on access to three sides of all beds. To this end, we recommend that units be formed by combining what we have termed 'wide-front' and 'narrow-front' bedsitting rooms. Above all, however, we urge that wherever possible, even in the case of nursing care, residents' capacities for actively assisting their fellows be exploited.

Finally, we wish to emphasize that, of themselves, our proposals are unlikely to secure resident independence, activity, privacy, or integration. Indeed, on each of these counts, we expect changes in staff/resident relationships consequent on staff shortages to be more influential. At best, the accommodation we have described may facilitate such changes. At worst, it may provide the conditions for continuing current practices, for example, differential allocation to units on the basis of administratively designated mental status (Harris *et al.* 1977). But even in the latter event, we believe that prospective residents are unlikely to be less advantageously placed than those in the traditionally designed and administered Homes we studied. At minimum, our proposals will increase the range of possibilities open to them.

References

AGE CONCERN (1973) *Age Concern on accommodation: Views on the problems of housing, with comments by the elderly.* London: National Old People's Welfare Council.

ALLEN, P. (1968) 'Accommodation for young people', *Architects' Journal, 147*, 847–54.

ALTMAN, I. (1975) *The Environment and Social Behavior: privacy, personal space, territory, crowding.* Monterey: Brooks/Cole.

ANDERSON, J. E. (1963) 'Environment and meaningful activity'. In R. H. Williams, C. Tibbitts and W. Donahue (eds) *Processes of Aging, Vol. 1.* New York: Atherton.

BARRETT, A. N. (1976) User requirements in purpose-built local authority residential homes for old people – the notion of domesticity in design. Ph.D. dissertation submitted in the University of Wales.

BARTON, R. (1966) *Institutional Neurosis.* Bristol: John Wright & Sons.

BATES, P. A. (1964) 'Privacy – a useful concept?', *Journal of Social Forces, 42*, 429–34.

BENNETT, R. G. (1964) 'The meaning of institutional life.' In M. Leeds and H. Shore (eds) *Geriatric Institutional Management*. New York: Putnam's.

BENNET, R. and NAHEMOW, L. (1965) 'Institutional totality and criteria of social adjustment in residences for the aged', *Journal of Social Issues, 21*, 44–78.

BROCKLEHURST, J. C. (1974) *Old People in Institutions – Their Rights*. London: Age Concern.

BROMLEY, D. B. (1974) *The Psychology of Aging*. Harmondsworth: Penguin.

COMMITTEE ON LOCAL AUTHORITY AND ALLIED PERSONAL SERVICES (1968) (Seebohn Report). Cmd. 3703. London: HMSO.

GOLDSMITH, S. (1975) 'Wheelchair housing', *Architects' Journal, 161*, 1319–48.

GOLDSMITH, S. (1976) *Designing for the Disabled*. London: Royal Institute of British Architects.

GUNZBURG, H. C. and GUNZBURG, A. L. (1973) *Mental Handicap and Physical Environment: The application of an operational philosophy to planning*. London: Bailliere Tindall.

HARRIS, H. (1976) Maintenance of social order in old people's homes, with special reference to spatial behaviour. M.Sc. dissertation submitted in the University of Wales.

HARRIS, H., LIPMAN, A. and SLATER, R. (1977) 'Architectural design: The spatial location and interactions of old people', *Gerontology, 23*, 5, 390–400.

KORTE, S. (1966) 'Designing for old people: the role of residential homes', *Architects' Journal, 144*, 987–91.

KOSBERG, J. I. and GORMAN, J. F. (1975) 'Perceptions toward the rehabilitation potential of institutionalized aged', *Gerontologist, 15*, 398–403.

LAWTON, M. P. and NAHEMOW, L. (1973) 'Ecology and the aging process'. In C. Eisdorfer and M. P. Lawton (eds) *The Psychology of Adult Development and Aging*. Washington: American Psychological Assn.

LEVI-STRAUSS, C. (1964) 'The principle of reciprocity'. In L. A. Coser and B. Rosenberg (eds) *Sociological Theory: A book of readings*. New York: Macmillan.

LIPMAN, A. (1967) 'Chairs as territory', *New Society, 9*, 564–6.

LIPMAN, A. (1968) 'Some problems of direct observation in architectural social research', *Architects' Journal, 147*, 1349–56.

LIPMAN, A. (1970) 'Accommodation for the elderly.' In *Modern British Geriatric Care*. London: Whitehall Press.

MASLOW, A. H. (1943) 'A theory of human motivation', *Psychological Review, 50*, 370–97; c.f. also W. H. HAYTHORN (1970) 'A needs by sources of satisfaction analysis of environmental habitability', *Ekistics, 30*, 200–3.

MEACHER, M. (1972) *Taken for a Ride, special residential homes for confused old people: A study of separatism in social policy*. London: Longman.

MINISTRY OF HEALTH (1950) *Report of the Ministry of Health for the year ended 31 March 1949*, Cmd. 7910. London: HMSO.

MINISTRY OF HEALTH (1962) *Residential accommodation for elderly people, Local Authority Building Note 2*. London: HMSO (c.f. also Metric Edition, 1973.)

MINISTRY OF HOUSING AND LOCAL GOVERNMENT (1966) *Old people's flatlets at Stevenage: An account of the project with an appraisal, Design Bulletin 11*. London: HMSO.

ONIONS, C. T. (ed.) (1972) *The Shorter Oxford English Dictionary on Historical Principles*. Oxford: Clarendon Press.

PARSONS, T. and SHILS, E. A. (1964) 'The basic structure of interactive relationship'. In L. A. Coser and B. Rosenberg (eds) *Sociological Theory: A book of readings*. New York: Macmillan.

PASTALAN, L. A. (1970) 'Privacy as an expression of human territoriality'. In L. A. Pastalan and D. H. Carson (eds) *Spatial Behavior of Older People*. Ann Arbor: Univ. Michigan Press.

PERSONAL SOCIAL SERVICE COUNCIL (1975) *Living and Working in residential homes: interim report of a working group*. London: The Council.

SCHWARTZ, A. N. (1975) 'An observation of self-esteem as the linchpin of quality of life for the aged: An essay', *Gerontologist*, *15*, 470–2.

SLATER, R. (1968) Adjustment of residents to old age homes. M.Phil. dissertation submitted in the University of Sussex.

SUTTLES, G. D. (1972) *The Social Construction of Communities*. Chicago: University of Chicago Press.

TOWNSEND, P. (1962) *The Last Refuge: A survey of residential institutions and homes for the aged in England and Wales*. London: Routledge & Kegan Paul.

TOWNSEND, P. (1975) 'Inflation and low incomes', *New Statesman*, *90*, 245–7.

TUNSTALL, J. (1966) *Old and Alone*. London: Routledge & Kegan Paul.

ZIPF, G. K. (1965) *Human Behaviour and the Principle of Least Effort*. New York: Hafner.

Part 5 Disability and Sickness in Later Life

25 On the natural history of falls in old age

J. H. Sheldon

The liability of old people to tumble and often to injure themselves is such a commonplace of experience that it has been tacitly accepted as an inevitable aspect of ageing, and thereby deprived of the exercise of curiosity. [. . .] An essential preliminary to further investigation is a knowledge of what actually happens, and the present paper is an attempt to meet that need by an account of the natural history of these falls.

The inquiry was directed at old people living at home, since the hospital population of old age has a heavy pathological bias, and, in addition, faces postural risks different from those of the community at large. This paper presents the results of an inquiry into 500 falls which happened to 202 individuals – 86 had been brought to the casualty department of the Royal Hospital, Wolverhampton, as the result of a fall, 59 had been admitted with a fractured femur, and the names of 57 were provided by the practitioners of the town. The inquiry was stopped when 500 falls had been described. This number is much less than the total falls sustained by these individuals, and reflects merely the number for which reliable information was available. Of the 168 persons seen at home, 34 were men and 134 women. The age distribution of the 202 was as follows: 50–59, eleven; 60–64, sixteen; 65–69, twenty-seven; 70–74, thirty-five; 75–79, thirty-nine; 80–84, fifty-three; 85 +, twenty-one. The frequency of the condition, its association with increasing age, and the ease of obtaining contact with a large number of old people so affected are obvious.

It proved surprisingly easy to classify the 500 falls, though the categories are not entirely self-contained.

Accidental falls	171
Drop-attacks	125
Trips	53
Vertigo	37
Recognizable C.N.S. lesion	27
Head back	20
Postural hypotension	18
Weakness in leg	16
Falling out of bed or chair	10
Uncertain	23

Source: *British Medical Journal*, 10 December 1960, pp. 1685–90 (extracts).

The very small number of falls out of bed is remarkable, and is in immediate contrast with their predominant importance in the hospital population of old people (Fine 1959), where the incidence of physical and, particularly, of mental defect is so much greater. The environment contributed a quota to the causation of 224 falls, whereas the cause lay within the old person in the remaining 276, though effective separation is difficult. Thus, while in some of the accidental falls a younger person would also have fallen, in many others balance would have been retained; for old people complain bitterly of inability to preserve their balance as they did when younger, saying, 'Once you're going you've got to go' – a remark which reveals a considerable problem in defective physiology.

Accidental falls

There were 171 falls (34 per cent of total) in 125 individuals, as follows:

On stairs		63
Missing last step or steps	15	
Poor illumination	13	
Vertigo	12	
Various	23	
Slipping		49
Falling over unexpected objects		16
Dark		12
Various causes		31

One-third of falls sustained by old people living at home are accidental in origin, and are of importance in that they offer the main target for prevention. Stairs, in turn, account for one-third of the accidental falls, and the complete contrast between this fact and the small amount of time actually spent at risk is a measure of the great hazard that stairs present to old people. The most frequent cause lies in missing the last step or the last group of steps in the mistaken belief that the bottom has been reached. This happens to us all from time to time, but in earlier years we are almost invariably able to preserve our balance, even if with some difficulty, and it provides a good illustration of the difficulty experienced by the older person in preserving a balance suddenly placed in jeopardy. Not only did one-quarter of the falls arise in this way, but six of the 59 fractured femurs (10 per cent) were in this group. The elimination of this particular hazard of the stairs is therefore a matter of urgency.

Next in importance comes inadequate illumination, whether the reason be defective vision or a fault in the actual lighting. In this respect the cellar steps and upstairs landings are especially apt to be at fault. Vertigo on the stairs accounted for twelve of the 63 falls. Some old people are apt to be giddy when looking down from the top of the stairs, but vertigo seems to be most dangerous when an individual is ascending, owing to the danger of falling backwards, with obvious risks of severe injury. There is need for improvement in the design of handrails for old people. Not only should they provide extra support at the top and bottom of the stairs, but the terminal shape of the rail should provide a special sensory cue which the hand will not normally reach till the feet have left the staircase at the bottom. A detached rail on both sides is ideal and should be of a size convenient for the sudden operation of the grasp reflex. The rail is often either so broad or so close to a wall that it is difficult for the hand to effect a sudden secure grasp in emergency. No fewer than twenty-eight of the 63 falls on stairs might have been prevented by good handrails and adequate illumination, which in turn might have eliminated the further risk of the staircase, new to the old person, which was responsible for one-tenth of the falls on stairs.

Loss of balance on a slippery surface accounted for one-quarter of the accidental falls, and half of these (21 falls) were caused by ice or snow, the commonest mode being that of the old woman who slips on her doorstep or in the back yard after a frosty night. It was pointed out by Boucher (1959) that the death rate from falls in old age was at its highest in Scotland, and thence declined southwards from a figure of 2,854 women per million living to one of only 1,439 for the South of England. The frequency of falls on ice and snow would seem to offer a reasonable approach to this curious geographical difference in mortality.

In addition to the well-known risk of the mat on slippery linoleum, floors slippery from something spilt and rubber shoes on wet pavements were also a source of danger. The domestic risks entailed by objects on the floor in unexpected places (grandchildren and pet animals being mainly at fault) account for one-tenth of the accidental falls, and in many instances darkness or poor illumination was an important contributory factor. Indeed, the small number of accidents directly due to darkness (for example, a fall in a dark bedroom during the investigation of a noise because of suspicion of burglars) bears no relation to the importance of inadequate visual information as a hidden but potent cause of accidental falls. The effect reaches beyond actual avoidance of the incident: when balance is in sudden jeopardy the point of no return is reached much earlier in the old than in the young, and a deficit in visual signals may further impair this already narrowed margin of safety. The danger is often intensified by the simultaneous presence of postural hypotension, as in getting out of bed at night to pass urine. Under such circumstances, even the least visual aid, as by a nightlight, can be most helpful to old people.

Drop-attacks

One hundred and twenty-five of the falls, occurring in 58 individuals, were classified as drop-attacks. [...] In a typical attack the individual suddenly and without warning falls to the ground, and many such persons have emphasized that they were at their normal avocations and feeling in good health at the time. So unexpected and so sudden is the incident that there is no time to prevent or to break the fall. There is no loss of consciousness, though, particularly in more advanced years, the victims may be dazed by the shock of collision with the ground, and are sometimes so surprised that they burst into tears.

Case 1 A woman of 86 was in her scullery peeling potatoes. She felt nothing wrong at all, but just fell down. She had actually peeled one potato and had picked up a second when the next moment she found herself on the floor, with a potato in one hand and the knife in the other.

They appear to fall under the unrestrained pull of gravity, and the speed of descent is such that injuries are common; in fact, twenty-six of the 58 old people concerned had sustained fractures or dislocations, while lesser injuries, particularly cut knees, are still more frequent. If not complicated by injury, the pattern of recovery varies in a curious way, being either immediate or delayed. These are about equally common, and are illustrated by the two following case reports.

Case 2 A woman of 61 was walking to church with a friend on each side when, as she says, she suddenly found herself on the pavement. Her friends were so surprised that they exclaimed, 'Whatever are you doing down there?' However, she got up quite easily and went on walking. She appears also to have had some partial drop-attacks, for she 'had been down on her knees three or four times'.

The pattern of recovery in the next case was quite different.

Case 3 A woman of 66 set out to go into town to do some shopping. She was walking along quite normally when, without warning, she suddenly fell forwards on the pavement. (She was not giddy, and knows that she neither slipped nor tripped.) She was quite unable to get up (though uninjured) and she had to remain some minutes on the pavement until a man appeared, when she managed to raise an arm to attract his attention. He, however, was quite unable to lift her, and, going off for help, was lucky enough to return with expert assistance in the shape of two dustbin men. With the additional help of a housewife who had just appeared, the four people were able to get her on her feet again. She stood where she was for a minute or so, and then managed to walk the short distance home with the woman holding her arm.

Several points arise from this history.

1 Difficulty of getting erect again

The difficulty of getting her erect again typifies the common experience of the younger relatives in these situations. They all agree that the patients are a 'dead-weight', and there is little doubt that the loss of power is associated with a loss of muscle tone – a flaccid state.

2 Distribution of loss of muscle power

The distribution of this loss is peculiar. It certainly affects the legs, and there is good evidence that the trunk muscles are affected. A very intelligent daughter stated that the main difficulty in getting her father, aged 84, on his feet after one of these attacks was that of lifting his trunk, for 'he has no strength in the body'. It will be noted that Cases 5 and 7 (see below) fell on their backs and were unable to turn over, although it is clear from the details that the arms were unaffected. That the arms normally escape in the typical senile drop-attack is shown by the following case report, which is typical of many.

Case 4   A woman of 79 was walking across the hall when she 'suddenly went down wallop'. She had the greatest difficulty in getting up, but managed to drag herself across the floor, and then 'hoisted herself up by the furniture'.

The histories show a remarkable agreement on the retention of sufficient power in the victims' arms to drag themselves across the floor and clamber up a suitable piece of furniture – while the legs and the rest of the trunk remain flaccid. It is suggested, therefore, that the drop-attack is caused by a sudden loss of tone limited to the anti-gravity muscles normally concerned in the maintenance of the upright position.

3 Duration of loss of power

The loss of power may be prolonged and of sufficient duration to endanger life in an old person living alone.

Case 5   A woman of 80 had made herself a cup of tea in the kitchen, and had put it on the table when 'down she went'. The kitchen clock registered 9.30 a.m. She fell on her back and could not get up until a neighbour came in at 5.30 p.m. She says the table moved whenever she tried to climb up it, and for the whole time she was unable to turn over on her face.

The duration of the loss of power for eight hours was cut short only by the timely arrival of help.

4 Recovery of function

We now come to what seems to me to be the most remarkable aspect of this whole series of events – that after, perhaps, some hours of effective paralysis, and after, perhaps, a considerable struggle to get the old person erect again – once there, immediate recovery of function occurs. In only one of the 125 falls did the individual fall down again after restoration of the upright position. Two case histories have provided a possible examination.

Case 6   A woman of 72 'fell down flat' in her bedroom one night while going to bed. She was unable to get up herself, and her husband was also unsuccessful. She spent the night on the bedroom floor and was in some distress by the time the doctor was fetched next morning. He also found it impossible to lift her until he had moved her so that her feet pushed against the skirting-board of the room, when 'he was able to lift her up from the back'.

Case 7   A woman of 86 was at the back of a large ground-floor room, when she suddenly fell down. She was unable to get up again and had to drag herself on her back across to the front of the room so that her feet could fall over two low steps into the garden path. She was then able to grasp some railings and stand erect.

In both these histories there is the strong suggestion that the decisive factor in recovery of function lay in pressure on the soles of the feet. This recalls the 'magnet response' or 'positive supporting reaction', which, according to Walsh (1957), is 'obtained most readily in decerebrate animals that have been subjected to a removal of the cerebellum'. In this state pressure on the soles of the feet causes extension of the limbs and tensing of the back muscles. The analogy with what happens to these old people is too close to be accidental, and it is suggested that it is by the operation of this low postural reflex that tone is restored to the anti-gravity muscles and the higher centres in the hindbrain are enabled to resume their normal control of posture and gait. This, if true, leads inevitably to speculation on the nature of a disturbance of central function that can cause such sudden and specialized loss of power and can then be restored to normal by the evocation of a lower reflex. One wonders whether the drop-attack may be based on a sudden loss of postural alertness – a sort of postural inhibition or sleep – based perhaps on a disturbance of function in the reticular substance of the brain-stem.

Provocative factors

In 96 falls with a good history the falls occurred during the following states of movement: walking normally, 36; turning round, 25; standing, 14; beginning to move, 8; rising from sitting, 8; throwing the head back, 4;

out of bed, 1. The one fall out of bed seems to have been a true drop-attack, and is of interest in that it may be relevant to the frequency of falls out of bed in the hospital population of old people.

Case 8   A woman of 81 was just beginning to get out of bed when she 'suddenly found herself on the floor'. There was no giddiness. The recovery was typical, in that 'she had great difficulty in getting up, and only managed this by dragging herself along the floor, and then up by the bed-rail'.

The circumstances in which the attacks occurred are so various that they must either be irrelevant or contain a common factor. If this be the case, the movement of the head and neck which in that particular individual affects the blood-flow in the vertebral arteries would seem the most likely cause. Sharply delineated as are the clinical features of the drop-attack, the falls of those who suffer from it are by no means limited to this mode. Fifty-one of the 58 individuals had had more than one fall; thirty-two had had other types of fall, while nineteen had suffered from drop-attacks alone. Thus in almost two-thirds of the victims the drop-attack could be regarded as but one manifestation of a more general decrease of postural control.

Trips

Trips were responsible for 53 falls in forty-one individuals. In fact, many more than this number were sustained, for, of all the modes of fall, that by tripping was easily the most apt to affect certain persons with special frequency and for the details of earlier falls to be forgotten. Indeed, some of the old people concerned had come to accept this liability to trip as part of their normal existence. It seems to be directly associated with age, for half of these subjects were in the 75–84 decade, and they all agreed (1) that they did not lift their feet as high as they used to, (2) that they found it almost impossible to recover their balance once they had begun to go, and (3) they were more likely to trip when tired or in a hurry. As would be expected, the most frequent single cause is the edge of rugs and carpets. ('I collect all the mats', said one old man of 84.) Kerbstones and steps in the house present a similar obstacle, and between them account for as many falls, while irregularities in the pavement are also a frequent stumbling-block. The underlying alteration in gait is obscure, but seems apt for experimental study. It may be part of the well-known gait of very old people, the 'marche à petits pas', which, as Critchley (1931) has pointed out, so strongly suggests an extrapyramidal origin.

Falls due to vertigo

These amounted to only thirty-seven falls in twenty-six individuals. This number – a mere 7 per cent of the whole series – is surprisingly small, for popular belief ascribes all unexplained falls in old people to an attack of giddiness. The reason is undoubtedly that the development of an attack of vertigo is usually slow enough to allow of safety measures – as by sitting down or holding on to something. For this reason only twenty-six of the forty-five persons in the whole sample who were liable to giddiness had actually sustained falls, and in twenty of the thirty-seven falls it was obvious that there would have been no fall had there been something handy to catch hold of.

This mode of falling is of special importance in late old age, for rather more than half the group (14 out of 26) were in the eighties. In some instances the subjective giddiness was accompanied by a sudden act of rapid, compulsive, and uncontrollable turning, which brought the old person at once to the ground. It has already been pointed out that the most dangerous of the falls due to vertigo are those that occur when an old person is going upstairs. The incidence of defective hearing and of tinnitus was almost double that found in the whole sample, figures of 58 per cent for defective hearing and of 41 per cent for tinnitus contrasting with 29 per cent and 20 per cent.

Falls due to disease of central nervous system

Twenty-seven falls occurred among twenty-one individuals. One-tenth of the sample were therefore concerned, and in some cases the number of falls was large, though an adequate history was available only for the last one or two. The conditions found were: subacute combined degeneration of the spinal cord, 3; paralysis agitans, 3; onset of cerebral thrombosis, 4; probable carotid or basilar artery thrombosis, 4; pre-existing hemiplegia, 7.

Falls due to throwing the head back

Twenty falls in seventeen individuals were the direct consequence of looking upwards with the head thrown back, and in seventeen of these twenty falls the old people were working with the hands above the head. Falls due to this cause may begin in late middle life, but they become increasingly characteristic of the later stages of old age: ten of the seventeen individuals were beyond the age of 75. Typical cases were:

Case 9 A woman of 86 had been advised not to reach above her head, but nevertheless she went out to hang up some clothes on the line, and as she started to do so 'at once went down with a wallop backwards'.

Case 10 A woman of 64 (who had had several drop-attacks) wanted to stitch a curtain at the top of a door and therefore stood on a stool while her husband held her. When she started to work above her head she was 'seized at once with an attack of giddiness' and a 'very queer feeling', so that her husband had to get her down. Had he not been there she would have had a nasty fall.

These falls carry a special risk of injury, for a common domestic reason for working with the head thrown back is to reach something high up in the room – such as an electric-light bulb – which may necessitate standing on a stepladder or a chair and so greatly reduces the security of stance. Many old people find that to retain balance with the head thrown back they need both to stand on a wide base and to hold on to something. When placed at sudden risk in this position old people are apt to clutch at whatever may be handiest, and so to bring some heavy object down on top of them.

Case 11 A woman of 87 began to have falls if she put her head back and worked with her hands above her head. She had always kept her hats on the top shelf of a wardrobe, and in trying to reach them she pulled the wardrobe over on top of her on two occasions. On another occasion she brought down a heavy iron saucepan and narrowly escaped injury.

Many old people have discovered for themselves the dangers of this posture and never willingly adopt it. The factors that may be concerned are undoubtedly relevant to the whole problem of falls in old age.

Falls due to postural hypotension

Only eighteen of the 500 falls were the direct result of postural hypotension – that is, of rapidly standing erect. Twelve falls occurred in the bedroom and four on straightening up – a particular hazard of the elderly gardener. The small number of falls ascribed solely to this cause bears no relation to its great importance in the postural life of old people, for many of them consciously adapt their habits to cope with it. Like inadequate illumination, postural hypotension has great importance as a hidden ingredient in other types of fall – as anyone will realize who has watched the initial uncertainties of balance of many old people when starting to move immediately after rising to the erect position. Of the 202 persons in the sample, twenty-nine (14 per cent) complained of postural hypotension, and had sustained 72 falls of various kinds.

Other types of fall

Of the remaining types of fall, sixteen occurring in twelve individuals were due to mechanical weakness in one leg, so that it was unable to meet an emergency such as that caused by stepping on a loose stone. These falls, in general, were due to factors carried over into old age from earlier years, such as loss of muscle from an attack of poliomyelitis or the effects of trauma. The relative infrequency of falls out of bed or a chair – ten falls in six individuals – is in striking contrast to their importance in the hospital population of old age. These falls, which are often based on mental confusion, are always of serious import and apt to be terminal features. Finally, twenty-three falls in twenty-one individuals remained unexplained – a surprisingly small number.

References

BOUCHER, C. A. (1959) *Geriatrics*, *14*, 293.

CRITCHLEY, M. (1931) *Lancet*, *1*, 1119, 1221, 1331.

FINE, W. (1959) *Geront, Clin.*, *1*, 292.

WALSH, F. G. (1957) *Physiology of the Nervous System*, p. 125. London: Longmans, Green.

26 The burden of rheumatoid arthritis: tolerating the uncertainty

Carolyn L. Wiener

Abstract

Being physically comfortable
and doing a simple chore
can raise one's spirits to
levels of supreme joy.

Persistent pain and wretched
tiredness brings one to
near despair.

In the next forty years, I
wonder how many variations thereof
I shall experience.

The above is excerpted from the journal of a 29-year-old woman, who has been afflicted with rheumatoid arthritis since age 15. It has become her practice to make such notations during sleepless, pain-filled nights. Her phrase, 'I wonder', only mildly captures the social-psychological burden of rheumatoid arthritis – that of tolerating the uncertainty that pervades all facets of the disease condition, and life with it.

All living requires tolerating a considerable amount of uncertainty – to state this is to state the obvious. But a study of the victims of rheumatoid arthritis provides an insight into the demands placed upon living when uncertainty is exaggerated beyond the usual level of toleration. [. . .]

Resource reduction as a source of variable uncertainty

The term 'arthritis' dates back to the days of Hippocrates, and literally means joint inflammation, i.e. joints which are hot, red and swollen. As popularly used to describe a disease, 'arthritis' is a misnomer, less than the full picture. There are many diseases that manifest arthritis as part of their symptoms, but rheumatoid arthritis, the disease under examination here, is now understood to be a systemic disease that affects the connective or supporting tissues which are ubiquitous throughout the body. The etiology of rheumatoid arthritis is unknown, but the result is that the

Source: *Social Science and Medicine*, 1975, 9, pp. 97–104 (extracts).

involved tissue becomes inflamed. When the disease attacks joint tissue, pain becomes the signal for patient and physician. In most cases, the onset is insidious, with ill-defined aching and stiffness. In about one-fifth of the cases, severe multiple joint inflammation develops suddenly at onset.

The victim of rheumatoid arthritis is faced with an intermittent reduction of personal resources – resources which are taken for granted by the healthy. Unlike some other diseases, the reduction can profoundly affect more than one kind of resource. A reduction of mobility may occur from the incapacitating effect of pain, and from the fact that weight-bearing joints may be so deformed or so acutely inflamed as to prevent the arthritic from wearing shoes and to make walking difficult or impossible. A reduction of skill may occur, attributable to three factors: increased pain, loss of dexterity and loss of strength. Joints which are affected by rheumatoid arthritis are not only swollen and painful, but have limited movement. If the disease of the joints of the fingers and wrists is progressive, it can lead to dislocation and deformity of the hands. A weakening and then wasting of muscle may occur above and below the affected joint, causing a loss of strength. Pots become too heavy to lift, handbags too heavy to carry, doors too heavy to open. And, finally, a reduction of energy occurs caused by the metabolic effect of the disease (its attack on connective tissues) and also by the circuitous quality of pain (pain drains energy and fatigue produces more pain). [. . .] The disease has been referred to as a 'rheumatic iceberg', in that the duration is lifelong even when so quiescent as to be no problem, but quiescence and flare-up are themselves unpredictable (Bland 1960).

The variability of progression, severity and areas of involvement cannot be stressed enough. For example, an arthritic may have reduced mobility but no impairment of skill, reduced energy but no interference with mobility, reduced energy one day and renewed energy the next and so on. Loss of skill will remain fairly constant, if it is caused by deformity, but it is variable if caused by swelling; the other resources, mobility and energy, can fluctuate. There is uncertainty about: (1) whether there will be *any* pain, swelling or stiffness; (2) the area of involvement; (3) the intensity of the disability; (4) whether onset will be gradual or sudden; (5) how long it will last; and (6) how frequently flare-ups will occur. Under this condition of variable uncertainty, two imperatives press their claims upon the arthritic: the physiological, which must be monitored for the pain and disability reading of the day, or even the hour; and the activity imperative, which must be acknowledged if one is going to maintain what is perceived as a normal life. Like two runners in a nightmare race, these two imperatives gain, each on the other, only to be overtaken again in a constant competition.

All of the individuals interviewed for this study were still coping with the demands these two imperatives were making upon them. When the physiological imperative gains a lead, they find that severe pain is more easily borne through withdrawal from interaction with others: 'I go off by myself . . . to cry, or swear, or both. If these flare-up periods increase, both in duration and frequency, the uncertainty problem will be resolved by the certitude of more bad days than good. The activity imperative, to extend the metaphor, will have lost the race, and the arthritic will have been moved into invalid status, and into increased isolation. The extent to which this becomes onerous is dependent on many intervening variables – age, family support system, economic independence, to name some. [. . .] But the very uncertainty which makes the disease so intolerable, also mitigates against acceptance of this invalid status, for there is always the hope of another remission. It is this dimension of tolerating which we shall examine next.

Social psychological tolerating strategies

The psychological strategy of hope

Faced with the whipsaw of a physiological imperative which reduces activity and an activity imperative pushing one forward, arthritics tolerate the uncertainty by *juggling the hope of relief and/or remission against the dread of progression*. Although they know the disease does not follow a decided downhill course, there is always the fantasy of the disease progression: dreading the next place and the next time it is going to hit. [. . .] They see others who are worse off and when they say, 'I'm lucky it's not in my . . .', the implication is clear. This leaves one constantly on the alert. Pain, when it hits in a new place, makes the uncertainty intolerable. Knowing the possibilities is one thing; having them occur is another. The arthritic must wait to see if the pain persists and while waiting the uncertainty is heightened. One begins to worry that the new pain is not really arthritis, but something even more serious, requiring professional diagnosis. Arthritics are inhibited by a selectivity in reporting symptoms: 'If I tell the doctor about all my aches and pains, he won't be listening when it's really important.'

The dread of a progressively worsened state brings with it a *dread of dependency*. [. . .] To illustrate, one woman, now 44, recalled the onset of her disease at age 22, her move to an apartment, and her struggle to continue working:

It was harrowing. When I got up in the morning my feet were so painful I couldn't stand on them. I would slide out of bed and with my elbow and rump get into the bathroom. I learned to turn the faucets with my elbows. [. . .]

Just such knowledge of the capricious behavior of the disease provides a psychological strategy to counter the dread: hope for remission or, at least, temporary relief. Often this is expressed in theories of causation, the hope that a remission can be correlated with something the arthritic can control, such as diet. However, a theoretical causal linkage constructed by the arthritic may be sustaining for a long period, only to be upset by another flare-up.

Another hope is directed toward symptom control efforts. Uncertainty as to how long the flare-up will last forces the arthritic to look beyond conventional medical treatment to folk remedies suggested by friends, kinsmen, other patients and by the arthritic's own reading. Self-doctoring ranges from ingestion of celery juice or massive doses of vitamin E, to plastic bags filled with powdered sulphur and wrapped around the feet at night, to a poultice of ginger root steeped in vodka and an alloy. [. . .] In addition, there is a trial and error approach to the use of applied heat, change of climate, diet and appliances. Even if relieved, arthritics are haunted again by uncertainty, for what they have attributed to a specific relief measure may indeed have been an independent spontaneous remission; but they continue to hope until next time proven wrong. [. . .]

The reversal of the hope for remission, i.e. the hope that the arthritis will perform 'on cue', is of course less common. But the fact that this hope can also be felt serves to emphasize the exasperating quality of tolerating the uncertainty. One woman reported that she waited six weeks for an appointment with an acupuncturist, and then was refused treatment because the disease was in remission and could be activated by the treatment. Even those whose deformity has made their invalidism appear to the outsider as irreversible have been socialized to the oscillations of flare-up and remission to such an extent that they continue to hope. An arthritic who was almost totally incapacitated by the progress of the disease had driven miles and waited four hours in the clinic for what turned out to be a refill on his prescription. He explained his patience to the interviewer, 'Maybe if you're around when they find something new, they'll try it on you.' [. . .]

Social strategies of covering-up and keeping-up

Another means of dealing with the problem of battling imperatives is to develop social strategies to assist one in *normalizing* life, i.e. suppressing the physiological imperative and proceeding with the activity imperative *as if* normal. The principal strategies employed are covering-up and keeping-up, which in turn generate problems of their own.

Covering-up, concealing disability and/or pain, while not a behavioral phenomenon peculiar to arthritics, is nevertheless an important component of their repertoire. [. . .] 'If anyone asks me how I am, I say fine.' [. . .] Covering-up is not a denial of the disease, in the psychological sense of the word. As described by M. Davis (1973): '. . . it is the rejection by the patient of the handicap as his total identity. In effect, it is the rejection of the social significance of the handicap and not rejection of the handicap *per se.*' [. . .] Interaction, so interrupted, impedes the arthritic's ability to view himself as he would prefer to be viewed by others.

There are various conditions under which covering-up is impeded. An arthritic who is subject to sudden attacks, such as a freezing of the back and the resultant immobility, is a case in point. This woman had such an attack while visiting her home town, found she could only walk at a creeping pace, some of the time only backwards:

People on the street would ask if they could help . . . the embarrassment was worse than the pain. I thought they would all think I was crazy or drunk.

Visibility – use of a cane or crutches, wincing when arising from a chair or getting out of a car – is another impediment to covering-up. [. . .] A young woman struggled to remove coins from her wallet with fingers that were badly skewed. She said poignantly:

I have just become aware of how uncomfortable people get around me. They don't want to be reminded of sickness; they are fearful for themselves, just as young people don't want to be around old people.

If covering-up is successful, a price may be paid, for the strategy drains already depleted energy: 'Do you know the stress you put your body to trying to walk straight so people won't see you can't walk?' There is increased awareness of pain and stiffness once within the confines of the home and increased strain on tolerating. Patients report that after situations in which they 'toughed it out', they give in to their fatigue and nervousness, dumping their irritability upon close family members.

Armed with their repertoire for covering-up, and lulled by their good days, arthritics struggle to keep the activity imperative ahead in the race, through efforts at *keeping-up* – keeping-up with what they perceive to be normal activities (preparing a holiday meal for the family, maintaining a job, participating in a family hike). They may carry through the moment successfully and then suffer increased pain and fatigue; the risk is taken precisely because of the uncertainty that such a price will in fact be extracted. [. . .]

Another problem occurs for those who have mastered the art of keep-ing-up by means of raising the threshold of their pain toleration. They may be slow to read the signs of body dysfunction, as, for example, one patient who walked around with a broken leg for a month, thinking the pain was arthritic.

Some arthritics engage in excessive keeping-up – super-normalizing – to prove a capacity, to deny incapacity or to recapture a former identity. Pain-free and energetic days invite frenetic activity, or catching-up, for the above reasons. The result is often (but uncertain again) that time is lost through increased pain and/or decreased energy the next day. Super-normalizing further ties in with the uncertainty of ascribing causes, as for example one patient who knows her condition is worsened during the summer, but is unsure if the disease is exacerbated by the weather or by her increased activities in her garden. Furthermore, some patients engage in super-normalizing as a device to distract them from pain. This may bring deleterious consequences – increased pain, increased fatigue and, in some cases, fever.

A successful repertoire for covering-up and keeping-up may at times turn out to be a mixed blessing. Relationships generally remain normal, but when the arthritic cannot get by, it is harder to *justify inaction* to others. [. . .] As with a tennis pro who found that he would be forced to cancel a lesson one day, only to be observed out playing the next; he began to worry that his club members were suspecting him of malingering.

Paradoxically, patients who are presenting a normal image to the world are nevertheless perplexed when they are not taken seriously by others. There is a longing for understanding, for a sensitivity from others, that goes beyond justifying inaction. An arthritic may be proud that 'nobody knows' and yet wish that 'somebody cared'. [. . .] As expressed by the patient whose journal was quoted at the beginning of this paper:

Pain is essentially private. Sometimes you wish for someone to understand and be patient with your pain. To allow you to have it!! I do not mean sympathy or pity.

The social strategy of pacing

Weaving in and out of the normalization repertoire is the governor of the activity imperative, *pacing* – identifying which activities one is able to do, how often, under what circumstances. The importance of this strategy lies in the fact that these are the activities which allow one to view oneself as normal.

Arthritics know it takes them longer to complete everyday tasks. [. . .] To quote one patient, 'I dress a little, lie down and cry a little and dress a little more.' They decide if they can only work a three-day week, or do housework for an hour; they know if they shop they may not be able to cook. Housework is not spontaneous, but planned around periods of respite. During remission, the arthritic may have resumed activities, or assumed new ones (for example, work, recreation, lodge and church), and then be forced by a flare-up into cancelling some or all of these. This all ties in with the variable uncertainty again; pacing is not a static decision, but must fluctuate with a monitoring of the physiological imperative. Along with pacing decisions run all the problems mentioned earlier related to justifying inaction.

Decisions on activities (which ones, how often) are also affected by the time lost in the rest required between activities. Rest is prescribed, but not always honored, for symptom control; however, when pain and stiffness are bad, arthritics find they have no choice but to lie down. For some, rest becomes a ritualized part of the daily regimen – an anticipatory device for coping with pain and decreased energy. Time expended in rest results in a further cut-back of desired activities. It also may lead to a contingent existence. Since covering-up and keeping-up have become an integral part of the arthritic's mechanism for coping, many prefer to rest and then make a fresh assessment of the physiological imperative rather than suffer the embarrassment of cancelling plans.

Re-normalizing: the adjustment to reduced activity

Re-normalizing, i.e. lowering expectations and developing a new set of norms for action, is directly related to the frequency and duration of flare-ups. [. . .] For the arthritic, this means settling for half a window being clean when the arm starts to hurt in the middle of the cleaning, or, as one patient put it, 'Sometimes I cannot open a jar; I'll bang it on the sink, and finally say damn it, put it away and have something else.' [. . .]

Increased frequency and duration of flare-ups will spiral re-normalization into lower and lower expectations. New coping mechanisms replace old mechanisms for tolerating uncertainty. For example, when constant use of a cane made covering-up impossible, one patient adjusted with a substitute philosophy: 'this cane opens many doors'. Resignation is expressed regarding the fleeting good days: 'It couldn't last.' If the flare-ups and the embarrassment of cancelling become too frequent, there may be a resultant change in life-style, such as a reduction in working hours or retirement, a move to a retirement home or the acquisition of a boarder-helper. Frequent cancelling of church or recreational activities, inability to visit or entertain friends, ends in withdrawal into a narrowed social world. The extent to which this becomes a movement into invalid status is variable, as explained earlier, but for those whose worlds are thus drastically circumscribed, boredom may become a problem, particularly if loss of skill deprives them of familiar avocations such as sewing and carpentering.

Eliciting help

Part of the step downward, of re-normalization, is accepting help. Arthritics may have to *elicit help* from others. [. . .] Once the need to ask extends beyond the immediate family, the act is weighted for importance. For example, one may consider asking a neighbor to unscrew the cork from a wine bottle and decide to forgo the wine, but, when pain and stiffness make public transportation a forbidding prospect, one will ask a friend to be driven to the clinic.

Eliciting help places increased strain on tolerating the uncertainty for it reinforces the dread of possible dependency. As perhaps the most extreme illustration, one woman stood without moving for two hours, when her back froze while visiting a friend in a convalescent home. [. . .]

The hesitation in eliciting help also stems from the fear that others may not be responsive. Problems of justifying inaction when others have stakes in action, as discussed earlier, surface again. [. . .] One such case was the patient who acknowledged she will only accept help from her son. His role was an emergent condition of his growing up, since the onset of her disease thirteen years ago:

My son was then five-years-old, and *he* had to take care of *me*. I'd sit on the side of the bed at night, and he'd put my legs up, *he'd* tuck *me* in. Many times he had to dress me from top to bottom. My older daughter and sisters have tried to help me but I don't feel comfortable having them do for me.

[. . .] Lastly, awkward and/or embarrassing situations of eliciting help may occur, which only serve to highlight dependency. One such case was reported by a man who was forced to ask a stranger in a public toilet to zip him up; his fingers are closed to the palms of his hands, and he had left his trusty button-hook at home. [. . .]

Since eliciting help is a tacit acknowledgement of the gain that the physiological imperative is making on the activity imperative, an additional weight on tolerating stems from the identity problems which arthritics suffer when their eliciting of help results in a role-reversal. [. . .] Male arthritics who have lost their dexterity must rely on wives to carry heavy objects, open garage doors, etc. Women frequently complained of their diminished roles as homemaker. [. . .]

Dependent as it is on duration and frequency of flare-ups, role reversal may result in a permanent change in the household's division of labor. Helping out has now become a new job. In these cases, tolerating the uncertainty has lessened and dependency need no longer be a dread – it is all too clearly a reality.

Balancing the options

In tolerating the uncertainty, the arthritic is ultimately engaged in a precarious balancing of options – options somewhat limited because of already reduced resources of mobility, skill, strength and energy. Indeed, a balancing is involved in all of the pacing decisions (weighing the potential benefit of acupuncture against the climb up two flights of stairs 'that will just about kill me', the potential withdrawal from church activity against the loss of social interaction). The options are constantly presenting themselves, each to be met with an *ad hoc* response: whether to keep-up and suffer the increased pain and fatigue; whether to cover-up and risk inability to justify inaction when needed; whether to elicit help and risk loss of normalizing, whether to re-normalize and decrease the need for covering-up and keeping-up. Furthermore, as explained earlier, there exists a constant balancing of the hope of relief and/or remission against the dread of progression.

At the same time another very worrisome balancing is going on. Since all of the patients in this study were being treated at a clinic, all were on a strict drug regimen. With no cure available, the drugs hopefully provide symptom control – to help the arthritic normalize. Patients with long histories of frequent flare-ups had undergone sequential trials of potent anti-rheumatic drugs, all of which can have adverse side effects. Some people had difficulty in recalling the sequence of these trials; frequently they were not told what was in their injections and did not ask. For them, the balancing was weighted in favor of relief at any cost: 'When you're hurting like that you have to do something.' Even after an accumulation of drugs, and faced with total hip replacement due to osteoporosis, one patient attested that she would have taken the drugs even if she had known the results: 'I'm glad to have had those years of life.' [. . .]

Knowledge of the specific possible adverse effects of a drug heightens the pressure of tolerating by placing an additional responsibility upon the arthritic ('I cut down on the butazolidin when I have a good week. Recently when I had a flare-up of neck pain I had to increase it again.' 'I know when I take more than sixteen aspirin a day my ears start to ring.') Pain increases one's vulnerability – an arthritic may rationally resist starting on a drug with known side effects, but when the pain becomes unbearable, such resolution is tempered by the uncertainty, in this instance, of duration: 'when the pain is this bad you feel like you'll never come out of it'. The tolerating burden is increased further by another uncertainty:

what 'works', i.e. keeps inflammation and pain controlled, one day or one week, may not work the next.

Balancing decisions are therefore constantly being reassessed. [. . .] Thus, about balancing – there is at best only temporary certainty. This, too, the arthritic must learn to live with.

Implications

To reiterate the self-evident proposition with which this paper began, all of life is uncertain. Living requires coming to terms with that uncertainty in much the same manner as described herein – by balancing options and making choices. Thus, arthritics were found in this study to be dealing with a universal aspect of the human condition, but *in exaggerated form and with severely limited options*. Further research could enlarge the scope of the framework presented in this paper, by theoretically sampling under different conditions, for example in another culture. The heuristic value of substantive theory is that such 'new theory' is not viewed as conflicting or invalidating, but rather as an extended explanation which can be incorporated into extant theory. Equally important is the consideration of the crucial variables of tolerating the uncertainty as they apply to other chronic illnesses, where they appear in different combinations and where uncertainty takes on varying degrees of significance. It is in this regard that the presentation of substantive theory, developed through systematic analysis of qualitative data, makes a contribution: not only in its practical use in the substantive area being examined, but in its application and adjustment to other situations with sufficient exactitude to guide thinking, understanding and further research.

Consider the normalization strategy of covering-up. Some arthritics can choose to employ this strategy because of the invisibility of pain, but for the individual with ulcerative colitis the uncertainty of the constant possibility of external evidence of diarrhoea may vitiate against this strategy. The relationship between uncertainty and covering-up for persons with ulcerative colitis more closely resembles the experience of those arthritics who are subject to sudden attacks, and those with decreased dexterity and/or visible deformity. Or consider the variable eliciting help, which for the arthritic was shown to diminish potential covering-up. For the person with ulcerative colitis, eliciting help takes on another dimension. Here eliciting help facilitates covering-up, for as Reif (1973) documents, many persons who have ulcerative colitis obtain the assistance of friends and associates to help them conceal disability, by sustaining normal interaction with others in situations where interaction would be interrupted by frequent or abrupt departures for the toilet. [. . .] If one looks at multiple sclerosis, one finds a more striking analogy to rheumatoid arthritis: the clinical symptoms vary greatly among patients, the course of the disease is highly uncertain, and patients share the dread of where it will strike next. Under these conditions, one finds social–psychological problems which intertwine all of the variables described in relation to rheumatiod arthritis, and, particularly in the early stages of the disease, a similar inability to read symptoms and a similar balancing of restricted options. The difference lies in the fact that, though the rate of progression is uncertain, there is no hope for reversal, creating further uncertainty as to whether expenditures for mid-disease needs, such as railings in the home to assist walking, are worthwhile. Space does not allow more than this brief glimpse at the applicability of these concepts. What is clear is that we are just beginning to grasp their implications as a key to understanding and explaining interaction that pertains to persons with chronic illness.

Regardless of the burden of tolerating the uncertainty, no one would suggest that persons so afflicted would choose the certitude of invalidism, and the attendant extreme dependency and lessened social contact. Nor are individuals with chronic illness asking for approbation for how they balance their remaining options. Rather, what they *are* asking, is for some comprehension on the part of those around them, and on the part of health professionals, of their situations *vis-à-vis* the general human condition. In the words of the previously quoted diarist:

> Being admired
> For handling a disease
> Palls
> Compared to
> Being loved
> For being human and frail.

References

BLAND, J. H. (1960) *Arthritis: Medical Treatment and Home Care.* New York: Macmillan.

DAVIS, M. Z. (1973) *Living with Multiple Sclerosis: A Social Psychological Analysis.* Springfield, Ill.: C. C. Thomas.

REIF, L. (1973) 'Beyond Medical Intervention: Strategies for Managing Life in the Face of a Chronic Disease'. Unpublished manuscript, Graduate Programme in Sociology, University of California, San Francisco. For abridged version see 'Managing life with a chronic disease', *Am. J. Nursing, 73,* 2, 262.

27 Problems in the treatment of hemiplegia

G. F. Adams

The treatment of strokes has attracted attention recently because there are many more of them, and because geriatric departments now offer what was lacking before, an effective system of treatment of the residual disabilities of strokes. Its essentials are *time*, measured in months, not weeks, because recovery is slow and few patients can adjust quickly to their disability; *special facilities*, space and equipment needed to take advantage of each phase of recovery; *staff*, doctors, nurses, therapists working as a team to condition the patient mentally and physically to make the most of the spontaneous improvement time usually brings; and *after-care*, as a hospital outpatient, in day-centre, or at home.

Progress towards recovery is the rule following cerebrovascular accidents. It may be incomplete if disability is severe, but failure to progress can usually be explained by a specific cause. In a search for such causes in a group of hemiplegic long-stay invalids (Adams and Hurwitz 1963), it became clear that the physical handicap alone was seldom responsible for failure to regain independence in walking and self-care (our criteria of 'recovery'); that the patients are often unaware of their shortcomings and cannot describe or explain them (attention being drawn to them usually by an interested and observant attendant who knows the patient well); and that apart from disorders of the special senses, common causes of failure are impaired intellectual capacity (such as defective comprehension, reasoning, or memory), loss of sensation in the limbs, or sensory disturbance involving body awareness or postural control. We have called these barriers to recovery from strokes. Understanding of the patient's difficulty is half the battle in treatment, and some hemiplegics remain bedfast invalids because their barriers have been unrecognised or ignored. [. . .]

Before discussing specific intellectual and sensory defects, impaired eyesight and hearing should be mentioned because although they are obvious sources of difficulties in rehabilitation, they are apt to be overlooked.

Sight. Defective vision may be corrected by glasses, or allowances may have to be made until the patient is fit for a cataract operation. Homonymous hemianopia tends to resolve with time, or the patient manages to compensate for it, but it is helpful to approach the patient from the side

Source: *Gerontologia Clinica*, 1967, *9*, pp. 285–94 (extracts).

with normal vision and to place the locker and other necessary articles where they can be seen easily, especially if the patient is still confused by clouded consciousness.

In non-dominant hemisphere lesions with parietal lobe involvement hemiplegics often ignore or disown not only the hemiplegic left side, but also the left half of their environment and are unaware of anything in the left field of vision. This defect may explain frequent falls and other mishaps because the patient walks into objects he cannot appreciate within the left field of vision, puts clothing on one side only, eats only half of the food on a plate, or reads only half of the writing before him. Unlike the patient with a straightforward hemianopia, who will search for the missing words in an apparently half-finished sentence, or look for the missing pieces of a puzzle or drawing, the victims of this disordered perception of external space are strangely unconcerned about their inadequate performance on the tests they are given. Space-blindness is a rare condition which may occur in isolation from the more frank physical signs of a vascular lesion and, therefore, is easily missed. The patient cannot assess the relationship of objects in space to his own body image; he no longer lives the three-dimensional existence that enables us to walk about in daylight and avoid bumping into things, or to walk straight to a chair, turn round and sit down. The space-blind patient sees the chair, makes for it clumsily across the room, fumbles around trying to bring the right part of his anatomy into proper relationship with the seat of the chair, and is as likely to finish by sitting on the floor as in the chair.

Hearing. A clouded or aphasic patient recovering from hemiplegia may be unable to indicate that his response to attempted re-education is handicapped by defective hearing, and observant nurses or therapists may first draw attention to it. Removal of wax, or a hearing aid brought from home to hospital, may make a great difference. Deafness may be conductive (middle-ear disease), perceptive (disorders of the inner ear), nerve deafness (damage to the VIII nerve or brain-stem), or central deafness (related to receptive dysphasia and impaired comprehension). Patients isolated by deafness become introspective, withdrawn, depressed and perhaps delusional. Difficulties in communication tax the patience of those who look after them. The patient whose handicap is perceptive deafness causing distortion of quality with intolerance of amplification resents being shouted at, but some time may elapse before the patient is fit to be tested for a hearing aid. Much patience, repetition and sympathetic understanding will be demanded of hospital staff or relatives during this interval.

Barriers with an intellectual bias include:

Defective comprehension. In the absence of disordered hearing mechanisms in the middle ear or of nerve deafness, this implies normal hearing with impaired interpretation of what is said; a central deafness or an auditory agnosia. Response from the patient may be variable, depending on the sense of well-being or attentiveness from day to day, or the patient may respond correctly to simple requests but fail with anything in the least complex. Reaction to sound or gesture may be associated with certain demands and acquired with practice, but without proper grasp of the full meaning of what has been said. In the early stages of recovery understanding is blunted owing to clouded consciousness, but this is distinct from a loss of comprehension which denies the patient the capacity to comprehend and interpret sounds picked up by normal hearing.

Perseveration. 'A response from the patient which is appropriate to a previously given instruction though not appropriate to the one just given' (Hurwitz 1966). This can be a most frustrating handicap to communication (involving speech) and to performance (involving thought and action).

Inattentiveness. Often a feature of clouded consciousness in early stages of recovery, of intellectual decline at a later stage, or of sheer exhaustion in old people debilitated by severe illness.

Memory loss. Loss of very recent memory has to be distinguished from inattentiveness. Hemiplegic invalids who fail to respond to instruction should be tested, for example by being asked to find an object they have been shown, which is then hidden for a time nearby, or by being given a name and address to remember and repeat ten minutes later.

Depression. Some very elderly patients lose interest in active life after a stroke and resist any attempts to restore them to it. Others who adopt a similar 'don't want to do it' attitude are depressed. Depression develops insidiously in old people, but response to treatment with modern mood-elevating drugs is often good, and the possibility of this diagnosis has to be kept constantly in mind.

Apraxia. Hurwitz defines apraxia as loss of the ability to perform a previously learned skilled act, although comprehension, motor power, coordination and sensation are adequate to do so. The movement made by the patient is coordinated but the whole meaning of the attempted act is lost.

Disorders of sensation. The intimate association between sensation and motor function was established by Sherrington, and others, who showed that a limb would be as if paralysed by section of its dorsal nerve roots, but if even one was preserved, especially the root carrying touch from the palm of the hand or sole of the foot, the motor deficit was minimal.

The sensory defects caused by cerebrovascular accidents may arise at cortical or subcortical levels involving the discriminative elements of touch, body awareness and sense of position in space, and the integration of sensory and motor impulses; at the level of thalamus and internal capsule with loss of all forms of sensation on the opposite side; or in the brain-stem with mixed patterns of dissociated anaesthesia.

Clinical pictures of disordered sensation vary from patient to patient, and in the same patient from day to day, because cortical changes are inconsistent and the distribution of atherosclerotic damage may be patchy. Concentration and cooperation tend to be erratic because mood and sense of well-being vary, depending on changes in the blood pressure and cardiac output of a circulation made unstable by the central effects of the stroke (Johnson *et al.* 1965). There appear to be two groups of sensory impulses with special influence on voluntary action and, therefore, on prospects of worthwhile recovery from a stroke. These are the impulses concerned with tactile discrimination and body awareness, and those relating to proprioception and postural stability:

1 *Touch and body image* A hemiplegic patient with cortical sensory loss is in special difficulty through being deprived of the unique sensory perception (stereognosis, discrimination and tactile localisation) normally provided by the hand. If recovery of this is poor, so also is the recovery of precision movement in hand and arm. Other special problems arising from impaired parietal cortical sensory appreciation are:

(*a*) *Neglect*, disuse of the affected limb, particularly the arm, despite good recovery of motor power and sensation. This will be referred to again as a special feature of dominant hemisphere lesions, being found more commonly in the right arm.

(*b*) *Anosognosia*, which means 'without knowledge of disease', occurs in varying degrees in different patients as a feature of non-dominant hemisphere lesions. Milder forms are evident in patients who recognise that an arm is paralysed when attention is drawn to it, but will say cheerfully 'it was working well yesterday', or 'it's because of the arthritis' in attempts to explain it. In fully developed anosognosia the patient refuses to admit to any weakness or disability in an obviously paralysed limb.

(*c*) *Denial*, is a more advanced form of anosognosia in which a patient disowns the affected arm and may ask to have it replaced with his own, gives bizarre explanations of its presence, or describes it by curious names.

2 *Postural stability* Hurwitz describes proprioceptive sensation as the basis of the servo system that continually signals and modifies length and tension in muscles. This maintains them at instant readiness and provides an essential component of righting reflexes and the initiation and integration of voluntary movement.

These disorders of sensation can present a wide variety of clinical pictures, but a few quite clear-cut 'syndromes' can be described because they have some value in prognosis and treatment.

At the level of the internal capsule the closely packed visual, sensory and motor tracts are especially vulnerable and lesions here cause dense hemiplegia with hemianopia and profound anaesthesia of the opposite side. This commonly follows embolic infarction owing to rheumatic heart disease or coronary thrombosis, and the prospects of recovery are better than in old people with infarction in an atherosclerotic cerebral circulation. When the ischaemic lesion mainly involves the thalamus, the thalamic syndrome of Dejerine and Roussay is produced with hemiparesis, severe sensory loss especially of proprioception, causing sensory ataxia (which reduces the patient to a floppy 'rag-doll'), pseudo-athetoid or choreiform involuntary movements ('thalamic dance'), and unremitting spontaneous pain with hypersensitivity to superficial stimuli.

Severe infarction of the non-dominant hemisphere often produces a characteristic clinical pattern. The patient recovers consciousness with hemianopia, dense hemiplegia, and hemianaesthesia (of the left side in a right-handed individual), but lacks insight into his predicament, may not admit to having anything wrong with the hemiplegic limbs, or may disown the paralysed arm. Sometimes this persists, even after quite good recovery of voluntary power in the arm, and the patient remains incontinent and fails to make any constructive attempts to walk. In other less severe instances, anosognosia and denial do not last more than a few days or weeks after onset, and with time, enough individual attention, and special emphasis in treatment on the sensory deficit, the prospects of recovery are good.

In contrast to this, some patients with vascular lesions of the dominant hemisphere recover quickly from a transitory right hemiparesis, but in later months 'go off their feet' despite minimal motor or sensory loss. Examination reveals traces of nominal or jargon dysphasia, a tendency to neglect the right hand, and a walking apraxia (Petren gait). The normal pattern of walking and postural control are both lost. The patient tends to fall backwards, and attempts to walk only with much difficulty. The feet seem to stick to the floor and even with help the patient can only shuffle shakily for a few hesitant steps before coming to a standstill. After much concentration and effort he may start again and repeat the same performance, and improvement is only gained with prolonged re-education and is short-lived if the patient cannot attend a hospital or day-centre permanently for supervision and exercises.

Apart from the transitory attacks of vertigo, diplopia, drop-attacks, weakness, paraesthesiae or falls that indicate vertebral-basilar insufficiency, some victims become bedridden for no better reason than the loss of confidence and initiative induced by too frequent falls; they may have no weakness, ataxia or focal cerebral signs to explain their disability, but they seem to acquire a new 'postural set' in their brain-stem and cannot stand upright. Instead they lean back at a dangerous tilt, and when they attempt to walk their legs appear to walk away from under their centres of gravity so that they fall backwards. Balance and walking exercises before a mirror to readjust postural fixation will do much for these patients, at least temporarily. [. . .]

References

ADAMS, G. F. and HURWITZ, L. J. (1963) 'Mental barriers to recovery from strokes', *Lancet*, 2, 533–7.

HURWITZ, L. J. (1966) 'Sensory defects in hemiplegia', *Physiotherapy*, 52, 238–42.

JOHNSON, R. H., SMITH, A. C., SPALDING, J. M. K. and WOLLNER, L. (1965) 'Effect of posture on blood pressure in elderly patients', *Lancet*, 1, 731.

28 Stroke: a diary of recovery

Douglas Ritchie

Douglas Ritchie used to broadcast during the last war under the pseudonym of 'Colonel Britton'. In May 1955, when he was aged 50 and head of BBC publicity, he sustained a severe stroke which produced paralysis and loss of feeling in his right arm and leg with complete loss of speech. To quote him (p. 174): 'when the stroke struck me my life became incomprehensible. Nobody would tell me – or I would not let them tell me – what was the matter with me. And when they did – or I would let them – my life was one of blank despair.'

His book grew out of a suggestion by a therapist that he should keep a diary. It tells the story of his progress, with many pitfalls and frustrations, to the stage when he could walk half a mile with the aid of a leg iron and sticks and his speech was greatly recovered, so that he could travel widely and address public meetings. He was then able to write, 'Now, at the age of sixty, I am healthy and independent (with the exception of my tendency to tennis elbow!) and, in recent years, my life has been full of surprises, full of excitement, and full of satisfaction.'

Throughout this period his wife was a continual source of support and comfort.

The stroke occurred at his father's house in Dorking. He was admitted to a nursing home where medical care was provided by a general practitioner, Dr Dorking and a consultant, Dr Wimpole.

When I had been in the nursing home a month I began to read. I read newspapers and periodicals before this, but it was simply a reflex action at first. My wife brought me some novels and I began to read them with some difficulty.

I could not remember very easily, but the real difficulty was in the style of writing. Of the first batch, I chose a book by Miss Ivy Compton-Burnett, who used to be a favoured novelist with me. The result was bad. I only read two or three pages when I had to stop. I picked up another book, as far as I can remember it was an old novel by A. J. Cronin, and it proved comparatively easy. Soon my wife obtained some books from the library. She could not get from me a list of books and so she chose for me writers for whom she knew I had a liking.

Henry Green, like Miss Compton-Burnett, was unreadable, although he was high up in my list before I had the stroke. L. P. Hartley was only moderate. If I had had an easier book I would have read it but this was the last of the batch. There were pages that were absolutely meaningless

---

Source: D. RITCHIE (1960) *Stroke: A Diary of Recovery*. London: Faber (selected extracts).

to me. [. . .] I had to settle for Maurice Edelman, whose books I had not read but whose lively style and whose straight-ahead manner of telling stories were what suited me now, [. . .] and very many novelists whose names I forgot the instant I had read them.

I puzzled over this. I had only to read a couple of pages when I knew it to be unreadable as far as I was concerned. Was it the style in which the book was written? Was it the straight-ahead manner compared with the allusive, complex manner? Or was it the things of the mind rather than the description of action that was the point? Or was it simply the grammar, the short sentences that were all my brain could accommodate?

I did not then come to any conclusion and if I had there would have been no speech or writing by which to impart such a conclusion; so it did not matter very much. I told my wife, in a series of nods and shakes of the head, that the novels ought to be simple, to be adventurous and not to be 'who dunnits' because my memory was poor.

At this time, too, I began to fly into sudden rages. The nurses were the chief target, and one of these, a middle-aged woman whose heart was over-flowing with love and kindness towards me, I could not bear in the room, even for a moment. In the first days in the nursing home I was grateful to her for her constant waiting on me. But she got into the habit of talking baby-talk to me. I think that was the beginning of it. [. . .] Once she even tried to make me eat some custard, holding the spoon. My sickly smile refused to come on my face on this occasion and she said: 'Temper, temper!'

My wife, who had an intuitive insight into what was troubling me, sought to calm me down. It was the nurse's manner; she was one of the most competent women there and if the matron was brought in, it would be the cause of a very disagreeable interview. I tried to say in what a fury I had been; but nothing at all came out except two or three words which I had used a day or so ago and which had nothing to do with anything. [. . .]

At that moment the nurse in question came in, carrying tea things. My wife immediately greeted her and asked how she was. From the nurse's condition of health, she turned to mine. Did the nurse think I was better? What appetite did I show? She hoped that I was not given any puddings, particularly milk puddings such as rice, tapioca and sago. The nurse began to reply but my wife stopped her with half a gesture and, with a female submission in which the nurse had to join, waited for the master to speak.

I wanted to laugh. Ev had, with a straight face, manoeuvred herself into an attitude (which was not hers at all) in order to show the nurse how mean and unimportant she was and how grand and important I was. But, of course, no sounds came except the word 'stick', which was the only word I had managed to get out since that morning. 'Stick,' I said. 'No.

Stick. Stick. No. Stick.' Sighing, my wife turned to the nurse and, with that air of haughty humility, allowed her to finish her sentence. [. . .]

I burst into laughter as soon as the nurse had left the room and my wife joined in, in relief at seeing me laugh for the first time since I had been in the nursing home.

I was choking with laughter when I realized I had lost control of myself. I do not think my wife was aware of it, but I think that it was from that moment that I began to feel that I had a serious illness. My paralysis and my inability to speak had not touched me – in a little while I would recover from these disabilities – but the loss of control of myself seemed to me a matter of the brain. Laughing was all very well, and the relief of it after the passion of rage which the innocent nurse had conjured up was quite understandable, but this laughter was sobbing and uncontrollable. However, my control was soon on again and I told myself it was nothing.

It was two or three days after that that the nurse enraged me more than ever. [. . .]

It had become the nurse's task to get me out of bed and into the chair. This unlucky nurse got me resting alongside the bed, and the chair, unbeknown to me, was just out of her reach. She stretched over to draw the chair nearer, and in so doing left me for a moment just as I sat down on nothingness. She could not pick me up off the floor and in a state of alarm rushed out to get some help. She brought back two nurses and between them they got me, in a state of some weakness but of more indignation, into the chair. The nurse had a guilty conscience and, though I could not separate myself from blame, I felt nothing should allow her into my room.

That afternoon when my wife arrived, I told her, with gestures and nods and shakes of my head, what had happened. The nurse was not entirely to blame, but I simply could not bear her in the room and I implored my wife to speak to the matron, taking the accident as the reason. Ev understood that I was at the end of my tether and she at once saw the matron and the nurse was forbidden to enter my room. [. . .]

Looking back to this period when I was in the nursing home, I realize that I was an impatient patient. It was a well-run establishment with kindly nurses. But I had not spoken for over a month and I was building up fast a dam without any outlet. I was perpetually being misunderstood. It was not so much the more familiar things that were being misunderstood – nods or shakes of the head were sufficient for these – it was the unfamiliar things, where conversation was necessary, that brought appalling silence. I did not know how much the paralysis had affected me, but even more I did not know how much the mind was coming adrift.

After two months he returned home to London, to the care of his own general practitioner, Dr Bloomsbury. After arriving home his uninformed assumptions that he would make rapid progress proved to be far from the truth.

The days which followed I can hardly remember. I gradually lost the feeling of being newly released, and there gradually grew upon me the feeling that Dr Bloomsbury, in whom I had full confidence, was going to leave me in the lurch.

Day after day passed without sign and I began to panic. I had little time, two full months had been wasted. A couple of days or four at the outside, and the doctor ought to be calling, arrangements should be made to get a physiotherapist, and all haste should be made. Now a week had passed, nothing.

Then the doctor came. I am not certain when he called. It may have been inside the week but it certainly seemed more than a week, more like a fortnight or three weeks. But I got excited. He came in, the usual grin missing from his face, and stood for a moment beside my bed. Then he asked my wife some questions and was gone.

When the front door had closed, I was eager to hear all that the doctor had said. Did he not ask for my blood-pressure? I motioned towards my arm. What questions did he ask?

My wife related all. It did not seem much. He had little time. He had been telephoned by Dr Wimpole, who had been fairly well satisfied with the progress up to date. The physiotherapist was away at the moment but he was expected back towards the end of this week. Dr Wimpole spoke highly of the physiotherapist.

I shook my head angrily at the continued mention of Dr Wimpole's name. What was Dr Bloomsbury's own opinion? What was the matter with me? It didn't matter what Dr Wimpole thought, or didn't think, what was the matter with me and how soon could it be cured? It must be called something. They thought in the nursing home it was called something – I never could make out what it was called – but they 'thought', not 'knew', and I was awaiting the truth, what it was, in words of one syllable. Dr Bloomsbury had charge of me; I was expecting that he would examine me – none of that pencil business under my feet – a proper examination – and that he would then tell me what he had discovered.

This is what I thought. By contorting my face into an agony of question marks, I was silently asking. My wife made an heroic attempt to answer these inquiries and complaints but all to no avail. I was silently silent for the next few hours.

The following days I changed my mind many times. At first I thought that the doctor was busy and that he had called on me to see how bad I was and to reserve a time to examine me properly. A day or two and he would call with the blood-pressure indicator and all the tools of his trade.

He would drink a glass of gin and french or whisky and the grin would go over his face and his advice, wise as it always was and very much in sympathy with me, would assist me to recover the use of my limbs and to speak.

Then I thought of the National Health Service. The doctor had treated me medically for several years without receiving a penny from me. Then I became ill in the country and for two months I, or my wife, paid the doctors privately for their services. When I returned to London I went to the doctor in whom I had confidence and whom I liked, and paid him exactly nothing. It was no wonder that he felt cheated.

Looking back to his visit, I felt now that he was unfriendly. He had stayed only the bare minimum of time. His normal affability was lacking and he was frowning. He was terse to my wife and left, coldly saying nothing. Heaven knew when he would return again.

Then again I changed my mind. This chap would not consider his pocket. He and I were friends, not close friends, but the sort of thing you would call 'in sympathy'. Of course, it would be a bit of a shock to him, my electing to go as a private patient when I was outside his beat. However, there wasn't anything to do about it now.

But it was odd that he never came.

Looking back at it now, two or three years later, there was not much the doctor could do. He had, as I had not, a clear idea of what was the matter with me. A cerebral thrombosis or haemorrhage. In other words, a stroke. To doctors by no means an unusual thing, and a thing that a series of visits could do nothing to help. It was a sad case, though to be expected given my pressure of blood, and the doctors had to give over to spontaneous recovery, to the arts of the physiotherapist, and, though I knew it not, to me.

But above all, it was most unfair of me to hold such base suspicions regarding the N.H.S. and private practice against any doctors without any evidence, and above all against Dr Bloomsbury.

His difficulties with speech continued to limit his relationships for a long time. The following passage concerns his relationship with other patients at the Camden Rehabilitation Centre which he began to attend nine months after his stroke. The events here occurred seventeen months after his illness began.

Among all the strokes, I only struck one who was cheerful. The rest were depressed like myself. He was paralysed on the left side, spoke well – he was a New Zealander so I thought, or an Australian – and not so badly impaired as I in walk or in arm movement.

I, as usual, at once disliked him. He got into conversation with the instructors, which annoyed me, because I could not. And his conversation was a cut above these others. He had obviously been to a good many other countries and he spoke to the chief physiotherapist, a Persian, about the Middle East and one of the patients, a young Nigerian student, about Africa.

A week later, I found myself sitting next to him during a break time in the gymnasium. He made some remark and I stuttered some reply. He, of course, noticed that I had little speech. He adapted his conversation to me and did not demand difficult replies. When possible, he was content with 'yes' or 'no'.

I asked him if he were a New Zealander. (The words 'New Zealander' came into my mind. Not like some words, which refused to come into my mind despite minutes or hours of reflections. Then it was just word formation. It had begun to become a little less slow. 'M-M-M-N-New-New-New-Zv-Zv-New-Zealand-New Zealand?')

'No,' said he in some surprise, 'I am Israeli. I am a Jew.'

He had served in the British Army during the war and had been a colonel. He was about 45 and lived in Tel-Aviv. He was a barrister. His name was Maklev.

I got to know him in the next few days and I liked him very much. I had Israeli friends, or friends who had relations in Israel, and I knew two or three people who knew him.

The Centre became a different place for me. Every break for lunch and tea, we would sit together and he would chat about the war.

The physiotherapist gave him his first tangible assistance . . .

At last the physiotherapist came. A fat, short man, about 40 or 45 years old, dressed in a blue serge suit. He was quiet and he had a good-tempered expression. He seemed to have hidden reserves of personality and I liked him immediately. He took off his jacket, folded it neatly and placed it on a chair, and then turned to give me his whole professional attention.

I was lying on the hospital bed, in my pyjamas, a blanket over me. He pushed the blanket to one side and examined my right leg and foot. He bent my leg and the knee gave sideways. He straightened my knee and then doubled my leg so that the knee came up and the ankle was nearly to my thigh. I emitted a groan, because the muscle hurt, and he looked pleased.

His expression was sympathetic because he had hurt me, and amused because the pain was not too great and he had struck me looking at him with amazement, as though the private fees I was paying him did not allow for groaning.

But above all, his expression was so intense. He was studying my face with such passionate interest the moment the hurt came. I laughed. It was relief that someone knew something about me. And the physiotherapist laughed too. I had confidence in him from that moment.

He came twice a week, always at one o'clock precisely and he stayed one hour. The nurse was in the room, too, so that when he was away she knew what to do.

At first he concentrated on the knee. He massaged and he bent the knee. He was so intense one day that the knee metaphorically shook at his coming. The moment that I saw the knee tremble in his grasp, I felt like cheering. The physiotherapist smiled in pure triumph.

About six months after his stroke he began to walk, but this was by no means plain sailing.

I began to feel my foot dragging. My idea was to keep the foot up by means of a piece of elastic running from the toe of my shoe to my knee. I managed to make my wife understand and she asked C. He replied that it was a calliper that I needed. He suggested a surgical bootmaker or one of the shops round Mortimer Street or Wigmore Street.

Ev got on to one or two of these and the price was so outrageous (for something that I would use for a week or a fortnight, so I thought), that we decided to call the doctor to give us advice. Ev telephoned him and he promised to give her a note to the National Hospital in Queen Square.

A day or two passed and Ev wheeled me to the hospital across Southampton Row. A couple of hours of waiting and then the doctor saw us. I stripped – or rather I was stripped by the nurse and my wife – and the doctor examined me thoroughly and, beyond a few kind grunts, said nothing. I dressed with the help of the nurse and meantime my wife had got the name of the hospital shoe-maker and had an appointment for us both to see him next week.

I was wheeled home in time for a late luncheon and a sleep. At any rate somebody is moving, rather slowly, but moving, I thought.

I spent the next three weeks grumbling about my calliper. I did not know at all what sort of thing a calliper was. The measurement was taken of my leg and foot and I was asked which shoes I would like. The shoe-maker explained that I might exchange the calliper for another pair of shoes only if they had the necessary fitment. My indignation arose simply because of the waiting. C had suggested a calliper one day, and weeks had passed, what with waiting at the hospital, the doctor being absent one week, and the shoe-maker being at the hospital once a week only, before the calliper reached me.

After my third visit to the surgical shoe-maker at the hospital I conducted a conversation with C, much to his surprise and my own. I usually kept silence with everyone, beyond a 'yes' or 'no', now that I saw the idiocy of trying to speak. But a blank rage filled me and I was yearning to find someone new to rage to. I started the exercises, meditating what words I should use, but suddenly I said (as far as I remember): 'F--king doctors! I don't-know-what-the-f--king-doctors-do. F--king-well-wait-wait-wait!'

I gazed at him in utter astonishment. He gazed at me. Then he started to laugh and I started too.

The swear words were not familiar to me. I used an occasional 'bloody' and 'bastard' in the office, but in the ordinary way I hardly ever used bad language. I certainly did not object to the use of obscene or blasphemous words; they are only used for cheap effect when the people who use them have little vocabulary.

I had little vocabulary then but I had to bear C in mind and to hear those words come trickling out of my mouth made me feel like a little boy using a forbidden word. So I laughed, too, but I felt my face going pink.

C remarked that he had not heard me talk like that. He jokingly advised me to spend more of my time at the hospital. Then I would keep my temper at boiling temperature and my speech would come back at record rate.

But the words would not come back. I thought them again but it was one thing to think them and quite another to say them. There was, I observed, a wide difference between thinking without words and actually thinking in words and about words. I could day-dream (and indeed I day-dreamed much too much both before and after my stroke). I could think, actively, without using words, and, coming down to earth, I rehearsed speeches silently. But there was the blank wall. The minute I rehearsed speeches with my tongue, even though I kept silent, the words would not come.

The medical director of the Camden Centre made a good impression on Ritchie.

Eventually he sent for me. Dr O'Malley, handsome, over six feet tall, I should judge, rotund, white-haired, though he wasn't more than 54 or 55, expensive clothes, suede shoes, and I, five feet eight tall, at least a stone or a stone and a half heavier than I should be, grey hair in front, in blue battle tunic, in too-tight shorts, bare legs, and with a calliper on my right foot. I felt like a concentration camp prisoner, with my tongue cut out, standing before the commandant. He had all my papers in front of him, my previous convictions, and he sat looking grimly out of the window.

But he turned round, gave me a charming smile, said 'Sit down, old chap,' and the picture had changed again.

I remember little of the conversation. Despite his bigness and his personality, which invaded me and all those in the Centre, he was strangely humble.

Towards the end, he asked if I wanted anything. I had previously asked Miss B whether there were any books about strokes that were easily read and she said she would speak to Dr O'Malley. With difficulty I raised the question and he promised me a book about psychiatry, containing several pages on aphasia.

I thought about Dr O'Malley the next few days. He had not said anything special. But the witch doctor idea was gone for good. And the date of my recovery, if any, depended on me.

He found Dr O'Malley's book on Aphasia very interesting and helpful, and commented:

There is a mystery about books on illness. Many doctors refuse to let their patients read them. They say that the more ignorant among them are bewildered by the medical terms, and feel that they are worse than is the case. I feel that there is something in this but very often the doctors are rationalizing and refuse to give information for the unconscious reason that their 'magical' or, in the modern style, 'scientific', power will pass away with the patient's knowledge. But knowledge is nearly always better than ignorance, for anyone, for patients as for doctors. The known, however bad it is, is nearly always better than the unknown. The patient, knowing what is the matter with himself, can help the doctor on his symptoms. He can keep a cool head, instead of a mind nearly panic-stricken with the unknown. His calls on the doctor are less frequent and he is far less prone instead of more inclined, to hypochondria.

By reading these books I, at any rate, was immensely helped. I was not only given things to do but – and this is much the more important thing for me – the reason for giving me things to do was apparent. Now I did not write in my diary nightly out of respect for my therapist, but because I knew that it was the only way to get writing back to normal.

Later on he became able to do much more for himself, but not without a struggle, as the next two extracts show (23 months and 26 months after his stroke).

Miss B suggested it was time I went to the Centre under my own steam.

I was aghast at this. I had not travelled except in an ambulance or a car since my stroke and considered that there were at least a score of patients who might try the bus instead of me.

Miss B made it clear that it was not to economize in the use of ambulances: it was to make me self-sufficient. 'You will not be content,' she said comfortingly, 'with an ambulance or a car when you finish at the Centre. You should try it now. I'll go with you for the first few times.'

I was still aghast. I would have been perfectly happy to go anywhere either in an ambulance or a car to the end of my life. And what was that about my finishing at the Centre? I thought I should remain around two years or three years more at the Centre. And I thought of the bus. They were not made for people with strokes. (They had half a bus in the Centre and made one step in and take a seat and step out. But I thought they were not serious.) Or the Underground. Before I managed to get myself in, the doors would have closed. . . . But I could not confess myself a coward – although I was one – and nodded when she suggested a date. The following was noted in my diary:

April 2. Miss B took me in the Underground and a bus to the Centre this morning. There was a considerable amount of walking at both ends of the Underground, Holland Park and Tottenham Court Road, but I managed all right. The steps out of Tottenham Court Road were the worst. The escalators were not bad. We took a No. 29 bus from Tottenham Court Road. All went smoothly. Like aeroplanes, it's all a question of taking off and landing – the journey is devoid of panic; the starting and the ending are the exciting parts. Of the two, I think the Underground is preferable.   (*35 minutes*)

And here is his account of his first journey to the Camden Centre on his own.

During that afternoon, my journey to Camden Road alone was horribly exciting. To anybody else it was entirely without incident.

I gave a lot of thought to it. In case talking proved impossible, I had 8d in my left-hand jacket pocket for the Underground and a sixpence for the bus. At the other end the bus, with me on it, stopped – or did not stop – at a request sign. If the conductor were there, I could motion him to stop. But what if the conductor were to be on top? Ah, then I had to be on the left side so that I could ring the bell from my seat. (On the right side there was no bell cord.) I had a frozen look on my face that would prevent anyone dropping a remark which demanded an answer, and a rather exaggerated routine with my stick to show the fellow travellers and, above all, the bus drivers that they must exercise especial care. Now that I had carefully considered everything my thoughtfulness – or excessive timidity, as someone might have called it – would be successful. I started now from Holland Park.

The four hundred yards to Holland Park Station – the 8d ticket without a word to the ticket clerk – lift down – a hundred, no, fifty yards through the corridor – train stopping at the platform while I am stumbling down the twenty or so steps – long wait on the seat until the next train came in – the luck I am in that the coach doors are exactly opposite me – the corner seat in which I just sit down in the moment the train starts – the look I give at the list of stations – an extreme effort in order to eject myself at Tottenham Court Road while passengers pour in – more steps up – more yards in the corridor – and now the escalators.

The top of the escalators – bad foot on the immovable one, good foot on the movable platform – steps, steps, steps, with passengers pouring down on top of me because I can only climb the stairs with the left bannister, and out into St Giles Circus – very crowded past Horne Bros., Lyons' Corner House, until the No. 29 bus stop, when I slacken, puffing, and lean against the concrete bus pillars, very tired, while four or five people queueing give me unfriendly glances. After nearly ten minutes, the bus comes along. I get on and take a seat on the left side before the bus starts. I take the sixpence out and in a whisper say 'Sixpence' to the conductor. Nobody says anything to me, and the conductor stays below when we come to Camden Road stop and helps me get off.

Camden Road is a wide road, with traffic whizzing by, but the zebra crossing is a mile and a half (or, more truthfully, a hundred yards) up and the Medical Rehabilitation Centre is just across the street, so I take my life in my hands and cross.

In the changing-room, I alternate between pride at my feat and a wish to tell everyone, and fear of my return journey.

At four o-clock precisely, I again board a No. 29 bus. The driver is in a hurry and so I have grimly to grab the handrail on the platform and not move until the next stop, the conductor at first protesting, then shrugging his shoulders and concluding that I am mentally deficient.

At Tottenham Court Road there is a machine which sells me an eight-penny ticket. I accomplish the escalators, take a corner seat in the train and watch with beating heart to see Holland Park turn up.

At my flat I sink into a chair and allow my wife, in her flu-ey dressing-gown, to praise me and to fetch a glass of whisky.

29 Old folks in wet beds

J. L. Newman

Last summer I asked one of the leading English geriatricians what views
he held, on the problem of incontinence. His reply was, 'We don't have
any problem with incontinence'; but later, when I asked one of his ward
sisters how many of her patients wet their beds, she looked around the
thirty-two beds and counted them, 'Eight,' she said. But they had no
problem with incontinence, and by the same standards nor have many of
us.

Before the visiting physician does his round there is a period of intense
activity in which the staff see that all is shipshape. If he turns the bedclothes down and finds a wet patch he pretends he has not noticed; the
sister hastily covers it up again, and when he has gone she may have
something to say to the junior nurse. How different if it had been blood;
then they would have been all eyes and interest. But blood would have
posed only a few problems in diagnosis, its treatment would have been
fairly simple, and the prognosis might have been quite good. But a patch
of urine cannot be readily explained – its treatment has proved beyond
most of us; and, as to its significance, it will make all the difference
between social acceptance and rejection with all that that involves in
prolonged hospital care and expense. One is respectable and the other is
not, but I have no doubt which is the more important.

Causes of incontinence

It will not be much good looking up 'Incontinence' in the textbooks,
because they are written by people who do not have any problem with it.
You will find in the books that hemiplegias and paralysis agitans are
causes of incontinence; but they are not – witness the number of victims of
both who are walking the streets without it. A hemiplegia will cause a
temporary loss of bladder control just as the operation of unilateral chor-
dotomy does; but it should pass off in a few days, and if it does not either
our diagnosis or our management may be at fault. It is the same with
Parkinson's disease, with all respect to Parkinson himself, who fell into the
error of saying it did. Why should the bladder be upset by a disease of a
section of the nervous system that plays no part in its innervation? It is
the same with many of the local conditions that have been blamed for

Source: *British Medical Journal*, 30 June 1962, pp. 1824–7.

causing incontinence – cystitis and caruncles, for instance. How can a little fleshy outgrowth at the urethral opening make any difference to the functioning of a muscle far removed from it? And as to cystitis, it makes you hurry up, but it does not make you wet the bed; again, witness the majority of its victims who do not.

Brocklehurst (1951) wrote a monograph on incontinence. He had to admit that most cases were inexplicable, but suggested that many were connected with a contracted bladder, and he treated them by progressive stretching under cystometric control. But why does the bladder become contracted? Is it the cause of incontinence or its result, the persistently empty bladder becoming contracted? Or is it a case of the 'local anatomical changes' or the 'senile degeneration of the bladder' which are alleged by some to be the cause of incontinence but which have never been seen by any pathologist?

I asked most of the geriatricians I met overseas what they thought about urinary incontinence, and most of them spoke about 'carelessness' or 'laziness', or, to use the expression of one of them, 'not enough in the top story'. Yet these old women who lie in wet beds unabashed are the very ones who will pull down their nighties hastily if you happen to uncover them, which is not suggestive of carelessness. And as to their top stories, they may be confused at times but they have their reasoning powers in plenty for most ordinary activities. Perhaps Dr Ewart, of the Vasa Hospital in Göteborg, came nearer to the truth when he added that besides simple carelessness some cases of incontinence might be a reaction against growing old. 'Let's be children again', as he said. I have long thought that there might be something in this, that it might be an end-result of the possible urge of the old to retrace the steps of childhood, first giving up walking, then having to be fed, and finally ending up by resuming a foetal position curled up, with the bed as the uterus and urine as the liquor amnii.

Treatment is naturally based on the particular theory of causation. The first attack is on the infection, if present, combined with an attempt to restore mobility; and if this fails, as it often does, recourse may be had to stretching the bladder or, empirically, to injections of testosterone. The miserable remainder who do not respond to any of these methods of treatment are usually relegated to long-stay annexes, where they will remain, making exorbitant demands on the nursing staff, a burden to everyone for the rest of their lives. But it is my belief that mental decay, senile or otherwise, plays practically no part in the genesis of incontinence. Of course there are some profoundly demented psychotics in geriatric wards as well as in others whose excretory habits are positively antisocial, but they are totally different, as anyone who has to deal with them will recognize, from the quiet apathetic old folk who simply lie in wet beds.

Classification

At this point I had better try to offer a classification of the different kinds of urinary incontinence by known causes, and the first thing to do is to differentiate between true and apparent incontinence. In the apparent group the first are those cases of precipitancy that cannot be satisfied in time. They are common in hospital practice, with immobility in bed and a lack of sympathetic and adequate nursing care as crucial factors, and with precipitancy, usually associated with infection, as no more than an aggravating one. Next are those conditions associated with polyuria, and one that is frequently overlooked is that which arises from nephrosclerosis. The kidney can keep down the level of nitrogenous waste products in the blood only by excreting increased quantities of unconcentrated urine, and it does this by day and night. These patients, if given hypnotics and not awakened during the night, may easily become the victims of an incontinence that is genuine but artificially induced. Another kind of incontinence is that which is associated with the supine position. 'I simply could not urinate lying down', wrote the victim of a coronary thrombosis in *Disabilities* (1952), 'It took me a week to learn the trick, and I advise everyone over 50 to practise it'. Some old men are not as lucky as he was. They get out of bed to try and an officious nurse thinks they are wandering and gets them back. The next thing is that the bed-boards go up and they are found next morning reeking of paraldehyde in a wet bed. That is why I always regard bed-boards with the most profound suspicion.

The causes of true incontinence of urine are more or less as follows; (1) *Neurogenic*: sensory, as in tabes; motor, as in bilateral upper motor lesions of whatever cause; combined, in paraplegia and cauda equina lesions. (2) *Traumatic*: in vesico-vaginal fistula. (3) *Bladder-neck disturbance:* displacement, causing stress incontinence; obstruction, by prostate enlargement or by constipation (and even pessaries). (4) *Dementia*, when profound.

Obviously this classification does not embrace all cases, and it remains to identify another, x, the unknown factor.

Stress and conflict

What I believe may be the answer to this problem came to me as I was reading Sargant's (1957) fascinating book *Battle for the Mind*:

Dogs, like human beings, break down when stresses or conflicts become too great for their nervous systems to master. At the point of breakdown their behaviour begins to vary from that normally characteristic of their inherited temperamental type and previous conditioning. The amount of stress or conflict that a dog can master without breaking down varies with its physical condition. A lowering of resistance can be brought about by such things as fatigue, fevers, drugs, and glandular changes. When the nervous system has been stimulated 'transmarginally' (that is to say beyond its capacity to respond normally) for long periods, a dog's responses eventually become inhibited, whatever its temperamental type, may be. . . . This transmarginal inhibition is protective and results in altered behaviour. Three distinguishable phases of increasingly abnormal behaviour occur: (*a*) The so-called 'equivalent' phase in which the brain gives the same response to both strong and weak stimuli. (*b*) The so-called 'paradoxical' phase in which the brain responds more actively to weak stimuli than to strong. (c) The so-called 'ultraparadoxical' phase in which conditioned responses and behaviour patterns turn from positive to negative or from negative to positive.

I thought of my incontinent old patients in the light of what I had read. 'The older the person the less easily can he improvise new conditioned responses to such changes in environment.' Could it be that in old age wetting the bed was one of the responses to break down under stress? What of those who repeatedly wet the bed, whose sheet is no sooner changed than they do it again? It might be that they are in a paradoxical phase, when their brains respond more readily to a weak stimulus from a filling bladder than to a strong one. I thought of Mrs B, an intelligent and cooperative woman of over 80 who had been working hard at her physical rehabilitation after a minor cerebellar thrombosis. Her balance was affected, and she fell and broke her hip. When she came back from having it pinned she was a completely changed character. She now took no interest in her recovery. When she was lifted on to a bed-pan she made no attempt to use it, but as soon as she was back in bed she would wet it, and would strike out at the nurses who came to attend to her. This may look to some like dementia, but to me it seemed a perfect example of the ultraparadoxical phase in which her response to the bed-pan had turned from positive to negative and to the nurses from negative to positive. How else could such a reversal of temperament be explained? 'One set of behaviour patterns in man can be temporarily replaced by another that altogether contradicts it; not by persuasive indoctrination alone but also by imposing intolerable strains on a normally functioning brain.'

Sargant goes on in his book to describe the application of stress to masses under religious pressure and to individuals as a deliberate means of inducing confession and political conversion. This may seem a long way from our treatment of an old person at home or a patient in hospital. But is it? When she is independent an old woman, or an old man, is treated, with at least outward respect. She performs every day countless acts as she has performed them for years, so that they have become ingrained into her whole system of life. She dresses in the morning in the clothes she chooses for the day; she sits down to her meals and helps herself to what she wants. She visits the lavatory, shuts the door, and locks it. She takes a couple of aspirins for her rheumatism; and so on through the day till she decides that it is time to go to bed, when she undresses with all the routine of washing and cleaning her dentures and finally putting out the light; simple repetitive acts backed by years of custom and convenience, but none the less the acts on which the whole pattern of life is built.

How different when she comes into hospital. No longer a person of consequence, she is ordered about by a chit of a nurse. She may be admitted into a single ward ('one method of altering a prisoner's normal conditioning is solitary confinement in the early stages of the examination'). She finds herself in an utterly strange environment among strange people. Strange men come into her room, talk to one another at the end of her bed about her, and leave without any explanation. She wonders if they are going to operate. Is her illness serious? Which of the nurses is going to look after her? and what is her name? (Pavlov could produce a breakdown by anomalies in the conditioning signals given. 'A hungry dog became uncertain what would happen next and how to face these confused circumstances. This could disrupt its normal nervous stability ... just as happens with human beings.')

'Nurse, nurse, may I have a bed-pan?' 'You'll have to wait a minute. I'm busy. We'll be bringing them round in a minute.' A minute becomes two, five, and then ... (Pavlov found that a powerful way of producing a rupture in higher nervous activity was 'to increase the time between the giving of the signal and the arrival of food. He found, in fact, that the dogs' brains revolted against any abnormal prolongation of waiting under stress. Breakdown occurred when a dog had to exert very strong or very protracted inhibition.')

She is ill. She is in pain. She would like an aspirin; but the nurse has taken hers away and she may not have one till sister brings it to her. (A fourth way of producing a breakdown was to tamper with a dog's physical condition by subjecting it to '... gastro-intestinal disorders, fever, or by disturbing its glandular balance'.) And so the patient's treatment in hospital goes on, with strict conformation to a new and largely incomprehensible routine that bears no relation to the ingrained pattern of life at home. Meals are taken sitting uncomfortably in bed, there is no friendly face of the family to be seen, lights are still burning after one would like to switch them off. Everything builds up to reinforce one or other of the methods of artificial reversal of behaviour patterns which Pavlov designed deliberately and which we apply all unconsciously. One final quotation: 'A further means of altering a prisoner's normal conditioning, especially one who has hitherto been a person of authority or consequence, is to make him wear old and ill-fitting prison clothes with trousers which he must support with his own hands, and to leave him unshaven. Such social degradation can prove most effective.' Surely this might have been written about hospital pyjamas with their 40-in cords to go round a 38-in. waist. And is not being fed a form of social degradation?

That, I believe is x, the unknown fifth heading in my classification of the causes of wet beds, alone principally, although, of course, there may be coexisting abnormalities to which geriatricians have hitherto attached an importance that I believe to be unjustified. That emotional breakdown can indeed cause incontinence was shown by the experience of some prisoners-of-war in the Korean campaign. 'Emotional isolation alone has a profound effect on most normal people. When a man is kept in confinement without trial and without hope he will, after a few weeks, become profoundly depressed. Life ceases to have any significance for one who has been debarred from every activity and deprived of every relationship which gave it meaning. Usually the prisoner becomes indifferent to his surroundings, apathetic, dishevelled, and incontinent' (Storr 1961). Is that so very far removed from our geriatric wards? It may be much nearer than we would like to think.

Environmental change

An objection against hospital management being the principal cause of incontinence may be that it is not entirely a hospital problem, that it often develops in the home – witness the demands for institutional care on account of it. The fact is that a patient does not have to go into hospital to be handled in a psychologically upsetting way, that very many old folk are needlessly babied, and hence humiliated in their own homes, and that we have not found a way of making the transition from employment to retirement, from activity to any degree of dependence smooth and gradual. All these things must tell and on occasion produce a breakdown in lifelong habits. Incontinence is very much commoner in hospitals and old folks homes than elsewhere, and I have found it relatively uncommon in communities of the same age as our hospital incontinents but living an independent life on their own. We need to know a great deal more about the incidence of incontinence in different groups, and to see if it can be correlated with the kind of care they receive and with such things as the retention around them of their own furniture and possessions. Several authors have commented on the way incontinence may follow a change in environment, usually from home to hospital but sometimes the other way – surely a further indication, if one were needed, that it is not dementia that is responsible.

Change in outlook

If I am right, the contracted bladder is the result of its never being allowed to become full because the equivalent or paradoxical phase will not let it. So we shall not treat incontinence with tidal drainage, antibiotics, and so on. What, then, shall we do? For the established condition I doubt if there is much we can do beyond follow the advice of one experienced ward sister with whom I discussed it. 'You've got to start housetraining them all over again,' she said.

But of course the main thing is prevention, and here I believe we could do a great deal by bringing the hospital environment into line with the individual instead of expecting the individual, at an age when he is least capable of it, to adapt himself to a preordained institutional routine which, if it is looked at dispassionately, often has little to recommend it. What we should try to do is to make this transition from independence to dependence a gradual one and not too rigid.

In the light of what we know about isolation (and isolation at home is one of the disasters of old age) I doubt very much the advisability of admitting a geriatric patient to a single ward. A two- or four-bedded one would avoid the risks of solitary confinement and allow the newcomer to profit by the experience of his fellows. Secondly, the patient must be made welcome and have someone who will take an interest in him, a sort of daughter substitute (and this is where frequent changes of nursing staff, though inevitable, are unfortunate). But at least real daughters can be more encouraged by avoiding restrictive visiting hours. Near relatives, especially if they are a part of the accepted home background, should be encouraged to come and go when they like, subject only to sister's permission, so far as is possible.

We need a drastic reorientation in our whole outlook on hospital care generally, and particularly in the admission ward. We should have a variety of available wraps; and if we must provide pyjamas they should at least be big enough, but ordinary clothes should be worn whenever possible, and proper shoes. We need day-rooms that cannot be appropriated as supplementary wards, dining-rooms in which all patients who can would be expected to take their meals sitting up at tables unless bed was prescribed, and not merely used as a means of keeping the patient quietly out of the way. They should have the food brought to them in dishes and should help themselves to what they want. In the same way they might be encouraged to help themselves to some of their own medicines instead of having to rely on someone else. To leave half a dozen aspirins in a pot by the bedside would be quite adequate control for this kind of drug.

We should need to awaken the hospital staff at all levels to the needs of the elderly patient, which are no less their own than the needs of the small child. They must have help when they need it and not when they do not. This applies particularly to feeding. No patient must be humiliated, and what can be more humiliating than to be fed when you are capable of feeding yourself? The very worst thing a nurse can do is to keep a patient waiting for a bed-pan. In their own way doctors are as great offenders. How often do you see them conduct a conversation out of the patient's earshot and then pass on? If a patient is worth considering at all he is worth a moment's personal approach. For many of them we have not much to offer except friendship and a kindly word; but if we used these powerful weapons oftener and to greater advantage we should be in a better position to ban the barbiturates and take away the cot sides. Finally, we must regard a wet bed as a challenge. It must not be accepted by the nursing staff as an objectionable trait in a senile patient. It should be reported to the doctor, and the first question he ought to ask himself is, 'What have we done wrong?'

Of course not all cases of urinary incontinence have anything to do with Pavlovian psychology: it is only a theory as yet that any of them have. But I do believe that the application of Pavlov's findings to the practice of geriatrics provides a reasonable explanation for what is otherwise quite inexplicable. It gives us a positive approach instead of the blind acceptance of 'senility' about which we can do nothing. It may even cause us to look at our own behaviour and accepted methods with a more critical eye and sometimes to replace antibiotics, tidal drainage, and hormones with vegetable dishes, pretty nighties, and a kind word.

References

BROCKLEHURST, J. C. (1951) *Incontinence in Old People*, Edinburgh: Livingstone.
  Disabilities (1952) London: The Lancet.
SARGANT, W. (1957) *Battle for the Mind: A Physiology of Conversion and Brainwashing*.
  London: Heineman.
STORR, A. (1961) *Sunday Times*, 4 June, p. 21.

30   Treatment of the 'irremediable' elderly patient

Bernard Isaacs

Here is a title as full of questions as a pomegranate is full of seeds. How does one treat the irremediable? If the irremediable is treated, is it irremediable? Is 'to treat' less than 'to remedy'? And why the contiguity of 'irremediable' and 'elderly'? Are all elderly irremediable? Are all irremediable elderly? These questions concern attitudes. They are important because attitudes rather than expertise determine the outcome of treatment.

Attitudes

There was a time, before I entered on that state of grace peculiar to the geriatrician, when the phrase 'treatment of the irremediable elderly patient' would have concisely defined geriatrics for me. Later, when I began to work in geriatric medicine, I would have indignantly rebutted the implication that anyone or anything old was irremediable; for did we not profess our faith in the liturgical phrase: 'an ill old person is ill because he is ill and not because he is old'? Now, after years of the pragmatic practice of my art, I welcome the recognition that we geriatricians, and not we alone, devote much of our activities to the treatment of the irremediable. Few diseases at any age are cured; most whisper to the patient of their continuing presence, long after the ink is dry on the discharge letter. The treatment of the irremediable is both a worthy objective and an accurate description of much modern medicine.

Who are the 'irremediable'?

First, who are they not? They are not, and must not be confounded with, the undiagnosed. They are not the confused, the incontinent, the senile. Confusion and incontinence are symptoms of impaired function of the nervous system and bladder. The words give no information on cause or cure. The term 'senility' offends the geriatrician; it requires an effort of will even to write it. In my mind's eye I see the word garbed in a cloak of

Source: M. WARE (ed.) (1974) *Medicine in Old Age*. London: British Medical Association, pp. 9–13.

black, with the blood of ill old people dripping from its lanky fingers. A melodramatic image perhaps; but how often has the attachment of this label to an ill old patient spelt the end of diagnostic and therapeutic endeavour, and condemned him to a slow death by stewing in his own urine?

Every ill person of whatever age has a right to a diagnosis; and only when this has been established is it possible to talk about remediability or irremediability. 'Senility' is not a diagnosis; it spells relegation for the patient and abdication by the doctor. I look forward to the day when the word 'senility' will have disappeared from acceptable medical terminology, as the word 'insanity' has done.

Irreversible disease

Many pathological processes which are common in old age are at present irreversible. These include neoplasm, atherosclerosis, and neuronal degeneration – one or more of which accompany most old people on their last long journey to the grave. It is among these sadly disabled people that the doctor seeks opportunities for effective intervention; and opportunities abound.

Treating the irremediable

A man of 69 was seen for the first time two months after the onset of a right hemiplegia, and after failure of a trial of rehabilitation. The patient was bedfast, there was no return of movement to the affected side, he had a catheter in his bladder, and he was unable to speak or to comprehend. He had been found picking faeces from his rectum and smearing them on his locker. He disturbed other patients by shouting. He had struck out at the nurses, and given his wife a black eye.

First the wife was interviewed. Who was this man? What kind of person was he? He had been a good husband, a loving father, abstemious, a steady and conscientious worker, a keen amateur gardener, a fit man, proud of his good health and work record, inclined to disparage those less healthy than himself. What did she know of his illness? What did she say to him when she visited? She talked to him; sometimes, she thought, he understood her; sometimes he pushed her away and turned his head away from her. Once he lifted his hand to her, a thing he never did in his life. Did she ever cry? She had gone home and wept to herself every night since his illness began, but hadn't told anyone. Did she think he was going to die? She didn't know, but sometimes she found herself half-wishing that he would, and that made her feel wicked. Had she told this to anyone? Not a soul. Had anyone told her what was likely to happen to her husband? No one.

Next the patient was examined. His tongue was dry, his rectum packed with hard dry faeces. There was a pressure sore on his heel; his urine was infected; his haemoglobin level had dropped. He couldn't speak or understand language, but he could pick up situational clues. He could sing 'Tipperary' with the words matching the tune; he could count up to ten if he was started off; he could correctly identify 'bottle', 'tumbler', 'spectacles'. He could build toy blocks one on top of the other. He could match dominoes. He had no movement in his arm or leg, but he could sit up in bed with minimal support. Suddenly, out of this irremediable situation, all kinds of opportunities of effective intervention were appearing, like crocuses piercing the wintry soil.

The nurses began first. They put him on a fluid chart, gave him adequate nourishing drinks, talking to him as they did so, telling him what they were trying to do, encouraging him to take the cup and drink himself, trying to find out what he would like – orange juice, milk, tea, beer, perhaps even a glass of whisky. They found his pipe, his false teeth, his razor and comb. They emptied his bowel, they gave him fruit. They put him in the bath twice a day, gave him a support to take pressure off his painful heel. They spigoted his catheter, emptied his bladder every two or three hours for a day or two, then tried him without the catheter, carefully showing him how to use a bottle, and ensuring that there was one where he could reach it on his left side. They sent for his clothes and shoes. They got him up, dressed, shaved, hair brushed, and showed him his image in the mirror. With the help of the physiotherapist they put him in a self-propelled wheelchair and taught him how to use his good foot to drive himself about.

The physiotherapist mobilized his limbs and trunk, stood him up with a support to give him the feel of the ground under his feet. The occupational therapist trained him to assist in his own dressing. The speech therapist discovered routes of communication by gesture and situational clues, and taught the relatives and the nurses how to exploit these. The doctor treated the accompanying urinary infection and anaemia, relieved pain, ensured sleep, conferred with relatives and with the therapeutic team. In the end the patient did not fully 'recover' – but he regained self-respect and a limited degree of independence. He became much less demanding and frustrated. He was able to go on outings, and could spend an occasional weekend at home. He took up indoor gardening and filled the dayroom with pot plants. We did not 'cure' him of his irremediable disease, but we were privileged to watch the tide of his personality begin to flow again over the dry sand of his disability.

Principles

All this required the full geriatric team. In the more usual setting of the patient's home or a general hospital ward the same basic principles apply. These are:

1 Listen carefully to the patient. He will tell you what needs to be done.
2 Make yourself available to talk to relatives in privacy. They too have needs.
3 Information is the fuel of opinion. So do not hesitate to investigate, but keep the investigation relevant to possible treatment.
4 No form of treatment should be rejected dogmatically; always the benefits should be weighed against the hazards. To secure comfort in the last days of life risks are justified.

Investigation and surgical treatment

The undiagnosed are often the unremedied; so no patient should be denied investigation. Evaluation of the haemoglobin, blood urea, electrolytes, and blood sugar is a minimum. A chest X-ray film may show unsuspected cancer, tuberculosis, or osteomalacia. Sternal marrow examination is well tolerated and should not be withheld on ground of age alone. Barium meals seldom lead to useful treatment. Barium enemas are more often helpful, but may be frustrated by non-retention or by faecal accumulations. Urine cultures often yield organisms, but their eradication less often relieves symptoms.

Surgery and anaesthesia are well tolerated, and should not be withheld if they offer hope of improvement in the quality of life. Post-operative rehabilitation may be very successful, and old people can learn to use colostomies or artificial limbs.

Relief of symptoms

Intractable pain is mercifully rare in the elderly. Its adequate control requires timely relief with non-narcotizing doses of potent drugs, a technique which needs organization, but which yields benefits by relieving the fear of having to endure pain.

Dyspnoea is more common and more difficult to control. Good posture is best obtained at home by nursing the patient in a chair. Adequate diuresis is sometimes resisted, because the patient and his relatives become exhausted by frequent potting. A catheter should be used without hesitation. Oxygen usually causes more anxiety and tension than it relieves.

Anorexia is treated by indulgence. Favourite foods and beverages are prescribed; and a glass of whisky or sherry acquires a new and glorious flavour through having been prescribed by the doctor.

Treating dehydration is important, since ill old people do not experience thirst. Their fluid intake should be charted, aiming at an intake of 1,500 ml a day. If they have difficulty in swallowing they should use a straw or a child's feeding cup. Their fluids can be given in the form of jelly or liquidized foods.

Constipation is compounded by lack of roughage in the diet, lack of physical exercise, poor somatic muscle tone and evacuating power, inadequate opportunity, and fear of discomfort, quite apart from any autonomic dysfunction. The provision of a commode which the patient trusts and is prepared to use is as important as the prescription of the correct laxative or suppository. Regular enemas are required; regular rectal examinations are even more important.

Sleep disturbances send the doctor off on a prescription odyssey, sailing from drug to drug in an endeavour to secure sleep by night and wakefulness by day. From time to time one stops all drugs and starts again at the beginning with one aspirin at 9 p.m. – and sometimes this works. The hot milky drink may secure sleep at night, but the full bladder may alert early waking.

Psychological features

Doctors are often urged to allow old people to die with dignity. I find this very difficult to do, since I associate dignity with black silk hats, the measured tread, the grave nod of the head – at very least with ambulation, continence, and mental clarity – features which are lacking as death approaches. Near the end of life some old people become undignified, remove their clothing in public, and revile their dear ones with obscenities. Others lose self-control and become irritable, demanding, and selfish; refuse to be left alone; moan repetitively; ceaselessly ask for drinks; or demand to be taken to the lavatory, do nothing, then wet themselves. These anxiety symptoms are hard for relatives to bear; and many have confided to me that the last months of a loved parent's life were the worst they had ever experienced.

These situations test to the utmost the doctor's capacity to treat the irremediable. He must listen, sympathize, reassure, explain. The relatives require our ears and our time, but the doctor can also give practical help by arranging day hospital care or short-term admission.

Conclusion

Much of medical work is concentrated on the final months or year of life. The curative role of the doctor is being attenuated. But equal or greater professional satisfaction can be found by the skilled and perceptive treatment of 'the irremediable'.

31 Psychogeriatrics

Klaus Bergmann

Psychiatric disorders occur commonly in the elderly and have characteristic features that merit special consideration. They are the concern not only of the psychiatrist but of the family doctor, hospital physician and hospital surgeon. Assuming that the population forecasts for 1992 are accurate, it has been predicted that 73.5 per cent of all beds currently available for men and 93.7 per cent of non-maternity beds currently available for women could be filled by old-age pensioners.[1] These figures exclude psychiatric beds. Although such extrapolations may not be fully justified, they do emphasise that the problems of the elderly will assume increasing importance in hospital practice. The stresses experienced by elderly patients are usually the result of complex interactions of physical disorder, social deprivation, emotional upset and mental impairment caused by organic brain damage (Figure 1).

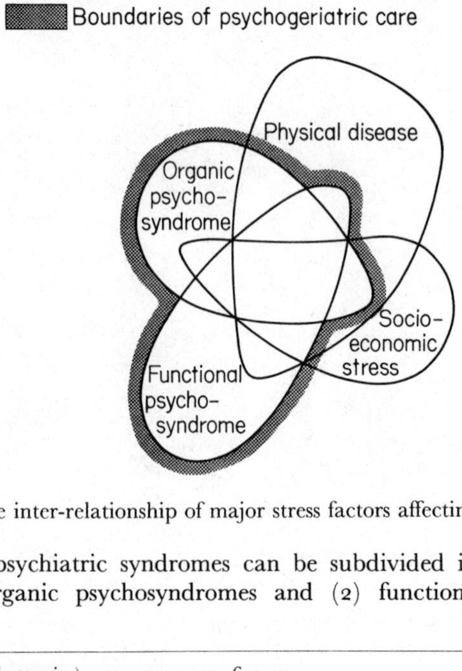

Figure 1   The inter-relationship of major stress factors affecting the elderly.

The major psychiatric syndromes can be subdivided into two main groups: (1) organic psychosyndromes and (2) functional psychosyndromes.

Source: *Medicine* (first series), 1972–74, *9*, pp. 643–52.

Organic psychosyndromes

Acute or subacute delirious states *

These conditions are characterised by a clouding of consciousness that ranges in severity from a mild perplexity and fluctuation of alertness and attention to a state in which the only response is an ill-directed restless one and which is near to stupor. Disorientation for time, place and person is always evident to some degree. Two important questions frequently arise: (1) How does one differentiate this condition from dementia? and (2) When a well defined and sometimes elaborate persecutory illness is a presenting feature, how can the underlying delirium be recognised?

When delirium is the predominant feature, only a short history of mental impairment may be obtained from relatives or friends. Marked variation in the degree of impairment can be observed at different times of the day and there is often a characteristic aggravation of the delirium towards the evening.

Where a well-organised paranoid illness is present the underlying delirium may be missed. If the patient expresses delusions of a persecutory type, perhaps accompanied by hallucinations, both visual and auditory, the minor fluctuations of consciousness, attention and orientation can be overlooked easily.

The causes of delirium

Systemic disease. Delirium may be caused by systemic disease, such as myocardial infarction, pneumonias, urinary tract infection and malignant disease.

Metabolic, biochemical and endocrine disorders. Generalised metabolic and endocrine disorders often cause delirium. The most important features to search for are: (1) disorders of thyroid function; (2) electrolyte disturbance, especially of sodium and potassium; (3) nitrogen retention; (4) abnormality of blood sugar; (5) anoxia or carbon dioxide retention; and (6) anaemias and vitamin deficiencies.

Iatrogenic causes. It is also important to remember that nearly all elderly patients have already received some medication before admission to hospital and often delirium can be iatrogenic.

Acute cerebral disease. It is often forgotten that when no systemic metabolic

* Synonyms: toxic confusional state *or* acute brain syndrome.

endocrine or toxic factors can be found, delirium can be caused by a localised and acute disturbance of cerebral function. When investigating a delirium, it is worth remembering that 'when it is not below the neck it is above the neck!'

Such conditions as cerebrovascular accidents are usually recognised readily by the accompanying long tract signs. However, infarction of so-called 'silent' areas of the brain may produce delirium without an obvious localising sign. Subdural haematomata, primary or secondary neoplastic deposits, acute or subacute inflammatory lesions and post-epileptic conditions may all be difficult to recognise in the elderly, especially if they have been living alone and no history is obtainable from a relative. In such conditions an electroencephalogram is often of considerable value.

Treatment

Tranquilisers. Treatment of the delirium is the treatment of the underlying condition. During the phase of acute disturbance sedation with major tranquilisers may be required. Where hypotension is to be avoided, thioridazine (Melleril) 25 mg tds may be the drug of choice. In violently disturbed, strong, active, elderly persons, chlorpromazine (Largactil) im 50 to 100 mg may be required. I prefer to use haloperidol (Serenance) 10 mg and procyclidine hydrochloride (Kemadrin) 10 mg iv as this does not induce severe hypotension.

Electroplexy (ECT). Uncontrolled delirium may continue after the underlying condition has been treated with apparent success. On some occasions one or two electroconvulsive treatments may be efficacious, but this must be administered with caution.

The dementias *

Definition and causes. Dementia may be defined as a global impairment of higher cerebral function. This includes such features as social behaviour, emotional control, visiomotor skills, the recognition of complex relationships, the ability to learn new tasks, and above all the ability to remember recent events. The natural history of the dementias is a progressive and downhill one. In the elderly the two main types of dementia are: (1) senile dementia and (2) arteriosclerotic dementia.

Senile dementia

Senile dementia sometimes called senile psychosis is characterised by an

---

* Synonym: chronic brain syndromes.

insidious and gradual onset of dementia in which the downhill progress is progressive and inexorable. In some elderly patients with senile dementia the clinical picture is said to take 'an Alzheimerized form'. This carries no pathological implications but implies that among the early clinical features of such a condition one would expect dyspraxia, dysphasia and other forms of parietal lobe deficits to be prominent.

Pathological changes. The pathological changes of Alzheimer's disease and senile dementia are indistinguishable. Macroscopically they include shrinkage of the gyri, widening of the sulci and dilatation of the ventricles. Microscopically the main features consist of senile plaque formation and neurofibrillary tangles.

Electron microscope studies have shed further light on the nature of these disturbances.[2]

Arteriosclerotic dementia

Those patients with arteriosclerotic dementia or arteriosclerotic psychosis have the following clinical features: (1) one or more strokes; (2) hypertension; (3) symptomatic epilepsy; (4) a stepwise course with plateaus of preservation; and (5) relatively good preservation of personality and affective response up to a late stage of the illness.

Pathologically, there is widespread evidence of cerebral infarction and softening either of large areas or multiple small areas. Attempts to measure cerebral softening suggest that arteriosclerotic dementia is unlikely to occur below a critical amount of softening.[3] Intercurrent delirious states are particularly common with arteriosclerotic dementia and may indeed be a presenting feature of this condition.

Functional psychosyndromes

Affective disorder in old age

Depressive illness is common in old age. The most important question to be asked is, is this depression a recurrence of similar attacks in earlier life or is this a depression starting in old age? The major features distinguishing the two types of depression are summarised in Table 1.

Treatment

Antidepressants. Elderly patients respond well to the tricyclic drugs. However, caution is necessary when prescribing them because of troublesome

Table 1   Analysis of depression in old age.

History and Clinical Aspects	First Illness Before Senium	Onset in the Senium
Family history of depression	Often found	No significant association
Current physical health	Average for age	Significant increase in physical ill health
Immediate response to treatment	Good	Good
Long term response	Good	Frequent relapses

Source: *Encyclopaedia of Psychiatry for General Practitioners*, Depression in the Elderly, p. 138 Roche Products Limited, London, 1972.

side-effects. These include postural hypotension, dizziness and falling glaucoma, urinary obstruction and sometimes iatrogenic delirium. In those cases where agitation is a prominent feature, drugs such as ami triptyline * 10 mg tds are helpful. Where lethargy, apathy and anergia are particular features, imipramine† 10 mg tds or protriptyline (Concordin) 5 mg tds may be more useful. One may increase dosages of all these drugs after seven to ten days. The use of mono amine-oxidase inhibitors such as phenelzine (Nardil) 15 mg tds may be justified in the elderly especially where one finds anxiety symptoms and atypical depressive pictures.

Electroplexy (ECT) is particularly valuable in elderly people, where psychotic depressive symptoms are prominent with self-neglect, dangers of starvation, dehydration and the side effects of decubitus. It is often less dangerous to give ECT than to increase tricyclic drugs to a toxic level. I cannot be emphasised enough that depression in the elderly carries a mortality risk from suicide and self-neglect and inanition.

The paraphrenias

Clinical description. When a delusional illness arises in a clear state of consciousness in later life this is usually given the name of a paraphrenic illness. Auditory hallucinations may frequently be present, and the delusions are often circumscribed, hang together logically and well and do

* Laroxyl, Lentizol, Saroten, Tryptizol

† Eight proprietary brands

not interfere unduly with the patients' ability to cope with life or with their personality.

Presenting features. The onset may be subtle and insidious shading imperceptibly from a cranky, strange personality, into a condition where a delusional idea is held tenaciously. Auditory hallucinations may arise in a clear state of consciousness followed by delusional explanations. As in earlier onset schizophrenic illnesses, primary delusions may arise out of the blue.

Paraphrenics readily attract attention as their behaviour is usually disturbed and gives rise to complaints from their family, if any, or from their neighbours.

Predisposing factors include prickly, hostile personality traits, a tendency towards a life style of self-elected isolation. The female sex predominates and sensory defect, especially deafness, is more commonly found than in other elderly people.

Treatment

Elderly paraphrenics require treatment for the rest of their lives and the condition rarely remits. It can, however, be well controlled with adequate doses of phenothiazines. It is often worth giving phenothiazines in much smaller doses than would be effective in younger schizophrenics and sustained release trifluoperazine (Stelazine) 2 to 4 mg bd may be adequate. In robust, elderly paraphrenics who live alone a trial of long acting parenteral phenothiazines may be justified. It is customary to use half the adult dosage in the first instance and anti-Parkinsonian cover may well be necessary. Day hospital care and supervision is of great help if it is available.

Neuroses of old age

Neurotic disorders in the elderly do not present either in the GP's surgery or the hospital out-patient clinic. They have a social invisibility which is related to the fact that the elderly no longer have the same demands made on them as younger patients. They are therefore less likely to be referred for psychiatric care.

Neurotic symptoms and hidden illness

There is a strong indication that hidden physical ill health may present as a depressive or anxiety reaction. Alternatively, it may flare up longstanding hysterical and hypochondriacal symptoms in such a way as to overshadow occult serious underlying physical disorder.[4,5] In addition, neurotic and minor affective disorder can be a potent factor in contributing towards an elderly patient's inability to cope when the physical examination does not reveal sufficiently severe factors to justify a given degree of disability.

Psychotherapeutic support of the elderly can be rewarding and economical; it can save the elderly patient from repeated and ill-directed investigation or the offer of ineffective social cures such as old people's clubs, extra home help and ungratefully received outings.

Natural history of psychiatric disorder in the elderly

One of the main questions bedevilling the treatment of the elderly is as follows: are all old people suffering from a central degenerative ageing process which has a unique picture in each individual, be it paranoid, depressive or delirious, depending on individual factors, life situations and psychodynamic considerations, or are the descriptive syndromes (see above) meaningful in terms of aetiology and prognosis?

Psychiatric diagnostic labels have been shown to differentiate most effectively for various groups of hospitalised elderly in-patients with regard to discharge, in-patient stay and death.[6] Further studies[7,8] have shown that the diagnostic descriptions mentioned above bear a close relationship to pathological data ascertained both retrospectively and prospectively at post-mortem.

Psychiatric morbidity among community residents

In order to get a true picture of the importance and the extent of psychiatric disorder within the community, surveys have been done in several centres. Some of the major morbidity studies from various centres in Europe and the United States are shown in Table 2.[9]

Although differences exist between these findings the similarity is impressive. It can be said that these findings represent approximately 5 per cent of severe organic psychosyndrome, 5 per cent of mild or early psychosyndrome and 10 per cent of functional disorder within all the communities surveyed.

Prevalence of organic psychosyndromes in the community

Detailed studies of community residents in two random samples carried out in Newcastle upon Tyne show the age-related prevalence figures for organic psychosyndromes (Table 3).

The relationship between the prevalence of definite dementia,

Table 2 Psychiatric morbidity studies among community residents.

	Sheldon 1948 $N=369$ Age$=65+$ (%)	Bremer 1951 $N=119$ Age$=60+$ (%)	Essen-Møller 1956 $N=443$ Age$=60+$ (%)	Syracuse 1961 $N=1592$ Age$=65+$ (%)	Primrose 1962 $N=222$ Age$=65+$ (%)	Neilsen 1963 $N=978$ Age$=65+$ (%)	Kay et al. 1964 Age$=65+$ (%)
Senile and arteriosclerotic psychoses	3·9	2·5	5·0	6·8	3·6 ⎫	3·1	4·6 ⎫
Other organic syndromes	–	–	–	–	0·9 ⎭ 4·5	–	1·0 ⎭ 5·6
Major functional disorders	–	4·2*	1·1	–	1·4	3·7*	2·4
Psychoses, all forms	3·9	6·7	6·1	6·8	5·9	6·8	8·0
'Mild mental deterioration'	11·7	–	10·8	–	–	15·4	5·7
Neuroses and allied disorders ·moderate/severe form	9·4 ⎫ 12·6	5·0 ⎫ 17·6	1·4 ⎫ 12·0	–	10·4 ⎫ 12·6	4·0 ⎫ 8·7	8·9 ⎫ 12·5
Character disorders	3·2 ⎭	12·6	10·6 ⎭	–	2·2 ⎭	4·7 ⎭	3·6 ⎭

* Includes constitutional and psychogenic psychoses I. Source: Key *et al.* (1964) *Brit. J. Psychiat.*, *110*, 146–58.

Table 3 Age-related prevalence of organic psychosyndromes.

Age	Both Sexes			Men		Women	
	N	CBS	$\% \pm SE$	N	$\%$	N	$\%$
65–69	253	6	2·3 ± 0·9	110	3·6	143	1·4
70–74	243	7	2·8 ± 1·1	91	3·3	152	2·6
75–79	144	8	5·5 ± 1·9	51	5·9	93	5·4
80+	118	26	22·0 ± 3·8	39	20·5	79	22·8
Total	758	47	6·2 ± 0·9	291	6·2	467	6·2

CBS = Number with organic psychosyndrome
Source: Kay *et al.*, (1970) *Comprehensive Psychiatry*, Vol. *11*, No. 1.

Table 4   Population by diagnosis and age.

Age (both sexes)	Normal	Functional	Chronic Brain Syndrome	Suspected Chronic Brain Syndrome	C-V Involvement without Dementia	Others	Total
65–74	350 70·1%	105 63·3%	15 31·9%	9 45·0%	14 63·6%	5 83·3%	498 65·5%
75 +	149 29·9%	61 36·7%	32 68·1%	11 55·0%	8 36·4%	1 16·7%	262 34·5%
Total	499	166	47	20	22	6	760

Source: Proceedings of the Vth World Congress of Psychiatry, Mexico, 1971.

Table 5   Percentage of subjects from Table 4 that developed organic Psycho-syndromes during the follow-up period.

	% Chronic Brain Syndrome Dead	% Chronic Brain Syndrome Alive	Total % Chronic Brain Syndrome	Total No.
Normal	1·3	1·5	2·8***	471
Functional Syndrome	2·4	2·4	4·8	164
Suspected Chronic Brain Syndrome	15·8	15·8	31·6**	19
Cerebrovascular Insufficiency	4·5	9·1	13·6*	22
Total	2·1	2·4	4·5	676
Subjects not traced at follow-up				17

Probabilities

$$**\text{p } 0\cdot01 \quad \chi^2 = 33\cdot9 \text{ df } 1$$
$$*\text{p } 0\cdot05 \quad \chi^2 = 4\cdot53 \text{ df } 1$$

} significantly higher.

$$***\text{p } 0\cdot01 \quad \chi^2 = 10\cdot31 \text{ df } 1 \quad \text{significantly lower.}$$

Source: Proceedings of the Vth World Congress of Psychiatry, Mexico, 1971

suspected or early dementias, cerebrovascular disease without dementia and functional psychosyndromes is shown in Table 4.

The percentage of subjects in each group that developed organic psychosyndrome during the follow-up period is shown in Table 5.[10]

It can be seen that even mild or suspected dementing syndromes have a grave prognostic significance and that functional psychosyndromes were not related to mild or insidious underlying organic brain disease.

Affective disorder

It has been shown that elderly patients with an affective disorder starting in later life do not achieve a return to normal social functioning when followed up over a period of years,[11] even if they respond well to treatment. The study cited demonstrated that 70 per cent of elderly depressives required further medical attention for affective symptoms within the first two years following treatment. This suggests that there is an especial social vulnerability accompanied by associated ill health which makes support of elderly patients with late-onset depressive symptoms a heavy task. They need not only psychiatric help, but physical care and social support. A point prevalence study of welfare home admissions shows that affective and neurotic disorder are highly represented.[9]

The dementias

The presence of dementia in an elderly person has the most sinister implications for his future viability as a community resident. A prospective study on a random sample of community residents showed that the demented patients were the victims of a higher mortality than previously shown.[12] They also occupied a very high number of bed days per person, not only in mental hospitals but in geriatric hospitals and welfare homes. This marked difference remained even when the subjects were matched with normal controls for age and sex.

There was also a qualitative difference; demented patients went predominantly to geriatric wards, welfare homes and mental hospitals whereas the normal controls spent most of their time in acute medical or surgical wards. Had future hospital care of any kind been solely predicted on the presence of dementia, it would have been correct in 58 per cent of the cases compared with an overall chance of admission of 22 per cent. The care of the elderly who remain in the community with their relatives may be gladly accepted.[13] However, it presents a very real increase on the burden they have to bear in terms of loss of leisure amenities, loss of income and an increased sense of strain. It was estimated that 87 per cent of patients with dementia and 61 per cent of patients with neurotic disorder were not known to their GP.[14] It is likely that most so-called acute emergencies or crises arise from this 'morbid pool' of psychiatrically disordered community residents.

Psychogeriatric care in general practice

The silent majority

The GP holds the central position within the Health service, coordinating hospital and social services for the benefit of his patient. We have seen that in spite of this the GP does not become aware of the size of the problem or the number of patients in his practice that are at risk. This is mainly because the model of the GP services is an 'on demand' service, and the elderly are characterised by their silence.

If a hypothetical group-practice of 20,000 patients is taken with the national average of patients over the age of 65 (12 per cent), one would expect 2,400 elderly patients. The predicted morbidity within such a practice would be as follows:

Chronic brain syndrome (senile and arteriosclerotic dementia)	6·7% =	161 patients
Early cerebrovascular involvement without dementia	2·9% =	70 patients
Patients with suspected, mild or early dementia	2·8% =	69 patients
Patients with moderately severe functional disorder (mainly depressives)	10·0% =	240 patients
Total 'Morbid Pool' within practice		= 540 patients

This represents 22·5 per cent of all patients over 65 within the practice.

Not all patients within the 'morbid pool' would be in need of treatment. Many may be well cared for, but from this group the GP can expect ill-defined crises, emergencies, late night calls, and disposal problems. Crises can present as clear-cut psychiatric or medical emergencies. Psychogeriatric care, however, concerns itself with that ill-defined borderland between such situations and I would like to describe some of the commoner ways in which problems may present.

Psychogeriatric emergencies

The sudden onset of a behavioural disturbance. An elderly person may present with a sudden disturbance of behaviour of a most dramatic kind. This may include shouting and swearing, smearing faeces, and often culminates in a violent attack on those neighbours, friends and family who try to help.

The social unmasking of a crisis. A mildly impaired patient may remain unknown to doctors or health visitors for a considerable period of time. However, when the patient undergoes a bereavement or the loss of a key relative owing to hospitalisation or illness then an acute crisis may present in which incapacity to cope, panic reactions and depression can all serve to mask the fact that the underlying mental impairment is an essential contributory factor.

Sudden emotional reactions. Elderly patients may appear to live satisfactorily,

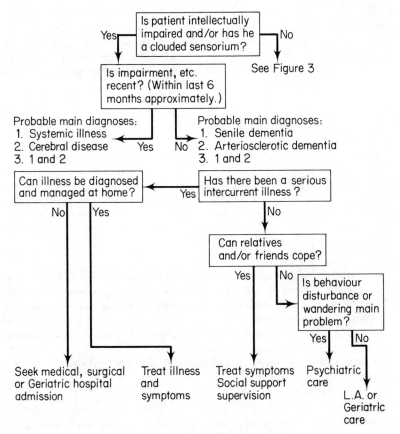

Figure 2   Management of psychogeriatric crisis.

coping with their social setting, and making few demands. Suddenly, within a very short period they become agitated, tense, panicky, demanding repeated attention and intolerably hypochondriacal. Often the last straw is several repeated and apparently unjustified night calls and when these occur, the patients' condition constitutes a crisis.

Family rejection and breakdown. This type of presentation can be most puzzling. A disabled and mentally impaired elderly patient who lives with a relative is suddenly reported as being 'impossible'. The description of their behaviour is always horrifying, incontinence is intolerable, faecal smearing may be prominently reported, abusive behaviour noted, and intolerable manners commented on. The total helplessness reported make it surprising that the patient should still be at home.

Characteristically, when one examines the patient's physical and mental state, the disability revealed does not match the history obtained. Any attempts to treat the reported disabilities at home are doomed to failure and whatever help is suggested does not seem adequate. It is, in my opinion, always best to bring out the question of rejection into the open as this permits the situation to be explored.

The inability to cope. The inability to cope does not always constitute a crisis. Often gradual mental deterioration accompanying the extreme physical frailty that is found with advanced ageing may lead to a situation where a patient cannot cope. Normally, this can be prepared for and should not constitute a crisis. However, when a previously independent person becomes untidy, dangerous with fires, incompetent in managing their finances, careless of hygiene or neglectful of personal nutrition then a crisis has occurred and attention is required.

Management

Such crises nearly always present in the first instance to the GP. A scheme is tentatively offered for managing such situations in a systematic way. It does not claim to be comprehensive and is guilty of oversimplification (Figures 2 and 3).

Management on the acute medical or surgical ward

Organic psychosyndromes

A recent study of the admission of patients of 65 and over to an acute medical ward [15] has shown that they have a high prevalence of psychiatric

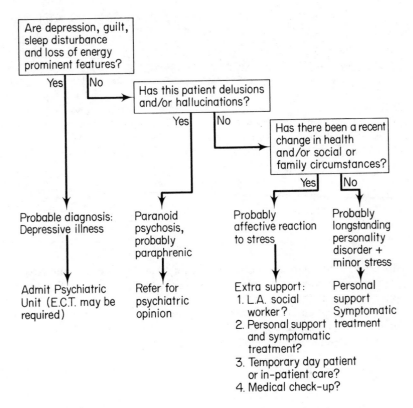

Figure 3 Psychogeriatric crisis without intellectual impairment.

morbidity. This excludes previously known psychiatric and geriatric patients (Table 6). The depressive patients largely pass through the medical wards unnoticed, though there is some evidence that depressives take longer before they can be discharged than those patients without depression. The main problem, however, is presented by patients with organic psychosyndromes of various types. Referral for a psychiatric opinion is usually for one of the following reasons: (1) behavioural disturbance; (2) failure to respond within the period regarded as the norm for the unit; or (3) 'disposal' problems.

Behavioural disturbance. Figures 2 and 3 give a general idea of how behavioural disturbances can be analysed systematically. The main problems on a medical or surgical ward occur when one encounters acute delirium in response to physical illness. This is the commonest cause of

Table 6   Breakdown of 65-year-old and over population admitted to an acute medical ward and fully assessed.

Diagnosis	Men		Women		Total	
	N	%	N	%	N	%
Normal	34	75·6	25	45·4	59	59
Functional (moderate and severe only)	5	11·1	13	23·7	18	18
Delirious	5	11·1	11	20·0	16	16
Dementia	1	2·2	6	10·9	7	7
Total	45		55		100	

disturbed behaviour and the interaction of acute delirium and more long-standing dementias in the elderly patient is often puzzling to the general physician or surgeon.

The main points to be considered in managing an acutely disturbed, mentally impaired elderly patient are summed up in Figure 4.

Three hypothetical patients are described:

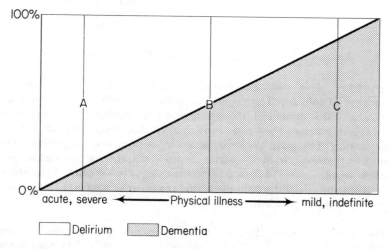

Figure 4   The interaction of factors contributing to disturbed behaviour in patients suffering from organic psychosyndromes.

Patient A – previous history of good preservation of personality, capacities and intellect, main contribution to behavioural disturbance is delirium. Precipitating illness likely to be clear-cut and severe.

Patient B – previous history of mild deterioration, some help required but well behaved, manageable and pleasant. Probably described by relatives as 'normal but a bit senile'. Disturbed behaviour probably the result of an interaction of delirium and mild dementia. Underlying ill health definite but perhaps not sudden or severe.

Patient C – five or six years history of gradual deterioration, requires help with dressing, feeding, could not manage his own affairs before coming in. Family already supporting maximally. Main cause of disturbed behaviour is dementia but some superadded clouding and disturbance of behaviour owing to delirium. Physical ill health likely to be trivial or difficult to ascertain.

The acutely disturbed patient with organic psychosyndrome

Immediate management. Such patients nearly always need sedation and this section deals with the main problems. Generous 'prn' doses of chlorpromazine (Largactil) paraldehyde or barbiturates may be temporarily effective in rendering the patient unconscious. In most cases the postural hypotension results in even worse behaviour if and when the patient recovers. An intolerable situation develops which swings from coma to frantic overactivity.

Regular sedation with, if possible, tranquilisers that do not cause severe hypotension may be more effective. One may try oral medication with thioridazine (Melleril) 25 mg to 100 mg tds in tablet or syrup form. The latter is extremely useful with patients who tend to refuse to swallow tablets, spit them out or hide them in their pyjama jackets. I have personally found an iv injection of haloperidol (Serenace) one of the most effective methods of quietening and controlling acute excitement and disturbance without producing postural hypotension.

The dose is 10 mg iv and it should be accompanied by 10 mg procyclidine hydrochloride (Kemadrin) iv to prevent dystonic reactions. Wherever paroxysmal or episodic bursts of behavioural disturbance are evident then one should consider the possibility of epilepsy or an epiliptiform equivalent. Anti-convulsant therapy may be very effective in such circumstances. I prefer sulthiame (Ospolot) 50 mg bd–100 mg tds to phenyl hydantoin or phenobarbitone (Gardenol, Luminol).

General care. Elderly patients who live alone and are admitted in delirium often have clinical or sub-clinical multiple vitamin deficiencies; evidence of atrophic glossitis, angular stomatitis, undue bleeding or bruising, keratotic or dry peeling skin should lead one to suspect vitamin deficiency. Intravenous high potency vitamins are worth considering in many cases and elderly patients with delirium should have the benefit of the doubt as such a course can do no harm and may well be extremely helpful. One can treat urinary retention, faecal impaction and unrelieved discomfort or pain, factors which may well contribute towards disturbed behaviour, with relative ease.

The disposal of the patient with organic psychosyndrome. Problems in this area lead to most misunderstanding and ill feeling between various branches of the medical profession. There is little doubt that a preliminary analysis of the situation will lead to a more effective use of geriatric physicians, psychiatrists and local authority social work departments.

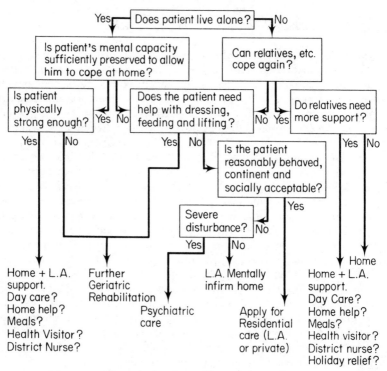

Figure 5   Disposal of patient with organic psychosyndrome.

Figure 5 is offered as systematising such an attempt. I am aware that many psychiatric colleagues, geriatric physicians and social workers may not agree with the proposals put forward. However, they could modify the criteria in order to make it correspond to their own organisational set-up.

Psychogeriatric problems on the orthopaedic ward

Presentation of patient

Increasing pressure is being placed on the orthopaedic ward by elderly patients. The largest proportion of these suffer from a fractured neck of femur. The condition has a considerable mortality and morbidity but with modern techniques survival is to be expected. Care and rehabilitation may occur over the next six weeks after which time the patient is probably reasonably mobile, ready for convalescence and then for discharge home. At this stage it often comes as a matter of shock and surprise to those who have cared for the patient that disposal is not easy. The patient may have to remain on the orthopaedic ward for a considerably longer period of time.

Product of neglect. There is little doubt that the orthopaedic service receives the end result of many failures in social, medical and psychiatric care. Neglected and lonely elderly patients, mostly women, arrive in casualty after a fall has been reported by the neighbours. The fall, however, is only the culmination of increasing difficulty in coping at home, self-neglect, unsteadiness, confusion at night and lack of supervision. Alternatively, in those who have been cared for by relatives or friends who have been strained to their limits, the fractured femur may act as the last straw. In such cases time is of the essence and the sooner the surgical unit is aware of the social situation the sooner they can arrange for suitable referrals, consultations and arrangements to be made.

The two most important questions to be asked are: (1) Is this patient living alone? and (2) What was the mental state of the patient before admission? Patients who live alone are an especially vulnerable group. They are more likely to be female, and more likely to be elderly. Unless competent young relatives live nearby, the friends and acquaintances that they have are often of increasing age and infirmity themselves.

Pre-existing mental impairment. The most important barrier to recovery is pre-existing mental impairment. This barrier will tend to negate even well thought out plans for social care, such as home helps, meals on wheels, regular visits from the district nurse or bath attendant and supervision by the health visitor. It is vital to find out how this patient managed her affairs before the fractured femur occurred.

Important questions to ask are: (1) Was she able to go out shopping? (2) Could she manage her finances independently? (3) Was the home reasonably well cared for? (4) What was the state of her hygiene? (5) How was her recent memory? (6) Had she activities and interests that suggested normal intellectual functioning? and (7) If deterioration had been noted, for how long had this been going on?

Social care. An elderly patient who had been coping well in all these respects before admission and who in the immediate post-operative phase turns out to be confused, disturbed, clouded, would be worth considerable medical attention as the delirium is probably symptomatic of underlying physical ill health, often amenable to treatment. When longstanding deterioration is evident from the previous history then although the delirium must still require treatment, active plans for future support which may well include a new need for social care will have to be started straightaway. Little relief, however, can be expected until the social, psychiatric and medical rehabilitation aspects of geriatric orthopaedic problems are provided for more adequately.

Conclusion

Some of the more important points of contact between the psychiatrist working with the elderly and his colleagues have been touched on. Perhaps undue emphasis has been placed on disposal. I make no apology for this as most elderly patients for whom psychiatric referral is requested are presented as such problems. I feel that the main use, however, for psychiatric assessment and care occurs at a much earlier stage with the elderly when vulnerability first becomes evident. A treatment plan has to be made in which I hope it has been shown that the mental state is often one of the most important determining features, whether it be treatable or has to be managed and relieved rather than cured.

References

General

KAY, D. W. K. and WALK, A. (1971) *Recent Developments in Psychogeriatrics*. British Journal of Psychiatry Special Publication No. 5.

POST, F. (1965) *The Clinical Psychiatry of Late Life*. London: Pergamon Press.

SIMON, A. and EPSTEIN, L. T. (eds) (1968) *Aging in Modern Society*, Psychiatric Research Report No. 23. Washington: American Psychiatric Association.

SLATER, E. and ROTH, M. (1969) *Clinical Psychiatry*, Chapter 10. London: Bailliere, Tindall & Cassell.

WORLD PSYCHIATRIC ASSOCIATION (1965) *Symposium on Psychiatric Disorders in the Aged*. Manchester: Geigy.

Special

1 KLEIN, R. and ASHLEY, J. (1972) 'Old age health', *New Society*, 6 January, pp. 13–15.

2 TERRY, R. D. and WISNIEWSKI, H. (1970) 'The ultrastructure of the neurofibrillary tangle and the senile plaque'. In *Alzheimer's Disease*, eds G. E. W. Wolstenholme and M. O'Connor, pp. 145–65. London: Churchill.

3 ROTH, M. (1971) 'Classification and aetiology in mental disorders of old age: some recent developments'. In *Recent Developments in Psychogeriatrics*, eds D. W. K. Kay and A. Walk. British Journal of Psychiatry Special Publication No. 6.

4 KAY, D. W. K. and BERGMANN, K. (1966) 'Physical disability and mental health in old age: A follow-up of a random sample of elderly people seen at home. Session 1 – Psychiatric and somatic disorders in old age', *J. psychom. Med.*, *10*, 3.

5 BERGMANN, K. (1971) 'The neurosis of old age'. In *Recent Developments in Psychogeriatrics*, eds D. W. K. Kay and A. Walk. British Journal of Psychiatry Special Publication No. 6. Chap. IV, pp. 39–50.

6 ROTH, M. (1955) The natural history of mental disorders arising in the senium, *J. ment, Sci.*, 101, 261.

7 CORSELLIS, J. A. N. (1962) *Mental Illness and the Ageing Brain. The Distribution of Pathological Change in a Mental Hospital Population*. Maudsley Monograph No. 9. London: Oxford University Press.

8 BLESSED, G., TOMLINSON, B. E. and ROTH, M. (1966) 'The association between quantitative measures of dementia and of senile change in the cerebral grey matter of elderly subjects', *Br. J. Psychiat.*, *114*, 797.

9 KAY, D. W. K., BEAMISH, P. and ROTH, M. (1964) 'Old age mental disorders in Newcastle upon Tyne. A study of prevalence', *Br. J. Psychiat.*, *110*, 146.

10 BERGMANN, K., KAY, D. W. K., FOSTER, E. M., MCKECHNIE, A. A. and ROTH, M. (1971) 'A follow-up study of randomly selected community residents to assess the effects of chronic brain syndrome and cerebrovascular disease'. Paper presented at the Vth World Congress of Psychiatry, Mexico.

11 POST, F. (1962) *The Significance of Affective Symptoms in Old Age*. Maudsley Monograph, No. 10. London: Oxford University Press.

12 KAY, D. W. K., BERGMANN, K., FOSTER, E. M., MCKECHNIE, A. A. and ROTH, M. (1970) 'Mental illness and hospital usage in the elderly: a random sample followed up', *Comprehensive Psychiat.*, *11*, 1.

13 GRAD, J. and SAINSBURY, P. (1965) 'An evaluation of the effects of caring for the aged at home'. In *Psychiatric Disorders in the Aged*, Symposium held by the World Psychiatric Association, pp. 225–45. Manchester: Geigy.

14 WILLIAMSON, J., STOKOE, I. H., GRAY, S., FISHER, M., SMITH, A., MCGHEE, A. and STEPHENSON, E. (1964) 'Old people at home: their unreported needs', *Lancet*, *1*, 1117 (Chapter 17 in this Reader).

15 EASTHAM, E. J. and BERGMANN, K. (1972) Unpublished observations.

Part 6   The Professional

32 Care of the elderly in general practice

C. Hodes

By mid 1971 the population of the retirement ages – 65 years and over, men and women – had increased by 15 per cent since 1961. By 1981 this population will have risen again by a similar amount.[1] The average list size per general practitioner is now about 2,500 and therefore he provides general medical services for 300 patients over 65 years of age, with about 100 of these being over 75. The development of the health team[2] in recent years has enabled the general practitioner to approach the care of the elderly more from the point of view of prevention and early diagnosis,[3,4] and new developments with social workers in general practice[5] may bring further benefits.

The assessment of the patient's needs and the organization of the care required are the essential tasks of the general practitioner. These needs may be known or unknown to the patient. At least six different aspects should be considered.

The primary care team

The general practitioner, the health visitor, and the district nurse together can provide the best care for the elderly in their own homes. Working from a common centre and sharing one medical record, there is adequate opportunity for exchange of information – which is so important in giving personal medical care to patients who often have some degree of mental confusion, in addition to the usual spectrum of diseases. Age is not a barrier to attendance at the surgery, and in fact the elderly patient should be encouraged to remain mobile and attend as required. Consultation with the health visitor and treatment by the district nurse should also be available at the surgery. Appointments – making and keeping – are easily overlooked by the elderly and it helps if they are always given an appointment in writing and a sympathetic receptionist fits them in without too much waiting if an appointment has not been made. Though willing relatives and friends may help increasingly with their own cars, more organized transport services[6] in general practice are required if the preventive approach is to increase.

Information about the services available locally should be kept at every

Source: M. WARE (ed.) (1974) *Medicine in Old Age*. London: British Medical Association, pp. 39–43.

practice. Local authorities often have booklets of services and can provide well-illustrated pamphlets on such subjects as diet and exercise; the health visitor is of course the best person to give out this information and can supplement it with individual consultation and with patient groups. Group discussions are also helpful in preparing for retirement,[7] and health education in the elderly should also be concerned with the prevention of accidents and fire safety. Local clubs, laundry services, washing facilities, chiropody, and meals-on-wheels are generally available and should be introduced to patients even if only required occasionally. Convalescent holidays are especially worthwhile in the elderly and whenever possible should include both husband and wife.

Nurses' role

The nurse has been identified more with the care of the elderly sick patient. She can be supported in her work in the home by bath attendants and male nurses, who are playing an increasingly important part in the care of the male geriatric patient. Night nursing may also be available and if required only for a short time can make hospital admission unnecessary. Visits to the home for routine injections can be used as a method of surveillance and any change be reported to other members of the team.

At present there is little in the way of domiciliary physiotherapy but the district nurse can give help with breathing exercises for the chest infection and continuing support for the patient with a hemiplegia. Aids to nursing – such as commodes, bed rests, and disposable bedding supplies – are always available. Laboratory services are now used extensively by general practitioners, and the district nurse can take urine and blood specimens in the home and return them to the surgery for collection by the hospital transport services. For haemoglobin estimation a Spence Haemoglobinometer is very simple and quick to use, in both the home and surgery, and when any anaemia is due to poor diet the health visitor can soon call at home with advice and help.

Practice premises

Practice premises have changed considerably in recent years and very large centres may present problems for the older patient. Cars should be able to drive up to the front entrance of the building, the doors should be wide enough for a wheelchair, and preferably there should be no steps. When all the members of the team have their own accommodation in the building referral is simpler and joint consultation can deal with problems quickly. A sufficient number of warm examination rooms allow the patients to dress and undress at their usual speed, and they can be helped by a receptionist or nurse; this also permits the general practitioner to carry on with other duties.

Good communication is facilitated by regular meetings between members of the primary care team. A high standard of record keeping is important and the problem-orientated record [8] may be found useful in geriatric care. All patients should keep with them at all times a treatment card, which can be used for repeat prescriptions and give useful information to any doctor seeing the patient as an emergency without the medical record being available.

Studies on the unreported needs of old people [9] and an evaluation of early diagnostic services for the elderly [10] have indicated the need for preventive care. To carry this out in general practice requires an age-sex register from which the geriatric register can be constructed.[11,12] Invitations for examinations can be sent to selected patients, and these screening examinations can be carried out by the primary care team in the surgery and in the home; treatment and follow-up are carried out as required. Special registers for high-risk groups, such as patients living alone and the surviving partner on the death of a spouse, are indicated.

Social services

The elderly patient depends on the social services as well as the primary medical care team to live in the community. The social worker's client and the general practitioner's patient are the same person, and working together can only improve the total care of the elderly. If the social worker can use the general practitioner's premises, regular communication is more likely and the preventive approach possible. The many benefits now available in the way of financial help and housing are best dealt with by the social worker. Psychogeriatric cases need the support of the social work services and patients recently discharged from hospital can be followed by a worker who is in close contact with the psychiatric services. The home help, in addition to cleaning and shopping duties, is a great support for the often depressed and isolated patient, and can alert the general practitioner if there is any deterioration.

When the elderly patient can no longer manage at home, the social worker will arrange alternative accommodation. This may be in a flat or bungalow with a supervising warden. If this is not sufficient, residential accommodation can be provided on a temporary or permanent basis. The temporary care may be used when a relative has to go into hospital or goes off on holiday; it may also be used for day care when meals are provided and occupational therapy is available. This also relieves the isolation of the permanent residents, brings them into contact with their community, and introduces the temporary residents to what might become their home.

By arrangement with the local authority, the general practitioner may provide medical care for the residents. In this work he can be supported by the health visitor and district nurse. It is useful to have an assessment chart for patients in addition to the usual medical records, which can be shared by the primary medical care team. The chart is used to record essential information about the patients, and to note changes which occur with time. The first part can be completed by the health visitor, and gives a score based on assessments of physical state, mental state, activity, mobility, and incontinence. If the score rises, the patient is deteriorating. The second part is completed by the nurse on admission and then periodically as indicated; there is a scoring system for hearing and the state of the feet.

Medical services

The geriatrician and his social worker in the local hospital are now very much part of community care and should be well known by the general practitioner. Domiciliary visits should be readily available without undue delay and requested for assessment and opinion, not only for admission. This prevents crisis from developing and allows the geriatrician to plan his admissions. The increase in the number of psychogeriatric patients in general practice gives rise to problems of regular medication and also to over-dosage; close supervision is required of patients living alone. The inclusion of geriatric and psychiatric services in new district hospitals will strengthen the support given to general practitioners.

Refractive errors are common and old spectacles may have been worn for many years; simple tests for visual acuity can be done in general practice but the detection of glaucoma requires special equipment and should be carried out by an ophthalmologist. During school holidays a technician with suitable equipment may be 'borrowed' from the local authority for sight testing in old people's homes. Hearing aids are usually given out by special centres and often involve further travel for examination and fitting; patients of any age may benefit by an aid and there should be regular supervision of its use and performance.

The community

The elderly patient usually wishes to continue to be independent and is supported by family and neighbours. The general practitioner can help by providing and introducing skilled help. The voluntary societies such as the British Red Cross and WRVS and help given by local groups such as Rotary are most valuable. Group practices and health centres can have groups of 'friends', who give help of all kinds to the elderly.

The patient

Old people often do not come forward for care – medical and social. This reluctance may be less in relation to the family doctor who is a familiar face, and the health visitor and nurse working with him are identified by the patient as part of the same care. An understanding of the patient's attitude is therefore important, and a health education programme can be introduced which promotes early diagnosis and the acceptability of any treatment offered. When an elderly patient is dying at home the primary care team needs all its skills. They can offer complete care when the patient may need them most and can continue to support the bereaved. [...]

References

1 DEPARTMENT OF HEALTH AND SOCIAL SECURITY (1971) *On the State of the Public Health*. London: HMSO.
2 ROYAL COLLEGE OF GENERAL PRACTITIONERS (1973) *Present State and Future Needs of General Practice*, 3rd edn. London: Royal College of General Practitioners.
3 HODES, C. (1971) *Journal of the Royal College of General Practitioners, 31*, 469.
4 WILLIAMS, E. I., *et al*. (1972) *British Medical Journal, 3*, 445.
5 GOLDBERG, E. M. and NEILL, J. E. (1972) *Social Work in General Practice*. London: Allen and Unwin.
6 LANCE, H. (1971) *Journal of the Royal College of General Practitioners, 21*, Suppl. No. 3.
7 HARTE, J. D. (1972) *Journal of the Royal College of General Practitioners, 22*, 612.
8 WEED, L. L. (1971) *Medical Records, Medical Education and Patient Care*. Cleveland, Ohio.
9 WILLIAMSON, J. *et al*. (1964) *Lancet, 1*, 1117.
10 LOWTHER, C. P., MACLEOD, R. D. M. and WILLIAMSON, J. (1970) *British Medical Journal, 3*, 275.
11 HODES, C. (1968) *Journal of the Royal College of General Practitioners, 15*, 286.
12 FORBES, J. A. (1969) *British Medical Journal, 2*, 46.

33 Management of incontinence in the home: the community nurse's view

Charlotte Kratz

The definition of incontinence is a simple one – 'voiding in the wrong place'. The task of the community nurse is equally simple – coping with the effects of this mistake. The manner in which she copes, or does not cope, will be determined by her assessment of the situation with which she is presented.

While this assessment takes account of the medical diagnosis, it is different from it, and it is also different from the assessment made by the nurse working in hospital.

Her first step is to gather any information which may be available to her. The general practitioner's records, letters from consultants, a talk with other members of the primary care team or the receptionist may all contribute to this. She is therefore as well informed as possible before she sets out on her journey.

She may know intimately the area in which the patient lives, but she will now approach it with a specific problem in mind. Is there a launderette nearby, how easily can it be reached, do people living in the area have easy access to drying facilities? Is the atmosphere humid and smutty, does the approach to the patient's house look neglected, or does he perhaps live in a high rise block of flats? All these factors may well influence the nursing care.

The nurse is therefore already in possession of useful information before she crosses the patient's threshold. Now she must take a good look at him. How long has he been incontinent? What kind of person was he before he became incontinent? Was he active and sociable, or a lonely old person? What does he think caused him to be incontinent? How does he feel about being incontinent – if indeed he is in a condition to express his feelings. What has the doctor told him about the incontinence and what, if any, treatment has been ordered for him? Has the patient got anything else wrong with him? Incontinence is a symptom of illness rather than an illness in itself. If so, what, if any, treatment is he having for that? A patient with cardiac disease may need different instructions on fluid intake than a patient with an enlarged prostate, and an adjustment in the timing of taking diuretics may make a difference between his having a wet and a dry bed at night.

Source: *Nursing Times*, 1977, *73*, 21, pp. 798–9.

In addition, the nurse will wish to assess the patient's physical and mental condition thoroughly and systematically. Has he a temperature or a raised blood pressure? What about ankle oedema or his general state of nutrition? Does he look anaemic, cyanosed or dyspnoeic? What about the condition of his pressure areas? And above all, what about his mental state? If the onset of his incontinence was sudden, he may well be mortified, or on the other hand unduly optimistic; if it is of long standing he may have resigned himself to being something of a social outcast, or he may just be unconcerned.

With all this information at her disposal the nurse will be in a good position to make a preliminary assessment of the needs of her patient. Perhaps he is a frail, emaciated elderly man with a long history of dyspnoea and a chronic smoker's cough. Obviously he'll have to be kept dry, but in his case it is especially important because his dyspnoea demands that he be propped up in bed and in his emaciated condition he is at increased risk of developing pressure sores. Or the patient may be a large, well preserved woman troubled for years with stress incontinence but now somewhat confused following a slight stroke. Perhaps the nurse should make sure her urine has been tested for sugar before making any other plans.

However, while the assessment of the need of the incontinent patient in hospital may well stop at this point, the nurse working in the community has not yet got past the preliminary stages of her assessment. She must now make a social assessment, taking into account the environment in which she finds the patient, the care available to him during her absence, and his economic circumstances. Where is the lavatory, are there steps to be negotiated, is the mattress or chair protected? Is the room so crowded that introducing a commode is well-nigh impossible? Or is he proud to the extent of being unable to tolerate the introduction of such an incriminating piece of equipment? What of his wife? Does she feel repulsed by sharing a bed with an incontinent patient, and if so how will this affect the patient's self-esteem or his physical care at night?

What about the confused woman with the slight stroke? A reducing diet may be a long-term remedy but it will not help her pregnant daughter-in-law with the immediate problem of keeping her in bed and changing her sheets.

In either case, what about the problem of extra washing that incontinence entails? Evidence of a washing-machine in the kitchen does not indicate an adequate supply of linen any more than the proximity of a launderette signifies either someone capable of transporting soiled linen there and back, nor an ability to pay for daily laundering.

The nurse working in the community will have to take all this information into account when formulating a plan for the incontinent patient's care. The patient's diagnosis may demand two-hourly opportunity for emptying his bladder, but his social context may indicate that such opportunity offered three times a day may be all that is realistic to expect. The nurse may be convinced that stepping up fluid intake will reduce bladder irritation and thus nocturnal incontinence, but the carer responsible for the patient in her absence may well disagree with her, or be unwilling to provide frequent cups of tea for a patient who intensely dislikes cold drinks – other than beer.

This leads to the next point in the care of the incontinent patient. However logical and desirable the nurse's plans for him may be, and however much she takes into consideration his social environment as well as his personal disposition, unless she can persuade the patient and his carer of this her plans will come to naught. The patient and the carer may be unwilling or feel unable to carry out the plan devised by the nurse. It is therefore wise that all three should jointly discuss and agree a plan of care.

It may be better to accept a plan which, while not perfect, will at least be capable of execution than to have a perfect plan which will not be followed through. Between them they should agree that perhaps for the next two days emergency measures are essential but that after 48 hours heroic efforts on the part of the family may become unrealistic and must be reviewed. Or it may be agreed that with tremendous effort on the part of everybody an attempt should be made to promote the continence of the patient during the day, while accepting that resources at night may make achievement of total continence unlikely. Alternatively, the nurse, the patient and the carer may regretfully come to the conclusion that, while the achievement of continence might in theory be a possibility, in practice it is impossible and continuous incontinence will have to be accepted.

Whatever the outcome of their deliberations, all plans – even the most long-term ones – should be reviewed at regular, specified intervals. Only in this way can the nurse hope to do as she was asked in the first place – manage the incontinent patient.

34 Rehabilitation principles applied to physio-therapy for the elderly

Helen Ransome

Introduction

With the widening of the scope of geriatric medicine in many countries and the awakening of interest in this discipline in others, I feel that we can hopefully expect that geriatric rehabilitation, too, will enter upon a new era. With the increasing proportion of the population of all countries lying in the age-group over 65, and the resulting predictable growing hospital-bed occupancy by this age-group, the prospect for our elderly and our hospitals will not be a bright one unless we do in fact enter a new era of rehabilitation for the elderly.

A young or middle-aged person who spends a period of some days or weeks in bed after, for instance, major surgery, will feel somewhat 'shaky at the knees' on first attempting to walk, but will probably, barring complications, quickly find his feet again and have a speedy discharge home – rehabilitation having been achieved quickly and efficiently without much effort on the part of the nursing or remedial care staff, or the patient. Let us now consider an elderly person in the same position. He will probably have some osteo-arthritis in hips, knees or spine, he may have Parkinson's disease, chronic bronchitis, hemiparesis as the result of a stroke (cerebrovascular accident or CVA), a previously pinned fractured neck of femur, or any one of a large number of physical conditions which he has lived with and despite which he has managed in the community before he came into hospital. He undergoes the surgery and then spends the usual amount of time in bed, then out by his bed in a chair, and then it is time for him to begin to walk again. What happens? He can't! He can't even get out of the chair! A busy medical or surgical ward, as are thousands of wards in Britain and other countries, does not have the time or staff, either nursing or remedial, to cope with this patient. So he is left, it being hoped that he will miraculously 'find his feet again'. It is murmured that he is 'too old' anyway to be expected to be mobile. Then one day his bed is declared 'blocked' and the geriatrician is called in to provide a permanent long-stay hospital bed for our patient, who now has considerable muscle wasting and joint stiffness and an attendant lack of function over and above his initial disablement, directly relatable to hospitalization. This appalling deterioration when it occurs makes rehabilitation once

Source: a shortened and updated version of a paper read at the Gerontology Session of the Westminster International Seminar, 1 July 1974.

commenced, even in a unit where functional geriatric rehabilitation is practised effectively, a much longer, costlier and harder procedure both in terms of patient pain (despite pain-relieving drugs, mobilizing is cruelly painful) and effort and in terms of use of rehabilitation resources. Under these conditions rehabilitation is also less likely to succeed. However, we hope that with luck our patient has not become too immobile to rehabilitate in the geriatric rehabilitation section where he has been moved by an enlightened geriatrician, one who believes that the combined onslaught of his 'team' may get the patient out of hospital and back into the community. The vital factor governing the patient's ability to return to the community, when medical and/or psychiatric problems have been solved, is his mobility. The first question from relatives or social workers trying to place the patient out of hospital is: 'Can he walk?'.

What has been happening while our elderly patient has been in bed and sitting in a chair by the bedside for those post-operative weeks/months? His arthritic joints which had for years been more or less stiff and painful when he woke up in the morning and when he sat in a chair too long, and which he kept mobile by being busy and active at home, have 'seized up' during this period of inactivity. The pain which he disregarded, and to disperse which he moved around at home, has got much worse. He is not busy either, so he notices it more. The slightly weak anti-gravity muscles which most elderly people possess have become much weaker through inactivity. The balance mechanism has not been used, so it has become unreliable. The rigidity of Parkinson's disease will cause further immobility. The patient with a previous stroke is in an even worse position, because the maintenance of his activities of daily living depended crucially, even before his admission, on his full daily use of the movement he had remaining after the stroke. Even an elderly patient with no previously diagnosed disabling disease will become surprisingly immobile in a short period of confinement in bed or chair. I include 'chair' here because merely sitting in a chair is actually little improvement on being in bed where mobility is concerned. Elderly patients who have suffered a new stroke, fracture or other basically physically disabling condition which precipitates their confinement to bed for a period of time have also, for the above reasons, a harder time rehabilitating than younger patients.

These specific physical problems suffered by the elderly confined to bed either at home or in hospital need a specific physiotherapy approach. Just as geriatric medicine has evolved to meet the challenge of the sick elderly person, so geriatric physiotherapy must now evolve, with the detailed assessment and treatment methods usually reserved for younger people being brought to bear on the physical problems of all elderly patients.

The team approach to rehabilitation has been proved a success. When applied to rehabilitation of the elderly this is equally true. The physiotherapist working in this field is only one member of a rehabilitation team consisting of the geriatrician or physician and his assistants, nursing staff, occupational therapist, social worker and speech therapist where required. Each of the members of this team has a vital role in the patient's rehabilitation, which must begin *immediately* the elderly patient arrives in hospital for whatever reason. It is from this moment on that the physiotherapist must observe the following rehabilitation principles: assessment, execution of a plan of action, setting realistic goals, continuous evaluation, and follow-up.

1 Assessment

For the physiotherapist the arrival of the elderly patient in hospital means an initial assessment.

1 Functional activities

Chair to bed transfer	Transfer from bed to commode
Getting into bed	Stand
Rolling to left	Stand up from chair
Rolling to right	Sit down in chair
Moving up and down in bed	Walk
Sitting up	Four-foot kneel ⎫
Pelvic raising	Getting up off floor ⎬ if relevant
Sitting balance	Wheelchair management ⎪
	Stairs ⎭

We must determine accurately how patients perform these functions, whether: alone, with supervision, or with help – of a person or of a walking aid.

2 Balance ⎫
3 Joint mobility ⎬ are also assessed in as much as they
4 Muscle strength ⎪ affect functional ability
5 Coordination ⎭

This assessment must take place immediately, even with an unconscious patient, as elderly joints lose range of movement alarmingly quickly. If the patient has arrived for surgery the assessment preferably takes place before surgery, to determine the usual level of the patient's functional ability.

An accurate initial assessment is vital to planning, specifically in regard to physiotherapy and generally with regard to the patient's future.

2 Execution of a plan of action

The plan is based on the assessment. Treatment must focus on the patient's weak points.

1 Re-educate functional activities involved in daily living listed under 1.1 above.

2 Re-train balance
3 Mobilize stiff joints
4 Strengthen weak muscles
5 Re-train coordination
⎬ as necessary and possible, to achieve maximum safe performance of functional activities.

Training is not 'treatment' done to a passive patient. The physiotherapist is often more of a teacher, e.g. teaching chair drill to a patient, who must be encouraged to want to re-learn the skill in order to become more independent. After frequent repetitions of simple instructions the patient should over-learn the skill in order for it to become automatic, e.g. 'wriggle to the edge of the chair', 'bring your feet back as far as you can' (knees should be bent to at least a right angle), 'lean forward', 'now push with your hands on the chair arms and stand up – keep on leaning forward'.

Re-training is a progression towards maximum independence, graded for each individual patient, easier movements and activities (e.g. rolling and sitting) proceeding in an orderly sequence to harder movements and activities (e.g. standing and walking). Advice may need to be given (e.g. about correct shoes or walking aid).

Movements and activities are done progressively:

1 With assistance – minimal.
2 Alone with supervision – it is crucial that, at this stage, a patient is not left alone. A fall can be catastrophic to the rehabilitation programme and the patient's confidence.
3 Alone without supervision.
4 With resistance – maximal.

Severely disabled patients need daily intensive physiotherapy. They and all elderly patients need to work to their individual maximum limit in order to gain improvement of function, be it of muscle strength or the vital capacity of their lungs. They do this work best with an individual physiotherapist, not equipment. The patient responds to and is motivated by an individually addressed request for movement. The elderly patient's rehabilitation is often slow-stream and this must be appreciated. Many general hospital teams reject the elderly disabled patient, who later rehabilitates in a geriatric unit where slowness of response is accepted.

Up till now I have talked about in-patients, who I hope in the new era could have this detailed rehabilitation, whether in geriatric assessment or rehabilitation wards or in the medical or surgical wards of the hospital. However, many areas now have Geriatric Day Hospitals where out-patients (and ideally the geriatric in-patients receiving rehabilitation) can come for whole-day rehabilitation. These patients, after physiotherapy assessment, fall into one of the following groups:

(*a*) some needing intensive general rehabilitation;
(*b*) a few needing intensive training of one function like getting up off the floor after falling;
(*c*) others who are basically still independent but slow and unsteady. Their needs may vary from general exercise, particularly for the anti-gravity muscles, to render them fully and confidently independent again, to increasing their stability by advice and help in the procuring of low-heeled supportive shoes or by the substitution of a walking frame for a stick;
(*d*) those who are severely disabled and who need maintenance exercise to keep them functioning at their maximum in the community, i.e. to delay their admission on a long-stay basis for as long as possible.

Because of the chronic shortage of trained physiotherapists and the large number of patients involved in a day hospital, these last two groups of patients need to work mainly with physiotherapy aides or helpers and use exercise equipment.

These out-patients come as often as their general condition dictates, from one to five days per week, most often two or three times, reducing as the patient improves; they can have their treatment increased again if they lose function. There are some younger, less disabled patients (e.g. 60–70-year-old stroke patients without complicating factors) who can, in fact, not merely achieve an adequate degree of rehabilitation, but, with intensive treatment, can progress to a near-normal functional situation, e.g. using an ordinary and less embarrassing walking stick instead of a more obvious quadruped.

Because of the nature of this functional rehabilitation, only very basic equipment is required by a physiotherapy department rehabilitating the elderly.

1 *For individual work:* exercise platforms (raised mats); adjustable bed; floor mats; exercise stools.
2 *For walking:* parallel bars; walking aids – numerous, various kinds and heights (including adjustable ones).
3 *Chairs:* stable chairs with and without arms; a spring chair, which is

useful for a few patients who cannot, because of severely limited mobility, get out of a conventional chair.

4 *Stairs:* preferably large with a turn at the top.

5 *Exercise equipment:* small static bicycles; rowing machines; shoulder pulleys.

6 *For classwork:* tape-recorder; bean-bags, balls, etc.

7 *Splints:* It is essential to have a storage cupboard full of various short and long calipers, and various sizes of shoes to receive the calipers, in order to lend them to patients before their own have arrived from the surgical-appliance fitter or while repairs are being carried out. Three to four weeks without a necessary functional lower-limb splint, e.g. toe-raising spring, can mean three to four weeks without walking, which, for the elderly patient, leads to deterioration and loss of morale.

8 *Infra-red lamp:* for occasional use in some cases of recent injury. In my opinion it is unjustifiable to use physiotherapists' and patients' time for palliative heat treatments to try and relieve chronic osteo-arthritic pain in the elderly. All geriatric patients have some degree of osteo-arthritis and attendant pain, and valuable time should be used to train them to adapt to living with their disability and to function despite it, with the help of pain-relievers where necessary.

9 *Ice:* for use with some inflamed arthritic joints – to reduce pain and swelling and to facilitate movement. Ice is also useful as an aid to the mobilization of some stiff joints.

3 Setting realistic goals

If a patient is accurately assessed his physiotherapy programme will ask neither too little nor too much of him, and he will certainly improve if working to his individual maximum even if working within severe individual limitations. While he is still improving, a plan for his future will be evolving. When he ceases to improve, a decision must be made by the rehabilitation team as to his future.

Where Part III or local authority residential accommodation is the goal for a patient, independence in the activities of daily living is mandatory. Even with patients for whom nursing-home or long-stay accommodation is envisaged, maximum functional independence will reduce nurse dependency.

On the other hand, with patients destined for home, the physiotherapist, as well as the occupational therapist and social worker, must know the home situation of the patient. Often she will need to make contact with the relatives and involve them in rehabilitation. Home visits and home assessments are a necessary part of the geriatric physiotherapist's work. After the home layout and the furniture have been seen, advice can be given which may be crucial to the patient's ability to live in that environment, e.g., a patient may be independent with a low bed and need help with a higher one, or vice versa, depending on the disability. The physiotherapist can suggest either the use of bed blocks or reducing the height of the bed as required. The elderly often find such changes difficult to organize, so that help as well as advice may need to be given in some cases.

4 Continuous evaluation

Continuous assessment will be needed as a sick elderly patient gradually recovers, so that his returning abilities can be immediately utilized. The withholding of help in the form of lifting, and the encouragement of the patient to use his arms to push with, and to reach for the bed being transferred to, can prevent the formation of the habit of dependence and will speed his return to functional independence. However, the attitude 'Let's do it for him, it's kind as he's old, and it's quicker' at first hinders recovery and may eventually block physical recovery completely. Every time someone does a movement for an elderly patient, of which he is capable himself, or someone helps him to perform an activity he can manage alone, another square inch of his 'long-stay' bed is being reserved. The choice is often between encouraging an elderly patient to become gradually responsible again for his own independent movement, which involves some effort on both sides, or consigning a human being to a permanent existence in a hospital ward.

The patient's response to rehabilitation is discussed at case conferences which the whole rehabilitation team attend. At these conferences the physiotherapist can consult with the geriatrician or physician to see if any medication, e.g. a pain-relieving drug, can be introduced to help the patient's performance, or to discover if a patient's current medical condition, for instance, low plasma potassium, is perhaps a key to poor performance. The interested doctor welcomes a physiotherapist's comments on patient's progress. Similar close cooperation is necessary with the occupational therapist, who needs to know, *inter alia*, when a patient has achieved sufficient sitting balance for dressing practice to begin. The social worker trying to find a home for a patient needs to know if he can manage stairs.

The physiotherapist must constantly communicate her aims and the patient's current level of function to the nurse, who must reinforce the physiotherapist's work during her continuous 24-hour contact with the patient. This will increase the overall speed of rehabilitation and ensure cooperation. The physiotherapist's opinion is, of course, only one of several interacting factors at all team discussions.

5 Follow-up

It is vital to maintain, in some form or other, contact with the patient and either his/her family or the staff of the old people's residential home, e.g. by means of day hospital or out-patient physiotherapy attendance after ward discharge, monthly attendance at day hospital review clinic after day hospital discharge, attendance at out-patient clinics, home visits from domiciliary physiotherapist, liaison with local authority staff such as health visitors or with district nurses, who will follow up soon after discharge. Occasional severely disabled patients can never be discharged – they are those who require continuous, life-long maintenance.

Summary

The role of the physiotherapist in the rehabilitation team for the elderly is to assess, at least maintain and, if possible, improve the patient's total mobility. This team membership is crucial to any form of rehabilitation and nowhere more crucial than when working with the elderly. Only with a constantly communicating team, with the patient at the centre, can the goal of returning the disabled elderly patient to the community with increased independence and improved quality of life be achieved.

35 The work of an occupational therapist in a geriatric department

Dorothy Thomas

Although one of the newer disciplines in the hospital world, occupational therapy has existed long enough to have developed the all-too-prevalent attitude towards geriatric work. A geriatric unit has been considered the Cinderella by the occupational therapist who more often seeks a career in orthopaedic, neurological, psychiatric and physical rehabilitation units. The reasons for this state of affairs may be legion but they may well hinge on what is expected of the therapist. Some units may only be visited by the occupational therapist once or twice each week. She is welcomed because she provides a much-needed transfusion of activity and mental stimulation, and a break in monotony, but, nevertheless, she remains a visitor. In other more dynamic centres she may have a department to which the patients are brought to work out the problems of personal dependence, such as dressing, feeding, and so on, but from the confines of which she is rarely encouraged to emerge.

In contrast there are other units where the occupational therapist may be a member of a well-integrated team, and it is here that she can find some of the most intensely satisfying work of all. Probably in no other field is she able to follow up a patient from home to hospital and share in the re-establishment of the same person at home again. Nor anywhere else can she contribute so largely in a programme that circumvents the need for hospital admission.

There is no one single discipline which can be entirely responsible for the patient's well-being and re-enablement, but in geriatric work the lines of demarcation must be less distinct, in order that continuity of purpose for the patient can be maintained throughout. For such teamwork the occupational therapist is particularly fitted; her practical skills and adaptability are perhaps obvious qualities. Her training in the psychological and physical fields ensure her ability to contribute to the basic plans that have to be made to enable elderly people to live as fully and as independently as possible. In few other spheres is there such opportunity for dealing with the 'whole person' as well as dealing with specific disabilities and problems.

Her knowledge of the basic human psychological needs for security, independence, usefulness and acceptance by the community help her to assess the individual person's difficulties in adapting to enforced limita-

Source: *British Hospital Journal and Social Service Review*, 19 April 1968, pp. 713–15.

tions, physical or environmental. This same training and knowledge also assist her in planning programmes to give opportunity to the person to adjust and compensate. It is not always possible to fulfil all these needs, therefore much discussion and judgment are called for by the team in order to balance the priorities.

The value of teamwork is never more clearly demonstrated than in attempting to provide an elderly person with some degree of security when ill-health and its attendant problems seem to threaten it. Fear, uncertainty and strangeness can be alleviated by the support and confidence of a team who are moving towards the same objective and who integrate with each other. For the same reason it is also imperative that relatives are incorporated and the patient is never allowed to feel that things are going on without his knowledge. This is sometimes done by arranging a special meeting in some realistic environment where all concerned are able to discuss and demonstrate the particular details connected with the plans for the future. In such an emotionally neutral atmosphere there is more chance of reaching really practical solutions.

Whatever may be the ultimate attainment of the patient it is important to aim at a basic level of independence. No person having reached maturity enjoys being dependent on others for personal daily living activities. Either the physiotherapist or the occupational therapist or both will work with the patient to enable him to move from bed to chair unaided, walk or wheel himself to the lavatory and manage there, wash himself, dress himself and feed himself.

This may seem a far cry from the early days of occupational therapy with its attendant image of felt toys and tangles of canework. (Although these still have their relevance in appropriate instances.) The occupational therapist in a geriatric unit knows that achievement boosts morale and confidence; she knows that time occupied by a patient with stiff joints in mastering the difficulties of dressing can be far more therapeutic than teaching the same patient some new craft for which there may be little use in the future.

Following assessment by the doctor, the occupational therapist may be required to visit the patient at home. She may visit alone or with a physiotherapist or with the social worker. In this way attendance at hospital, with the usual long waits, and hazards of transport, can be avoided, for although facilities are available in the hospital for assessment of the patient, it is often found that only in the individual person's home are the real problems exposed and solutions worked out. Considerable time may be spent, away from the patient, in discussing the progress, the social background, investigating possible adaptation to furniture or equipment, making some of the simpler 'aids', as well as seeing relatives and visiting the home. In some areas cooperation is possible with the local authority welfare department so that alteration to the home or provision of equipment can be undertaken before the patient is discharged from hospital. In other areas some of the work may be done by a technician from the occupational therapy department.

Independence for personal needs, however, is not enough. Only a robot would wash and dress each day with great effort but without the likelihood of being seen or going somewhere to do something purposeful. Such routine daily activities can only be the first step. There must be other activity and what this is will depend on the person's particular circumstances. If possible it should be useful activity, not just useful to the participating individual but to others – other patients, the family, the ward, the hospital or some outside organisation.

For a person who wants to be able to live at home, entirely alone or alone for most of the day, the ability to obtain, prepare and cook meals will have special importance. To begin with the occupational therapist may encourage the patient to help make tea for a group of patients before extending the exercise to that of preparing part of and then a whole meal. Even if the patient is only able to prepare the vegetables, help with washing-up or set the table, this is something that can be done for the family, something that can be done for others. Other related activities will, if realistic, be included in the programme, such as walking outside, crossing roads and shopping.

Perhaps, when thinking of particular known geriatric wards, it is difficult to imagine the kind of activity which can be useful, and which can be done by the patients and which can be done in the ward or day-room. No person can maintain a satisfactory existence in isolation and in a ward it is not easy for an elderly person to talk to his neighbour if a bed intervenes or to become interested in activity unless stimulated by company. It is, therefore, necessary to provide a situation where the patients can be grouped together. Activities or projects which can be completed reasonably quickly by the combined efforts of the group are most suitable for people who may tire quickly or forget the purpose if it is prolonged over too many sessions. It is important that the work is simple, that the whole project can be broken down into a variety of parts demanding different ability and different effort on the part of the patients. Having assessed the patient's ability, both physical and mental, the occupational therapist is able to allocate the various tasks. She is also able to organise the work so that each patient can work to his own time without upsetting the remainder of the group; always bearing in mind that the influence of the group, whether by praise or complaint, can be more beneficial than any encouragement or persuasion by a member of staff. If her work is well planned each patient can have a sense of achievement at the end of a session when the result of their combined efforts are reviewed.

In some centres work from factories can be used but where the group may fluctuate in capability and in numbers participating, the therapist often finds work of a suitable nature within the hospital. Such work as packing for the Central Supplies and Sterilization Department, labelling bottles for the pathology department, making paper bags for lining soiled-dressing bins, is very suitable. The latter has been found to be particularly valuable as it entails such a variety of movement, from standing to cut the large sheets of paper down to applying the last dab of paste. Whatever the activity it is important that there is no hard and fast date-line for completion as such conditions tend to sacrifice the patient for the work, there being too many variables to be able to estimate and guarantee 'output'. The occupational therapist may keep two or three projects going at the same time as a precaution against monotony, or she may intersperse the sessions of work with sessions of 'social recreation' – music to movement, games, films, and so forth.

Any doubt about the need for daily programmes of this kind can best be judged by visiting a ward on a Monday morning after two days of 'rest'. To be able to establish and maintain activity on such a scale, however, requires special empathy on the part of the nursing staff. The normal ward routine does not usually allow for patients learning to become independent, let alone forming work groups if no day-room is available! It breaks across all the rules and regulations, it involves calculated risks of falling, of losing clothing, water being spilled, beds being pushed out of alignment, to mention but a few of the disturbances. It is done and can be done where there is teamwork. And there is much to commend the activity in the ward, instead of a day-room, where the bedfast can focus their attention on movement more stimulating than trolleys and bed-pans!

During this time the relatives, or those closely connected with the patient, will have talked to some of, or all of, the team and will have seen for themselves the patient's capabilities. Not only will they have observed, but where necessary will have been given the confidence to allow the patient to continue to maintain such independence and interest once away from the hospital environment. Activity within the home or at a work-centre or a day-centre must be provided if the patient is to be permitted to live as satisfactorily and as fully as possible.

To make her contribution to the work of the team concerned with the geriatric patient the occupational therapist must not only be skilled in her own discipline, but she must also be prepared to spend considerable time in coordinating her work with that of the other members of the team. No team is ready-made, it demands the full strength of each link in the chain.

36 The chiropodist's role in the care of elderly people

H. Youngman, G. French and M. Witting

The function of a chiropodist in the care of elderly people is a combination of advice and actual treatment which may take many forms. The advice may be on measures which will prevent trouble arising. It could be said that this kind of advice begins as early as routine inspections of children's feet at school clinics. Surveys have shown that such things as hammer toes and 'bunions' and some other deformities are initiated by wearing shoes which are too large, too small, or of a casual type in childhood or adolescence. Advice is also given on how to care for the feet when something has gone wrong with their shape or function, and this together with padding and other treatment of various kinds helps to take people into an active old age.

Chiropody is currently provided by the National Health Service in Britain for two main groups of people. It may be provided in hospitals where it forms part of the general treatment of certain diseases and the chiropodist treats only those patients referred to him by the hospital consultants. These patients may be of any age, including the elderly, if their systemic disorders are likely to produce additional complications in the feet. The major provision of chiropody in the Health Service, however, is in the community division, where treatment is available to the so-called priority classes of which the elderly number by far the greatest. (The others are expectant mothers, physically handicapped and, nowadays, in some areas only, school children.)

In most parts of the United Kingdom, therefore, a chiropody service is available to elderly people, but it may be liable to certain restrictions in the frequency of treatment, usually because of shortage of trained staff. The service is usually offered in clinics, which may be held at health centres or in separate premises, but most Health Authorities also provide a domiciliary service for those patients who cannot get about. There are also mobile chiropody units in some rural areas, where an equipped van calls at outlying villages on a regular basis. Another way in which treatment can be provided is to allow the patient to visit the surgery of a private chiropodist at a set fee which the chiropodist then claims from the Health Authority. To obtain treatment from a clinic it may only be necessary for the patient to call in, and an appointment will be made on production of

Source: previously unpublished paper, written for this Reader.

a pension book, Clinic staff will usually also know what arrangements need to be made for domiciliary visits and whether any scheme exists in the district for attending the surgeries of private chiropodists.

Many Health Authorities send a chiropodist on regular visits to Homes for the Elderly, but the matron obviously is the best person to approach if chiropody is needed. Elderly people in long-stay hospital units are eligible for regular chiropody, which should be provided by the hospital chiropodist, as of course it should be for those of the elderly who attend hospital out-patient departments for specialist care of such conditions as diabetes, arthritis, nervous diseases and circulatory disorders. Chiropodists in hospitals need a note of referral from the consultant in charge of the case, but it is rarely necessary for the patient to have to ask; the consultants generally are keen to initiate chiropody treatment when it is required, provided that there is a chiropodist at the hospital.

Not all hospital patients qualify for treatment as of right, however, and priority is given to serious cases whose foot troubles arise out of their general condition. Although in the community division patients do qualify by age, more and more Health Authorities are having to introduce assessment systems to determine the degree of clinical need or urgency involved. It may be that some old people will be referred to nail-cutting clinics or asked to look after themselves. There is no reason why a healthy old person with good eyesight and reasonable mobility should not continue to cut his own toe-nails provided that they have not grown thick or deformed. If a daily bath is not possible, old people should be encouraged to wash their feet daily with ordinary toilet soap in comfortably warm water. Long soaking in harsh substances such as washing soda should be discouraged. Many elderly people have rather dry skin and after drying the feet thoroughly may apply a mild emollient such as toilet lanoline. 'Medicated' plasters, sprays or powders should not be necessary and the advice of a qualified chiropodist should be sought before recommending any form of 'self-treatment'. Although rough, hard skin may be smoothed with a pumice stone while bathing the feet, the treatment of corns, callosities or any other conditions should be left to the chiropodist.

When treating apparently healthy elderly people the chiropodist will have two main aims. These are:

(a) to keep them as mobile and independent as possible for as long as possible;

(b) to watch for early signs of the onset of what may become serious or disabling conditions, and if these are observed, to refer the patient as quickly as possible to his or her doctor.

A very important part of a State registered chiropodist's training involves the recognition of signs or symptoms which may precede or indicate the presence of a serious medical condition. An example of this is the tissue breakdown which does not heal as quickly or completely as would normally be expected, and when tests are carried out the patient is discovered to be a diabetic.

The commonest problem which the patient will meet is likely to be painful corns and callosity, sometimes complicated by self-medication and/or sepsis. Perhaps a brief explanation of how and why corns and callosity are caused will be helpful here. The outer part of the skin is called the epidermis. The normal reaction of the epidermis to increased wear and tear is to become thicker. On the foot (and on the hand also when used for unaccustomed manual work) when pressure (i.e. work) increases, the epidermis becomes noticeably thickened. When the production of callosity increases to the point where it becomes first, uncomfortable, and later, painful, we call this pathological callosity. Corns are areas in the callosity where the concentration of forces is greatest, causing a small area of the callosity to become condensed, hard, and painful, and the corn may contain fine nerve fibres or blood vessels or be tied down by fibrous tissue. In almost all cases, therefore, the presence of corns and callosity indicates that overloading of that part of the foot is taking place. If the lesions are on the upper surface of the toes it means that there is excessive pressure from the shoe; if under the foot an abnormally large proportion of weight is being transferred to the ground at that point. Usually this happens over prominent bony structures. Short-term treatment for corns and callosity is simply to remove the thickened epidermis with a scalpel. This gives partial relief immediately in many cases. But this is only palliative treatment and the epidermis will thicken again quite rapidly unless the underlying cause or causes are removed or treated. Chiropodists try to discover and treat not only the immediate cause of a condition but also the underlying factors which may predispose to its recurrence.

The most common cause of corns and callosity is undoubtedly pressure from footwear. Many painful and sometimes dangerous conditions arise because of stretch nylon socks or stockings which, the manufacturer claims will fit a range of sizes. Man-made fibres are very strong, and while the toes will undoubtedly push out the garment to the required length, the sock or stocking will exert a corresponding back-pressure on to the toes and at the same time press them tightly together. This deforms the toes and also prevents correct toe function, which is a very important part of the normal working of the foot. The foot of the sock or stocking should be as long as the patient's foot without being stretched before he puts it on.

A patient's feet spend approximately two-thirds of their life inside shoes or slippers of one kind or another. It is therefore also very important that these should be correctly fitted and of the right type. A chiropodist will explain the need for adequate length, width, depth of toe box, and, most important, an adjustable fastening such as laces, which will grip the foot around its narrowest part. Even a flat-heeled shoe, if it has no adjustable strap or lace, can be very deforming. A fastening prevents the foot from sliding forward as the patient walks and so helps to prevent shoe pressure from causing deformities. Even slippers are better if they fasten.

Shoes which have uppers made from man-made materials are, on the whole, best avoided except in waterproof footwear, because being impervious to water they do not allow evaporation of sweat. Sweat retention makes the skin less elastic and more liable to split, and predisposes to infection. Here we are up against the cost factor. Elderly people have limited resources, and plastic shoes tend to be cheaper than leather. An important part of a chiropodist's treatment is to advise a patient as to the kind of footwear which he or she should wear, and sometimes also where to obtain it.

Another cause of corns and callosity is bony deformity of the foot. Even otherwise healthy people may have damaged or deformed feet. The most common deformity of shod races is *hallux valgus*, in which the big toe moves over towards the outer side of the foot, taking up much more than its share of the available room in the front of the shoe, with consequent compression and probably deformity of the four smaller toes and the formation of what is known in everyday language as a 'bunion'. *Hallux valgus* is, however, most often caused by shoes which are badly fitting or otherwise unsuitable. Other kinds of deformity can be secondary to general conditions such as old poliomyelitis, the muscular dystrophies, leprosy, *talipes equino-varus* (club foot), and some neurological conditions. In all deformed feet the relationship between bones is altered, movement at joints is restricted or non-existent and muscles function badly, or not at all. Shoe pressure is increased over distorted joints.

The aim of the chiropodist's treatment is to help the foot to function as effectively and painlessly as possible. Initially this will be done by applying adhesive padding cut into appropriate shapes to remove excessive pressure from painful areas, to try to correct the position of the skeleton, to realign joints and thus allow muscles to work more effectively.

When maximum improvement has been obtained and any acute condition has settled down, the chiropodist may make what is known as an appliance for the patient. This is a pad or pads which have been either placed on an insole so that it can be worn in the shoe, or covered in leather, or dipped in latex and then worn attached to the foot by elastic loops. These are much longer-lasting and more hygenic than adhesive padding, and in the long run are more economical. Patients who have appliances do not need to return for treatment so frequently. Unfortunately appliance-making facilities and technicians are only available in a few areas at present. Chiropodists are able to make appliances of many types, from simple insoles to dummy toes and moccasin fore-foot appliances for amputees. They can also make a false bursa to protect a 'bunion', and special plastazone boots or sandals for patients whose feet have been disorganised by rheumatoid arthritis, and for diabetic patients and leprosy cases where after-care of healed ulcers is needed. Complicated appliances for severe deformities are moulded on to a plastic cast of the patient's foot, either in a vacuum-forming machine or a special oven, and then built up where necessary with additional padding.

Problems with nails also bring a patient to a chiropodist. These can be problems of eye-sight, mobility, abnormality of shape, or the presence of other serious systemic conditions which necessitate great care in even routine cutting. The blind or partially-sighted are an obvious group who need regular routine care. Many middle-aged people who need glasses for reading also find it difficult to cut their own toe-nails. Reading glasses focus at reading distance which is too close to enable the patient to see the toe-nails clearly. Arthritic changes in hips, knees, and spine make bending difficult and in the fingers and wrists make it difficult to grasp scissors, so that help at regular intervals is necessary.

The nails in themselves can be a problem. If they have become excessively thickened it may be impossible to cut them with scissors. This can be dealt with very easily by the chiropodist by reducing the thickness with an electric drill similar to that used by the dentist. The shape of the nail may be changed, the sides becoming rolled under and inwards so that the side of the nail is invisible, covered by the soft tissues. This kind of nail deformity is potentially dangerous. It will probably be found that for years the patient has been cutting away the side to relieve discomfort. This is only palliative, the pain returning as soon as the nail grows again. The chiropodist will persuade the patient to allow the nail to grow forward until it is long enough to be cut straight across at the free edge, which is the correct and safe way to cut toe-nails. Correction of the excessive curve can often be achieved by fitting a nail brace made from sprung dental wire, very similar in principle and effect to the brace a dentist uses to realign a child's teeth.

If a nail of any kind is cut by the patient himself or by someone else, so that a spike or splinter of nail is left at the side, this sharp spike may penetrate the skin as the nail grows forward and cause a true ingrown toenail. This is particularly likely to happen where the nails are very curved transversely, or where they have been cut too short or too far down at the sides. The splinter of nail causes an ulcer in the groove at the side of the nail, and a nasty inflamed toe with a mound of red repair tissue partly covering the nail may result. The chiropodist will give the patient an injection of local analgesic and remove the splinter together with a section of nail right down to the base. Then the cells from which that part of the nail has grown will be destroyed by using chemicals or a small, safe, electric current. That section of the nail will then never grow again, and the patient will be left with a perfectly acceptable but narrower nail which is much more comfortable.

When a doctor sends a patient to a chiropodist, either in hospital or in private practice, there is again the need for cooperation in the form of adequate information in the introductory letter on any relevant medical history or treatment. This is particularly important in the elderly who, because of their age, may be expected to be affected to some extent by normal ageing processes. Changes occur in the feet as part of the general bodily disturbance associated with some diseases as for example, in rheumatoid arthritis, and in old age these changes may be complicated by the onset of osteo-arthrosis or a reduced arterial supply to the lower limb. Medication for such things as rheumatoid arthritis also may cause problems. If a patient is taking steroids the signs of inflammation which are a warning of the presence of infection may be very slight, allowing the infection to become established. Steroids also retard the healing processes as part of their effect on inflammation.

Elderly patients who would otherwise be considered to be in normal health may have residual effects from such things as poliomyelitis, peroneal muscular atrophy, strokes, or meningitis. Chilblains are particularly likely to occur in people who have had poliomyelitis. Here the chiropodist may be able to help quite a lot by advice on how to prevent chilblains coming and by local treatment if necessary, in addition to preventive medication by the patient's doctor.

The first signs of many serious illnesses manifest themselves in the feet and legs, either by changes in the way the patient walks or by the production of a lesion with a typical history. Parkinsonism and multiple sclerosis cause changes in walking which, when considered with other signs and symptoms, show the doctor that there is a need for investigation. A painless ulcer which will not heal may initiate investigation which will disclose diabetes mellitus, vascular disease, the later stages of syphilis or some other serious conditions. Chiropodists who see a patient at regular intervals are particularly well placed to observe these signs and to send the patient at once to the general practitioner for advice.

37 Casework with the older person and his family

Margaret Milloy

In casework with the aging, as in any other area of casework, the worker's primary goals are to develop a sound psychosocial diagnosis and to carry out a satisfactory plan of treatment. [. . .]

Perhaps social workers have tended to provide less than equal service to the older person because they have geared their actions to his reality needs or those of his family without undertaking a proper diagnostic study of his total situation. Their conscious or unconscious conviction seems to be that the older person can progress in only one direction – down. Seeing only death in his future, they wonder, What is the use . . .? They often appear to feel that it is more worth while to work with a younger person in short-term ego-supportive casework than to work with an older person whose needs may be similar. [. . .]

The concept of aging as a developmental stage related to previous stages and carrying with it certain specific tasks is particularly important in thinking about diagnosis. According to Robert Peck, old age poses three tasks: the achievement of ego differentiation as opposed to work-role preoccupation, of body transcendence as opposed to body preoccupation, and of ego transcendence as opposed to ego preoccupation.[1] Charlotte Buhler, as paraphrased by Margaret Blenkner, seems to see one goal in the last stage of life as 'finding an inner fulfillment, an inner meaning and integrity',[2] that enables the individual to face death with the sure knowledge that he has contributed to the future of his family and to society.

Obviously, it is the rare client who comes to a social agency having achieved this goal, and here is where the worker's diagnostic and treatment skills become most important. To what extent can the caseworker help him accomplish the tasks before him? What kind of help, aside from that geared to reality needs, does he require? What capacity does he have for mastery? In this regard, Blenkner makes a plea for social workers to be less concerned with the older person's defenses and more concerned with his capacity to cope with the myriad changes taking place within himself and his environment, which form the basis for the developmental tasks mentioned above. She asks the social worker these questions: 'If one accepts the developmental frame of reference, what is more important to diagnose or evaluate in an older person; his particular resolution of the

Source: *Social Casework*. 1964, *45*, 8, pp. 450–6 (extracts).

Oedipus complex or his philosophy of life? Which is more likely to offer you a dynamic you can use in treatment?'

What does the caseworker diagnose, which of his tried and true methods can he use, and how can he expand his conceptual framework to include age categories that, for the most part, he has dismissed with a pat generalization? [. . .] Stanley Cath[3] speaks of certain basic anchorages that people form throughout life: (1) an intact body and body image, (2) an acceptable home, (3) a socioeconomic anchorage, and (4) a meaningful purpose in life. These four anchorages provide the structure within which the individual performs the required developmental tasks at various stages of life; and the degree of success with which tasks are performed and crises met spells the difference between good and impaired health.

Cath states that throughout life, but particularly in the latter years, a balance is struck between external and internal depleting and restorative forces; and that all these anchorages are vital to the individual's ability to maintain balance. From these anchorages also comes the 'feedback' – the memories, relationships, and so forth that reinforce the individual's sense of his own worth and help to maintain his balance. In a sense Cath is talking about the nature of the ego and its capacity to cope with both internal and external stress, and about ways in which its functioning can be strengthened. In terms of casework with the older person Cath's formulation implies that the worker's proper concern is not so much the pathology of the client as those ego and life forces that are still intact or capable of restoration. The caseworker needs to acquire a longitudinal view of the client in order to determine the strength of his anchorages, how well they have served him, and how adequate they are in the present. In other words, if the worker views aging as a developmental stage, he needs to evaluate both the individual's success in mastering the tasks and crises of previous stages and the residue of unsolved problems complicating his mastery of current crises.

Much of the foregoing also can be viewed in terms of the adequacy and continuity of the older person's role functioning at various age levels. To what extent are previous role discontinuities affecting his current problems? How much conflict is there between his and society's expectations in regard to his role performance in his various statuses – for instance, his performance in his roles as husband, father, son, older person, unemployed man – and in regard to his roles as related to his race and religion, his education, and his occupation? As a husband and father, a man is expected to be strong, supportive and giving – the employed head of a household who is active in decision-making. As an old, unemployed man, he is expected to be cheerful, nonassertive, and satisfied with his income from Old Age Assistance, Social Security, or his children. Perhaps he is expected to be a baby sitter for his grandchildren; perhaps a substitute homemaker if he is a widower, or a household helper to his wife if he is a husband. Obviously, the transition from one set of roles to the other cannot be accomplished without great pain and anxiety, not only for the older person but also for those who are affected by his role definitions or participate in them as does the adult child when he feels he should assume the role of a parent to his own parent. It is the caseworker's responsibility to understand this problem area and gear the treatment to it.

Inherent in this discussion are questions that have to be answered about the client's character, his ego-functioning, and past and current traumas to which he may be reacting. How much depletion is irreversible because of the death of loved ones and an inability to cathect substitutes or because of the loss of health? To what extent can the caseworker hope to help the client restore his capacity to function? What objects in the environment can be used as cathectic substitutes? If there are children, how can the worker help to free them and the parent from the old, unsatisfying, unworkable ties and strengthen the positive aspects of their relationship?

It is not easy for the worker to accomplish these aims of casework with the older person, particularly because so many older people seek help only at a point of considerable crisis. Often, unfortunately, they seek help only when there has been so much irreversible loss that the worker can do no more than assist the family in making a plan for the client. The points that follow, however, need to be given consideration in treatment.

The first point concerns the worker's own attitude toward old age and his ability to empathize with the needs of his clients. In order to be able to help older people, the worker must first have resolved his own feelings about death, not only the death of his loved ones but also his own. Much of old age relates directly to real losses – of family and friends, of job, of money and status – to impairment of the body or body functioning, and to anticipated death of oneself. Unless the worker can recognize the client's losses and empathize with his sense of bereavement, he cannot be tuned in to the client's need to deal with these losses, to cathect new objects or face an irreparable loss realistically. The worker has to be able, moreover, to tolerate the extreme – sometimes overwhelming – social and emotional isolation in which so many older people live and not to be drawn into it if, as sometimes happens, he perceives in the client what he fears to be his own future. This aspect of counter-transference, which has perhaps not been recognized or dealt with sufficiently, certainly deserves much consideration.

It is important for the caseworker to understand the handling of grief and mourning. The client may express specific grief reactions or a generalized depressive reaction. For whom or what is he mourning? Is he reacting to a former or a current loss? Is his grief reaction 'normal', or are there aspects of morbidity present? If it is a normal, acute grief reaction, perhaps the best help is empathic listening and recognition that the client may need to withdraw temporarily because he is preoccupied with guilt; if someone close to him has died, he may seem to have lost an 'anchor', a habit pattern of daily living related to the lost person, and he may appear not quite oriented. But he will not have lost touch with reality, and he will need reassurance, expressions of interest from those around him, and help in making new connections.

As a person progresses from normal grief, where the preponderant feelings toward the lost object are positive and warm, along a continuum of increasing ambivalence, intervention may be needed to help him release negative feelings of loss and desertion. If he can really 'suffer' the loss, he will be much freer afterward to express hostile feelings and will have less feeling of guilt in connection with them; through this experience he will be able to withdraw his tie to his lost object. If, however, he is encouraged by family and friends to repress his feelings of loss and 'keep a stiff upper lip', resolution of the negative feelings will be extremely difficult, if not impossible, because of the repressed guilt associated with them.

With the majority of older people, mourning is a reaction to both current and past losses. The caseworker's task, then, is to support the client's capacity to master the current trauma. After sensitively exploring earlier experiences of loss, the worker relates these to the current situation by responding either verbally or in a kind of 'double talk' – that is, responding to deeply felt emotions at the same time that he discusses conscious feelings. To the degree that the client can be freed emotionally from his ties to the lost object, he will be able to reach out and form new ties to living objects that constitute a measure of restitution.

The worker has to make an unusually heavy emotional investment in the older client – not a personal one, but a feeling, professional one – through which the client learns that he, his thoughts and his feelings, are truly important. If the worker fails to make this kind of controlled investment, the client may interpret his various attempts at ego-restoration as empty reassurance, attack, or pressure to do what seems impossible. If the worker is able to make the investment, he can use supportively many techniques that are effective with younger clients – confrontation, clarification, and interpretation, for example – to help the client accept his world and cope with it. The difference between working with the young and the old in this respect is a quantitative one; the aging person, in comparison with the young person, usually has much less energy to invest, partly because he expends so much in coping with his everyday problems of living. Moreover, unlike the younger person, he tends to despair and to have relatively little hope that what he does will benefit himself in the future. A larger emotional investment by the caseworker is therefore necessary to achieve the same results.

The client-worker relationship is achieved as a result of various types of communication. [. . .] 'Often the only way in which we can communicate our continued interest and concern to very sick patients is through touch – and a sensitive worker can always tell when this is appropriate or when it would be too threatening for an inhibited patient.'[4] [. . .] Social workers have always been taught that physical contact with clients, except young children, is unprofessional; but with the aged and sick it should be regarded as a specific technique of treatment that springs from the worker's empathy with the client and a desire to let him know that he matters. Without this empathy, this controlled emotional investment, physical contact is a gesture that is meaningless or one that may even be harmful.

Although the worker needs to make an investment of feeling, he must be alert to the dangers of overinvesting himself to satisfy his own personal needs. [. . .]

The proper use of community resources

So far, the provision of psychological services has been discussed, but many older persons have also an acute need of concrete services. Probably the more varied the agency services provided, the more social workers are able to reach out to people in need. [. . .]

Social workers should use the special services available for old people with discrimination. The two most important criteria for utilizing any services (with the exception of protective services) are (1) Will using the service increase or maintain the client's capacity for mastery? and (2) Will it tend to lessen his sense of isolation and increase his feeling of being needed? For instance, a part-time homemaker can help an isolated person maintain his independence and so delay or obviate the necessity of providing domiciliary care. This is a very important service to him and the community.

Family agencies should have both a philosophy and a policy regarding the protective care of older people. LeRoy Levitt points out the great importance not only of making 'an adequate, flexible, utilizable medical diagnostic evaluation' before taking any legal protective measures but also of recognizing that certain disorders fluctuate and change after a diagnosis is made.

A knowledge of symptomatology is not as important as information about the modifiability and the medical, environmental, or emotional changes required. The double play of quick diagnosis, then disposition to hospital, commitment, nursing home, or guardianship is interfered with by such an attitude. It is medieval to think of a psychosis at any age as a problem of competency or confinement, just by virtue of the diagnosis. There are as many kinds of senescent problems as there are people with such problems.[5]

Levitt goes on to comment on the reparative capacities of the aged and the seriousness of depriving a person of his civil rights, a move that should not be made without plans for regularly reappraising his initial state of incompetency and the new clinical condition. This principle is just another aspect of concern for the older person, carried forward to a period when he has suffered greater depletion and possibly organic change.

Questions about plans for living arrangements often arise in working with most older people. Can the older person live in the community? If so, with what protections? Does he need institutional care? If so, what kind? Can he use a foster home? What kind of protection does he need? Inherent in all questions in this area is the fact that each person is different from all others; he is a product of his own unique life experiences and has to be understood in that light. Therefore, plans for living arrangements should be based on the principle that as long as a person gains more gratification than pain from living in the community, it is better to help him remain there. Many older people seek entrance to an institution at a point of crisis occasioned by the death of a spouse, a caretaking child, or an important friend. The point of crisis may follow the onset of a disabling illness, with the result that the distress of the client is aggravated by a fear of encroaching weakness. In these circumstances he is apt to regress and focus on his weaknesses and his need for care. The social worker, then, must carefully evaluate all indications, however minor, of his interest in the world and his wish to participate in it.

When a person enters an institution, it becomes the center of his world, and outside relationships take on a lesser meaning. In even the best institution, independence and a sense of mastery must be curtailed. Therefore, by supporting him and by assuring him he will be helped to enter an institution when he needs to, the social worker encourages the older person to live independently as long as he can safely manage it. The word *safely* refers not only to physical safety but also more important, to emotional well-being.

One client was so hostile and attacking in her overwhelming need to be given to that she drove one person after another away from her. The consulting psychiatrist thought that even though living alone in miserable surroundings was physically dangerous to her, her hostile attempts to meet her insatiable needs could be managed better in the community than in an institution where she would probably 'use up' everyone available quickly.

Another client took in a roomer who helped to care for her house. Her need for independence was fierce and unrelenting. She was in great danger of falling or of having some other serious accident, and the social worker consulted a psychiatrist and a lawyer to determine the medical and legal responsibility of the agency for initiating proceedings for protective care. The psychiatrist thought that the client's denial of her dependency longings was one of her most important defenses. To break down this defense would literally destroy her; she had to be allowed to live alone until an incapacity forced her to recognize her need for care.

In both instances the social worker kept in close contact with the clients and made plans for them to be institutionalized when the change was indicated.

Lest the worker consider his responsibilities in working with the older person global, he should recognize, as he does with younger clients, that when personality damage is too great there may be nothing he can do to ameliorate the situation, at least with the current state of knowledge and staff pressures. The worker must make a moral judgment about the use of his time and, after proper evaluation of the needs of the client, either discontinue service entirely or, when necessary, provide only tangible service without psychological treatment.

Working with the adult children

The world is full of families in which there is a minimum amount of discord and a maximum amount of respect and love between generations. The older person participates in the total life of such families, and they usually do not seek treatment at social agencies unless the advanced age of the parent creates an acute problem. However, many of the people who come to social agencies have severe intergenerational conflicts, sometimes dormant until the need for plans for care of the parent becomes criticial. For many years social workers have been struggling with the question of how to reach out and help adult children with the feelings aroused at this point by the needs of their parents. The whole gamut of unresolved parent–child relationships can be stirred up again in such situations. With as much skill and sensitivity as social workers can muster, they have not been able to help these clients appreciably.

The adult child who is usually able to use casework help in relation to his unresolved conflicts about his parents is an individual whose role as a son or daughter has become secondary to his role as marital partner or parent. He requests help in solving marital or parent-child problems, and some resolution of his own ambivalent tie to the parent is a necessary ingredient to his getting help and managing his current roles more effectively.

What of the adult child who comes seeking help for his aged parent? There is a popular notion that as parents become less capable there is a reversal of roles between parent and child. I do not believe that the roles are reversed. Rather the older person and his child undertake new roles, and they both must learn to cope with the new situation. As the adult child assumes a new primary role with his parent, he may not have the energy to invest in an introspective, uncovering type of treatment. Both internal and external pressures are so heightened when he feels he has to take responsibility for his parent that he cannot afford to dissipate his energy in other directions. Assuming a new role is fraught with much conflict, partly because of the adult child's need to hold on to the cathected object that, in reality, has undergone considerable change through the aging process. If he allows his own strong, negative feelings to emerge, he creates an intolerable situation not only for himself but also for the aged parent, whose realistic problems must be dealt with positively. At this time the adult child's primary task is not to engage in introspection but to help the parent meet his reality needs.

If this formulation is correct, the adult child who asks for help in relation to an aging parent can be assisted in several ways, short of involving him in treatment for himself. One of the most important is in separating reality from the mass of feelings that color it. The social worker can be most supportive if he can help the client understand that his parent is not a child for whom he must assume complete responsibility: the parent is an adult, who, although suffering from serious limitations, has a right to make decisions and to take responsibility for the consequences of those decisions. The worker can lift a great burden from the adult child by helping him see that he does not have to act as if he were omnipotent. He also can help him look at alternatives realistically and share the responsibility of decision-making plans directly with the parent. By insisting on discussing plans directly with the parent, the worker can strengthen the adult child's ability to support his parent and to refrain from taking on too much responsibility.

In conclusion, it is worth while to repeat a warning against stereotyping older persons simply because they share one common characteristic, advanced age. Older people differ in their personalities and needs, in their internal and external resources, and in their capacity for change and growth. If social workers are to help them make the most of their remaining years, they must deal with them as individuals and not as undifferentiated representatives of a social category.

References

1 PECK, R. F. (1956) 'Psychological Developments in the Second Half of Life'. In

J. E. Anderson (ed.) *Psychological Aspects of Aging*, pp. 42–53. Washington: American Psychological Association.

2 BLENKNER, M. (1962) 'Developmental Considerations and the Older Client.' Paper presented at a Symposium on the Relations of Development and Aging, Fifteenth Annual Meeting of the Gerontological Society, Miami Beach, 8–10 November 1962 (unpublished).

3 CATH, S. H. (1963) 'Some dynamics of middle and later years', *Smith College Studies in Social Work*, *33*, 97–126.

4 LAMBRICK, H. M. (1962) 'Communications with the patient', *The Almoner*, *15*, 199.

5 LEVITT, L. P. (1963) 'Health: Current Practices, Responsibilities, Resources, Problems, Issues, Gaps, Recommendations.' Paper present at a general panel session, Seminar on Protective Services for Older People, Arden House, Harriman, New York, 10–15 March 1963; in *Seminar on Protective Services for Older People*, p. 110. New York: National Council on the Aging, 1964.

38   How to help the bereaved

Lily Pincus

Shakespeare lets Hamlet's mother say: 'Thou knowest 'tis common, all that lives must die'. It is therefore equally common that bereavement through death has to be faced as a fact of life. Yet, however honestly it is faced, bereavement brings about a crisis of loss, probably the most severe crisis in human existence. In this situation of inevitability and crisis, what help does the bereaved need, and what help can be offered?

We know from the accounts of bereaved children how vitally important the attitude of those around them, their teachers their relations, is for their recovery from the crisis of loss. Although the adult mourner is not so totally dependent on his 'outer world' and more able to understand the reality of his bereavement, many of the people to whom I spoke have told me how lost and bewildered they felt, how frightened about the 'grave departures from their usual attitude to life', and that they did not know to whom to turn ›for help. Some were afraid of going mad, or of getting themselves into irrevocable situations, such as hastily giving up their home. Many developed symptoms of physical illness, but even if they did not go to see their doctor or some other helper, their symptoms were a disguised request for help of some sort. [. . .]

The experience of counsellors for the bereaved confirms that help is most needed and most effective in the period immediately after the funeral. It is when the first numbness and the distractions preceding the funeral are over that the pain of loss is most severe. At that time, too, adjustments to the changed life have to be made, and the bereaved needs somebody to hold his hand, just as the baby who experiences loss needs to be firmly and lovingly held. [. . .]

The immediate task may consist chiefly in letting the bereaved talk, letting him tell all the details of the last weeks and days again and again, and just listen in the knowledge of how important this is. The need to talk, to complain, 'to mope', to 'get it off my chest', and to be listened to, is great.

In a climate of trust the bereaved may become able to talk about his feelings of guilt about having failed or harmed the deceased, or not having loved him enough. He, the bereaved, may be frightened by his occasional feelings of hatred, perhaps a wish for the patient to die quickly, to 'get it over with', so that he has now no longer to watch and participate in the

Source: *Social Work Today*, 1975, *6*, 13, pp. 392–5 (extracts).

suffering. There may also be guilt about the fury against the dead person who has left him with all the pain of loss. To have these feelings accepted and understood as a normal part of bereavement is true therapeutic help that a counsellor or good friend can give.

The need for a person who is simply around and quietly gets on with the various tasks which otherwise the bereaved would have to do – thus setting him free to grieve, may be equally great. In his grief, he may be as self-centred as an infant, and totally unaware of the needs of the other person, who after some time may be desperately in need of a cup of tea or completely exhausted. It is not easy to be a helper in bereavement. Our usual way of behaving may not be relevant for the bereaved. True help consists in recognising the fact that the bereaved has a difficult task to perform, one that should not be avoided and cannot be rushed. He has not only to accept the ultimate loss of the loved person, he has also to assimilate the experience of having been in touch with death. John Donne's words will always be true: 'Any man's death diminishes me because I am involved in mankind'. Colin Murray Parkes has said: 'There is an optimal "level of grieving" which varies from one person to another. Some will cry and sob, others will betray their feelings in other ways. The important thing is for feelings to emerge into consciousness. How they appear on the surface may be of secondary importance'. While the mourner is in great need of sympathy, pity is the last thing he wants. Pity puts him at a distance from and into an inferior position to the would-be comforter. 'Pity makes one into an object; somehow being pitied the bereaved person becomes pitiful.' [1]

Any sensitive friend can provide comfort for a mourner by regular contact at times of special vulnerability. A telephone call at the moment of waking may take the sting out of the early morning depression that another day of loneliness and misery has to be faced. If this call can be counted on every day at the same time it may be of great therapeutic value. [. . .] The regularity of such arrangements is what is most helpful, because it is the routine of married life, often little things taken for granted, which has been lost and is so sadly missed.

All such help derived from affectionate understanding of the needs of the bereaved, whether given by counsellors, neighbours or friends, can be termed therapy in bereavement situations in which there is no evidence of complications. If there are signs that all is not going well, if the bereaved is suffering from lasting physical symptoms, excessive guilt or anger, persistent depression, or uncontrollable grief, then more direct therapy may be indicated.

Absence of grief is such a sign. Yet those who cannot mourn are also likely to deny any need for help. 'Therapy is only for mad people,' said one such widower. This man, in his forties and in good physical health, had devotedly and tenderly nursed his dying wife. Immediately after her death, he plunged into work, moved and got busy with arrangements for himself and his children, intent on keeping the stiff upper lip and denying any needs of his own. He became angry and upset with his children who showed clear signs of disturbance after their mother's death. He not only was unable to help them but alienated them and kept away from them as much as possible. Six months after his wife's death this man contracted a terminal illness and died.

It may not be the bereaved himself but rather the people around him, who first sense that all is not well. An example of this was a recently widowed woman of 72 who since her husband's death had caused much trouble in her local clinic by turning up at all hours and shouting abuse at the doctors who, she claimed, had killed her husband and were now killing her. The puzzled doctors felt that this woman needed frequent home visits and asked a social worker to call on her. On his first visit, after knocking at the door, the social worker heard energetic movements in the flat, but when the woman opened the door and recognised the caller, she collapsed into his arms. She seemed to have to impress on him her need for support. Her first verbal communications were complaints about being let down by everybody ever since the death of her 'angel-husband'. She produced photos of him and also of her only daughter, who had married a Swiss and lived abroad. She, too, was described as an angel. Everybody else was nasty; her friends exploited her, her neighbours annoyed her, nobody cared for her or was prepared to help her.

What help she needed she could not say but it was clear she expected the social worker to provide it. On each of his subsequent visits she collapsed into his arms when he arrived but as soon as he had guided her to a chair, she got up, went into the kitchen to make tea for him, and showed that she was perfectly capable of looking after herself. On the one and only occasion when – early in their contact – the social worker brought one of his students with him, the widow showed her disapproval of this interference in their relationship by dropping the tea-tray and then collapsing on the floor. She needed one person to herself.

Soon, the stories about the angel-husband began to change. It emerged that for many years and up to his death he had been having an affair with another woman and had on several occasions deserted his wife. When he died suddenly she must have felt that her hate and resentment about his desertions had killed him, and transferred this self-accusation on to the doctors and all the others who had 'killed' him and would now 'kill' her. It also emerged that the 'angel-daughter' showed no interest in her mother. She had gone abroad when she was still very young, there was little contact, and she had not even come home for her father's funeral.

Obviously, no-one could stand this woman's demands and confused communications – her anger had driven everyone away. The social worker was well aware that he must not repeat this pattern. He had to watch his own reactions, in order to stick by her in spite of all her frenzies and provocations. Only then could he hope to help her to show her pain and anger more directly and not act it out so madly. He understood that this woman had probably always felt unacceptable and insecure, and since her husband's death which she saw as his greatest, most punishing act of desertion, her anxiety about her own badness had become overwhelming. Her only chance of recovery was to feel understood and accepted as she was. After she had been able to tell the truth about her husband, and face her hatred of him and her resulting self-hate, she no longer collapsed when the social worker came to visit her and did not feel so persecuted by all the people around her.

For elderly and dependent mourners neither short-term bereavement-focused therapy, nor more conventional psychotherapy, which aims at increasing insight, is appropriate. Their need is for a long supportive contact on a counselling or social work level. Once a trusting relationship has been securely established, other helpers may be included, and the agency may then become 'the good object'. This widening of the contact can help to avoid a degree of dependence which throws the mourner back into the original grief situation at the slightest threat of termination, or on any occasion when the individual helper is not available. Careful timing, however, is very important. In the case we have just discussed, the social worker brought his student along too early, and his client protested justifiably. She felt that this visit was not planned for her sake, but as a teaching-opportunity for the student.

Not many bereaved show their need for acceptance and love in such a bizarre way. Yet many, perhaps all, feel at times that they have lost their own loving self with the loved (but also sometimes hated) person. Extreme ambivalence, the fear that the hate is greater than the love, makes it impossible to integrate the lost person and thus complete the mourning process.

In his paper 'Mourning and Melancholia' Freud said: '. . . although grief involves grave departures from the normal attitude to life, it never occurs to us to regard it as a morbid condition and hand the mourner over to medical treatment. We rest assured that after a lapse of time it will be overcome, and we look at any interference with it as inadvisable or even harmful'.[2] This paper was written in 1914, before the first world war. In Freud's Jewish middle-class background mourners were likely to be less isolated than they are in our time and place, and death and bereavement were still acknowledged facts of life. In addition, there has been since Freud's time some change in the practice of psychotherapy. Many therapists now put great stress on the human and supportive relationship of the therapeutic situation, and it is this aspect of psychotherapy which is most important in work focused on bereavement. Yet therapeutic intervention should only be considered in exceptional cases, and normal mourning should not be regarded as an illness which requires treatment. [. . .]

An important feature in all short-term bereavement work is the firm focus on the crisis of loss. We are not treating an illness or attempting to affect personality disorders, yet it is imperative to understand what problems in the mourner's personality and in his pattern of relationships have been highlighted by the crisis. These cannot be resolved in short-term therapy but the specific problem which each person brings into the bereavement crisis has to be grasped by the therapist and the mourner. Only then can the bereaved hope to distinguish between his immediate and previous, real or fantasied, losses and abandonments, the pain of which has been stirred up by the actual present loss and has made the response to it so frightening.

In all therapy one of the major aims is to help people towards more satisfactory relationships in the broadest sense. In bereavement work this is of paramount importance. The bereaved often feels that with his lost object he has lost all that is good in him. In this situation of self-doubt he is faced with the task of adjusting his ongoing relationships, and having sufficient trust to risk new attachments.

To offer help in this difficult task is implied in all types of work with the bereaved. Often it is expressed in encouragement to join clubs, attend evening-classes, 'get out of his shell'. A frequent suggestion is to do some charitable work, for to have nobody to care for is one of the great deprivations of bereavement. Such advice is absolutely right and valid in uncomplicated grief situations. Often, however, such suggestions end in disappointment and frustration both for the well-meaning adviser and the bereaved, who may be unable to get out of his shell just because he is shut up inside himself, struggling to deal with a more than average amount of guilt, anger and agonising regret, and retreats into denial and unreality.

The greatest obstacle towards making new relationships after bereavement and being able to live again meaningfully, is the ambivalent feeling about the deceased and the denial of one's own hating self. By denying the hate the mourner impairs the love, and with it the capacity to be in loving contact with other people.

In some cases this aspect of therapeutic work can be done by a lay person who cares for and understands the bereaved and offers him the degree and quality of compassion and reliability which will enable him to regain hope. Only when this has been achieved can he risk a new attachment. This should not be an attempt to replace the lost one, but rather an expression of renewed confidence that life is still worth living and meaningful relationships are still possible.

New life-affirming attachments may take a wide variety of forms, according to the needs of the individual bereaved. It may be a job, an interest, a cause or a child, perhaps a new grandchild. Or it may be a new committed relationship with a person of the same or the opposite sex with whom the bereaved can share his life, someone who will both give and accept care.

The majority of bereaved people will return to a new life without therapeutic help after they have mourned their dead in a way appropriate for them. A general climate of acceptance of the importance of mourning will support them. If that climate is lacking the completion of the mourning process may be hindered or delayed.

The task of mourning, and returning to life with renewed strength, may take a long time, often much longer than the traditional year. It is important for the bereaved and for those around him to know and accept this, but also to know that the phase of mourning will pass.

References

1 PARKES, C. M. (1972) *Bereavement*, p. 162. London: Tavistock.
2 FREUD, S. (1917) 'Mourning and Melancholia'. In *Standard Edition of the Works of Sigmund Freud*, Vol. 14, p. 244. London: Hogarth Press.

Part 7 On Working Together

39 Coordination between health and personal social services: a question of quality

Adrian L. Webb and Martin Hobdell

Introduction

Two powerful objectives – the provision of good quality care and the provision of cost-effective care – tend to strengthen the search for ways of ensuring a high level of coordination between the social services. [. . .] This concern with coordination is especially strong in Britain in the case of the health and personal social services. [. . .]

One response has been to concentrate on inter-service planning in the hope that this will give rise to an effective set of services and prepare the way for better coordination at field level. Another has been to develop machinery to ensure that joint consultation occurs across professional and service boundaries in cases where children appear to be seriously at risk of neglect and maltreatment. More generally, seminars and discussions have been provided to prepare staff for their new roles in the reorganised health service – including their responsibilities for liaison with other social services. These occasions have brought staff together across service boundaries, but mainly at senior levels and spasmodically. [. . .] It is unfortunate that in Britain we have hardly begun to analyse what it is we are urging upon practitioners; why it is we are doing so; how much we think it is worth paying for better coordination; or how we might recognise good coordination – or teamwork – when we see it.

The one certainty in an uncertain field is that students of social administration in Britain need to analyse systematically the subject of inter-service coordination. This paper can only make a small beginning. I will outline the broad task as I see it and then provide, by way of illustration, a comment upon the conceptual confusion which lies behind the current enthusiasm for 'teamwork' in the social services.

The task

Good coordination is only one facet of a more general search for ways of improving the quality of services. The concern for quality is even more powerfully expressed through the pursuit of specialisation. The first ques-

Source: Eurosocial Report No. 4 (1975) *Interaction of Social Welfare and Health Personnel in the Delivery of Services: Implications for Training.* Vienna: European Centre for Social Welfare, Training and Research, pp. 26–38 (extracts).

tion to be asked, therefore, is what relative contribution effective, or simply better, coordination might make to the overall quality of service offered to the client? Is it the case that the pursuit of excellence in narrow specialisms merely passes the task of service coordination on the client, to his long-term detriment? Alternatively, is it the case that British social work needs a sharp increase in the level of specialist skills at this point in time, rather than an irrelevant and diversionary expedition in search of the Holy Grail of inter-professional collaboration? What is the nature of the trade-off between these constituents of quality of service? How is their impact on the client to be measured so that an optimal trade-off can be struck? These are the primary questions to be asked of the coordination issue and they have virtually not been posed in Britain as yet. We certainly have not begun to construct the equations which would link various types of organisation and professional practice with the quality of service received by the client.

The second half of our task, assuming that better coordination is a worthwhile goal in some situations for some of the time, is to identify the characteristics of good coordination and its determinants. What features of professional practice would lead us to say – 'that is effective coordination'? How does one judge? Do we expect effective coordination to result in measurable changes in the rate of referral of clients, in the length of time they remain on agency files, in the completeness of their recovery or rehabilitation as assessed by professionals or by themselves, or in the balance of time spent on cases by different types of professional workers? A plea for coordination can reflect a belief that expensive professional time is being wasted, that the uncosted time of clients is being wasted, that 'success' rates are too low and failure is too common for professional comfort, or that the client's wants and expectations are not being fulfilled. It is not that these different variables cannot, or are not, measured, nor that they are necessarily in conflict with one another; the basic problem in Britain at the present is that we have not yet agreed upon what it is we are seeking to achieve by better coordination. It may be that clients can afford the time and have the skills to put packages of services together to suit their own needs, or it may be that the capacity and opportunity to do this is a major factor in the full utilization of social services. Better coordination may therefore be of great importance in the equalisation of benefits received by rich and poor, or it may be the height of irrelevance in the face of gross inequality. The experience of such projects as the Community Development Programme has tended to divert attention away from coordination and towards the underlying inequalities of wealth, income and control over life chances. However, this does not tell us much about the role of coordination as a minor means of adjusting inequalities. Nor do we yet know in what circumstances improved coordination may enhance the impotence of the client in the face of professional omnipotence. These are not the kind of issues on which to seek consensus; but we are still at a prior stage – we have yet to expose many of the problems because we have to discuss the assumptions and expectations which lie behind the search for better coordination.

Once we have established alternative sets of objectives we can then begin to identify the characteristics which seem to promote or inhibit particular types of collaboration. There is clearly substantial conceptual confusion to be sorted out before we reach the stage of choosing organisational structures and professional practices which will promote chosen, objectives. I now intend to illustrate the extent and importance of this confusion by examining the currently popular notion of teams and teamwork as an expression of good coordinative practice. Britain has a long historical tradition of fostering the 'team spirit', but the whole purpose of good team spirit in competitive sport is to maximise the likelihood of defeating less cohesive teams. One could often be forgiven for thinking that this particular objective is precisely that which underlies teamwork in the social services. Let us therefore turn to this subject and see what it reveals about the nature and problem of good coordination.

Teams and teamwork: an example of conceptual confusion

Definitions

In the health and social services a professional's definition of a professional is that of a person who by virtue of training is expected to take an overview of an individual case. Specialised and detailed information may be obtained from many others to create this overview; in this context, however, the role of these other workers is seen as supplementary to that of the professional. This is a rather different definition of a professional person to the narrower one given, for example, by Carr-Saunders when he argued that a profession may be defined as an 'occupation based upon specialised intellectual study and training, the purpose of which is to supply skilled service or advice to others'.[1]

The notion of professional that we are using refers to the breadth of interest or responsibility taken in a case, rather than simply to the acquisition of knowledge and training. The definition of a para-professional hinges accordingly on the absence of responsibility for taking the wider viewpoint. A para-professional may offer highly skilled help or just a sympathetic (and untrained) ear; but whichever the case may be, he or she is not expected to be responsible for the integration of a wide range of help into a cohesive treatment strategy. These definitions obviously accord well with the professional's view of the nature of teamwork. They are the type of definitions which emerge as teamwork develops and treatment planning or coordination, become a conscious and skilled task. They are not always unambiguous in interpretation, however, and precisely one of the difficulties that can arise when people attempt to work together is that they fail to agree on who is or is not eligible for professional status, or on what type of overview of a case is appropriate. We will return to this point later.

Having begun by defining professionals and thence para-professionals, it would be logical to go on to define what is meant by a team, but this I will not attempt to do in global terms. It has obviously been implied, however, that we are referring to people working together – people who have to, or whom it may be judged should, interact with each other in order to provide health or other social services. Within this area of work situations a continuum may be noted which ranges from the very close interaction – frequently based on physical proximity in a particular room, building, or geographical area – of people who know each other well, to the most tenuous of spasmodic working relationships.

There has been a considerable growth in the use of the language of teams and teamwork and an expanding body of literature and research is being devoted to teamwork in this field; but the language is used in two rather different ways. First, in a descriptive 'tone'; whereby a group of people seen to be interacting frequently in an objective sense, or considered to be interacting to good effect, is said to be a team. Second, in a prescriptive 'tone'; whereby the implication is that particular groups or types of workers ought to be interacting frequently and to good effect. This latter is the important one in the sense that it reflects aspirations which we really do not yet know how to fulfil.

A taxonomy of teams

Let us begin by employing terms familiar in the context of the family and distinguish *nuclear* and *extended* teams; an approach which immediately takes us back to our definitional problem. A nuclear team is in one sense readily understood, it is the type which occurs at the close-knit, high-interaction end of a continuum of work relationships. But do we demand that such a grouping of people work well together before we call them a nuclear team, or merely that they interact frequently? Let us settle for the simple notion of working closely in the measurable sense of being in close proximity and interacting on work related issues. What determines the *quality* of teamwork is the problem; representing a considerable area of ignorance to be overcome in the long term. However, in the present discussion the question that remains is how one distinguishes nuclear from extended teams. Being on a continuum, there is no sharp distinction; but the principle is clear, some groupings of people do cooperate effectively even though they do not work in close proximity, do not meet regularly, and only communicate on a relatively infrequent basis. They work in a way which warrants the use of the term 'team', but their work relationships are characterised by infrequent or formalised contacts, rather than by frequent and informal contacts. Many of the factors which influence the effectiveness of nuclear teams may also operate in the case of extended ones, but some variables are importantly different. For example, how often does a linkage between people have to be activated for it to be used as and when this is appropriate? What types of training keep open relatively infrequently used linkages or pathways between professionals? How does one fit a new specialism or profession into an extended network where people meet rarely and therefore cannot be expected to adapt quickly to such developments? These are questions which become increasingly important as one moves along the continuum from nuclear to extended teams. For the moment let us concentrate on the more easily distinguished nuclear team and return to the extended team later.

We have already noted that the language of teams is frequently used prescriptively, but what is it that people expect teamwork to achieve? For what purposes are teams created or advocated? Two related purposes can be immediately identified – *to overcome the disadvantages of specialisation by improving coordination*, and *to exploit the advantages of a division of labour by facilitating specialisation*. These purposes can be pursued jointly, but they can also be articulated in isolation from each other and lead to the growth of quite different types of teamwork. In the first instance we are dealing with a team of individualists, in the second with a team of mutually interdependent specialists. To make the analogy with sport, where the word is used most freely, the team of co-equal individualists (generic social workers, doctors in a group practice, etc.) is rather like a team of tennis players, whereas the team based on a division of labour resembles a football or cricket team. The purposes, role relationships and structures of these teams differ. The tennis team is designed to ensure a flow of collegial support – to maintain morale among people who are individually facing tense situations – and to guarantee good coordination in particular circumstances. The division of labour team is designed to orchestrate different types and levels of skill. It too may be highly relevant as a morale boosting institution, but when, as in dental and other medical teams, there are distinct differences in the status of the various workers this may be highly problematic.

The attempt to identify different notions of teamwork can now be generalised. We have been talking of teams which differ on two dimensions – the homogeneity or heterogeneity of skills, and of tasks. This can be represented diagrammatically (Table 1).

Table 1   A simple taxonomy of teams.

| Tasks | | Skills | | |
		Homogeneous		Heterogeneous
Homogeneous	(1)	Family practitioner in a group practice, or team of generic social workers.	(3)	?
Heterogeneous	(2)	Social work team with individual specialisation. Group practice including some specialisation.	(4)	Health centre team, dental, other social service teams including professionals and para-professionals.

The first case (1) represents a team of co-equal individualists, or *collegial team*, such as we have already mentioned; it is particularly in tune with the expectations of many professional workers. The second (2) is a *specialised collegial team* in which specialisation by task does not necessarily imply the existence of a skill gradient or hierarchy. The third (3) may involve such a hierarchy but is basically an unlikely, or unstable, type of team in that the same task is shared by people with different types, or levels of skill. One possible example is the hierarchy of hospital doctors from houseman to consultant. The presumed differential by level of skill is formalised in a hierarchy but the tasks performed by the members of this hierarchy may overlap to such an extent that they are difficult to differentiate. A hierarchical system founded on a strong professional and tutelage tradition would seem to be one of the few justifications for, and guarantees of, a team in which the formally recognised differences in skill vary more than perceived variations in the work done. For this reason one might refer to it as an *apprenticeship team*. Another example is that of social work before the Seebohm changes. Some, though not all, of the specialisation among social workers was challenged precisely because it was accompanied by a substantial overlap of activities at the field level. This was an unstable team situation. Finally, the fourth (4) cell in our taxonomy represents what may be called a *complex team*. This is not to imply that other types of teams are necessarily more simple affairs, but to underline the congruence of two factors: *both* skills and tasks vary in this team situation. In particular, such teams can encompass multi-professional and professional/

para-professional work relationships. Hierarchical divisions can occur within professions; between professionals and the para-professionals with whom they work; or between professions of different status or seniority. In addition, there are likely to be various 'horizontal' divisions along the boundaries of specialisms or professions, each of which may interrupt the smooth flow of work, may be reinforced by role conflicts or misunderstanding, and may be a potential source of further hierarchical divisions. There can be a rich harvest of bitterness and confusion, as well as smooth coordination and a productive division of labour, in complex teams.

The complex team is probably that which most people envisage when they think of teamwork in the health and social services but, as we have seen, it is only one type in the health and social services and not necessarily the most frequently encountered. Nevertheless, teamwork across professional boundaries is needed – for example, between social work, medical care and the educational system – if whole person care is to be possible and the optimal use of skills is to be attained.

The implications of para-professionals in teams

The difficulties mentioned above may become particularly acute when para-professionals are brought into the team. Collegiality as a guarantor of high morale and easy working relations, can be jealously guarded by the same profession that unthinkingly subordinates even the most skilled para-professionals to a menial status. Here we touch upon a cluster of administrative, political, and moral issues which lie at the heart of any discussion of teams – particularly the complex ones. These issues bear directly on the quality of care provided to the patient or client. One reason for caution in the creation of teams is that groups of workers (such as midwives, health visitors, or social workers) who operate in semi-autonomous collegial teams, may work less effectively if they find they are expected to act in a para-professional role when absorbed into multi-disciplinary teams. They may also unintentionally visit some of their new frustrations on their patients or clients. A major problem is that when workers from different professions are brought together in teams, even the objectives of the service they are to provide are rarely the subject of agreement in advance. While highly abstract statements of goals may achieve consensus, this breaks down on closer examination. As Lefton and Rosengren have argued, different professions look at the same patient or client in different ways and this can be the basis for misunderstanding at best, or bitter conflict at worst.[2]

Problems arise because the different views of patients', or clients', needs enshrined in different professions are all equally valid in their own right, but they imply different priorities and decision structures. Each professional group naturally has a vested interest, as well as a belief, in upholding its own orientation or viewpoint. For this reason alone there can often be no simple agreement about objectives, about the validity of any one profession's claim to seniority, or, therefore, about decision-making. This is equally true for para-professionals, who may well claim that they come closer to the client and that they possess a more detailed knowledge of his or her personal needs, feelings, and anxieties. But if agreement on objectives is one fundamental stumbling block to effective teamwork, the *ad hoc* growth of specialisation is another. Both professional and para-professional workers have frequently developed similar or overlapping skills, as in the case of physiotherapists and remedial gymnasts. Demarcation disputes which might otherwise lie dormant for long periods of time are precipitated by attempts to establish teams.

The disadvantage of the generally unplanned move towards teamwork is not that planning will minimise these kinds of setbacks, but that the issues involved will not be considered in any depth. Resolving problems by invoking entrenched attitudes, precedents, or the power and prestige of the more well established professions may be a useful short-term expedient, but it is a poor basis on which to form teams. The growing interest in teams underlines the weakness of the traditional divisions between different professional groups and between professionals and para-professionals; it is not sufficient to create teams in which these divisions are replicated without question. Ideally teams should be developed for specific purposes and, unless the working life of a team is to be brief, it is important to anticipate the problems of sustaining the team in the field. Much of this sustaining process must be built into the team in the form of management structures and styles which will maintain team morale. As has been implied, one of the key areas here is the method and manner in which decisions are made in the team. The work of Davies and Francis [3] has shown that in the hospital team the decision to discharge a patient is seen ultimately to lie with the consultant. Other members of the team are seen to have differing levels of influence over this decision. It seems important to question whether this can be considered an ideal arrangement; both from the point of view of the patient and the team itself.

In industry, at least, there has been much debate over the effects on output of different organisational structures and styles of management. Two models stand out: the more traditional hierarchical one; and the participatory one advanced by Likert and others. [4] In one sense, teams composed of professionals and para-professionals could be a means of resolving this debate. The team offers a forum for pooling knowledge in a participatory approach to making decisions. This is particularly important when there is a high degree of specialisation and when the scale of an organisation makes for impersonal or hierarchically structured relationships between workers. A collegial method of making decisions allows optimal use to be made of the varied skills, experience, and sources of information in a team. One advantage of having para-professionals in teams with professionals is that they can frequently bridge the gap created between professional workers and many of their patients or clients by differences in social status and the use of specialist jargon. The para-professional can lend weight to the clients' circumstances and viewpoints in decision-making. This idea is not new, nor is the para-professional role described without inherent difficulties.

However, where particular groups of workers claim the sole right to make decisions because of their overview of individual cases, it is hardly surprising that tensions develop between them and other professionals or para-professionals with whom they work. For such decisions affect both the work that the team does and the conditions under which it is carried out. The situation may be further exacerbated when the 'duty' to make decisions is advanced as a justification for large pay and status differentials. The 'junior' professions and para-professionals are considered accountable to their more prestigious colleagues, but they are rarely credited with responsibility for either the patient's (or client's) well-being or their own actions. The nurse, ambulance driver, or home-help may have to cope with patients or clients in distress as frequently and continuously as, if not more so, than their professional colleagues. Yet the responsibility they bear is not given due recognition and their knowledge of patients or clients is often not utilized to the full. Status and pay differentials are also often reinforced by the disproportionate number of women in para-professional roles. A woman's position as a para-professional in a team led by a male professional appears to be doubly difficult; not only are there the prejudices against women to be overcome, but also those against para-professionals.

Unfortunately, the development of collegial decision-making is difficult when teams are themselves embedded in institutions with strong hierarchical traditions, such as large hospitals. This difficulty is increased when management, in an attempt to provide a better career structure and to rationalise the allocation of resources, institutionalises a rather rigid hierarchy of skills such as that in the nursing profession. This imposed hierarchy may stifle collegial decision-making, but it may also isolate even the para-professionals from the patient or client. As they become more 'professionalised' and ascend a career ladder, the client is all too often seen to be below the lowest rung.

Perhaps the most profound constraint on the expansion of teams based on a collegial rather than hierarchical distribution of decision-making is the absence of a legitimating ideology. Although there are exceptions, such as the therapeutic community, there is little to guide or support groups who do wish to establish new role relationships and structures in team situations. To relinquish an essentially hierarchical approach to decision-making is to step into a disorienting void. There are few principles or axioms against which to chart a course. It is therefore worth suggesting that two considerations should feature strongly in the organisations of teams. The first is consumer sovereignty – by which is meant a far greater attentiveness than is customary to the patient's or client's own definition of their needs, the resources which they can muster and their supplementation by the service agency, and to the patient's or client's satisfaction with the treatment received. This does not amount to a subservient gratification of the client's every wish; resources are in short supply and must be rationed on principles other than the strength of the demands made by individuals or groups. Nevertheless, it does mean avoiding two approaches to patients or clients that are all too common and are strongly embedded in the historical development of our social services: first, the tendency to treat the patient or client as a passive recipient of service; and, second, the parallel tendency to perceive the patient or client in isolation from their immediate social world – a process which is accentuated in those services where the patient or client is rarely if ever seen in their own home environment.

The second consideration – matching that of consumer sovereignty – is what might be called the 'authority of relevance'. The struggle between professional and bureaucratic ideologies has produced a distinction between the 'authority of position' (or hierarchy) and the 'authority of knowledge' – the latter being the organisational principle enshrined in the professions. With the growth of teams, and especially professional/paraprofessional teamwork, we need to modify this latter principle. The professional emphasis is on mastering and contributing to a body of theoretical knowledge. It is therefore not surprising to find that the principle of 'authority of knowledge' becomes dominated by the academic status of the body of knowledge possessed by the professional and by the length of the training required to obtain it. One consequence is the tendency we have noted for teams to be riven by covert, or overt, struggles over which is the senior profession, which professional view of the patient or client should prevail, and which profession should take the lead in decision-making. Where one group of professionals work together with paraprofessionals, these questions are not asked – at least not openly. Yet no profession is so comprehensive in its scope as to fit its practitioners to be the appropriate leaders of teamwork in all circumstances. A variety of types of information are needed, including that gleaned by those who work closely with patients or clients on the mundane tasks of caring. The broad lateral view of the client's social context is needed as well as the narrower view taken, for example, by the surgeon in an emergency.

Similarly the home-help's awareness of the client's concern for his cat, or his embarrassment at asking for help with laundry because of incontinence, is as relevant to a feeling of well-being as is the physician's knowledge of his illness or the social worker's awareness of his fear of death. Consequently, the right to contribute to decision-making must arise from the *possession of knowledge relevant to the client's own feelings of well-being.* Not from the possession of a particular body of theoretical knowledge. It is this assertion that I would grace with the title – the principle of the authority of relevance.

It must be acknowledged that the pendulum can swing too far the other way, in which case there is a danger of increased security among para-professionals who believe they are expected to carry a disproportionate amount of responsibility in relation to their knowledge and skill.[5] However, there is good reason to argue that this is most likely to happen when para-professional workers are not considered to be part of the caring team, but are nevertheless required to work closely with patients or clients. Their inclusion in the team is a step towards providing the supportive structures that can make substantial responsibilities compatible with limited training.

To summarise, even a rapid glance at the question of teamwork reveals great complexity and confusion. The confusion arises because some of the current interest in teamwork revolves around the development of para-professionals, or the attempt by professionals to gain control over para-professionals, and the resources that they represent. At the same time, the notion of teamwork is applied to the search for inter-professional coordination across service boundaries. Precisely one of the problems confronting inter-professional teamwork is that professionals who, as leaders of one type of team, have become used to controlling the work of para-professionals seek to recreate the same pattern of relationships in inter-professional teams. More simply, the degree of hierarchical organisation, the steepness of hierarchies, and the styles of management practised within different social service organisations vary. Professionals working within different organisational settings have to overcome these structural barriers to coordination. Similarly, it is not at all clear that the promotion of closer knit, 'nuclear teams' within organisations permits or encourages the development of 'extended teams' which span organisational boundaries. Teams can be linked by 'outposting' members of one professional group to work closely with members of another profession – e.g. the attachment of social workers to general practitioners. But this can undoubtedly create tension and conflicts of loyalty, with potentially damaging effects on the individual workers and the relationships with their professional colleagues.

More fundamentally, the argument is quite simply that the uncritical assumption that better teamwork means better coordination, which in turn means better service for the client, is a naive premise that we are very close to adopting in practice. Teams should only be designed to serve specific purposes, they should be consciously designed to fulfil that purpose and their members should be specifically trained to work in a team setting. All the while, the creation of a particular type of team approach should be monitored to assess its effect on other areas and types of coordination. Most important of all, perhaps, the allocation of decision-making responsibilities and powers must be examined not only to assess the effect of particular patterns of decision-making on team morale and satisfaction, but also to gauge the effect on the client's well-being. In this sense the greatest barriers to teamwork are not merely ignorance, role uncertainty and confusion, or unclear objectives and ill-designed structures; the barriers are also those of modifying professional constructions and perceptions of the world, the balance of power which exists between one profession and another, and that which exists between professions and clients. To modify these variables requires resources – resources for training people to work in teams, for the careful planning of teams, and for 'buying off' professional monopolies. This brings us back to our initial question: what is better coordination worth; is it worth paying a high price to achieve it?

Conclusions

There are many detailed issues to be resolved, such as the role of different types of teamwork in promoting coordination between professionals and between professionals and the para-professionals who work alongside them. Once the contribution of different types of collaborative approach have been identified, we still have to translate this knowledge into structures, processes, guidelines and training programmes. But logically prior are the questions about the relative contribution of different types of improvement in the delivery of services to the quality of the services received by clients.

Is it more important in the British case to improve coordination by integrating the activities of social workers and related groups of workers such as home-helps, occupational therapists, social work aides, residential and day-care workers; or is it more profitable to promote interaction between social workers and doctors or other professional groups. In short, should we concentrate on strengthening the newly emerging nuclear teams within local authority social services departments and on what basis – a hierarchical or collegial basis; or should we seek to create extended teams which cross service boundaries? Can we try to do both at once; are they compatible? Even more fundamentally, should we forget the problems of coordination – with the exception of a few especially sensitive issues such as that of children in risk of physical harm – and concentrate on raising the professional standard of social work? This latter course could conceivably do more for collaboration between doctors and social workers than hastily improvised structures and procedures designed to induce the early birth of mutual professional accord and effective communication.

The simple answer is that we do not yet know which of the many options to pursue, nor have we yet tried systematically to assess the options themselves. The reason for this is that we are still ambivalent about our objectives in seeking better coordination and unsure about the nature and determinants of what is perceived from the clients' point of view as a good quality service. We are surely right to experiment with alternative patterns of inter-service collaboration, but it will not take us far unless these more fundamental issues are simultaneously faced and answered – at least in part.

References

1 CARR-SAUNDERS, A. M. (1928) *Professions – their Organisation and Place in Society*, Clarendon Press.
2 LEFTON, M., and ROSENGREN, W. R. (1966) 'Organisations and clients: lateral and longitudinal dimensions', *American Sociological Review*, *31*, 802–10. For more general discussion of the inter-professional variable in teamwork, see REHR, H. (ed.) (1974) *Medicine and Social Work*, Prodist; BROOK, A. and STRAUSS, P. E. (1971) 'Mental health social workers in general practice', *The Practitioner*, March 1971; HUWS-JONES, R. (1971) *The Doctor and the Social Services*, Athlone Press; FORMAN, J. A. S., and FAIRBAIRN, E. M. (1968) *Social Casework in General Practice*, Oxford University Press; GOLDBERG, E. M. and NEILL, J. E. *Social Work in General Practice*, Allen and Unwin.
3 DAVIES, C. and FRANCIS, A. (1974) 'A critique of Friedron on professional dominance'. Paper delivered to the British Sociological Association Medical Sociology Group, May 1974.
4 LIKERT, R. (1961) *New Patterns of Management*, McGraw-Hill; ALGIE, J. 'Management and Organisation in the Social Service', *British Hospital Journal*, *80*, 1245–8; ROWBOTTOM, R. (1973) 'Hierarchy or . . .?', *Public Administration*, *57*, Autumn 1973.
5 For discussion of a related problem see: LEVISON, P. and SCHILLER, J. (1966) 'Role analysis of the indigenous non-professional', *Social Work*, *11*, 95–101.

40   Social network diagram

R. Capildeo, Christine Court and F. Clifford Rose

Abstract

A diagram that shows at a glance the social network and support of patients was found useful in a follow-up study of patients with strokes. We believe that the diagram would prove valuable in medical case records and should be an essential part of medical-social reports, particularly for patients at risk of losing their independence.

Introduction

Medical case records often contain little information on the social background of patients and give little idea of the environment or problems a patient convalescing from an illness may face when returning home. When referral has been made to a social worker the reports are often kept in a separate file in the social work department and may be so detailed that the patient's dependency is not readily appreciated. In view of the persisting shortage of skilled social workers and the frequency with which social problems prevent patients from being discharged from hospital it is important to have a summary of a patient's social circumstances as soon as possible after admission.

In a domiciliary follow-up study of patients with strokes a social network diagram was devised to show how the patient was supported at home by family and friends. The diagram was found useful in indicating the social needs of any patient, particularly those at risk of losing their independence, so that the necessary help to maintain these patients at home could be arranged – for example, home aid, domiciliary services, or contact with hospital or area social workers. We describe here the social network diagram and give two illustrative case histories.

Method

On a sheet of paper a box is drawn to indicate the patient's home. When the patient lives in a flat in a converted house boxes are drawn to indicate the flats immediately above and below the patient's flat. When the patient

Source: *British Medical Journal*, 1976, *1*, pp. 143–4.

lives in a purpose-built block of flats other boxes are drawn only when immediate neighbours are frequent visitors. All persons, whether family, friends, or others, living in the patient's home are included in the box; other relatives are named on the right side of the page and friends on the left. Lines of communication are drawn to indicate contact with the patient and also the direction of contact. A solid line is drawn when a relative or friend visits the patient daily, but when visits are less frequent the line is dotted, with abbreviations above the line to indicate the frequency of the visits – for example, $3/7$ = three visits a week; $2/52$ = a visit every two weeks. Other lines of support, such as Meals on Wheels, a district nurse, etc., are drawn on the left side of the page, again with the frequency of the service above the line. Means of support that have been lost are shown by a cross through the appropriate line.

Case histories

Case 1

A 91-year-old woman was admitted to hospital on 13 July 1973 after a right cerebral infarction causing dense left hemiplegia. She had had diabetes for six years, was receiving insulin, and had been attending the Charing Cross Diabetic Clinic for three years. She was transferred to the West London Rehabilitation Unit after three weeks, being discharged home after a further three weeks. There had been no recovery in the left arm, although the leg had improved enough for her to walk with a Zimmer frame and the help of one person. At home, further progress was made despite osteo-arthritis of the left hip. One year later she was able to walk slowly unaided. She could also wash and dress herself and continued to exercise her left arm despite there being no recovery of power.

Social circumstances The patient was a widow living on the ground floor of a two-storey terraced house owned by her son-in-law. Her part of the flat, to which she was confined, was not self-contained and consisted of bedroom, sitting-room, out-side lavatory, and kitchenette. The social network diagram (Figure 1) shows strong social ties. Upstairs was her daughter, who had recently developed diabetes, son-in-law, granddaughter, and great-granddaughter, who all helped to look after her, especially at night. During the day another daughter came to look after her, doing the shopping and household tasks; both daughters were able to give insulin injections when the district nurse could not visit. The rest of the available family members visited at least weekly. Clearly the family had made all the arrangements necessary to look after the patient.

Comment. Although this patient had suffered a stroke at the age of 91, it was possible to discharge her from hospital because of her strong social network. A commode was initially provided because she could not manage the two steps to the kitchenette followed by one step to the outside lavatory. She continued to make progress at home, and when the follow-up domiciliary visit was made all the members of the family were present, as they wanted to see and tell the stroke team how well she was doing, especially with her exercises, which they encouraged.

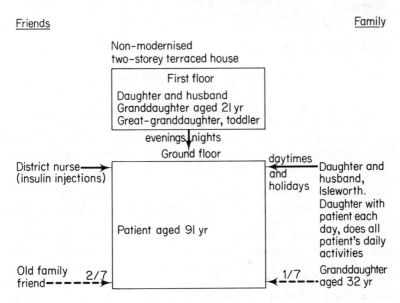

Figure 1   Social network diagram in case 1.

Case 2

A semi-retired bank clerk aged 64 was admitted to hospital on 15 May 1973 after a right posterior parietal infarction causing left homonymous hemianopia, left hemiparesis, and left sensory inattention. During his hospital stay moderate to severe dementia was found by psychometric testing and angiography showed that the ventricles were dilated. He had a ten-year history of hypertension, although he was not receiving treatment at the time of admission. He was discharged home after five weeks with a persisting visual field defect and left sensory inattention, the left hemiparesis having resolved. His mental state had not improved and he was emotionally labile. The hypertension was controlled with methyldopa 250 mg thrice daily, bendrofluazide 5 mg daily, and Slow-K 600 mg twice daily.

Social circumstances. The patient's wife was 63 years old and they had no children. They had lived for twenty-six years in their two-storey terraced house, where there were inside and outside lavatories and fifteen stairs up to the first floor. The social

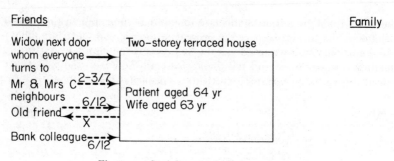

Figure 2   Social network diagram in case 2.

network diagram (Figure 2) shows that they had no family and could rely only on a neighbour, who visited daily and looked after the patient when his wife went out. The patient did not improve at home and his dementia increased, causing frequent concern for his wife, who had fears of not being able to cope. Visits to an old friend were no longer possible.

Comment. This case shows that provided the spouse can cope it is possible to discharge home a patient needing considerable nursing care. With deterioration in this patient's condition his wife made the home environment smaller, so that he used fewer rooms and would not get lost. The area social services supplied incontinence pads and a laundry service. When the patient's wife was out a neighbour sat with him. Without the full-time care of his wife the patient would have needed permanent hospital care; it was anticipated, as his wife grew older and became less able to cope, that this would be necessary within two years. Because of this, so that he could be placed on a waiting list for a bed in a hospital for the chronically ill and be admitted as an emergency case to this type of bed if the need arose, a specialist domiciliary visit was arranged, but just before this consultation took place the patient suffered a further stroke and died.

Discussion

Doctors have become increasingly aware that they cannot treat a patient's illness without regard to his social environment. The problems of discharge from hospital are often social, and if information regarding these is obtained as soon as possible plans may be made well in advance of discharge. The general practitioner could include a social network diagram with his letter at the time of admission to hospital, particularly when the patient is already receiving domiciliary or community services. If this has not been done the admitting houseman can quickly compile the diagram while clerking the patient and interviewing the relatives.

The particular value of the diagram is that the patient's social environment may be seen in detail at a glance, which lessens the need for lengthy social reports, reducing the pressures on the medical social work department. It is applicable to any patient admitted to hospital who is potentially at risk as well as to disabled or elderly patients at home. Any breakdown in the home environment may be identified easily and appropriate support given, thereby avoiding unnecessary admission.

The social network diagram is a suitable framework around which the rest of the social history can be built, and the diagram should be included in every patient's medical records, preferably on an easily identifiable social history sheet.

41   Care of the sick: professionalism versus love

Julius A. Roth

Sociologists have assisted in generating much nonsense about the normative aspects of professional–client relationships. The normative structure commonly applied is associated with the writings of Talcott Parsons,[1] but elements are repeated so often by social scientists of a wide variety of persuasions that they have become accepted lore and are so passed on to students. The fact that the normative assertions are contradicted by empirical studies – that is, studies which deal with what people do rather than surveys which deal with what people say they do – does not prevent the assertions from being repeated.

Let us look at two related normative prescriptions that are endlessly touted in the health care scene: Universalism (as opposed to Particularism), and Affective Neutrality as characteristics of the professional–client relationship. The true professional, so the argument goes, treats all clients as equally worthy of his ministrations, and variations in effort are justifiable only in terms of variations in complexity and seriousness of the client's problem. However, empirical evidence shows that this is *not* a working norm. Observations of health professionals at work show that moral evaluations are constantly being made of the clientele and that these evaluations often directly affect the treatment offered and care management proposed.

In the past, most of the evidence of the effect of such moral evaluation came from studies in the area of mental illness where clients whose values deviate most widely from those of the professionals are most likely to be called 'sick' but are given no effective 'treatment' nor allowed to take part in decisions made about them. Some critics maintain that such moral biases are possible because mental illness management has no technology[2] or because the whole concept is a myth and merely a facade for moral judgements.[3] But it is clear that similar evaluations with similar effects occur in other areas of health care. In tuberculosis treatment, alcoholics and other 'bums' are more likely to be hospitalized, are hospitalized longer, are more likely to be denied hospital privileges, more likely to be locked up under public health control laws, and more likely to be refused treatment for 'lack of cooperation'.[4] In rehabilitation units, the greatest staff effort is focused on the young, the person with family and job, the person able to pay for care, the 'well-motivated' (that is, the patients who appear to endorse the staff treatment ideology and behave in a 'coopera-

Source: *Science, Medicine and Man*, 1973, *1*, pp. 173-80 (extracts).

tive' manner).[5] Such moral evaluation is not dependent on long-term acquaintance. In the fleeting relationship of the emergency ward, there are preferences for and against categories of age, ethnic and class status (to the extent that these can be determined by the patient's appearance and his answers to standard questions), and presumptions of moral behavior inferred from the patient's physical complaint with a particular bias against drunks, illegal drug-takers, welfare cases, and women showing evidence of attempted abortion. Favored treatment, on the other hand, will go to friends, colleagues from the medical world, police, firemen and other emergency personnel who often come into contact with emergency room staff.[6] Even the kind of care you get in an ambulance (and indeed, whether or not you will be transported at all) depends in part on how you are dressed, whether or not you have alcohol on your breath, what neighborhood you live in, your general appearance and demeanor, weight, and the circumstances of your injury or illness.[7] [. . .]

Affective neutrality is not a standard characteristic of health professional–client relationships. On the contrary, negative affect is common and it often negatively affects the care provided the client. Positive affect is less common, but when present, usually improves the care provided the client, largely because the client in this instance is not just a client, but a friend whom one really cares about in a special way. Of course, some sociologists who would concede this point would argue that it is irrelevant because their model of professional service is not intended as a description of everyday events, but as an ideal type which may serve as a measure of 'how professional' a given person, occupational group, or service organization is. Those interested in policy action will carry this argument another step and say that we should make a deliberate effort to bring our health services (and other services) more closely in line with the model of affective neutrality and universalism. Organizational structure, rules and procedures should be established which make it more difficult for affective relationships to develop or to be brought into the health care situation. Aside from the fact that such programs would be difficult to enforce, there is also the question of whether they are worth it. What would a successful outcome be? The reduction of inconsiderate treatment and neglect of persons and categories of people that the professionals do not like? But what would replace it? Routinized efficiency in which all clients would be treated alike because none of the professional caretakers cares particularly what happens to *any one* of them. It seems much more sensible to me that, instead of trying to eliminate affect from the care and treatment relationship, we harness positive affect to do the bulk of the task. The way to avoid job and career routinization is to put the caretaking tasks in the hands of those for whom the patient is always a special case, namely the people who love him.

Let us consider the matter of caring for a sick person. There are signs to watch for, perhaps equipment to check on, medicines and other treatment to give. When such care is turned over to hired hands (as it routinely is in hospitals in our society), it is scarcely surprising that a great many errors (mostly errors of omission) are made.[8] The patient is the victim of job routinization. He is not the special case of anyone who has his interest primarily at heart. He is dependent on people who will tend to him if they remember, if they consider it appropriate to their job, if he has not demanded 'too much' from them already, and if they do not have too much else to do. Here indeed is affective neutrality at work with scarcely inspiring results.

Why should we go to great lengths to eliminate from the caring process those whose positive affect can be used to improve the care of the patient (including the patient himself in so far as he is physically and mentally capable of self-care)? A person who loves the patient would not treat him as one of many who must be fitted into the routine. He would treat the patient as a non-routine special case deserving his undivided attention. He would take special care to detect appropriate physical signs, to make sure equipment is functioning properly, to see that medicines and other treatments are given correctly and at proper times. The chance of error, carelessness, and neglect would be greatly reduced.

Though love of the person one is taking care of is of great value, it also helps if one is competent to carry out his task in a technically proficient manner. The caretaker who does not know what he is doing can inflict damage instead of rendering aid and comfort. The best combination is a high degree of competence and a loving relationship with the patient. This might seem like a rare combination and therefore not very helpful as a policy statement. However, once we concede the value of such a combination, we can address ourselves to speculation about the best ways to approximate it.

Analytically, there are two ways of proceeding to produce a combination of love and competence among health caretakers (and the same would apply to other areas of service to humans):

1. Take those who have been trained in a given line of work and apply themselves to it day after day (the presumed competent) and teach them to love their charges.

2. Take those who have a loving relationship to a given sick person and train them to provide competent care.

I contend that the first of these two procedures has not been and probably cannot be successful and that the second is by far the more practical of the two. (Note that I do not say the more efficient, but the more practical in the sense of actually providing personalized care with a minimum of neglect and mistakes.) The first approach has been tried

again and again without significant result. [. . .] In our present-day occupational context, it is unreasonable to expect such personal concern. It
is much more reasonable to expect workers in large and complex organizations to routinize most work with their own convenience in mind, to
avoid those tasks which they define as outside their territory, to neglect
the immediate needs of many of the clients for the sake of efficiently
organizing service to a large number of human units, and often deliberately to reduce service to persons who have dared to make 'extra'
demands or raise criticisms of the service.

On the other hand, if we want *each* client's needs to receive special and
individual attention, it makes sense to place that care in the hands of
people who are *already* committed from their established positive relationship to treat the client as a special case. Then we need not worry about
routinization and neglect or that the standards of efficiency of a larger
organization may dictate compromise with best service to a given
individual. We need concern ourselves only with making sure that the
caretaker is competent to do the tasks properly. This means providing the
information and skills necessary to the care required.

The solution may at first appear impractical. If our local plumber
develops a brain tumor, should we train his wife to perform brain surgery?
No, of course not. But if we consider all the tasks involved in caring for the
sick on a continuum of complexity with brain surgery at one end to
bringing a drink of water to a thirsty patient at the other end, the bulk of
the tasks will be piled up near the drink-of-water end of the scale. Much of
the care needed in any given case requires no more expertise than most
of us pick up in the ordinary course of our lives. Very often this requires
nothing more than providing creature comforts to a partially disabled
person, something that professional health workers are notoriously neglectful of. Sometimes it is a matter of watching for signs, checking equipment, providing minor treatments. A person can often be equipped for
such tasks by just a few minutes of instruction. As tasks and the information required become more complex, more training time is required: for
example, taking a blood pressure, giving an intramuscular injection,
familiarizing oneself with a complex treatment regimen. The amount of
time and trouble involved can easily be exaggerated, however, and often
is. The work of doctors, nurses, laboratory technicians, and others in the
medical world has been made to appear so esoteric that we forget that
when their tasks have been broken down into their elements, many of
them can be learned adequately in a few hours.

We are still left with the question of how much time and effort we are
willing to expend to teach non-professionals to look after the health of
their loved ones (including self-help). This is the kind of question which
can never be given a definite answer, although it will be answered in any

given case at a given point in time. The more convinced we are that care by primary group members has important advantages over completely professional care, the more trouble we will be willing to take to pass on the necessary information and skills.

Once we accept the notion that pre-existing positive relationships should be used in providing health care, we can consider how this principle might be applied to situations other than the case of a specific sick person. One thing we might do is make a much greater effort to provide medical information and skills to the public at large as part of their schooling, through television teaching, and other methods. People already do most of their own diagnosing and treating with the help of family members, friends, workmates, and others they associate with every day. We should strive to make them more proficient so that they will be even less dependent on professional help and better able to evaluate that help when they call upon it.

Another approach is to produce a large number of part-time healers and health advisors scattered throughout our population so that virtually everyone would have immediate access to at least one among his kin, friends, neighbors, workmates, or voluntary association members. These people would receive sufficient training to enable them to deal with most health issues with a much higher degree of proficiency and expertise than the average citizen. *They would not work at a health service job*, but carry on whatever other work or household activity already took up much of their time before they were selected for health training. They would be on call by people who know and trust them when health advice or aid is needed. *They would not have clients*, but would serve their friends, neighbors, work associates, and fellow lodge or church members. They would not collect fees or make other charges, though they might be paid a small retainer from public funds and would also be supplied with necessary equipment (e.g. clinical thermometers, otoscopes, sphygmomanometers, appropriate therapeutic agents, informational literature, etc.) at public expense. Not only would they handle most health problems that arise (those not dealt with by the person himself and his lay friends and family), but when they refer a member of their circle to a specialist, they would continue to act as the patient's agent and thus assure better attention from the full-time professional. The work of medical aids ('barefoot doctors') in China is suggestive here.[9]

Perhaps I can clarify the role of agent-advocate with an illustration from auto repair. If we know nothing about auto repair, but know our car is not working right, we may bring our car to a professional mechanic and ask him to repair whatever is necessary. We all know this is a very risky business; that our action leaves us wide open to being cheated. The mechanic can make some superficial repairs which soon leave us with worse trouble; he can make unnecessary repairs; he can charge us for things he has not done at all or overcharge for parts he has used and things he has done. We have no way of protecting ourselves because we are not competent to evaluate his work. How can we reduce the risk of being cheated? We can consult a friend who is knowledgeable about auto repairs even though he himself cannot make the repair because he does not have the equipment or does not wish to spend his time at such work. Our friend can help to diagnose the car troubles and suggest what work will be required. He can also comment afterward on what the professional mechanic has done and whether his charges are reasonable. Even better, our friend can accompany us when we take our car to the mechanic and present the problem for us. [. . .]

We are constantly seeking the advice and intervention of friends and acquaintances to help us control the actions of the professional stranger and to evaluate his efforts, whether our problem deals with bodily health, psychic health, social relations, house purchases, or TV repair. And when we are in a situation where we are unable to obtain intervening advice or intervention from someone we trust and are therefore forced to be completely dependent on a purely professional relationship, we are typically very uncomfortable and worry about the outcome, especially if the issue is important to us. And there is good reason for our discomfort – we in fact have no good basis in such a situation for judging whether the professional will take effective action on our behalf. I am arguing that the process of using friendly agents as advocates in dealing with professional specialists, which we now use in a haphazard manner, be deliberately built into the organization of health care. [. . .]

I think we should first discard some of the pervading prejudices of our money economy. The notion that you can buy anything if you are willing to pay enough has proved fallacious and nowhere more so than in the area of personal service. We must throw overboard the common formula that we can improve the output or the quality of work of a group of workers by paying them more or that we can recruit a higher quality of worker by offering higher compensation. If we have an institution in which the needs of the inmates are frequently neglected and where they are treated in a brutal manner, the usual reformist response is that we cannot expect anything better from such low-paid untrained workers, and to improve conditions we must substantially raise the salary schedules and provide some training for the staff. I would contend that all that we are likely to get with such a solution is more expensive neglect and brutality. I believe that concerned and loving care cannot be purchased; it must be volunteered. So long as we rely primarily on hired hands for the care of the sick and rejected, that care will *at best* be mediocre and marked with frequent error and neglect, and at worst will be vicious and brutal. Love cannot be taught or pounded into hired hands, but the same end might be achieved, at least to some extent, by replacing the hired hands with dedicated volunteers. [. . .] With the help of some training in relevant information and skills, such volunteers might well take over much of the care of people without friends or family with a great advance in both compassion and devotion to duty compared to the paid staffs we now largely rely on.

References

1 PARSONS, T. (1939) 'The professions and social structure', *Social Forces*, *17*, 457.
2 PERROW, C. (1965) 'Hospitals: Technology, Structure and Goals'. In J. G. March (ed.) *Handbook of Organizations*. New York: Rand McNally.
3 SZASZ, T. (1960) 'The myth of mental illness', *Am. Psychol.*, *15*, 113.
4 ROTH, J. A. (1969) 'The Treatment of the Sick'. In J. Kosa, A. Antonovsky and I. K. Zola (eds) *Poverty and Health*. Cambridge, Mass.: Harvard University Press.
5 ROTH, J. A. and EDDY, E. M. (1967) *Rehabilitation for the Unwanted*. Chicago: Aldine-Atherton.
6 ROTH, J. A. (1972) 'Some contingencies of the moral evaluation and control of clientele'. *Am. J. Sociol.*, *77*, 839.
7 DOUGLAS, D. J. (1969) Occupational and therapeutic contingencies of ambulance services in metropolitan areas. Ph.D dissertation, Department of Sociology, University of California, Davis.
8 ROTH, J. A. (1972) 'The necessity and control of hospitalization', *Soc. Sci. & Med.*, *6*, 425.
9 HORN, J. (1971) *Away With All Pests*. New York: Monthly Review Press.

42 'No need', they said: the hazards of setting up a Good Neighbour scheme

Katharine Pindar

Mr Bob Barrett, the local farmer, was I had heard a strong Methodist, a vigorous parish councillor, and a popular and effective man in our Oxfordshire village of some 900 people.

'I think we ought to do something for the elderly in Shipton', I said, appearing on his doorstep one autumn afternoon. He was sympathetic. We discussed the problems that the forthcoming winter (of 1973–4) might bring to the elderly – particularly a likely shortage of coal, and power cuts, because of strikes. I told Mr Barrett about the Age Concern Good Neighbour schemes, and he promised to bring up the matter at the Parish Council.

There was no heating in the village hall on the night of the next Parish Council meeting, and, by the time the problems of Shipton old people were raised under Any Other Business, the seven frozen councillors would have agreed to anything. It was simply decided to hold a separate meeting of councillors and representatives of village associations, for which Mr Barrett offered his house.

Before the meeting I pressed on Mr Barrett a document which I hoped would give him a framework for action. This recommended dividing the village into areas, each committee member taking an area and visiting all retired people within it. A simple questionnaire should be filled in for each household, noting whether people lived alone, were isolated, frail, had transport problems, what means of cooking and heating there were, and so forth. I envisaged the committee members then finding good neighbours on the spot, both to keep an eye on the isolated and frail and to meet specific requests for help.

Mr Barrett however politely brushed my master plan aside: such a formal scheme would not do for a village, he explained. I could see his point, but was consequently obliged to put over my – and Age Concern's – ideas piecemeal during the meeting. And it was evident that as a newcomer and 'townee' I did not carry much weight.

As chairman of the meeting, Mr Barrett first described existing services for the elderly in Shipton. There were home helps (but no meals-on-wheels), an Evergreen Club (meeting only in summer), a Christmas hand-out of £2 per household from a local charity, and a night-watching

Source: *Age Concern Today*, Summer 1975, no. 14, pp. 9–11.

service to relieve the tired relatives of sick old people, set up by the local retired doctor – a masterful character who had pooh-poohed my sugges-tion of a Good Neighbour scheme on the ground that it was only the ones who did not need help who would ask for it.

When the meeting got down to discussing the needy retired of the village, at first the well-informed locals seemed to be able to name every senior citizen in the place and to think that none of them needed help. They allowed only one definite exception, a ninety-year-old whom I shall call Miss Kemp, who lived alone in an isolated bungalow – but you could not help her, the locals added, because she was much too difficult.

This was not encouraging; and soon the meeting was wandering aim-lessly in the wide open field of possible needs. I mentioned fuel problems and loneliness; someone else thought pensioners should be told of financial benefits; meals-on-wheels and hospital transport were brought up; then general interest was roused in the emergency sign schemes which someone had seen in operation.

The men continued to be sceptical about the extent of need, but some of the ladies, including the Secretary of the Evergreens, a lady herself retired and living alone, said they believed senior citizens suffered both from loneliness and practical problems. Then one young woman parish councillor inquired whether those present covered the village geo-graphically. No decision had been taken on dividing the village into areas (or on anything else, for that matter), but at this question everyone fell amicably into naming the village streets and associating those present with them. When no one was present from a particular area, the know-ledgeable villagers were able to suggest others who might help. The turn-ing point was reached; we elected a chairman, and the Good Neighbour scheme had crept into existence.

Everyone was vague about the new scheme's functions, but the need to tell the local paper about it obliged a definition. The Chairman an-nounced that we were going to help elderly residents cope with the prob-lems caused by the fuel, transport and power crises of the winter. We had decided to recruit twelve volunteers to cover the twelve areas of the village and keep in touch with elderly residents. 'We want to be ready', explained the Chairman importantly.

We were ready, but for what? In fact, village people were so provident that nobody ran out of coal or froze in front of a dead electric fire or sat in the dark without candles; in fact my own elderly neighbour, who has always looked after me, loaned me some paraffin. The Chairman had a disappointing winter waiting for emergencies and resigned in the spring.

But the Secretary of the committee – myself – had of course an entirely different concept. The sympathetic ladies recruited the rest of our volun-teers, and I went round privately, talking of the need to keep in touch, to visit, and to uncover needs through visiting. In my own area I found out where and who all the senior citizens were, and began to visit those old and frail and on their own, the housebound and the sick, who gave me a kindly welcome.

There had attended our meeting a newly-retired couple called Gibbs. After the meeting Mrs Gibbs went quietly away to seek our Miss Kemp, the 'difficult' housebound ninety-year-old. She became her firm friend, her mainstay, for there were no relatives living anywhere near. She goes in at least twice a week, and always on Sundays if at home, for Miss Kemp, with a home help six mornings a week, had commonly seen no one between Saturday morning and Monday morning.

Two other Good Neighbours also now regularly visit the old lady, among other benefits providing patient ears for her tirades against her home help. For it is true that she is awkward and ungrateful and tedious in her reiterated complaining, and I was fiercely lectured for allowing a new visitor to call on a Saturday afternoon when she had her feet in a bath! But of Mrs Gibbs she has grown genuinely fond.

As for the rest of the Good Neighbours, I could not discover that they were doing any visiting. 'They know they can always come and see me', a prominent councillor told me. He did not realise that his elderly neighbours would not ask for help, however gratefully they might accept it once offered.

So the winter passed, and I prepared myself for the probable disappearance of the Good Neighbours at the annual Parish Meeting held in March: for what achievements could we point to? However I prepared a little speech about winter always being a time of problems for the elderly and neighbourliness without a Good Neighbours scheme being insufficient, and asked the Gibbs to be present. To my surprise, there was no opposition to the motion that the scheme should continue: evidently the village had decided that if we wanted to run a well-intentioned though patently useless scheme that was up to us. Mr Gibbs was elected Chairman, and we established an object, 'To keep in touch with all frail or isolated retired people, to see and meet their problems as they arise.' We were to resume meetings the following October (1974).

By then, however, my satisfaction had abated. How was I to persuade my fellow Good Neighbours to do anything in face of the general cry of 'No need'? They knew so much more about the village senior citizens than I did. So I set out on a door-to-door canvass of the village. 'I'm calling on behalf of the Good Neighbours', I would announce, 'looking for the retired people of the village. We want to ask if we can do anything for you this winter?'

This question worked like magic; every face would brighten into a gratified smile, as each senior citizen assured me that though he personally was all right at present, it was good to be asked, heartening to learn that an organisation like the Good Neighbours existed in case of future need. Among the younger people too there was almost universal approval and many offers of help. A pleasanter task could not have been found.

I made a little map as I went, with notes on the circumstances of each senior citizen, roughly dividing them into those who clearly needed no help and those with whom it seemed advisable to keep in contact. The retired people asked me what sort of help we could give, and I said that we would keep in touch, come and help in sickness or bad weather, provide transport where needed, and organise social events if desired.

Social events were easy to talk about, and the idea of a Christmas party went down well. Then one lively, jolly old lady, obviously socially-disposed but living alone, asked if we could arrange a little social meeting in an afternoon. The Evergreen Club met fortnightly on summer evenings, and she suggested that people might like a fortnightly meeting on winter afternoons.

So it proved. Luckily, Shipton has a block of warden flats in the centre of the village, with a good-sized common room. I went to see the residents, and we held a preliminary meeting. I collected suggestions of villagers who could give talks or show slides, and undertook to arrange the programme, while the Good Neighbours would also provide transport for those unable to walk or prevented by bad weather. In no time at all the 'Wednesday Club' was a flourishing concern with over twenty senior citizens attending each meeting. It has met happily each fortnight since November, even surviving a talk by the widely-respected but mischievous old doctor, who chose as his theme 'Voluntary euthanasia'.

Meanwhile the Good Neighbours had held their own first meeting of the winter, when I revealed that my survey had shown many over-60s would be glad of someone calling now and again during the winter to check all was well. During the following months we replaced inert with more active Good Neighbours, and ensured that everyone knew who were the retired people in his area. Most of our meeting, however, was devoted to planning a Christmas – soon becoming a New Year – Party, when I announced how popular the idea had been. We arranged to hold first a fund-raising coffee morning with bring-and-buy and raffle. This was a great success, largely because of the support of the retired people themselves, who also invariably held a small raffle at the Wednesday Club to swell our funds.

In the event the New Year Party cost very little, because all the food was provided free by Women's Institute members, who responded most generously to an appeal at their meeting. We also found plenty of private cars to transport the senior citizens to the village hall, so there was little cost beyond making small presents to the entertainers. As the day neared my chief anxiety was that I might have over-estimated the demand for the party. However, when I entered after collecting passengers a splendid sight met my eyes. All round the gaily-decorated hall, by pretty little tables loaded with sandwiches, sausage-rolls and scones, sat between forty and fifty senior citizens. The hall was full, the Good Neighbours perched on the stage stairs and leaning out of the kitchen.

I slipped into a chair and began to enjoy myself. The children's ballet performance was delightful, the tea substantial, the game of guessing old farm implements hilarious, and the solo singing by a local baritone and the community singing that followed generally enjoyed. It was a most successful party. We promptly decided to make it an annual event. Besides being something for the elderly people – some of whom had had dismal Christmases – to look forward to, it was a psychological success, putting us on the map. A prominent councillor who had been threatening to resign significantly changed her mind after the party.

But still, to me, visiting was the most important part of our work. One afternoon I found Miss Kemp in a terrible state. She was sure 'the social security' were depriving her of a week's supplementary benefit: one book had finished a fortnight before the next began. It was impossible to check this because the later book had been sent back for an alteration. But I promised to ring 'the social security' next morning, and gradually soothed her. In fact there was no missing week, the later book had started correctly; but the visit of a Good Neighbour at that moment had saved the old lady a night of worrying and distress.

Two elderly sisters lived together, devoted to each other and ignoring their neighbours. Last September the elder had to go into hospital, where she has remained. The Good Neighbours, official and unofficial (for we have never denied the existence of the latter), have managed to take the younger sister the twenty miles to the hospital nearly every week. Moreover this sister, who has neither relatives nor friends in the area and was now consequently quite alone, was, after the utmost urging by everyone in touch with her, including her doctor, persuaded to come to the Party. She enjoyed herself, and is now a regular attender at the Wednesday Club.

Nearby lives another uncommunicative old lady, who resolutely refuses to join any village organisation, muttering about gossip and backbiting. She was happy so long as she could go on the bus two or three times a week to see friends in neighbouring villages, especially as she (perversely) enjoyed the company on the buses. But this winter, illness confined her to the house. A Good Neighbour now visits her, as does a young woman with children, one of the first to offer to help us, and we have also brought an old friend from the other end of the village to call.

The Dunns did not need visitors: they were active and had a car. But when Mr Dunn went down with bronchitis, they suddenly found they could not get the weekly bread supply, which he had always fetched in his car from a neighbouring town. They asked a Good Neighbour to bring it for them.

And fetching bread was finally to prove the value of my village canvass, when the bread strike was on. Rather late in the week – for we are not yet as streamlined as we should be – we appealed to the bakery of the nearby town to bake extra bread for Shipton's old people, who were entirely without it.

On the Saturday morning we fetched, cut up and distributed a dozen loaves. It was painfully little, although the senior citizens accepted it like ambrosia and us as the angels bearing it; and we had to decide who should have some and who not. My maps and lists provided the basic information for this difficult task, telling us who was housebound, and who had no relatives or mobile friends to help. Similarly we are able to distribute more or less equitably the free firewood provided by a small carpentry business in the village.

Nobody asked us to fetch bread during the bread strike. It was typical of the patient endurance of the village senior citizens that, although I saw several of them at the beginning of the strike week, no one mentioned the lack. It is a general rule that they will not ask, we must find out. It was only by chance that I discovered recently that a lady I have been visiting regularly for eighteen months had never, in two years, been able to visit a dear friend living in the next village. Yet most weekends I am about in my car and could have taken her.

No need! no need! said the sceptics. But the Good Neighbours know that the more time we devote to the senior citizens of Shipton, the more we shall find ways of making their lives easier and pleasanter; and that is enough for us.

43 Camden old age pensioners*

Betty Harrison

The author has been a full-time trade union official for twenty-five years, first in the Fire Brigades Union for seven years and from 1946 to 1964 in the Tobacco Workers' Union. [. . .] Since retirement, she has been very active in the old age pensioners' movement. She has been treasurer of the Camden Old Age Pensioners' and Trade Union Action Association, and claims that her trade union experience has been invaluable in her work in the old age pensioners' movement. This article is based on an interview with Marjorie Mayo.

Could you describe how the branches of the Old Age Pensioners' Union were set up and organised in Camden?
We held a meeting in the Town Hall, where a lot of people came, and we signed them up. We agreed that we should make a charge of 5p a year. We then had to go out to try and get members in other ways. The first meeting was organised by the Camden Trades Council and Camden Borough Council. The Trades Council invited people and I think that there were almost more Trades Council people and Labour Councillors there than pensioners. The information had also gone round by word of mouth, and we had a few names and addresses of people who were interested.

We then went to luncheon clubs and talked to people, many of whom joined. Then, during the summer of 1972, some members stood outside the Post Office in Kentish Town. Those who lived in the Regent's Park area had an easier job because there is a big estate there and they could go round to the houses and flats.

But in Kentish Town we couldn't do it quite like that so we stood outside the Post Office on the days when the pensioners went to draw their money, and gave out duplicated forms. The first part of these forms said who and what we were, and what our objectives were; the bottom part was an application to join, and we signed some of them up there and then outside the Post Office. One of our members in Kentish Town then had the idea of asking the Consumer Aid Association in Kentish Town Road to lend us a table and a chair. [. . .] Sometimes we had people lining up to sign on. When we had quite a number of addresses on these forms, we called a local meeting in Kentish Town. We found that some of the people who signed belonged to the Holly Lodge Estate, so we got in touch with

Source: D. JONES and M. MAYO (eds) (1975) *Community Work Two*. London: Routledge and Kegan Paul, pp. 192–202 (extracts).

one of the men up there who had come to the first of our meetings and gave him the names and addresses of the people from that area who had joined, and he formed a branch there. We then wrote to all our local Kentish Town addresses, which added up to over a hundred people, and asked them to come to a meeting. We had been given permission by the Director of Social Services in Camden to use Social Service Centres, and the Leighton Road Centre agreed to let us have our meeting there. On this particular occasion, we posted the notices, and out of over a hundred people we got forty-seven to the first meeting – from that we more or less formed our Kentish Town branch. I must add that on my initiative we didn't make it into a formal branch. I have found that if you have these organisations with a chairman and secretary, the rest of the members tend to sit back and let those three or four people do all the work. We don't to this day have a committee; all problems are raised at the full branch meeting and everybody takes part in discussing them. I agreed that I would more or less guide these meetings without actually being chairman, and that if there was any correspondence, I would do it. We have gone on like that ever since.

Now some of the other branches have been organised in different ways. The Regent's Park branch, for instance, found it much easier to organise themselves, for the reason I have already mentioned; there is also a community centre on the estate, where they held their first meeting. They formed their branch formally with a chairman and secretary and treasurer. And if that's their way of working, well that's all right, too, although I think personally that they get less participation from the majority of their members than we do.

Then Task Force and the Neighbourhood Centre in Malden Road started to form a branch in that particular area. They took a leaf out of our book and went outside the Post Offices and they had one or two big blocks of flats which they could canvass for members. They called a meeting at the Neighbourhood Centre and asked me to go and speak when their branch was formed. Here again, they had a chairman and secretary and a committee, and within a fortnight half the committee resigned, which meant there were only two people left; then the chairman had to give up because he fell ill, so they were left with no one in the way of officials. But they were still determined in wanting a branch, so they found a new chairman and secretary, and at the present time perhaps fifteen or so people go fairly regularly.

Local branches have been formed all over north-west London now, and I have been along to speak to them. The only trouble as far as I am concerned is that because I am articulate and have some experience of organisation through my trade union background, anybody who's starting up a new branch wants me to go and talk to them, and this has meant quite a bit of work. But most of these new branches have got off the ground now, with one exception. The Task Force people had spoken to the organiser, who was in charge of a lunch club at the Maiden Lane Community Site, and so we too went along to speak there. Task Force showed a couple of very useful films they had made of interviews with two or three old people, and then I spoke. We got about seventeen people interested who wanted to have a chairman and secretary and form a committee and, as far as I knew, they were going to go on all right. The next thing I learned was that the whole branch had collapsed. When I enquired – and this is only heresay as I didn't experience it myself – I found that the Claimants' Union had gone there to talk to them. Apparently they had not understood, being in the main young people, what old people are like and how they respond to things. Because they had made a fighting speech about making claims and making appeals on their claims and all this kind of thing, the old people were terrified by this, as they could see themselves constantly in tribunals or something; so they shied away from the whole thing. [. . .]

How do you recruit new members, and how do you organise the meetings to keep up their interest and active participation?
We keep getting new members all the time: not so much by standing outside shops and post offices: in the winter, anyway, old people can't really be expected to do that: but by people who are already members bringing in their neighbours and friends. One of the things we've done in our Kentish Town branch, which I think has kept the branch going very healthily, is that we have had a succession of speakers on various subjects. One evening a young man brought some folk records along which we enjoyed very much: but we've had serious speakers, too. For instance, when people have talked about problems with social security, I suggested that we ask the manager of the local Social Security office in Kentish Town to come and speak to us. Well, he did, and gave us a very good lecture. Then, of course, our people were able to tell him of our difficulties with Social Security. [. . .]

Can I ask you whether it is more difficult to organise older people because they are less mobile, and, if so, how you cope with that problem?
Yes, this is a problem. You see, we don't have the same people coming now as when we first started. The same number come, and some of these are original members who have kept coming, but the membership changes because old people get so that they can't come out, some of them go into hospital for various things, and some of them die. But we have tried to keep in touch with all our members, whether they can come to meetings or not. There's one woman whose husband died a few months

back, for instance; some of our OAPs went along to the funeral and then brought her to the branch, because she didn't want to come on her own at first. Now she comes regularly because she feels that we are her friends. Anyone who is sick or in hospital we will make a collection for, and then two of our women go down to see them. We have found that it is our women who mostly go out to see people and this kind of thing. Although we have a large number of men members, they don't fancy going to hospital to see a sick woman. Our members also keep in touch with their neighbours, and this is one reason why they keep bringing neighbours along to join. We do have a steady flow of new members, usually two or three at each branch, so that we are growing all the time. If we have to call a special meeting to discuss any particular problem, we get out a circular – I usually do that – but we don't have to post it. I give a bunch of notices to various people in different parts of the area we cover and they deliver them in person. Now when they deliver them, they don't just put them through the door; they usually take the opportunity to ring the bell and talk to the people and say: 'You haven't been to the meetings recently; are you sick or something, or do you need some help, or should we call for you?' So we have a whole social network, and this is very beneficial to our members. [. . .]

Out of all these issues you take up, could you rank them in order of their importance for your organisation?
Well, all these social problems, however important in themselves, are incidental to the main work of the organisation. The main issues are usually connected with housing – lack of hot water, workmen taking weeks to come along and do repairs – but the real issue is lack of money. Our main aim is to increase the pensions of old people, with the ultimate objective of getting a pension related to the average earnings in industry. [. . .] We are working for this because we want to do away with people going to Social Security to ask for the money to buy another blanket. We don't want them to have to ask for the telephone to be paid for, either, or the television licence. All these demands are also in our programme. But we are different from other organisations such as Care for the Elderly and Good Neighbours because we don't want these things as charity or hand-outs. We feel that the old age pensioner has earned them as a right, particularly this generation of OAPs who fought and won two World Wars for this country, who suffered unemployment and came out of that, who fought for, and won, a Health Service and the Beveridge Insurance Plan. These things had to be fought for, too, they were not just handed out as a generous bonus. Now our generation of pensioners built up the wealth of this country in order to be able to do these things, and therefore

we are entitled as a right to a sufficient pension to live a decent life in the community with dignity.

What kind of support have you had from other parts of the organised trade union movement in this campaign?
As I have already mentioned, our Camden Pensioners' Association is sponsored by the Trades Council, which sends a representative to our Committee. They have given us money from time to time, because the 5p from the members doesn't go very far and we have to get money from other places, too. We have also had money from the Co-op Political Committee. In our Association, we have organised deputations to the Social Services Minister, and have had a demonstration outside Buckingham Palace. Together with other pensioners' organisations from all over the country, and the TUC, we also organised a lobby in November 1972 at the House of Commons, with a big meeting in the Albert Hall. [. . .] And so it was from that Association that the demonstration of 20,000 people was held in Blackpool. The TUC passed not only the resolution of support but also a resolution that it would consider industrial action to help us. [. . .]

Has this political campaign involved you in any difficulties with some of your members because you might be seen to be too closely identified with one particular political party?
No – we haven't had the problem of some of us thinking we are becoming too much identified with the Labour Party. Most of our people just feel that they want this decent pension so much that they are prepared to let anybody or any party help them. [. . .] It's a great step forward that the trade unions have now definitely committed themselves, instead of just passing resolutions as they did in the past. Some of the unions, particularly the Transport and General Workers' Union, have also set up OAP committees of their members because the pensioners themselves have now become more active and have forced the unions to accept that they must help the pensioners. We have said to them that they will be OAPs themselves one day and have an interest in organising to rectify the present position before they get to that stage. On this point of links with the unions, it has been infinitely important that people like myself have been active trade unionists and known how to talk to trade unionists. In fact, most of the people active in the OAPs' organisation up and down the country have been ex-trade-union officials. [. . .]

What about link-ups between the pensioners and other organisations and agencies, particularly those based on community rather than workplace issues?
We haven't been very active with other organisations in the community –

for instance, tenants' associations – maybe because old people have come to us rather than them thinking we understand their problems better. The Social Services departments have given us some help in providing a room to meet in, as they have done elsewhere in the borough, I understand, but that is all. They don't come to our meetings or discuss anything with us. We would like them to come if they didn't try to run the thing. I'm not saying they're not doing a good job, in the main, but our experience of these people is that they think they know best. Agencies in the community, which are there to help, often like to tell people what they think they ought to do. Well, the old people have been told for too long what to do and what not to do, and one of the basic characteristics of our organisation is that we don't tell them what they ought to do. We ask them what they want, and what their problems are, and we discuss these together. And it is because we discuss these together we are getting somewhere. Now, I'm not sure if I ought to say this, but although some of these other voluntary organisations have been very helpful, they also tend to try and tell the branches what they should do. [. . .]

Do you have any words of caution for community workers, then, as to how best to be helpful to the pensioners?
I'll speak about the voluntary agencies first, although it applies to community professional workers, too. They are very kind, but old people don't want to be set apart, and this is one of the things in our Camden organisation that we've really stressed: old people need to be, and should be, an integral part of the community. The Social Services can help by providing home helps, district nurses and other assistance. But one of the biggest things for people confined to their houses is the loneliness: I think the professional workers should be discussing this particular problem, not just seeing that the district nurse goes to visit. This is what happens: she goes and maybe stops half an hour, the home help goes and stops maybe an hour; but the elderly are awake twelve hours in a day as a rule, and what do they do with the rest of their time when they can't get out of the house? There needs to be discussion on how this problem can be tackled. It's not easy; all they have is the television, and they get sick of it sometimes because it can't talk back to them. And I know some of the community people say: 'She talks my head off when I go.' Well, why? Because it's the only talk she's having. I think they should at all costs avoid segregating people, and try to persuade an old person who lives next door or up the street, who can go out, to get to know someone who can't. Old people want gossip. Community workers should help to put old people in touch with the local network rather than tell their organisations what to do. The trouble with a lot of the clubs run for old people is that they are run *for* them and not *by* them. And so, in a way, the clubs actually cut them off

from the rest of the community. If someone comes along to try to make them active to fight for a better pension, it's not liked at all, because the clubs are run on the basis of keeping the pensioners passive and treating them like nitwits who don't understand the problems of the day; just entertaining them with outings and Christmas parties, etc. Whereas what we're trying to do in the Camden Pensioners' and the British pensioners' organisations is to involve the pensioners in the community so that they know what's going on – they have something to contribute, they have a wealth of experience and knowledge which could be invaluable, if only it were properly used.

44 Three organisations – one cause

National Corporation for the Care of Old People

The elderly comprise a much larger part of the population today than ever before. Moreover their social and economic circumstances are less favourable than those people in middle and younger years. It is therefore not surprising that a number of national organisations have arisen since the War to argue the case for improvement, and/or to provide facilities for old people.

Three such organisations are: Age Concern, National Corporation for the Care of Old People and Help the Aged. These organisations believe that they each have worthwhile though somewhat different roles to play; that even if there were any overlap between them the work to be done is so considerable that the efforts of all of them are necessary and their cooperation on certain matters is helpful.

It was the National Council of Social Service that first saw the need for a national body to champion the cause of old people. In 1940 it established the National Old People's Welfare Council (NOPWC) under whose encouragement many local groups began to flourish.

In 1944 the Nuffield Foundation decided that the circumstances of the elderly needed special study, and its report *Old People*, published in 1947, became a classic. As a result of the recommendations of that report, the National Corporation for the Care of Old People (NCCOP) was established to carry on the study process and to administer funds made available to start experimental services.

In 1962 Voluntary and Christian Service saw the need for a new initiative in fund raising from the public, launched Help the Aged (HTA) and quickly demonstrated that goodwill towards the elderly could be turned into cash support, particularly to meet specific needs.

Finally, in 1971, NOPWC (which had by then become independent of the National Council of Social Service) saw that modern circumstances required a new look and new methods if the movement was to make an impact on certain aspects of social policy, and took on the new title Age Concern for that purpose.

It has to be noted that whereas HTA has worldwide functions, NCCOP relates only to the United Kingdom, and Age Concern is the title given to four independent bodies, Age Concern England (ACE) and equivalents for Scotland, Wales and Northern Ireland.

Source: NCCOP (1977) *One Cause*. London: NCCOP on behalf of Age Concern, National Corporation for the Care of Old People and Help the Aged.

Age Concern has most of the national organisations in any way concerned with old people in membership and special opportunities occur for cooperation with NCCOP and Help the Aged. Age Concern's governing body and executive committee are elected by the movement. HTA and NCCOP, on the other hand, have management committees in part nominated by their parent organisation, and in part self-appointing.

All three organisations are registered charities.

It is not surprising that the basic aims of the three bodies are the same. HTA speaks of 'relief of the needy aged', a philosophy of 'active independent old age' and the aim of securing 'better conditions and rights for old people'. 'Our job, by conviction and by a passionate involvement', says its 1975 Annual Report, 'is to restore old people to their rightful place in society. Respected, involved, giving as well as getting, active full members of the community.' NCCOP and ACE would accept these objects as their own, though the implications in the UK are bound to be different from the implications, for example, in Africa and India, in which HTA is also involved.

Not only are the implications of these aims different in different parts of the world, but the three bodies approach them from different angles, and the following paragraphs explain and illustrate these approaches briefly.

Age concern

Age Concern organisations are local groups which came together because they saw local needs which they thought that a new voluntary association could help to meet, or because in larger areas a cooperative effort of existing organisations seemed required. They use the help of many thousands of voluntary workers. Their interests range from meals services to better housing, from social clubs to visiting the elderly at home, from heating in the home to better arrangements for admission and discharge from hospital. These local groups now number over 1,000.

Regular visits to housebound old people help them to feel part of the community. Many groups can offer visiting schemes, good neighbour and street warden services, transport for hospital visits or to day centres and club entertainments. Many organise holidays and day outings and give all kinds of practical help – such as filling in forms, fetching a prescription, or collecting the weekly pension. Volunteers help the elderly to claim their rights to an adequate income and advise them of the other services that will help make their lives more comfortable. Age Concern's home visitors are now estimated to number 60,000.

The four national headquarters – Age Concern England, Scotland, Wales and Northern Ireland – provide local organisations with advice, information and literature. They prepare reports on the needs of the old and present them to local and central government, commercial and voluntary organisations, so that the views of the elderly are known and can be acted upon. A quarterly magazine *Age Concern Today* is published, as well as a wide range of publications for volunteers and professionals in the caring services, and educational material is made available for schools. The four national Age Concern bodies brief MPs and make sure that the interests of the elderly are upheld in any legislation that may affect them. They scrutinise all measures being considered by Parliament which relate to pensions, social security benefits, taxation, transport, heating and housing. In 1974 a manifesto on the place of the retired and the elderly in modern society was published.

Age Concern pioneers new developments for the elderly by either joining with other bodies or initiating its own experimental projects or study groups. Recent developments have included the setting up of a radio unit at the Age Concern England Headquarters, where tapes are produced for BBC or commercial local radio programmes as well as for training volunteers and for use in clubs or day centres to entertain and inform the elderly. Age Concern also promoted evaluation of an emergency telephone scheme for the elderly set up in Gateshead.

Age Concern's new research unit will ensure the application of rigorous techniques of appraisal to future experimental projects. Continuous investigations of the views of the retired and elderly themselves will be used as a base for future policies and programmes.

In the process of bringing local groups and other national organisations into council to coordinate their views, Age Concern may rightly claim to be the largest voluntary movement for the elderly in the UK.

National Corporation for the Care of Old People

NCCOP is essentially an organisation established to promote new experiments and to think about problems and policies. It was started to work out the implications of the enormous increase in numbers of old people, for the health and social services, for housing and on matters relating to work and retirement. It is a small centralised organisation without local branches or groups.

The Corporation's advisory council is composed of experts in many fields. It decides what matters require study, and what action should be taken when the results of the studies are available. This action may take the form of further research, or advocacy of new government policy, or practical experiment. NCCOP has often been able to attract funds to implement such action.

Studies in the housing field, for example, resulted in a publication *Housing in Retirement* in 1973, and a research project was undertaken by a university with NCCOP funds, whose report was published as *New Housing for the Elderly*. This last report broke new ground in giving authoritative comments from the users of specially-designed dwellings for old people. The Corporation also made a practical contribution to meeting housing needs of the elderly by setting up the first national housing association for this purpose, the Hanover Housing Association, which has been very successful and now provides over 4,000 dwellings.

NCCOP was also able to commission a major research project on other services. It was undertaken by the Government Social Survey, and resulted in *Social Welfare for the Elderly*, a report used extensively for reference on the needs of old people. Another report, *Services for the Elderly at Home*, dealt with several kinds of domiciliary services, and indicated where further provision was required. On the side of practical experiment, NCCOP has brought in the National Research Development Corporation and the two bodies are jointly developing a device which it is hoped will enable old people who are alone to summon assistance easily in any emergency.

Because NCCOP must maintain contact with research in gerontology (i.e. the process of ageing) if it is to carry out its main functions, it is well placed to keep a register of such research for use by others. It has produced and published *Old Age, a Register of Social Research* annually since 1955, and this is widely used as a reference book. The Corporation is also providing the secretariat for the newly-formed British Council for Ageing, which for the first time brings together people from the academic disciplines and clinical fields which contribute to gerontology, such as geriatric medicine, biology, sociology and psychology. The Corporation has a small specialised library, which can be used by outside enquirers who cannot obtain the information they need from elsewhere.

Although new thinking and new experiments are the primary functions of the NCCOP, it has acquired others, which are undertaken largely because the Corporation is uniquely placed to perform them. Thus, another charitable Trust asked it to undertake a study on its behalf of the care of the mentally infirm. Another Foundation asked the Corporation to use its special knowledge of old people's residential homes to administer some of that Foundation's money to improve and modernise such homes: more than £1 million has been allocated for this purpose since 1974. NCCOP has recently formalised its willingness to advise voluntary and private residential homes by establishing Homes Advice, a service which will include the issue of short publications on matters such as staffing, finance and fire precautions.

Grants, whether with money from other Trusts or from the

Corporation's own limited funds, are used to encourage innovation. For example, voluntary bodies were helped to provide flatlets for old people before 'sheltered housing' was in existence; to provide chiropody before the Health Service did so; to provide day care before local authorities entered this field. Current studies of transport problems of the elderly and of the care of the mentally infirm may suggest experiments in these fields which the Corporation can help to launch.

NCCOP does not offer a direct service of advice to individuals on personal problems.

Help the Aged

The approach initiated by HTA was different again. It saw enormous need amongst the aged, both at home and overseas, and a goodwill amongst thousands of people in Britain which could lead to generous giving if those needs were powerfully presented to them. Help the Aged took on that role of presentation through appeals, press and advertising campaigns, and quickly became the largest fund-raising body in the UK working for the relief of the needy aged both in the Third World and in Britain. It employs full-time staff for fund-raising and research to discover needs with a view to fund-raising work. It seeks to involve the whole community in its work. It has been able to make financial contributions to hundreds of welfare projects in this country as well as contributing to overseas programmes in 70 developing countries. In the UK Help the Aged is now raising money for medical research and rehabilitation following disabling illnesses.

Overseas, Help the Aged was able to point to such obvious needs as for food, clothing or medical services, especially following natural disasters, war or political upheaval; at home its appeals were necessarily more sophisticated and at first were concentrated on the need for new sheltered housing for the elderly, to give effect to which it started its own housing association, now independent and known as Anchor Housing Association. Otherwise it has provided finance through bodies with which it has no formal connection, undertaking specified kinds of work, particularly by promoting day centres, to alleviate loneliness. In its overseas work HTA supports existing relief teams rather than incur further expense by setting up its own operation. Aid is channelled through voluntary workers in the field including church groups, Red Cross, United Nations and many other accredited agencies.

Recent activities in the United Kingdom are numerous. Through its newspaper *Yours*, HTA encourages voluntary work of a fund-raising nature and sets up local committees for this purpose. Gift shops are also promoted throughout the country as part of the fund-raising work. At the present time HTA is initiating fund-raising in Canada, the USA, South Africa and India to provide more help for the Third World and is working to encourage the involvement of individuals, churches and groups in its campaigns to provide a fuller life for the aged overseas. A particularly important recent development is the training of fund-raisers by HTA in India; a thousand pounds spent in this way can be multiplied many times over by the effort of Indian nationals working at Indian rates. In many parts of the developing world there are areas of relative affluence and by exporting expertise in fund-raising new funds are released.

In the UK, HTA campaigns vigorously to secure better conditions and rights for old people, issuing statements and reports. Its newspaper *Yours* informs and stimulates the elderly. It has produced and promoted a Good Neighbour Charter. It makes representations to governments regarding pensions and allowances. It works closely with the Ministry of Overseas Development concerning aid and development overseas and has produced and promoted a World Famine Charter. HTA has cooperated with five other voluntary organisations in discussions with governments on the universality of poverty. Educational material is made available for schools through its own Education Department.

Help the Aged offers a direct service of advice to individuals on personal problems from its head office but more particularly through *Yours*.

All three organisations seek outside financial support. For HTA this is the very reason for its existence, raising funds which can be distributed according to the urgent needs of the day: it gets no government grant, and raises money almost exclusively from the public. Age Concern does get a government grant, because of the direct welfare work it undertakes, but needs also to appeal to the public, because its grant covers only a proportion of its expenditure. NCCOP does not receive a government grant and does not normally make appeals to the public: much of its work is paid for by trusts or foundations but it does need to build up a capital fund to keep in being the basic organisation without which it could do nothing, and it seeks contributions and legacies for this purpose.

The 1975 accounts of HTA show in that year it raised £4,800,000 in appeals and in the value of gifts in kind. [. . .]

Age Concern in the year 1974/75 had a grant of £55,000 from the Department of Health and Social Security, and raised £207,000 from other sources. It distributed £63,000 to local groups and other bodies, leaving £218,000 for its own work.

The NCCOP accounts for 1974/75 show that it had an income of £119,000. Of this £56,000 was spent on outside projects, and £38,000 on its own activities. These activities included the disbursement of £208,000 for another trust to voluntary residential homes.

Part 8 Older People in Care

45 Old people in care

Paul Brearley

Social workers concerned with admitting elderly people to care are usually involved in finding a balance between conflicting needs and wishes. As the Williams Report suggested, residential care is likely to be seen as second best by the person who is being admitted, however comfortable the home, or however well the admission is managed. The notes that follow are offered as guidance to the social worker involved in providing care for the elderly person.

Reasons for admission

A request for help may take many forms, from an apparently straightforward request for grandma to be looked after while the family takes a holiday in the summer, to a series of demands from neighbours, doctor, and health visitor, that an old lady must be removed from appalling circumstances immediately. In whatever way the situation is presented the social worker's first task is to collect the relevant facts in order to put together a clear picture of what is happening.

One important consideration here is the time factor: it is a recognised and recognisable fact that older people tend to be slower and that they need more cues before they feel able to take action or make a decision. The problem then becomes one of balancing the elderly person's need for time with the more pressing physical needs for care, warmth, food, or support which are likely to exist in the situation. The necessary skill is to be able to create a less pressured situation in which problems can be seen realistically.

To identify the sources of pressure is therefore a priority. The great majority of people applying for admission to old people's homes do so because of an inability to care for themselves, or an anticipated inability to care for themselves in their present environment. The underlying factors are predominantly related to the standard of accommodation and to the state of health. Problems arise because of a cluster of circumstances – an accumulation of difficulties which gradually arise over a number of years. In addition to this background of predisposing factors many admissions to residential care for the elderly seem to be related to precipitating, short-term factors, such as the illness of a daughter, or changes in family circum-

Source: Supplement to *Community Care*, 27 October 1976.

stances. It is often possible to provide substitute supports – home helps, neighbours, etc. – on a short-term basis to create the necessary breathing space. The elderly person can be given space and time to relax for long enough to think more clearly about the alternative courses of action.

In collecting information the social worker should be able to draw on many different sources, as a member of the agency team and the team of health professionals in the community. It is very important to recognise that illness in the elderly can show itself in atypical ways. Sudden behaviour changes, confusion, and physical changes, for example, should be investigated by the doctor as well as the social worker. This may sometimes create difficulties if the doctor is not currently in touch with the old person or if the patient is unwilling to undergo a medical examination. It is therefore vital for close liaison between social worker, health visitors and doctors to be established to facilitate communication in difficult situations.

The home help is another important contact between the social worker and the elderly person. She can act as an early warning system for the social worker in reporting difficulties before they reach the crisis stage. As well as this she can also help to build up the picture of the development of difficulties and give an indication of their cause. Similarly district nurses, volunteers, and other community workers are an important part of the team approach to the assessment of the circumstances in which the elderly person is found. What should be avoided at all costs is the situation in which several people visit the elderly person but never communicate their separate views and concerns to each other to provide an overall view.

The elderly client

The elderly person himself is, of course, the most important component of the situation. This may sound too obvious to state but it is easy to lose sight of the client in the crisis situation in which neighbours, family, doctor and counsellors – often with complete justification – are exerting pressure for action. Sometimes the situation created is one of panic reinforcing panic and the overall perception may bear little relation to the elderly person in the middle and his real needs.

In dealing with the client living alone, with little family or community support, the social worker's main contribution can be to reduce the pressures that have been described and to help in clarifying first of all what the areas of difficulty are and secondly what the alternatives for action are. This may involve taking the pressure of demand and anxiety from those in the surrounding community away from the old person and dealing with them separately. It is more likely to involve filtering the demands through to the client in a way that he can understand. A realistic decision about the future cannot be made in total isolation from the needs of those who will have to provide care and support.

Most families do wish to continue looking after their elderly relatives. It is precisely this determination to continue caring which sometimes leads families to push themselves beyond their limits. Occasionally problems arise because of long-standing family difficulties: more often they arise because the demands made by an increasingly frail parent become more than the family can deal with alone. One difficulty for the social worker in the family situation lies in disentangling the needs of the elderly person as an individual from his needs as a member of the family. It is again easy to lose sight of the individual in concentrating on the whole situation. The necessary skill here is once more that of balancing the needs of the family for relief, while helping them not to feel guilty about what they may see as abandoning responsibilities, with the need of the elderly parent for care, while helping him to avoid a feeling of rejection.

What type of care?

Residential care is a form of provision that segregates the elderly. Recent research in the field of social gerontology has suggested a number of different strands in thinking. Early disengagement approaches argued that ageing is a process of mutual withdrawal in which society demands less of the older person who in turn finds satisfaction in reduced involvement with others. This was not to argue that old people cannot be involved and integrated with others, but that it is possible for them to lead contented lives while segregated from wider social relationships.

In its original form this approach is now rarely defended: research has shown that the majority of old people are integrated into their local communities by the services they receive and give in return to others. Nevertheless a significant minority are segregated by a number of formal and informal pressures in society – compulsory retirement, poor living standards, stereotyping, labelling as 'pensioners', 'senior citizens', etc. – and do need help and support from outside their immediate social network. Professor Peter Townsend has argued convincingly for the provision of a wider range of community services for the elderly to enable them to remain integrated within the larger community.

The social worker should therefore be prepared to look at the *alternative forms of care* with the elderly person and his family and to match these as far as possible with the needs that have been identified. In entering the situation he should state clearly what his powers and responsibilities are and what objectives can be achieved. There is nothing to be gained from presenting an unrealistically wide range of options. Nevertheless one of the principal deprivations experienced by the ageing is the loss of freedom of choice, and in order to restore choice new options must be opened up.

The development of sheltered, or purpose-built housing for the elderly, for example, has offered new possibilities, although one argument against such provision has been that it, too, separates out the elderly as a special group. Studies have shown, however, that both segregated and integrated forms of housing can be satisfying to elderly tenants, providing the individuals themselves feel that they have freely made the choice to move. This last point seems to be the key factor in the provision of all forms of accommodation: if the old person feels rejected or compelled he is far less likely to experience a move as satisfying.

Admission to residential care

If admission to residential care is inevitable, following a full assessment, then as far as possible the elderly person should be fully involved in discussion of the reasons for the inevitability. Sometimes this will not be possible because of the inability of the old person to understand intellectually the reasons, but only very rarely – in acute emergencies – should lack of time prevent full discussion. Most social workers will be familiar with the kind of situation in which pressure is exerted to avoid such discussion.

Sometimes families avoid open discussion and try to pressure the social worker into a collusive position – filling in an application form in the kitchen with the daughter and then pushing it in front of the mother for signature with a very brief explanation. It may sometimes be appropriate to do this but more often this is a sign that they are avoiding the pain and anxiety involved in open discussion. The social worker, in colluding, will only help to build up a more painful time when they are faced with the reality of admission. Other difficulties are associated with communication problems linked to sensory loss – especially deafness. The solution in such cases seems to lie in patience and a determination to get over the message in a careful and sensitive way.

Residential accommodation is provided for those who by reason of age, infirmity or any other circumstances are in need of care and attention which is not otherwise available to them. The 1948 National Assistance Act provided this very broad base for care which may be provided as either short-term or long-term admissions. One relatively unexplored possibility is that residential homes can have a rehabilitative effect. Some people are admitted to care following a period of apathy and neglect, and given warmth, companionship, and good food they improve considerably. If this is recognised and short-term admissions arranged to take advantage of this, residential care can become a much broader resource.

Short-term admissions are also, of course, arranged to give families relief, or a holiday, or to enable them to decorate the house, etc. If the admission is to be for a short term the nature and length of the stay should be clearly agreed. If the family return at the end of their two-week holiday and refuse to accept the old person back home this can only cause distress for all concerned. One answer to this problem is increased family support to prevent them reaching a hopeless or desperate position.

A formal application for admission to care should be made then only after assessment and full discussions have taken place. To make an application and be placed on a long waiting list is frustrating and depressing: waiting lists are an effective way of avoiding taking action. Once the application is made and accepted, admission should follow fairly soon and the social worker's next step is to prepare the elderly person *for leaving home in the right way*.

Michael Meacher has described the plight of the old person who is given little explanation of what he has applied for and at very short notice is 'taken for a ride' by the social worker to a place he has never seen before. Little wonder that when asked if he knows where he is he cannot answer appropriately and is labelled 'confused'. A step by step approach is necessary to provide a clear explanation. It should always be possible for the elderly applicant to visit the home before admission and a return visit by the residential worker to the client's home should also be a possibility. In this way the elderly client does not appear on the doorstep suddenly as 'the new resident' but can present himself as an individual with his own background needs, and likes and dislikes.

At this time the elderly client will be anxious not only about the future but also about what he is leaving behind. Arrangements must be seen to be made for property that is to be left behind. If appropriate, the house and furniture should be protected and preserved in case the client wishes to return home, and this will at least give a feeling of security. Otherwise suitable arrangements should be made for disposal of the property, with the client's full involvement where he wishes for this. Property to be taken to the home should also be discussed: no one entering a new situation wishes to take the wrong clothes.

The actual move from the old home to the new may be arranged in any convenient and comfortable way. If the family can be involved they should be encouraged to help but the social worker must judge each situation individually: he should certainly be involved both immediately before and after the admission if not with the actual transport: continuity is important.

Emergency admissions

There will inevitably be some emergency situations – fire, illness, etc. In such cases preparation is impossible and extra effort must be made after admission to discuss the past and future in terms of realistically achievable alternatives. Similarly there will inevitably be some situations when clarification and discussion prove fruitless and the social worker must decide what to do in the face of persistent refusal or denial of entry, or where the elderly person is clearly in need of care but is unable or unwilling to recognise this.

Some elderly people will need to be protected in their own interests. When a person is suffering from grave chronic disease, or is old, infirm or physically incapacitated and is living in insanitary conditions and cannot care for himself and is not receiving sufficient care from others, the local authority may, on these grounds, apply to a magistrate's court for an order for the removal of the person to a suitable hospital or other place and to be detained there. Usually such an order will be for three months and must give a week's notice of removal, although emergency orders valid for three weeks can be made on medical recommendation with immediate effect.

Admission to a new home inevitably involves new kinds of stress for elderly people who are usually coming from already difficult situations. In addition to the emotional stress, entering a large group of people exposes the newcomer to physical risk in terms of infections, etc. In arranging transfer from hospital to residential home the social worker should be particularly aware of these physical risks.

The nurse has an important part to play in such cases. She should give the patient at least two days' notice of impending transfer, discuss fully with him the reason for the transfer and the advantages of the new accommodation. All property should be packed in front of the patient and, if possible, with his help – it is particularly important that dentures, spectacles, and hearing aids are not left behind. The social worker should be able to arrange the transfer and to provide continuity from one environment to the next: to give a link and a reference point while the elderly person resettles. It is important also to give clear explanations to the family.

Settling in

He should be met by the person in charge of the home and shown his room and helped to meet a small number of other residents. Entering the new group will involve learning about both the formal and informal relationships of the existing systems. The formal rules should be accessible in written form and it should be possible for resident and residential worker to establish clearly the possibilities and limitations of the situation. The word 'contract' has been suggested for this initial agreement and whether it is seen in such definite terms or not it is important for all to have a clear understanding of the limits.

Fitting into the informal structure of the group is a less clear-cut process. If the residential worker has met the client previously and knows something of him he can then be introduced to the group in terms of some common ground, mutual friends, etc., to give him an opening from which to build.

Once the elderly person has arrived at the home it is also important that the fieldworker does not abandon him and his family at once. There will be an inevitable settling-in period, the length of which will vary. For many clients the fieldworker can provide a link with the past and an opportunity to discuss the appropriateness, or inevitability, of the move after the event. To leave the elderly person at this time may only serve to emphasise the feeling of rejection by the community and the idea of having been 'put away'. This follow-through may only involve one visit to 'tidy-up' or it may mean several visits to help the client adjust to the new home as well as the loss of the old. Continuing support for relatives may be just as necessary for a while. Finally, it seems essential to maintain a review system for old people in homes: some people live in homes for up to ten to fifteen years and social workers should recognise the right of older people to continue changing.

In conclusion I suggest the following points are of central importance: *A full assessment* is essential following a request for help: this involves subsidiary questions: How much time is there for action? Who wants the action to be taken? How far can the elderly client be involved? What is the relevant information? What are the realistic options?

If admission is inevitable the social worker must ensure the elderly person leaves his home or hospital in the proper way: An explanation and discussion of the future with the client and with his family; at least one visit to the proposed home; adequate arrangements for the protection and disposal of property; adequate warning of the impending move.

If admission is an emergency, or if compulsion is necessary, disruption should be minimised by continuing discussion and support.

Reception should be properly arranged by giving previous information to the residential worker who should prepare the home for the new resident. *Continuity of contact* should be maintained by the social worker where this seems appropriate.

46 Improving geriatric care in hospital

Royal College of Nursing

The little book from which these extracts come is a report of a Joint Working Party of the British Geriatrics Society and the Royal College of Nursing. The Working Party was concerned with the problem that although much information is available on the medical, nursing, social, remedial and other aspects of the care of elderly patients, there are still many places throughout the country where, despite the fact that staff are concerned, kind, and have the best intentions, patients are treated inappropriately, inadequately or inhumanely.

Because of this discrepancy between available knowledge and observed shortfall in quality of care, the Working Party re-stated the philosophy and objectives of patient care, and outlined the basic needs which must be met for both patients and staff so that practice may be consistent with philosophy and the objectives fulfilled.

Care and quality of life

[...]

21 The essence of care is to be concerned with the well-being of others and to attend to those needs which affect their welfare and quality of life. [...] Quality of life for the elderly requires the recognition of the old person as a unique individual with a need for creative activity, for privacy and fellowship at appropriate times, and with the right to be consulted and to choose in all matters affecting his health and welfare. The patient has rights in common with any individual and should not have to feel beholden to anyone for the treatment he receives. The quality of the geriatric patient's life in hospital results directly from the standard of care received and is affected not only by what happens but also by how it happens. No single aspect of care will ensure well-being; it is only effective when it is comprehensive.

Objectives

22 [...] The prime objective of geriatric hospital care is to diagnose and treat the patient's illness, to help him overcome his disabilities and to enable him to leave hospital and if possible to return home. Where this is

Source: ROYAL COLLEGE OF NURSING (1975) *Improving Geriatric Care in Hospital*. London: RCN, pp. 11–29 (extracts).

not feasible the object is to enable the patient to live as full and worth-while a life within the hospital as his infirmities allow and finally to die in dignity and comfort. [. . .]

Patient needs

27 [. . .] Needs are interrelated and can be described broadly as physical, psychological and social. The elderly patient in hospital is usually frail in body and mind, he may be quite severely disabled, have difficulty in expressing himself clearly and sometimes he will be unable to perform basic human functions without assistance; his physical requirements must not be underestimated.

Physical needs

Food

[. . .]
29 The majority of patients need something to eat and drink after teatime; they cannot wait until breakfast the next morning. Provision of a good choice of food and an adequate fluid intake throughout the day and in the evening is essential. Many older people cannot manage large meals; small meals with between-meal snacks, can better meet the patient's needs and can be provided in consultation with the caterer and dietitian.
30 Enjoyment of food is dependent on dental comfort and attention to mouth and dental hygiene is very important.
31 Many patients and their relatives express appreciation of or dissatis-faction with a hospital on the basis of the quality of catering; even in a hospital where there are few amenities, everyone has meals. As an event in the day, patients can look forward to an appetizing meal, served at the right temperature. Meals present an opportunity for patients to have a familiar social experience, that of sitting in company to eat, drink and talk together. Patients can miss the type of food, the 'treats', to which they were used when these do not form part of normal hospital diet but there is no particular reason why from time to time these cannot be provided, only an imaginative approach and a cooperative relationship between the groups of staff concerned is required.

Sleep

32 With advancing years, sleep and rest patterns often change. Many

elderly people need a short nap during the day. Participation in varied and interesting activities in the daytime is an effective way of ensuring a reasonable night's sleep.

33 Sleep is easily disturbed by noise caused by some types of footwear worn by nurses and other staff, also by conversations and clattering equipment. Attention to reduction of noise at night does much to ensure a good night's rest. Common domestic noises emanating from handling cutlery, crockery and cleaning equipment should be lessened. [. . .]

35 Single rooms designed for noise reduction, but ensuring adequate observation, are ideal for some patients; however, for those who are in an open ward, it is essential to provide adequate bed-spacing [. . .]

36 Restlessness and inability to sleep are sometimes a sign of discomfort due to a full bladder or bowel. The patient may therefore need relief before he settles.

37 Sleeping drugs should be avoided if possible but persistently poor sleepers should be subject to medical review.

Health

38 The elderly patient has been admitted to hospital because of ill health or infirmity and his physical condition may vary from day to day and from week to week. Relevant and up-to-date patient notes must be kept by the staff.

Medical review

39 When a patient is first admitted to hospital, he is likely to be examined frequently. When he has been in a long time, examinations become less frequent but periodical reassessment remains important. In particular, his medicine should not be unthinkingly renewed week after week, but should be reviewed regularly and the drug prescription sheet updated as necessary by the medical officer responsible. Senior medical staff should visit all wards regularly and up-to-date notes should be kept.

Personal care

40 All patients need facilities for the elimination of body waste products in comfort and privacy, the recognition of this need helps those who are continent to remain so. Those who are incontinent experience deep embarrassment and a sense of shame. They should be given help and encouragement to build up confidence and every possible assistance to establish continence, if this has been only temporarily lost, and then to maintain it. This requires an immediate response to any request from the patient for

w.c. facilities and, in the absence of a request, enquiry at frequent intervals. The ability to maintain continence directly affects the morale of the patient.

41 Most people take pride in being and feeling clean. They have their own patterns of bathing and washing. In hospital, people need the facility to maintain their regular standard. Patients should wash themselves if they are able to do so. Others should be encouraged to do as much as possible for themselves. An adequate and conveniently placed supply of hot water must be available; a plentiful supply of soap, towels, toothpaste and dental fixative are obvious essentials. Privacy for washing and bathing should be seen as the basic right of the individual.

Environment

42 Everyone requires a congenial environment and the elderly are no exception; the surroundings in the hospital need to reinforce the therapeutic approach of hospital personnel. Bed and daytime living space are equally important and each must be of adequate size; the day area should provide for flexibility to accommodate varying members and to allow different types of activities such as dining at table. Adequate waiting and quiet interview space are essential. Endeavours to create homely surroundings are appreciated by patients [. . .]

43 It is important that space in hospital is purposefully used. Journeys between sleeping, w.c., living and dining areas provide opportunities for patients to walk short distances at intervals throughout the day; but distances must be reasonable if the patient is to be independent.

44 To feel secure is of great importance to patients in hospital. Confidence that one will improve in health and well-being and come to no harm facilitates the recuperative process. The patient's environment should give him a sense of security and cheerfulness. Soft furnishings should be in bright colours, flowers should be fresh and the floors should not only be safe but look safe to walk on. Falls, which so destroy the patient's confidence, are less likely when he can take his time in moving from place to place. Appropriate furniture facilitates movement and wheel chairs for those who are confined to a chair ought to be individually prescribed to take account of varying abilities. The patient needs also to be secure from fire; furnishings should be flame resistant and fire precautions should be reviewed from time to time.

45 Old people are particularly sensitive to cold, therefore a warm, comfortable and draught-free environment is essential. The patient needs an atmosphere that is well ventilated, free from persistent odours and is warm and light. Adequate clothing will help to prevent loss of heat and it is best

for the patient to be fully dressed; his dignity will be enhanced if he is in his own clothes.

Psychological needs

Identity

46 The ability of a person to impose his personality on his environment is easily lost in hospital. An old person's awareness of himself as an individual can be weakened if he feels that he is taken over by the regimentation of institutional living. The likelihood of failure to get himself across can be minimized if care is taken to enable him to manifest his own personality. If staff can spend time giving him a welcome when he arrives, introducing him to other patients, showing him the geography of the ward, listening to him with care and calling him by his own name, this will help to maintain his own identity.

Self-esteem

47 For most people self-esteem is strengthened by the esteem in which they are held by others. Individual self-regard is associated with being able to do a job well, having enough money, having status in a group, being needed and having a role. For the elderly, some or all of these factors may be lacking. [. . .] In hospital, staff need to perceive the old person not only as he is but as he knows he was. Interest in the patient's past occupation and achievements and in his family can do much to raise his spirits and help him to find a new role which is congenial and so to regain his self-esteem.

Affection

48 The need to care about others and be cared about, to feel and give affection and love, is fundamental and universal. There is no evidence that people ever lose the need for warmth and affection in their lives.

Independence

49 Independence and self-care are taken for granted by most people, as is the ability to walk about and the freedom of action and choice which this allows. Loss of mobility, from whatever cause, is traumatic because it places the person concerned in a dependent, restricted and frustrating situation. Where locomotor impairment is associated with impaired reach

or grasp, there is almost total dependence on others. Old people whose independence is threatened in this way need special help to overcome their disabilities and it must be recognized that their recovery, even if achievable, is likely to be slower than if they were in a younger age group. They need encouragement to gain confidence in their own ability, to regain a measure of independence and to be able to set goals for personal self-care.

Spiritual

50 Spiritual needs mean different things to different people. They reflect an awareness on the part of the individual of an inner strength which sustains and motivates him. Religion is, for many people, an important element in their lives, from which they derive comfort and inspiration according to the strength of their individual beliefs. Others realize their spiritual needs outside formal religion. Whatever the individual's source of spiritual support, provision to meet this need is fundamental to the quality of life of most patients in hospital.

Understanding of bereavement

51 For elderly people the sense of loss and mourning associated with the death of a spouse, member of the family or close friend is painful and often followed by a prolonged period of grieving that may be accompanied by loss of purpose, self-neglect and illness. Old people whose illnesses are rooted in grief need to be treated with sensitivity and compassion. Many will, with attention to their total needs, regain a sense of purpose and the will to carry on, while, for others, the death of a companion of many years may only hasten their own decline, and they may die in resignation and perhaps thankfully. Those who care for the elderly need to be able to accept that death is an inevitable outcome of living; that, as an event, it is a failure neither for them nor for their patient.

52 Patients also feel grief at the loss of one whom they have come to know well in their own midst. This may well make them more actively aware of their own situation and the inevitable end. Patients need to share their grief and their concerns with relatives and staff. Such sharing establishes a mutual understanding and provides support in the face of a deeply felt loss.

Social needs

Relationships

53 People, with rare exceptions, have many interpersonal relationships.

The patient may be part of a close-knit family unit, and/or have some close friends; he may be accustomed to conversing with trades people, neighbours, church members, the family doctor and others. He probably has a role in his local community which provides a familiar pattern of people, places and events. Morale and the sense of well-being are closely associated with having such a place in the community. The elderly patient, especially if he is in hospital for a long time, needs a substitute niche in the hospital situation which affords him opportunities to enrich life through established relationships and familiar activities.

54 Most people are endowed with some degree of humour which leavens their relationship. Sharing jokes with the elderly can release much tension and dispel some of the starch, the solemnity, and the doing-good-grimly attitude that can pervade the atmosphere of long-stay wards. The grouping of patients according to their needs and their individual choices facilitates a sharing of interests in which the staff can join. The patient appreciates the opportunity to see others of all ages; therefore it is important to have free visiting throughout the day and evening to enable visiting by both those at home and those at work.

Interests

55 Elderly people have a range of interests and activities as diverse as any other group. Some like to spend most of their time taking part in activities in the company of others. Others are by nature reserved and enjoy doing things on their own, such as reading, listening to music, doing craftwork or simply contemplating.

56 Shared activities, such as talking, playing bingo, watching sport, taking part in community singing, and going on outings, along with daily living (getting up, eating, washing, going to bed) and receiving visits from family and friends are the fabric of the life style of most people. Contraction of interest with advancing years may be inevitable for some but, for many, opportunities to maintain interests, to give as well as to receive, add zest to life, a measure of fulfilment and a purpose for living. Interests and activities are vital in hospital and other institutions, where lack of opportunity for activity may result in apparent disinterest and apathy on the part of the patient.

Privacy

57 Although most people thrive in the company of others, are stimulated and involved, some are naturally reserved and prefer to spend time on their own. Privacy is the right of the individual and must be preserved in hospital. [. . .]

Radio and television

58 Radio and television can contribute much to the enjoyment of many elderly patients and may help to retain their interest in external matters. For other patients, however, the media can prove obnoxious and noisy. The discriminate use of mobile television sets, radios, tape recorders, all with earphones, in selected parts of the ward is appreciated by a large number of patients, especially if they can choose the programmes. Colour television is a real joy, and enables greater involvement with the personalities on the screen. Television can perhaps best be provided in the day room, but there must be facilities for transporting those patients who wish to watch it.

59 The patients' wishes and preferences about the use of radio and television need to be ascertained, and it must be understood that the equipment is solely for the patients' benefit.

Telephone and post

60 The telephone provides a social outlet for the patient by allowing opportunities for him to talk to relatives and friends and to keep in touch with the outside world. The telephone also provides useful practice for the patient due to return home, who may be entitled to receive a priority telephone provided by the local authority. Regular collection and delivery of mail keeps the patient in touch with the world and makes him feel secure.

Money

61 The patient should handle his own money if he can; an understanding can usually be established with the relatives about this. Having some money gives him an opportunity for choice if the hospital has a shop where he can spend it and it also gives him a sense of security. Where the patient is unable to manage his money and has no relations to do it for him, the hospital finance officer is responsible for its safe keeping; he should make sure that it is spent for the patient's benefit and according to his wishes. [. . .]

Recognition of people's feelings

65 The elderly, as a section of society in Britain, have little economic

influence or power and do not enjoy the high status accorded them in some cultures. The attitudes people adopt towards the elderly appear to indicate a belief that, along with the observable characteristics of advanced years such as grey hair, wrinkles, slower movement, less acute hearing and eyesight, the capacity to feel deteriorates and emotions become blunted.

66 When people enter their declining years they become acutely aware of their diminished status and vulnerability. They have shared society's evaluation of old age when they were younger so that, paradoxically, their situation in retirement has been structured or reinforced by their own earlier perceptions of old people. However, many old people, in spite of economic deprivation, lead full and interesting lives. Their personality and experience enables them to accept the inevitability of ageing with courage and serenity.

67 A wide range of feelings is common to everyone, although the way people express them, and the values different societies attach to them, vary significantly. Feelings that people have are an integral part of their wholeness; they are internal or involuntary responses to those around them and to their environment. Feelings can be denied, hidden or suppressed but still remain powerful determinants of behaviour which are impossible to measure and difficult to predict. Unlike physical and intellectual attributes, there is no real evidence that feelings diminish, either in intensity or range, as part of the normal ageing process.

68 The pleasure felt by anyone when complimented by another on his appearance, an achievement, or a skill is the same kind of feeling whether he is nine or ninety years old. Being noticed, greeted, introduced to people, enquired about or asked for help or advice, all boost morale, give satisfaction and promote feelings of worth and a sense of identity.

69 Sharing affection, humour, company, conversation, ideas and tasks gives warmth and fellowship. People who are confident that they are loved, accepted and respected usually feel secure; they emanate contentment and well-being.

70 Grief, loneliness and anxiety, feelings of unworthiness, of an inability to cope and of not mattering to anyone else are painful emotions which, if experienced over a long period, erode morale, diminish motivation and frequently result in illness.

71 Anger, jealousy and suspicion are disturbing emotions which distort the perception of others.

72 Loss of independence, of self-determination and privacy, or the diminished control of bladder or bowel generate feelings of helplessness, frustration, humiliation, shame and embarrassment. Being ignored or belittled, regarded as simple-minded, talked down to or patronized engender misery and suffering.

The individual's response to his feelings

73 Some people respond to misfortune or insensitivity with determination to overcome their disadvantages. Others face their problems with hostility and aggression and some may curl up and withdraw into apathy, even to a state where they can no longer communicate. In hospital some old people fight against their situation and are often regarded by the staff as 'difficult'; these are the patients who may well give up the struggle and then lapse into apathy. This state of apathy is often attributed to senility rather than to the emotional distress caused either by illness or by the failure of staff to respond to the patient's total needs.

74 Old people are vulnerable to ill-health and loneliness. The clinical needs of those who are admitted to hospital are treated but recovery from an acute phase of illness or trauma is not always accompanied by spontaneous recovery of either independence or a feeling of well-being.

75 For many old people, admission to hospital is the culmination of a long period of struggle against declining health, adversity and increasing fear of becoming dependent on others, or against isolation and loss of interest as companions and contemporaries die. They are a prey to worries about things such as whether they will ever feel fit again, be able to manage on their own, be a burden on their family and friends or, perhaps worst of all, be 'put away' in an institution. This is in contrast to younger patients, whose families and employers need them; they have little doubt about their role when they return home and are therefore strongly motivated to take part in their own recovery and discharge from hospital.

76 Failure to progress according to clinical expectations is often a manifestation of emotional discomfort or disturbance. Worries and the negative feelings of old people, whether caused by real or imagined problems, should be explored and treated so that they can understand and accept their situation and prospects, and be helped to make realistic plans.

Staff's reaction to patients' feelings in hospital

77 It is necessary for the staff to recognize and respond to the patient's emotional needs. Patients who are to be transferred to continuing care units should be well prepared and given the information and reassurance they require. On arrival they need to feel welcome and of significance. They should be introduced to staff and other patients, not only their immediate neighbours but people from the same neighbourhood or those who share common interests. They should be asked about their personal preferences and wishes and about their normal daily life pattern.

78 Having ascertained patients' needs and preferences, staff should ensure whenever possible that these are met. They should also give information

about essential facilities which are available for patients' use. Staff should use judgement about how much information an individual patient can absorb at any one time and continue to explain where he is and why for as long as it takes him to settle in.

79 If staff can perceive the elderly as fellow human beings with common feelings and needs, the way they care, cure and rehabilitate will be enlivened by imagination, consideration and unfailing courtesy. A few patients may appear to be incapable of any feeling; even so, 'to treat others as you would wish to be treated' should always apply. Where patients cannot or will not communicate it is impossible to assess their feelings, wishes or perceptions but it is wise and humane to assume that they are able to feel and think. Staff should develop an awareness of their own feelings and sensitivity to those of patients, thus ensuring that care is not marred by a lack of knowledge and understanding of people. [. . .]

Promotion of urinary continence

Physiological factors

105 An ageing bladder has a small capacity and tends not to empty completely. There is often little warning of the need to pass urine.

106 Frequency of micturition at night is common in old age. The patient may have to empty his bladder within an hour or two of going to bed and even though he voided at bedtime, he may need to go as often at night as he does during the day.

107 Bladder control is more likely to be achieved if the patient is offered the opportunity to pass urine at regular intervals; for some the interval may be as little as every two hours.

108 Older people easily become dehydrated and the presence of urinary incontinence is not a reason for drastic fluid restriction, but it is unwise to give large quantities of fluid in the late evening.

Clinical factors

109 Acute urinary infection may be associated with incontinence and should be treated; chronic urinary infections may or may not be associated with incontinence.

110 Drugs may contribute to a patient's incontinence and his prescription should be kept under review. Diuretics, because they increase the flow of urine, should be used with care; they should be given early in the day so that the effect has worn off before night. Sedatives and tranquillisers reduce the patient's alertness and may contribute to incontinence.

111 Diabetes, because it causes polyuria, may interfere with bladder function but bladder control will usually return when the diabetes is treated.
112 Impacted faeces or a loaded rectum can cause urinary retention with overflow incontinence. Any patient who is incontinent should have a rectal examination to exclude this cause.

Environmental factors

113 It is essential that a suitable call system is available and within reach of the patient, so that he may call the nurse when he wants to pass urine, and he should be encouraged to use this call system.
114 Whenever a patient is unable to reach a w.c., he should be provided with a commode by his bedside. There should be enough commodes in a ward to leave one by the bedside of every patient who might need it.
115 The use of bedpans should be avoided whenever possible. Male urinals on the other hand are acceptable and they should be left within the patient's reach.
116 Privacy is essential for this most intimate function. Every bed should have individual curtaining but, where this is not yet available, screening is essential.
117 The patient needs an adjustable height bed in a low position to enable him to sit with his feet on the floor so that he can get up readily.

The water closet

118 The w.c. must be within 10 m (40 ft) of the patient if he is to get there in time to avoid accidents.
119 W.c.s. should be clearly labelled and it may be an advantage to paint the door a distinctive colour. Access must be clear, the floors must be dry and must be seen to be non-slip. The approach should be well lit and free from obstacles.
120 To suit all patients the area of the w.c. should be 2·75 m^2 (30 ft^2). This provides space for the patient to manoeuvre a wheelchair or walking frame. There must also be room for someone to accompany him. The doors must be wide enough to admit wheelchairs. Handrails should be provided and the position of the wash-hand basin must be carefully chosen to avoid obstruction of the wheelchair. There should be a call bell so that the patient can summon help.
121 The w.c.s should not all be at the same height but 45 cm (18 in) high suits most patients. They should be provided with upright and horizontal rails.
122 Interleaved or soft toilet paper is preferred by most patients.

Treatment

123 If measures to prevent incontinence do not succeed, drugs are available to reduce irritability of the bladder and to improve the condition of the tissue surrounding the urethra.

124 When incontinence persists protective garments should be used. The common practice of leaving patients all day in pyjamas or without their knickers because of incontinence is to be deplored. Protective underwear, disposable knickers and washable trousers should always be available.

125 Of particular value to women are Kanga pants which have a waterproof marsupial pouch holding a disposable absorbent pad on the outside of the garment. For the management of dribbling incontinence in women, a cellulose pad may help.

126 For a few patients, an indwelling catheter draining into a bag is the only effective treatment but it should be used as a last resort. [. . .]

Promotion of mental well-being

Communication

128 [. . .] The staff must be willing to listen and the patients must be able to see, hear and understand those around them.

129 The elderly may not understand speech as easily as they did when they were younger. It is therefore important that they are spoken to slowly and simply and given time to understand what is said. An important conversation should be conducted away from noise and distractions. The use of hands to express a point is helpful. It is best to speak face to face, with both parties sitting or standing. Very occasionally, gentle holding of an old person's hand may be necessary to gain his attention.

130 Hearing deteriorates with age and may make communication difficult. The ability to receive high pitched sound disappears first and staff should address elderly people in a low firm voice. Hearing can often be improved by the removal of wax from the ears. If a patient has a hearing aid it is important to ensure that it is in working order. The battery must be checked regularly and the device should be clearly labelled with the patient's name. Both staff and patients need to understand how to use a hearing aid. The staff should speak clearly and quietly into the receiver. Those patients who do not have a hearing aid should be referred to an audiologist. Wards should be equipped with devices to facilitate conversation with a deaf patient. This may be an electrical converser with microphone, amplifier and earphones or a simple conversation tube made by attaching a short length of tubing to a large plastic funnel.

131 Like hearing, so eyesight may deteriorate in old age. Most old people have spectacles and enquiries should be made about them. It is often necessary to ask an ophthalmologist to check an elderly person's eyesight and to prescribe new glasses. Spectacles should be labelled to prevent loss; and should be kept clean and readily available to the patient. If they are broken, arrangements should be made for immediate repair.

132 Good illumination is necessary and the elderly usually need stronger lighting; reading material should be as clear as possible; large clocks, large calendars and large print books are important. Contrasting colours help people to see better; bright colours on a dull background stand out clearly.

133 If physical barriers to communication are removed, it is easier to converse with the patient and to understand his feelings and anxieties.

134 Anxieties may provoke depressive illness and various forms of disturbed behaviour. Some people may become restless, agitated or aggressive, others querulous and demanding with innumerable bodily complaints. Yet others may become apathetic or withdrawn and fail to respond to the proper treatment for their physical condition. Too often such behaviour is attributed to 'senility' and the underlying psychological disturbance is overlooked.

47 Care of the dying

Cicely Saunders

The problem of euthanasia

In 1967, Hinton wrote: 'It seems a terrible indictment that the main argument for euthanasia is that many suffer unduly because there is a lack of preparation and provision for the total care of the dying'.

Since 1936 when the first Bill to legalise euthanasia was debated in the House of Lords this subject has been discussed repeatedly in the press and radio and on television. [. . .]

In April 1976, the Royal College of Nursing's Representative Body discussed the whole question of 'mercy killing' and passed a unanimous resolution that the RCN approach all appropriate medical bodies urging that all recognised therapeutic measures be taken in the case of patients in the terminal stages of disease to alleviate pain and suffering.

[This chapter] discusses the relief of distress in dying patients. [It] concentrates on patients with terminal malignant disease, although much that is written will be applicable to other situations.

There have been many therapeutic advances in the past twenty years and some of them have added to our problems. As often happens, we discover how to do something, and only later *when* to do it. No treatment which can be used to sustain life during the acute phase of a remediable illness or trauma carries with it the automatic commitment to use it just because it is technically feasible. It may be totally inappropriate for those who are irremediably ill.

Many nurses, continuing their caring role, have found themselves unhappily involved in treatments which they felt were only prolonging and even adding to their patient's distress. There is an increasing sense of responsibility in all concerned with such decisions. One hopes that doctors will more often include nurses and others who know patients and their families better than they do in these discussions. Too often, inappropriate treatments are instituted because the problem was not properly foreseen and no one person has been prepared to take responsibility.

Roman Catholics draw a distinction between ordinary and extraordinary means of treatment. One of the few recognised guidelines was given by the Pope. On 24 November 1957, Pope Pius XII was asked by delegates

---

Source: *Nursing Times*, 1976, *72*, pp. 1003–5, 1133–5, 1203–5, 1247–9 (extracts).

to the international congress of anaesthetists in Rome the following question about artificial respiration: 'Does the anaesthetist have the right, or is he bound, in all cases of deep unconsciousness, even in those that are considered completely hopeless, to use modern artificial respiration equipment?' He answered, 'Since these forms of treatment go beyond the ordinary means to which one is bound, it cannot be held that there is an obligation to use them.' [. . .] The Pope defined extraordinary means as whatever 'cannot be obtained without excessive expense, pain or other inconvenience, for the patient or for others, or which, if used, would not offer a reasonable hope of benefit to the patient' (Papal Allocution 1957).

Wherever possible, a patient and his family should be involved in such discussions and it may be that where the patient is unconscious some statement made beforehand may help in giving the doctors (and the family) an indication of his wishes.

There are several suggested forms of a 'Living Will' in circulation.* They help in revealing a person's general wishes but cannot indicate ahead with any certainty what he will want when he reaches the unknown situation. If such a statement were given legal force we should then perhaps face the danger that everyone who did not complete and carry such a 'Will' might be deemed to expect his doctors to do all they could to prolong his life.

What has justifiably been called 'furor therapeutics' or 'meddlesome medicine' could in fact become the norm from which one had to contract out. The present flexibility in which doctors are increasingly making decisions *not* to carry out every treatment technically possible where it is inappropriate would then once again be made more difficult.

This has not been the only development [. . .]. There have also been many valuable additions to the pharmacopoeia and a sounder knowledge of how to use the drugs available has been developed. [. . .] Some of the basic issues have become more complicated and I would add two further questions to those asked [. . .] 'Is euthanasia morally right?' and 'Is there really no other way of relieving the distress of patients in the terminal stages of cancer?' I believe now that we should also ask, 'Do patients ask for euthanasia?' and 'What would they do and feel if mercy killing became a legal option?' [. . .]

Most of us can recall situations when we have wished death could have come more quickly to a patient (though we have sometimes changed our minds when the end finally came with a rightness of its own), but it remains my conviction that if we had taken any step deliberately to hasten death we would have assumed a responsibility which is not ours.

The Christian imperative is to care and to heal. Healing does not only

---

* Obtainable from the Human Rights Society or The Voluntary Euthanasia Society.

mean assisting someone to get better. It may mean easing the pains of dying or allowing someone to die when the time has come. [. . .]

Christians have been occupied in the relief of suffering and in establishing hospices and hospitals from the beginning of the era. More recently they were the first to establish centres for the control of pain and the relief of indignity in dying.

Many things we see are hard to reconcile with our faith in a loving God. There is no complete or easy explanation but there are some clues to the full answer which we will find only in eternity. We find ourselves in a world in which chance and randomisation have made evolution and development possible but have at the same time opened up the possibilities of genetic and other disasters. We also see that those qualities we salute as the greatest – sacrificial love, generosity and courage – are possible only in a free and thus dangerous world. The Christian believes that the God who made this world entered it in the vulnerability of the Incarnation, shared and transformed suffering, and still shares it in the persons of all His children. [. . .] We are given the vision of Jesus crucified, 'bearing our griefs and carrying our sorrows'. That vision brings us to the point where we change our questions. 'Why should this happen . . .?' changes to 'How can I help – with God's grace?' or 'What can I do in this situation – which He shares with me?'

On the other hand, it has been suggested that a man should have the choice of opting out of a situation which he believes is an intolerable burden for himself and for those around him. Captain Oates walking out of the tent to give a last chance to his companions has often been referred to in the context of such voluntary euthanasia. We do not all remember the entries in Scott's journal which show the background to this act of self-sacrifice and which throw a somewhat different light upon it.

Sun March 11, 1921
Titus Oates is very near the end, one feels, . . . Nothing could be said but to urge him to march as long as he could. One satisfactory result to the discussion: I practically ordered Wilson to hand over the means of ending our troubles to us, so that any one of us may know how to do so. Wilson had no choice between doing so and our ransacking the medicine case. We have 30 opium tabloids apiece and he is left with a tube of morphine. So for the tragic side of our story . . .

Fri March 16 or Sat 17
. . . He said 'I am just going outside and may be some time'. He went out into the blizzard and we have not seen him since . . . We knew that poor Oates was walking to his death, but though we tried to dissuade him we knew it was the act of a brave man and an English gentleman. [. . .]

From a letter
We have decided not to kill ourselves, but to fight to the last for that Depot, but in the fighting there is a painless end.

The friends of Captain Oates could never have suggested to him that he should make his decision of sacrificial love. They did all they could for him until his last day. Certainly we need to look carefully at the suffering we may cause by failing to recognise the difference between acute, chronic and terminal care and the occasions when each care is appropriate and to spread widely the knowledge of relief developed over these past years.

But even more, like Oates' companions, we need to encourage the attitude which conveys to the dying person: 'You matter because you are you. You matter to the last moment of your life, and we will do all we can to help you not only to die peacefully, but also to live until you die.'

Control of pain in terminal cancer

Most of us know that the late onset of pain and other symptoms is one of the reasons for the poor prognosis of certain sites and forms of malignant disease. It is not so well known that pain is by no means an inevitable characteristic of advanced cancer. Many of the public and not a few nurses believe that those who die of their disease will endure severe and mainly untreatable pain before their death. These expectations may lead to much suffering. People live in fear of the onset of pain and, if it occurs, because it is thought to be inevitable, no complaint is made and no relief given. As a district nurse said sadly to us on a day visit, 'They don't know how much pain they are supposed to have.'

The few studies that have been carried out in this area suggest that of those who die of all forms of malignant disease some 50 per cent are unlikely to experience pain at all. Another 10 per cent may be expected to have mild pain only. The remaining 40 per cent of these patients, and of those who need admission to special centres such as hospices probably 60 per cent, will need help for severe or intractable pain. But it must not be forgotten that 'intractable' does not mean 'impossible to relieve'; its meaning is 'not easily treated'. Successful treatment may call for much imagination and persistence but pain can be abolished while the patient still remains alert, able to enjoy the company of those around him and often able to be up and about until near his death. [. . .]

It is my opinion that the cardinal rule in the treatment of patients is to give drugs *regularly* from the start. A four-hourly interval is probably the routine of choice for most of the commonly used drugs. Pain should never be allowed to take control and regular doses of analgesics should be initiated as soon as a patient is at all worried by it. It is not safe to rely on patients to ask, for either they will wait too long (and once pain has become really severe it is a potent antagonist to any drug) or else they will ask too soon and dependence may become a problem.

If a patient receives prompt relief from the start and knows that he can rely on the next dose appearing on time, he does not increase his own pain by fear and tension. There must, of course, be some latitude and when pain becomes more severe no-one should have to wait until the 'right time'. Sometimes a milder analgesic by mouth in between doses is enough. Apart from this, an increase of the regular dose is nearly always to be preferred to the shortening of the time interval.

The work observed at St Luke's Hospital and introduced in St Joseph's Hospice was developed at St Christopher's from 1967 onwards. There it was found that for large groups of patients a narcotic by mouth in a cocaine elixir (e.g. diamorphine elixir BPC) with the addition of a phenothiazine (either prochlorperazine (Stemetil) 5mg or chlorpromazine (Largactil) 12.5–25mg) was the most consistently reliable analgesic. Doses varied from 2.5mg as the maximum dose for 16 per cent of all patients to 60mg and over (2 per cent of all patients). A dose of 20mg by mouth was all that was needed by over 80 per cent of all the patients referred to the hospice for pain control during its first eight years. It was shown that tolerance is not a practical problem and that, handled in this way, this group of drugs can be given orally and continue to be effective for weeks and months on end. So far in a series of controlled clinical trials no observable clinical difference has been found between morphine and diamorphine when given with Stemetil but further work is continuing in assessing the ingredients of the so-called (and most variable) 'Brompton Mixture'.

We begin with the weaker analgesics, and mild and moderate pain is often surprisingly well controlled by Aspirin, tablets of codeine compound or dextropropoxyphene co. (Distalgesic) given regularly. An effective mixture was made by dissolving the first two drugs with 1–2ml of Nepenthe at St Luke's and St Joseph's.

Pethidine is unreliable by mouth, and by injection it is not only an unacceptably large volume but its action is of only two to three hours' duration. Levorphanol and methadone may both be somewhat capricious in their effects and we are not yet so certain of their duration of action as we are of that of the opiates. New analgesics are constantly being introduced and it is important to evaluate our own experience with them. At St Christopher's the most consistently satisfactory drugs for moderate to severe pain have been Diccnal (dipipanone co.), phenazocine (Narphen) and oxycodone (Proladone) suppositories.

All these drugs suit some people, but those who look after large numbers of patients with terminal cancer continue to say that they always return to the opiates. They are given for distress of various kinds (e.g. dyspnoea, thirst, intense weariness) and they are unrivalled when used with skill and confidence.

Regular small doses are started by mouth if possible, and even when nausea makes injections necessary for a few days, many patients can then be given their drugs orally again. At St Joseph's we began with Nepenthe, morphine or diamorphine in a mixture with added alcohol and cocaine. At that time we began with twice-daily doses for a few patients, but for most the four-hourly routine was needed from the beginning. Injections were used for severe pain where oral drugs were inadequate, when a patient suffered with persistent vomiting and for the last few days if he could no longer swallow easily. It was my opinion in 1959 that there was little to choose between morphine and Omnopon in equivalent doses and that diamorphine was really needed for persistent painful coughing and for some patients who seemed to vomit after all other drugs.

This clinical impression concerning diamorphine has not been confirmed by the controlled clinical trials at St Christopher's. It is essential to test one's own enthusiasms, especially when they affect drugs unobtainable in many areas. It was important to discover that diamorphine was not irreplaceable but that other narcotics could be equally as effective when used according to the methods described above.

Nevertheless, St Christopher's continues to use diamorphine [. . .] A number of patients need to change to injections, if only for their last 12–48 hours and its solubility then makes it a drug of choice. Doctors do not always know the size of the injections they order nurses to give to cachectic patients.*

Psychological tolerance to the opiate drugs hardly ever develops if they are given regularly as part of a general, attentive approach. Physical tolerance is not really a dependence problem, and develops slowly if at all. Only occasionally did we give more than 60mg of morphine or its equivalent in 1959 and we found that most patients needed much less. Such doses would remain effective for months and sometimes for years. [. . .]

Dependence or addiction, the continual craving for injections, hardly ever occurs and we found at St Joseph's that the rare patient who was admitted with this problem responded almost immediately when amiphenazole was added to an adequate dose of the opiate. Later observations have led us to believe that in nearly every case such patients have had an inadequate dose of the narcotic concerned. Once a routine dose of the correct level has been established the 'craving' has gone. It has been relief of pain the patient has been demanding and once his own optimum is reached the dependence problem is over, though, of course, the dose

---

* Diamorphine is extremely soluble. 100mg will dissolve in 0.2ml. Morphine is considerably less soluble and the maximum strength available is 30mg in 1ml. If pethidine is used it generally requires three-hourly injections as it has a much shorter action. The maximum available is 100mg in 1ml.

may need adjusting or 'titrating' if pain increases as the disease spreads. Patients need their own optimum dose, no less and no more.

I cannot emphasise too strongly that an automatic, rapid increase of the dose of an opiate is not the best nor the kindest way of dealing with intractable pain. Such action so often demoralises the patient and may indeed increase his anxiety and mental distress. We do him a great and unnecessary disservice when we thus take away his dignity and his ability to face up to his illness, and watching him may be a terrible experience for those who love him. We may produce much the same effect by thoughtlessly decreasing the interval between doses. On the whole it is better to keep to a four-hourly régime and although three-hourly may occasionally be right for an individual patient, medication given one- or two-hourly is out of control.

Side-effects, though these are minimised by properly balanced doses, can still be troublesome. Constipation calls for constant vigilance and individual assessment. Nausea and vomiting seem to occur more often in women than in men, but may subside spontaneously and almost always respond to phenothiazine anti-emetics. Heavy sedation is rare and personality changes are absent with these methods. Excitement is a very rare phenomenon and respiratory depression is scarcely a problem where dosage is well balanced. Lack of ability to concentrate on reading does trouble some patients.

Much of our total pain experience is composed of our mental reaction and most of these patients need some tranquilliser or sedative. The opiates in themselves may be sufficient, but this is by no means certain, as this action is variable. We find at St Christopher's that most patients benefit from a drug of the phenothiazine group, and alcohol may be a help as well as a pleasure. If a patient is enabled to relax, his need for analgesics lessens correspondingly. Diversion may be the best pain-killer of all.

Most patients think that cancer and death are inevitably painful. [. . .] Any who know their diagnosis should be reassured on this point. Our reassurance together with our confidence in our own methods will do more than anything else to make it true that the pain of terminal cancer can be controlled in every patient.

The nursing of patients dying of cancer

Some of the patients dying of cancer have only a short time of illness or weakness and present few nursing problems. Others are cared for well by devoted families who ask only for minimal professional advice or help. But there are some people who suffer long dependence or whose many symptoms make great demands on all around them.

Much of the nursing is the same as that needed by any very ill patient but there are some problems that frequently cause difficulty and some nursing skills which can deal helpfully with them. Most of the suggestions given below will be shared between the nurse, the doctor and the family. For example, help for a symptom such as nausea will include the nurse's observation of the patient's anxiety, the doctor's knowledge of anti-emetics, and the family's awareness of the patient's favourite (and unfavourite) dishes. [. . .]

Anorexia is one of the commonest symptoms of malignant disease and its treatment and an improved food intake make an enormous difference to the patient's general state and even more to his morale. Glucocortico-steroids are frequently used, either prednisolone (enteric-coated) 2.5mg × 2 *tds* or prednisolone 5mg *tds*. Here the nurse can make a great difference by offering small helpings on small plates, as far as possible giving the patient's own preferred type of food. Sometimes it may be 'subliminal' nausea and an anti-emetic may help.

Intractable vomiting and/or nausea [. . .] may be due to mechanical obstruc-tion or bleeding from the growth, to pressure on the gastro-intestinal tract or to biochemical upset, and there may certainly be a psychological element. At times it is a side-effect of drugs being given for other symp-toms.

The opiates and other potent narcotic analgesics may all cause nausea or vomiting. [. . .] This effect may wear off after a few doses or the ad-dition of an anti-emetic (or more than one) is usually sufficient. Patients have their own idiosyncrasies and eventually it may be necessary to try another narcotic and drugs by suppository (such as Proladone) before deciding that injections are the only satisfactory route for a particular person. Once a patient no longer has any nausea it is worth while to try returning to oral medication. This is often successful and is usually a great relief to him.

There are various anti-emetics now available and the phenothiazines are probably the most valuable at this stage. Prochlorperazine (Stemetil) 5–10mg, promazine (Sparine) 25mg or chlorpromazine (Largactil) 10–25mg are listed in ascending order of sedative effect. [. . .]

If these prove inadequate it is probably better to add another anti-emetic of a different type rather than to increase the dose. Cyclizine (Marzine or Valoid) 50mg orally or intramuscularly, *bd*, is often effective, and so is metoclopramide (Maxolon) 10mg, especially if it is given about one hour before meals. Both these drugs as well as the phenothiazine may all be needed.

When vomiting is obstructive and cannot be abolished completely because the lesion is high in the gastro-intestinal tract it is usually possible to control the nausea. Both the pain and the vomiting of malignant large bowel obstruction should be controlled in its terminal phase by the use of adequate analgesics and a combination of anti-emetics. In these cases Dioctyl forte tab. 1–2, *tds* are sometimes used until it appears that obstruction is complete. Lomotil tab. 2 *qds* may have a place in the control of painful colic.

Dysphagia may be so severe that anything taken by mouth may cause retching or a spill over into the lungs. A nurse may help most of all by observing what an individual patient finds easiest to swallow. Local anaesthetics may be tried with care and iced drinks are often welcome and a help in encouraging patients to take other drinks or semi-solids. Celestin tubes with their large lumen do not block up so frequently as did the Older Southey's or Souttar's tubes but fizzy drinks may be needed to shift an injudicious meal which has become stuck (typically ham and salad).

These patients need scrupulous and frequent mouth care, constant mouth-washes, (often a favourite 'gargle' should be beside them permanently). Monilia is an added insult and prevention by the use of amphotericin (Fungilin) lozenges is to be preferred to a resort to the cure by nystatin emulsion. These patients are among the most courageous and uncomplaining of all, but they do hate having unsuitable food offered to them unthinkingly.

They almost always need some sedation for anxiety and at times we may need to be generous or even bold in our doses at the end.

Dehydration of a mild degree is comparatively common among dying people [. . .] but there are many dehydrated dying patients who do not need the interference of intravenous infusions purely for relief of thirst. In fact, feelings of thirst and other discomforts are usually controlled by the opiate drugs which relieve terminal pain so well. Ice to suck, frequent sips of water or a favourite drink is almost always enough to relieve these patients of the dry mouth which is often their only complaint.

Hiccups occur for many reasons and are irritating and exhausting. [. . .] If they become a problem injections of chlorpromazine are usually effective. If they persist and carbon dioxide is not available, it is worth trying to make the patient breathe in and out of a paper bag.

Itching is common with a patient suffering from obstructive jaundice and can make his life intolerable. Initially it may be worth using calamine lotion with phenol up to 1 per cent. Eurax ointment often helps and the patient may be persuaded to rub this in instead of scratching. Hydrocortisone cream may help but topical antihistamines or local anaesthetics should not be used. [. . .]

Some patients are just hot, itching and sweating because they are wearing unaccustomed materials. Most people are more comfortable in cotton nightdresses rather than the nylon confections sometimes bought specially for hospital use.

Mouth care is important for all ill people even where the mouth is not involved with growth. Many drugs cause dryness and much ingenuity may be needed when they cannot be changed. Pineapple chunks and sweets which take some gentle chewing, an acceptable choice of slightly acid drinks, or just frequent sips of water, iced if preferred, may all help. Lip-salve and bland creams are best for dry, cracked lips. Sepsis must be treated appropriately and much discomfort thus avoided. Hydrocortisone pellets (Corlan) and Bonjela will ease painful ulcers.

Dyspnoea is worrying when it is mild and can be terrifying if it becomes severe. These patients are usually helped by a drug such as diazepam (Valium) given regularly as well as by specific measures.

Broncho-dilators may ease breathing even when there is little, or no, evidence of broncho-spasm. [. . .]

Antibiotics may ease distress if the dyspnoea is associated with a cough with purulent sputum. Septrin, ampicillin and chloramphenicol are all used. On the other hand, the indiscriminate use of antibiotics may merely prolong the terminal phase and increase the distress of dying.

Pleural effusions are not usually aspirated at this stage. It may be a distressing procedure and give little relief. Since the advent of cytotoxic drugs we do not encounter them so often, but a patient who has had regular aspirations may be reassured that the fluid will find its 'own level' and then stop filling up further.

In cases of large effusions and extensive carcinoma of bronchus the above measures are unlikely to be sufficient to ease distress and opiates must then be used freely. The diamorphine or morphine elixir may be adequate. More often injections combined with a phenothiazine or diazepam (Valium) will be needed. If their use shortens life this is not at all the same as the deliberate choice of a drug for its lethal properties and nurses should have no hesitation in giving adequate doses. Relieving the distress of dying has always been part of both medical and nursing care.

These patients are not often helped by oxygen. Most hate a mask and even light spectacles are not easy for them to endure. An open window or an electric fan is more effective. [. . .]

When a patient is dying, intramuscular hyoscine 0.4–0.6mg is given with an opiate to dry up the excessive secretions which may accumulate.

It will almost always eliminate the death rattle so distressing to relatives and to other patients, if not to the dying person himself.

Coughing may keep a whole ward awake, especially among male patients. Hot drinks are a comfort and a help, and linctus seems to work better given with very hot water. [. . .] Smoking should not be forbidden at this stage and is, in fact, an effective expectorant. It can be very trying to other patients, however. [. . .]

Insomnia. The ritual of hot-water bottles (not too hot for the debilitated or limited of movement), hot drinks, a well-timed bedpan, the change of position and a firm settling down on the 'right' side, real quiet and properly shaded lights all help to give a good night's sleep. At home there is all the comfort of one's own bed; in hospital the knowledge that one will not disturb a tired relative if one wants anything, but instead a nurse who may have time to talk. [. . .]

Sedatives are frequently needed with the evening analgesics, but should not be given automatically. Opiates should rarely be used for sedation only and a hypnotic may be added to them when they are needed for pain control. [. . .]

Alcohol and a warm drink may well be all that is required to give a good night's rest to many patients.

Once adequate pain control is established, patients often say they are sleeping better than for months. Some will sleep through for seven or eight hours but if they consistently wake with pain, and if they are having doses in the higher range, they will need a midnight dose at the routine four hours, and should be woken for it. The pain threshold is raised in sleep and it may take quite a severe degree to break through sedation, and the first morning dose may then not really be sufficient to give quick relief.

Urinary complications. Frequency may call for the treatment of infection by antibiotics or tab. emepronium (Cetiprin) 100mg *tds* or 200mg *nocte*.

Retention and incontinence are treated with indwelling catheters if possible. [. . .] Condoms may be useful, especially for nocturnal incontinence.

Bowels are an ever-lasting source of interest and worry to many healthy people and may make life intolerable to the very ill. Many are admitted with problems of constipation and come from hospitals or from home with impacted faeces, often suffering from the misery of overflow.

Patients do best with a combination of softening and peristalsis-inducing aperients. [. . .] Many patients have their own favourite aperients, which work best for them. Glycerine suppositories may be needed or a disposable phosphate enema. A manual removal is sometimes necessary. A well planned diet (perhaps including bran if it is tolerated), an adequate fluid intake and prompt nursing action at the right moment may solve this problem without medication.

Fungating growths need not be offensive. Liquid paraffin is the best lotion and Eusol 1:4 is added if there is sepsis. An antibiotic spray, e.g. Polybactrin, may be indicated. Some homes use yoghurt and other culinary remedies. [. . .] Non-adhesive dressings should be used and old linen may be the kindest dressing for a large area. It is often impossible to be so gentle when using forceps and for an exquisitely tender area it may be kinder to abandon them. [. . .]

Pressure sores can be cured even at this stage, but are far better prevented. They may well give more pain than the cause of the illness itself and it is not an easy pain to cure. Regular care is the first necessity and most nurses have their favourite applications. Many patients have very dry skins which need suitable care.

Patients should be encouraged to get up as long as possible and the physiotherapist has a great deal to offer. Unexpected activity and mobility can be achieved for some patients while others find passive movements and massage exceedingly comforting. [. . .]

Once patients are bedridden they must be moved gently and frequently, all the more when the number of comfortable positions becomes limited. Sheepskins and Ripple beds with special care to the heels should prevent sores for many patients but with a few it is almost impossible to keep decubitus totally at bay.

We have found at St Christopher's that the London Hospital canvas back slings, used with a number of soft pillows, are probably the most comfortable for our patients. By this time people must be allowed their own foibles and idiosyncrasies and these can be catered for. Near the end they are most often at ease on their sides with pillows well tucked down their backs and resting shoulders and necks.

Patients may be allowed some independence about washing and bathing. They vary tremendously in their toilet needs and in what they like, be it a plunge bath, a bed bath, a shower, or a degree of 'neglect'. Apart from backs, mouths and eyes they should be given some freedom in the matter. Said one old man on admission, 'You won't wash me, will you? They washed me to death in the last place.' Touch, which is so comforting to most, is an intrusion to a few.

The needs of the dying have long been summed up as 'tender, loving care'. This means respect of independence and individual foibles, coupled with these few suggestions and all the other nursing skills I have omitted.

The last achievement

It is not so much death itself as the actual process of dying that most men fear, but the reality when it comes is almost always painless and peaceful for a patient who dies of malignant disease. Mental and physical pain usually recede during the last few days before death and almost always in the last hours. [. . .]

After some years of experience in two hospices – one where patients were moved out from a twelve-bed ward to single rooms when they were dying and another where they almost invariably remained in their four- or six-bed bays – we had to plan our wards for St Christopher's. We believed that the comfort of company for the dying patient himself and the peaceful and reassuring sight of a dying person who was not restless nor in pain and never left alone so greatly outweighed any anxiety for the other patients that we would adopt the second policy. We have rarely regretted it, although we now believe that the opening of our final ward of single cubicles will be welcomed by some of our longer-stay patients and by those patients and families who come in for a few days only.

Dying patients do not like to lie flat on their backs and they are usually unable to move themselves. They should be turned gently and frequently if they are restless. They need to be propped up so that the head is well supported and many are best curled up on their sides with plenty of pillows. They are often afraid of the dark and need light and fresh air. They hate imprisoning bedclothes, and their restlessness is often an at-tempt to throw them off. They may need sponging and rubbing, as they often sweat profusely as their extremities gradually become cold and clammy. Thirst is their last craving; they do not need infusions but sips of iced water; regular cleaning of the mouth and salve to the cracked lips can still be comforts. The 'death rattle' of noisy tracheal secretions can nearly always be stopped by an injection of atropine or hyoscine if it is given with an opiate at the right moment.

The need for analgesics and hypnotics may increase but often this will decrease as death approaches. They should not be withdrawn entirely, though they may be given in lower doses, if a patient becomes unconscious or comatose. If they are stopped abruptly patients may become restless and distressed with withdrawal symptoms. It is better to continue giving the drugs that were needed previously as four-hourly injections to the end. We can then be certain that a patient is not suffering when he can no longer communicate this to us.

Even if a patient lingers in this stage and can make no flicker of recog-nition, he may well know who is with him and find comfort in their presence. Hearing is the last sense to go and we should tell the relatives this and be very careful not to forget it ourselves.

Most patients are unconscious at the moment of death and some seem to drift into this state unaware of what is happening. One sister who has cared for these patients for over twenty years tells me, however, that she is convinced that the great majority know at the end that they are dying and that they accept it peacefully. I have known several who wanted to talk only a few hours before they died. They were not frightened nor unwilling to go, for by then they were too far away to want to come back. They were conscious of leaving weakness and exhaustion rather than life and its activities. They rarely had any pain but felt intensely weary. They wanted to say good-bye to those they loved but were not torn with longing to stay with them.

Some have said to me that they hoped 'it would be in their sleep', and this is something we can promise with little fear that we will be wrong. All the same, we must be ready to use really adequate sedation for the occasional patient who gets a sudden increase of pain or who feels that he is choking or suffocating, but almost always unconsciousness precedes death. [. . .]

The care of the dying should not be an individual work but one that is shared. Shared with relatives, with all the various members of the staff, spiritual, medical and lay; and, as far as we can, with the patient himself. Where this is so we are left with the sense of completion and fulfilment which makes this such a rewarding branch of medical and nursing care.

References

HINTON, J. (1967) *Dying*. Harmondsworth: Penguin.

Papal Allocution to a Congress of Anaesthetists, 24 November 1957, *Acta Apolstolicae Sedis*, 1027–33.

SAUNDERS, C. M. (1975) *The Nature and Management of Terminal Pain*. Medical Practitioner Recording Service – Tape.

SCOTT, R. (1913) *Scott's Last Expedition: Journal* (Vol. 1); *Collection of reports of scientific works under supervision of Dr Wilson* (Vol. 2). Smith Elder (absorbed into John Murray (Publishers) Ltd.)

TWYCROSS, R. G. (1974) 'Clinical experience with diamorphine in advanced malignant disease', *Internat. J. clin. Pharmacol., Ther., Toxicol.*, 9, 184.

TWYCROSS, R. G. (1975) 'Diseases of the central nervous system. Relief of terminal pain', *Brit. med. J.*, 2, 212.

Index

Index

Acknowledgments

The editors and publisher wish to thank the following for permission to reprint copyright material in this book:

Cambridge University Press for 'The history of aging and the aged' (from *Family Life and Illicit Love in Earlier Generations*, by Peter Laslett, CUP, 1977); The Gerontological Society for an abridged version of 'Predictors of longevity: a follow-up of the aged in Chapel Hill', by E. B. Palmore and V. Stone (from *The Gerontologist, 13*, 1, 1973, 88–90), an abridged version of 'Compulsory versus flexible retirement: issues and facts', by E. Palmore (from *The Gerontologist, 12*, 4, 1972, 343–8), and 'Homes for old people: towards a positive environment', by A. Lipman and E. Slater (from *The Gerontologist, 17*, 2, 1977, 146–56); Nursing Times for 'Speculations in social and environmental gerontology', by D. B. Bromley (from *Nursing Times, 73*, 16, 1977, 53–6), 'Management of incontinence in the home: the community nurse's view', by C. Kratz (from *Nursing Times, 73*, 21, 1977, 798–9), and abridged extracts from 'Care of the dying', by C. Saunders (from *Nursing Times, 72*, 1976, 1003–249); George Allen & Unwin (Publishers) Ltd for an extract from *On Growing Old*, by A. L. Vischer (Allen & Unwin, 1966); Martinus Nijhoff's Boekhandel en Uitgeversmaatschappij B.V. for 'That was your life: a biographical approach to later life', by M. Johnson (from *Dependency or Interdependency in Old Age*, edited by J. M. A. Munnichs and W. J. A. van den Heuvel, Martinus Nijhoff, 1976); Routledge & Kegan Paul Ltd for an extract from *The Family Life of Old People*, by Peter Townsend (RKP, 1957), and an abridged extract from 'Camden Old Age Pensioners', by B. Harrison (from *Community Work Two*, edited by D. Jones and M. Mayo, RKP, 1975); The Lancet and the senior author for 'Old people at home: their unreported needs', by J. Williamson *et al.* (from *The Lancet, 1*, 1964, 1117–20); The British Medical Journal for 'Tolerance of debility in elderly dependants by supporters at home: the significance for hospital practice', by J. R. A. Sanford (from *BMJ, 3*, 1975, 471–3), 'Domiciliary care for the elderly sick – economy or neglect?', by L. J. Opit *et al.* (from *BMJ, 1*, 1977, 30–3), a slightly abridged version of 'On the natural history of falls in old age', by J. H. Sheldon (from *BMJ*, 10 December 1960, 1685–90), 'Old folk in wet beds', by J. L. Newman (from *BMJ*, 30 June 1962, 1824–7), 'Social network diagram', by R. Capildeo *et al.* (from *BMJ, 1*, 1976, 143–4), and for three extracts from *Medicine in Old Age*, edited by M. Ware (British Medical Association, 1974): 'Role of day hospital care', by J. C. Brocklehurst, 'Treatment of the "irremediable" elderly patient', by B. Isaacs, and 'Care of the elderly in general practice', by C. Hodes; Age Concern, England, for ' "No need," they said – the hazards of setting up a Good Neighbour scheme', by K. Pindar (from *Age Concern Today*, no. 14, 1975, 9–11), and 'Falling through the social services net' (from *Age Concern Today*, no. 15, 1975, 19–20); The Open University for 'Poverty and the elderly', by D. Jordan, 'Mobility and the elderly – a community challenge', by M. Bury and J. Barker, 'The chiropodist's role in the care of old people', by H. Youngman *et al.*, and 'Rehabilitation principles applied to physiotherapy for the elderly', by H. Ransome; Pergamon Press Ltd for an abridged extract from 'The burden of rheumatoid arthritis', by C. L. Weiner (from *Social Science and Medicine*, *9*, 1975, 97–104), and for an extract from 'Care of the sick – professionalism versus love', by J. A. Roth (from *Science, Medicine and Man*, *1*, 1973, 173–80); S. Karger AG for an abridged version of 'Problems in the treatment of hemiplegia', by G. F. Adams (from *Gerontologia Clinica*, *9*, 1967, 285–94); Curtis Brown Ltd for selected extracts from *Stroke: A Diary of Recovery*, by Douglas Ritchie (Faber, 1967); Medicine, The Monthly Add-on Journal, for 'Psychogeriatrics', by K. Bergman (from *Medicine*, London (1st series), *9*, 1962, 643–52, reproduced by permission); Hospital and Social Service Publications Ltd for 'The work of an occupational therapist in a geriatric department', by D. Thomas (from *British Hospital Journal and Social Science Review*, 19 April 1968, 713–15); Family Service Association of America for a slightly abridged version of 'Casework with the older person and his family', by M. Milloy (from *Social Casework*, *45*, October 1964, 8, 450–6); British Association of Social Workers for an abridged version of 'How to help the bereaved', by L. Pincus (from *Social Work Today*, *6*, 1975, 13, 392–5); European Centre for Social Welfare Training and Research for 'Co-ordination between health and personal social services: a question of quality', by A. Webb, a paper presented at a seminar organised by ECSWTR 'Interaction for social welfare and health personnel in the delivery of services: implications for training', Strobl, Austria, November 1975, Eurosocial Reports No. 4 (1975); The National Corporation for the Care of Old People for an extract from *One Cause* (NCCOP, 1977); Community Care and the author for 'Old people in care', by P. Brearley (from *Community Care* (Supplement), 27 October 1976); The Royal College of Nursing for selected extracts from *Improving Geriatric Care in Hospital* (RCN, 1975); Winthrop Publishers, Inc., for three extracts from *Aging in Mass Society: Myths and Realities*, by Jon Hendricks and C. Davis Hendricks, copyright © 1977 by Winthrop Publishers, Inc., and reprinted by permission; Her Majesty's Stationery Office for selected extracts from 'The elderly', by D. C. L. Wroe (from *Social Trends*, no. 4, 1973, reproduced with the permission of the Controller of Her Majesty's Stationery Office); Prentice-Hall, Inc., for an edited extract from Donald O. Cowgill and Lowell D. Holmes, *Aging and Modernization*, © 1972, pp. 305–23, reprinted by permission of Prentice-Hall, Inc., Englewood Cliffs, New Jersey, USA; Jonathan Cape Ltd for an extract from 'Tomorrow and Tomorrow and Tomorrow', by Kurt Vonnegut Jr. (from *Welcome to the Monkey House*, by Kurt Vonnegut); Farrar, Straus & Giroux, Inc., for 'The double standard of aging', by Susan Sontag, copyright © 1972 by Susan Sontag and reprinted with the permission of Farrar, Straus & Giroux, Inc.; New Society for 'Age discrimination', by R. Slater (from *New Society*, 10 May 1973, 301–2), and an abridged version of 'Living with old age', by P. Harrison (from *New Society*, 1 November 1973, 265–8): these two articles first appeared in *New Society*, London, the weekly review of the social sciences.